LAW AS FACT

AUSTRALIA

The Law Book Company Ltd.
Sydney : Melbourne : Brisbane

CANADA AND U.S.A.

The Carswell Company Ltd.
Agincourt

INDIA

N. M. Tripathi Private Ltd.
Bombay

ISRAEL

Steimatzky's Agency Ltd.
Jerusalem : Tel Aviv : Haifa

MALAYSIA—SINGAPORE—BRUNEI

Malayan Law Journal (Pte.) Ltd.
Singapore

PAKISTAN

Pakistan Law House
Karachi

LAW AS FACT

BY

KARL OLIVECRONA

SECOND EDITION

LONDON
STEVENS & SONS
1971

First Edition - - 1939
Second Edition - - 1971

Published by
Stevens & Sons Limited
of 11 New Fetter Lane in
the City of London and
printed in Great Britain
by The Eastern Press Limited
of London and Reading

SBN 420 43250 7

CONTENTS

PREFACE

When I had gained the inestimable freedom of an emeritus professor, my first thought was to prepare a new edition of my *Law as Fact*, which appeared in 1939. My intention was to revise the book thoroughly and make such modifications and additions as would suggest themselves to me. But I soon had to change my mind. The additions would have been numerous and sometimes rather long; during thirty years one has occasion to learn a little more. To make a great many insertions would have meant breaking up the flow of the argument, and it would have been difficult to present the new material to the best advantage.

The proper thing to do seemed to be to cut loose from the old book and write a new one. My views have not changed in any important respect. But much more had to be said, and the exposition had to be differently arranged.

The question of title remained. The book here presented is no second edition in the usual sense; it is an entirely new book. But the fundamental ideas are the same and it was impossible to find a title indicating their main content as well as the original one did. The book is therefore called *Law as Fact*. This title tells what I am aiming at: to fit the complex phenomena covered by the word law into the spatio-temporal world.

An Italian edition by Dr. Enrico Pattaro, Rector of the Collegio dei Fiamminghi in Bologna, is to be published simultaneously by Etas-Kompass in Milan. A Japanese translation by Professor Hamao Abe of the Osaka University of Foreign Studies is nearing completion. I take the opportunity of thanking the two translators warmly for their unselfish labour.

I have had numerous discussions with Professor Abe and I am grateful to him for many observations on the text. Thanks are also due to Mrs. Mary Wentz, B.A.(London), English Lecturer in the University of Lund, for kindly revising the style. The Swedish

Council for Social Science Research has contributed towards the costs for making the manuscript ready for print.

My greatest debt of gratitude is to my wife for unfailing support and encouragement during many years and for being the very best of secretaries.

KARL OLIVECRONA

University of Lund
January 1971

FINDING A STARTING POINT

THE purpose of this book is to explain the nature of what we call the law of a human community. The interest is focused on the situation typically prevailing in modern Western society. So-called international law is, on the whole, left outside the scope of the investigation. Ancient forms of law are only occasionally considered.

A difficulty immediately appears when we propose to elucidate the nature of the law. That is how to avoid circularity.

The object of inquiry is said to be 'the law' of a modern community. But does not this imply some knowledge of what the law is? How else could any object of inquiry be designated by this expression? But then the inquiry seems to presuppose previous knowledge of its object.

We are apparently caught in a dilemma. One seems to be unable to define the object of investigation without already being familiar with it.

Not surprisingly, therefore, works on the nature of the law often begin with a definition of the concept of law. If a definition is not proffered, a concept of law is usually presupposed as a necessary starting point.

The dilemma has not escaped observation. It has been noted and accepted as unavoidable. This, for instance, is the position of the German jurist-philosopher Ernst Bierling. He expressly says that a definition of the law must be part of the introduction to a treatise on the principles of jurisprudence though it can only be the result of a whole series of investigations.[1] You must know beforehand what you can only know on the basis of your studies.

If such were really the case, the science of the nature of the law would be in an awkward position. It would of necessity have to move in a circle. What purpose could it then serve? And if different authors start from different suppositions concerning the law, as they actually do, how could it be ascertained which view, if any, would be the correct one? The science of the nature of the law would seem to be lost in a quagmire.

Such a defeatist view is not warranted. It should be possible here, as well as in other branches of science, to define the object of

[1] *Juristische Prinzipienlehre* (1894–1917, reprinted in 1961) 19.

inquiry without anticipating the result. This means framing the questions without making any assumption concerning the answer.

In raising a scientific question one always starts from something which is supposed to be known. The question is called forth by an unpleasant feeling of having a gap in our knowledge. It is an incitement to make a search in order to fill the gap. The investigator is like an explorer standing on the frontier of new country, never trod by human feet. He assumes that the earth does not abruptly cease at the horizon but stretches forth with plains or hills or water as it may be. He sets his course by means of the compass and goes to see what is to be found there.

Let us take an example from natural science. When the investigation of lightning began, before the time of Benjamin Franklin, the situation can be supposed to have been of roughly the following kind.

A certain celestial phenomenon called lightning was well known. People had many times seen a flash in the skies followed by thunder; this was called lightning. When some curiosity concerning the nature of this phenomenon began to be felt, one could first ask whether it usually appears under special atmospheric conditions, at certain times of the year, at localities with peculiar geological properties, and so on. What was known from the start was the celestial spectacle as it appeared to the eye. Its relationship to some other known phenomena such as changes in the weather and the composition of the soil was the first object of investigation. No assumption concerning the result had to be made.

Curiosity was further extended to the causes of the flash of light and the thunder. The general advance of natural science made it possible to relate the celestial occurrences to other known phenomena, especially to the newly discovered manifestations of electricity, and to the laws of light and sound. Hypotheses were formed and tried experimentally. This did not mean that any results of the inquiries were anticipated. A working hypothesis is a guess concerning the unknown made on the basis of some known facts with the intention of its being verified or falsified by experiments. Like the explorer's compass, a hypothesis serves to indicate the direction of the investigation and to give it a systematic character. As the science of lightning and natural science in general proceeded, new hypotheses could be formed on a broader basis of known facts.

An assumption concerning the causes of the light and the thunder was made when these phenomena were ascribed to the action of a god who threw his thunderbolt in anger to punish human beings. This was no working hypothesis. It was an assertion concerning reality based on pure speculation, and it could lead nowhere. As long as it was held to include the explanation of lightning, no progress in knowledge could be made.

When we propose to investigate the nature of ' the law ' we cannot start from some visual impressions as happened with the study of lightning. A ' law ' is not to be seen, nor is a ' right ' or an ' obligation '. But we know that people talk of laws and rights and obligations.

The man in the street may lack pretensions to any particular knowledge of ' the law '. Nevertheless, his mind is stocked with a considerable supply of ' legal ' or ' juristic ' notions, and he makes use of many ' legal ' terms in his daily life. He holds that he is a ' citizen ' of a ' country ' (a ' kingdom ' or a ' republic ') with its own ' government ' and ' parliament ' or ' diet '. He knows that certain texts called ' laws ' are issued by these authorities. How this is done he probably does not know in detail; his ideas on the subject may be very dim. But when the papers announce that some new ' law ' affecting his trade has been brought into being, he takes it for granted that everything has been done in the right way. He takes care to make himself acquainted with the new law; for he knows that everyone has to obey it; unpleasant consequences are likely to occur if the law is disregarded.

Furthermore, our man is firmly convinced that he has a number of ' rights ' and ' duties '. He ' owns ' a house where he lives with his family; but he has a ' loan ' from the ' bank ' on which he must pay ' interest '. He is obliged to pay ' taxes ', to send his children to school, and to do a lot of other things. He has the right to ' vote ' at the ' elections ', to be ' paid ' for his work, to get his old age ' pension ', and so on. In case of a dispute with another man about his own right and the other man's duty, he can go to a ' court ' to have the matter settled by a ' judgment '.

The legal notions are not of importance for the day's activities only. In the evening, when the citizen listens to the radio or looks at his TV, he will not be able to understand the news unless he is familiar with the existence of other countries which have their respective governments and ' boundaries '. Even when he bids good night to his ' wife ' a legal notion is involved.

The common language and the content of the common mind may

serve as a starting point for our investigation. We have some immediate knowledge of these things just as people had some immediate knowledge of the celestial phenomena from which the study of lightning once began. We therefore have the necessary factual basis from which the inquiry may proceed.

The course of the inquiry may be set in different directions. One possibility is to study the common mind itself by analysing its notions and tracing their history. This could lead to a more extended knowledge of our ideas concerning 'the law' and the language used to express them. The object of the inquiry could be described as legal ideology.

Another possible course is to go beyond the common mind and ask what empirical realities we find where the legal notions are applied. This inquiry is not concerned with ideology but with objective facts.

We can ask, for instance, what we find where people say that a 'frontier' exists between two countries. On the map a line is drawn; the land on the one side is called country A, the land on the other side country B. If we proceed to the localities corresponding to the map, we may find different things: some heaps of stones at regular intervals, a clearing in the forest, a stretch of barbed wire, a road block. We are told that these different things are supposed to mark out the border-line on the ground. As the arrangements are obviously not made for fun, we ask what purpose they serve. The answer is that the frontier has to be made perceptible to people because it is of importance in many ways: one must not cross the frontier without a passport, a sum of money must be paid for certain goods brought from the one country to the other, the 'police' and other 'authorities' are different on both sides of the frontier, and above all there are different military establishments on each side. One can go on to ask how the frontier has come to be drawn in this way. It appears to be the result of a 'peace treaty'. Furthermore, we may ask why the proclamation of a 'frontier' in that way can have such effects as have been described. The treaty was made by the 'representatives' of two 'states' and was supposed to end a 'war'. For some reasons which have to be studied the conclusion of the treaty has exerted a profound influence on the behaviour of people. Furthermore, we are told that the significance of the frontier is regulated by 'legislation'. Now a great many questions emerge: what happens where people talk of legislation, what exists where we speak of a state, and so on. One question leads to another without end.

In a corresponding way we can start the investigation from another point. We may ask, for instance, what actual situation we find in the case where somebody is said to be the ' owner ' of an object, what situation we find when somebody is held to have a ' monetary claim ' against somebody else, what a ' court of justice ' is, or what a ' judgment ' by such a court is. Whatever point of departure is chosen, we are soon led to the same questions about the ' state ', its ' representatives ', its ' legislation ', and so on. New facts are collected and related to previously known facts. Thus the range of our knowledge is successively enlarged. The investigation proceeds step by step from known facts. No assumption is made concerning what is not yet known.

A third course of inquiry would be to begin with the theories about the nature of ' the law ' and try to ascertain their content of truth. This would eventually lead us to the same questions as were just mentioned.

One feature is common to all three courses of inquiry. At the beginning, current notions and current language about the state and legislation, about rights and obligations, are taken as facts. From these the search is started. We do not pretend to have any previous knowledge as to what the state is, what legislation means, or what a right or an obligation is. What we know is the way people talk about these things. Therefore no circularity occurs.

Of the three courses of inquiry the last one offers certain advantages. It is better to start with the more precise ideas of acute and learned jurists and philosophers than with the more vague notions of the common mind. The point of departure will then be the present position of legal theory.

The theories of law are usually divided into two groups which carry the names of natural law theory and legal positivism. For the most part this classification is taken to be exhaustive; every theory of law is put into the one group or the other.

The term natural law theory is usually applied to every theory in which a ' law of nature ' is supposed to exist and which is concerned with the elucidation of this law. Such theories have been known from Antiquity to our time. The theories collected under the name of legal positivism have in common the rejection of the notion of a natural law. They are of comparatively recent origin. If we disregard certain precursory views in Antiquity, legal positivism began to appear in the eighteenth century and gained strength during the nineteenth century. It largely superseded natural law theory and was for a long time widely regarded as *the* scientific theory of law. During recent decades, however, a remarkable renaissance of natural law theory has taken place.

A common characteristic of the theories reckoned as belonging to legal positivism is the tendency to realism. It seems suitable, therefore, to begin the investigation with a scrutiny of legal positivism. But legal positivism emerged in opposition to natural law theory. It has to be seen against the background of the idea of a 'natural' law as the basis of 'positive' law.

CHAPTER 1

LEGAL POSITIVISM AND NATURAL LAW THEORY

THE distinction between legal positivism and natural law theory is connected with the notions of 'natural law' and 'positive law'. These are of different origin. The idea of a natural law derives from Antiquity, but the notion of positive law was developed during the Middle Ages. Exactly when this took place is not known.

As regards *terminology* the following might be stated on the basis of recent research. In Antiquity the term 'positive law', *ius positivum,* was not employed. One single instance (from late Antiquity) of the expression 'positive justice', *iustitia positiva,* has been recorded.[1] The expression *legem ponere,* to lay down a law, from which the term *ius positivum* derives, makes its appearance as a legal term in the sixth century.[2] Since that time it was often used.[3]

The expression *ius positivum* has been found in a work by Abelard from about 1140.[4] This is the first instance on record. Probably the expression was not invented by Abelard; he writes as if it were well known.[5] The equivalent expression *iustitia positiva* is used by another author in a work from 1130.[6] For all we know, both expressions may have been employed for a long time before that date. In any case it is certain that the term *ius positivum* was in general use in the thirteenth century.[7]

[1] In Chalcidius' commentary to Plato's Timaeus. See Kuttner, 'Sur les origines du terme "droit positif"' in the *Revue historique de droit français et étranger* (1936) 736 ff. The commentary became important during the Middle Ages as one of the few sources through which the works of Plato were known. See Gagnér, *Studien zur Ideengeschichte der Gesetzgebung* (1960) 221 f.

[2] In the legislation of Justinian. See Gagnér 209, 207, where two instances in the Codex are mentioned (2,58,2 pr. and 3,1,13 pr. and the equivalent expression *legem condere* in Codex 1,14,12,3). Ullmann points out several places in Justinian's Novellae, where the expression *legem ponere* occurs. (29 *Tijdschrift voor Rechtsgeschiednis*, 1961, 122 ff.)

[3] Ullmann 124 f.

[4] Kuttner 730. Kuttner suggests that the term was borrowed from Chalcidius' commentary.

[5] Abelard says: *Ius quippe aliud naturale, aliud positivum dicitur*. (Gagnér 212.)

[6] This has been discovered by D. van den Eynde, 'The terms "*ius positivum*" and "*signum positivum*" in Twelfth-Century Scholasticism', in 9 *Franciscan Studies* (1949) 43 f. (Cited from Gagnér 223.)

[7] Ullmann 124. The expression is found in papal legislation from the first half of the century. It is also used by St. Thomas; *cf.* Aubert, *Le droit romain dans l'œuvre de Saint Thomas* (1955) 105 ff.

Abelard defines 'positive law' as law that has either been instituted by men for their utility or honour or is based solely on custom or the authority of writings.[8] In this definition the concept of 'law' is presupposed. 'Positive' law is distinguished from natural law by having its origin in some human activity. This need not necessarily be an act of legislation; Abelard includes customary law and law based on authoritative writings under the term 'positive' law. But in some way 'positive' law must have been laid down or 'posited' by men.

This is the general sense of the term 'positive law'. It should only be added that many writers (not only theologians) have reckoned with divine positive law side by side with human positive law. By divine positive law is meant such law as God has specially given with limited application; examples are the injunction against eating the fruits from the tree of the knowledge of good and evil and the prohibitions of the Mosaic law against certain kinds of food.[9]

In contradistinction to positive law, 'natural law' generally means a law that has not been posited. Even if it is ascribed to the will of God, it is supposed to have always existed. Its validity is not thought to be limited to a certain people or a certain time. The law of nature is timeless and universal.

At this stage of the inquiry nothing more can be said about the notions of natural law and positive law. Not even the common notion of 'law' can be discussed now.

In the 'natural law theories' a law of nature in the sense indicated is overtly assumed. In the theories comprised under the name of 'legal positivism' its existence is denied.

Classical Natural Law Theory

Since 'legal positivism' was launched as the truly scientific alternative to the 'classical' natural law theories of the seventeenth and eighteenth centuries, the latter theories form its immediate background. To understand legal positivism it will not be necessary to go farther back. It would be entirely beyond the purpose of the author and the requirements of the argument to write a history of natural law thinking from Antiquity to our own days.

Even with regard to classical natural law theory a restriction is possible and desirable. A systematic exposition of the natural law

[8] See Kuttner 730.
[9] Thus Gronovius in his commentary to Grotius 1,1,10,2.

theories of two centuries is not necessary to depict the background of legal positivism. One or two examples of influential theories will be quite sufficient for the purpose. I propose to choose those of Grotius and Pufendorf. They are typical of natural law thinking and their importance for the development of legal theory has not been surpassed by any other theories.

The reasoning of these scholars necessarily started from the general political situation prevailing in their time. Europe was divided into a number of independent 'states', each one with its supreme authority, the 'sovereign' or *potestas civilis.* No overriding authority on earth was recognized. Each state had its particular 'law', the *lex civilis,* which was thought to be binding on the citizens.

The principal questions to which the situation gave occasion were the following. What is the basis of the *lex civilis*? On what is the authority of the sovereign grounded? Is there also a law that regulates the relations between the sovereigns, or are they living in a state of lawlessness?

We shall try to follow the trend of the argument. Since the *lex civilis* is a kind of positive law, *ius positum,* or *ius voluntarium* as Grotius said, we have to begin with the notion of positive law.

The notion of positive law

The notion of positive law presented no great problem. Grotius is very brief on this point. The *ius voluntarium* is so named because its origin is in the will of men or God. The *ius civile* stems from the will of the sovereign. It consists of the sovereign's prohibitions and precepts. Its duration is dependent on his will.[10]

Pufendorf is more explicit. Every positive law is grounded on the authority of a superior. Human positive law consists of the commands of the sovereign. It is, indeed, nothing but his will, through which he prescribes how the subjects are to act.[11]

The binding force of the law

According to the teachers of natural law every law, properly so

[10] *De iure belli ac pacis* (ed. Amsterdam 1712 with comments by Gronovius) 1,1,14: (*Ius*) *civile est quod a potestate civile proficiscitur. Potestas civilis est, quae civitati praeest*; 1,1,13: *Ius voluntarium . . . ex voluntate originem ducit: estque vel humanum vel divinum.* Cf. 2,4,12,1.

[11] Pufendorf, *De iure naturae et gentium* (ed. Frankfurt 1744 by Mascovius) 1,6. *Cf.* Welzel, *Die Naturrechtslehre Samuel Pufendorfs* (1958) 53[10].

called, has binding force, *vis obligandi*. This belongs to the essence of law.[12]

Grotius expresses himself very briefly on the nature of this binding force. He never defines it; his meaning is to be gathered from the use which he makes of the term.

The binding force of the law implies that the law creates obligations in those who are subject to the lawgiver. What it means to be under an obligation appears clearly from Grotius' discussion of how an obligation is assumed through a promise.[13] He explains that the promisor ' alienates ' part of his freedom. This is analogous to the translation of the right of property to an object. The promisee acquires the right to claim the execution of that which has been promised. It becomes morally necessary for the promisor to accede to the claim. In this sense his inner freedom is restricted. What he alienates is part of his inner freedom of decision.

Pufendorf has the same view on the effect of a promise.[14] He provides more extensive information on the nature of obligations. An obligation, he says, is a moral quality through which one is compelled to do, accept, or suffer something (1,1,21). A comparison is made between an obligation and (outward) constraint. Through constraint one is induced to perform a disagreeable action because one is threatened by some evil in case of opposition. The will is affected externally only. An obligation, on the contrary, affects the will intrinsically. It puts a moral restraint on our will in prohibiting us reasonably to act in a different way. Furthermore, one is forced to recognize that one will be justly exposed to some evil when acting contrary to the obligation.[15] Constraint is based solely on natural forces; an obligation cannot be engendered by such forces only, because it requires certain reasons which act upon the human conscience.[16]

[12] Grotius 1,1,9,1: (*Lex est*) *regula actuum moralium obligans ad id quod rectum est.* Pufendorf 1,6,4: *Lex commodissime videtur definiri per decretum, quo superior sibi subiectum obligat, ut ad istius praescriptum actiones suas componat.* 1,6,5: . . . *in definitione legum . . . a superiore proficisci, et in se habere vim obligandi.* *Cf.* Hägerström, *Recht, Pflicht und bindende Kraft des Vertrages nach römischer und naturrechtlicher Anschauung* (1965) 59 f.

[13] 2,11. *Cf. Hägerström* 70 ff.

[14] See the discussion in 3,5.

[15] 1,6,5. *Cf.* Hägerström 59 ff.; Welzel 53.

[16] 1,6,10: *Diversa quippe sunt cogere et obligare. Illud solis viribus naturalibus potest effici; hoc vero nequaquam. . . . Obligatio enim praesupponit tales causas, quae intrinsece hominis conscientiam ita afficiant, ut ex propriae rationis dictamine iudicet non recte, adeoque non iure sese resistere.*

The great problem

If the binding force—which is essential to the law—consists in an internal restraint on the will based on reason, one might suppose that the teachers of natural law could have argued in the following way. Reflection shows us that men can live and enjoy the advantages of civilization only in a community regulated by rules. We must therefore accept prevailing rules and feel bound by them, even if we dislike some of them. Reasonably, we cannot take the position that the system of legal rules as a whole deserves no respect, because that would mean delivering society to anarchy; we could only say that we ought to work for the reform of the law in such parts as we think bad; evidently, the reform could only proceed step by step.

Such an argument would have been plausible if the binding force of the law was actually to be based on 'reason'. (Whether the argument, in that case, would have been conclusive need not be discussed now.) But there was one obstacle to taking this simple line of thought. The teachers of natural law made an assumption which called for another ground of the binding force of the law. This was the assumption that all men are by nature free and therefore equal.

When men live in society under law, their freedom is restricted, and the organization of society implies inequality. How, then, could this state of things be reconciled with the assumption of original freedom and equality? How could the free and equal individuals have introduced restraint and subordination on themselves? This was the great problem.

The double meaning of freedom

No reason was adduced for the assumption of original freedom. This tenet was held to be undoubtedly true.

What freedom implied was not explicitly stated. From the reasoning two different connotations of the term can be gathered.

On the one hand it is evident that freedom meant absence of actual, outward restraint. A man in chains or a people under the dominance of a tyrant was not free.

On the other hand there was another kind of freedom which could not be affected through outward force. This 'freedom' was a moral concept. It involved freedom from obligation. But an obligation was an inner bond on the will. Freedom from obligation therefore meant an inner freedom.

No human being possessed by himself the power of imposing an obligation on another. Every man was, under God, a sovereign to himself. His realm, his inner freedom, could not be touched from outside.

The necessity of a social contract

Among human beings there was only one conceivable way of restricting the original inner freedom of one man in favour of another. This was voluntary submission.[17]

For this reason mutual consent was required for the formation of society. Those who form a group or associate themselves with a group, Grotius says, have either expressly promised, or must be understood to have promised, to obey the decrees of the majority or of those upon whom authority has been conferred. This express or tacit contract, which has afterwards been called the social contract, is the source of the binding force of positive human law.[18] The power of the law to restrict the inner freedom of the members of society, as distinguished from the power to exert outward compulsion, derives from voluntary submission under a lawgiving authority.

No attempt is made to describe the social contract as having been concluded then and there. It is not depicted as a historical fact (and it would obviously be difficult to explain how a contract entered upon by people living hundreds of years ago could be binding on those living now). The meaning is that consent *must* be submitted since the law *has* binding force and since the binding or obligatory force can only derive from consent.

The reason for the binding force of the social contract

The assumption that the members of society had voluntarily agreed to associate and subject themselves to a supreme authority was not, however, sufficient. It ought also to be explained how they could bind themselves through their own action. Binding themselves would mean restricting their inner freedom. How could this be an effect of their own will? The individuals could declare their intention to take part in a society and to obey the decrees issued by an authority that had been established by mutual agreement. But if

[17] Pufendorf 1,6,12; 3,5,3. *Cf.* Welzel 68.

[18] Grotius prol. 15 and 16. Welzel (65) discerns four steps in the formation of society according to Pufendorf: (1) the social contract, (2) the decision on a constitution, (3) the choice of a ruler, and (4) the contract of subjection.

they were pleased to change their will, how could the earlier resolution be a hindrance to that?

Grotius says that there must of necessity be some mode of putting oneself under an obligation; and no other natural mode than an agreement could be devised (prol. 15). But this argument seems to presuppose that there is a rule making the agreement binding on the parties. The obligatory force of the mutual promise cannot stem from the will of the parties alone. There must be a rule which stands above the sovereign individuals, which has the power of putting restraint on their inner, inviolable freedom. This is a rule of the law of nature. In the law of nature the source of the binding force of a promise is supposed to be found. The social contract is the mother of positive human law, Grotius says, and the law of nature its grandmother (prol. 16).

The law of nature

According to Grotius the law of nature consists of certain general maxims such as the necessity of abstaining from what belongs to another and of repairing any damage that one may have culpably caused (prol. 8). Pufendorf propounds a general principle of natural law: that everybody ought to contribute to the maintenance of a peaceful community with all others, in accordance with the disposition and purpose of humanity. From this principle all special maxims of natural law are to be deduced (2,3,15). For both authors one of the most essential and inviolable maxims is that everybody should keep his word and fulfil what he has engaged himself to do through a promise or an agreement.

The maxims of natural law are held to follow from the sociability of man which gives rise to a tendency to act in such a way that living in a peaceful community becomes possible. The maxims express the fundamental rules that must be generally observed among men if this end is to be achieved. They are evident to reason.

In the first place, therefore, the maxims of natural law are maxims of reason telling us the correct means to a certain end. If we want to have a peaceful life in society, we have to act in certain ways. This implies, however, no obligation, no restraint on one's inner freedom. So far the maxims are of the same kind as the maxim that one has to put on warm clothes to protect oneself from cold weather. How, then, can the maxims obtain obligatory force?

Grotius first says that the social nature of man is the source (*fons*) of the law of nature in the strict sense, which includes the principles of abstaining from what belongs to others, of keeping promises, etc. (prol. 8). This would be true, he states in a famous passage, even if we dared to maintain that God does not exist or that He does not care for human affairs (prol. 11). Though the law of nature flows from the internal principles of man, it can however be ascribed to God because it was His will that we should be endowed with such principles (prol. 12).

So far what can be gathered from the exposition is only that man, as a rational and social being, is capable of grasping the fundamental rules necessary for life in society and has a propensity to act according to them. But in the view of Grotius, a law consists of prescriptions or commands, issued by a superior. He therefore leaves a gap in the theory. The actual tendency to follow certain principles indicated by reason is no law. It remains to explain how prescriptions binding on men are established in conformity with those principles.

Grotius passes over that difficulty in silence. But his conscientious commentator Gronovius has noted it and makes an effort to fill out the theory. He remarks (to prol. 8) that the social inclination, fortified by tacit or express pacts, is turned into law (*transit in ius*). This probably reflects Grotius' own train of thought: he glides over from the idea of man's social nature to the idea of prescriptions to follow the principles of life in society.[19]

> When Grotius derives the law of nature from man's desire to live in a community with others, this would seem to imply that the law of nature is based on utility. But this would be a dangerous position. It might then be argued that the social contract would be binding on each individual only in so far as it is useful to him. But in that case, he could not truly be said to be under any obligation. The obligatory force of the law would be dissolved.
>
> Grotius is careful to prevent this conclusion. He maintains that we would strive for society even if, without it, we suffered no want at all. It is true that the Creator has willed that we, as isolated individuals, should be weak and lack many things required for proper living. But His reason for this is that we should be all the more strongly impelled to cultivate society. Positive law, it is true, has been established with a view to utility. But the binding force of the social contract, which is

[19] This ' logically illegitimate transition from *Sein* to *Sollen* ' (A. H. Campbell in 21 *Modern Law Review,* 1958, 566) has often been pointed out. Welzel says (39 f.) that classical natural law doctrine transforms certain human inclinations into norms and therefore occupies ' eine unheilvolle Zwitterstellung zwischen Sozialpsychologie (Soziologie) und objektiver Wertlehre des Rechts (Rechtsphilosophie) '.

the basis of positive law, is not dependent on utility. It has an absolute basis in the unconditional desire for life in society (Prol. 16). Gronovius comments to Prol. 8: *Homo appetit societatem, quia ea iuvatur et conservatur: et si nihil iuvaretur, ac sibi sufficeret, eam appeteret tamen.* He adds his own reason why men should desire to live in society. It is not enough to possess many things, he says; there is no real joy in it unless you can show to others what you have: *naturaliter enim gaudia testem requirunt.*

In textbook accounts of Grotius' doctrine he is generally represented as simply having grounded the law of nature on the social nature of man, it being overlooked that he actually has a better theory—a theory explaining the origin of the law of nature as a set of prescriptions or commands. Reason *shows* us, Grotius says, that an act is morally reprehensible or necessary from being at variance or in accordance with our rational (and social) nature and that it *consequently* is forbidden or enjoined by God. The law of nature consists of God's commands and prohibitions.

Cf. Hägerström, Recht, Pflicht 45 f. The crucial passage 1,1,10,1. runs as follows: *Ius naturale est dictatum rectae rationis, indicans actui alicui, ex eius convenientia aut disconvenientia cum ipsa natura rationali* [*ac sociali, cf.* 1,1,12,1] *inesse moralem turpitudinem, aut necessitatem moralem, ac consequenter ab auctore naturae Deo talem actum aut vetari, aut praecipi.* Strangely enough, eminent authors in citing this passage cut off the latter part (from *ac consequenter*). (For instance Dunning, *A History of Political Ideas*, 1928, 165 f.; Verdross, *Abendländische Rechtsphilosophie*, 1958, 104.) Grotius is usually said to have separated legal theory from theology and founded a rationalistic theory of law which is independent of a religious basis. (Thus for instance Dunning, *loc. cit.*) This is due to a misunderstanding. It is true that Grotius says that the law of nature is immutable to such a degree that it could not be altered by God himself (1,1,10,5). But the reason for this is that God cannot create anything which is contradictory. Just as he cannot cause that two times two should not make four, he cannot effect that anything which is intrinsically evil should (at the same time) not be evil. But God can alter that to which the law refers. If He ordains that somebody should be slain, the act will not be a crime (1,1,10,6).

As related above Grotius holds that what he says about man's social inclination being the source of the law of nature would be true even if God did not exist. This follows from his theological position on good and evil. Since there are acts which are good or evil in themselves, independent of God's free will, man's reason would enable him to distinguish between good and evil even if there were no God. *Cf.* on the usual misconception as regards the position of Grotius Wieacker, *Privatrechtsgeschichte der Neuzeit* (2. Aufl. 1967) 226, 290. (Professor Villey has pointed out that what Grotius says in prologue 11 is reminiscent of the *Meditations of Marcus Aurelius,* 6,4. See *La formation de la pensée juridique moderne*, 1968, 612 f.)

Pufendorf is more consistent than Grotius. He rejects the thesis that the law of nature would subsist even if God did not exist. On this impious hypothesis the maxims of reason would not be *obligatory*; they would be observed only because this would be to one's advantage just as following the prescriptions of a doctor. To give the maxims binding force as law, a lawgiver is required; and a law can only be given by a superior (1,6,1 ff; 2,3,19). The law of nature is given by God, as reason clearly shows. God has given us a nature such that we cannot maintain ourselves without living in society. Therefore it is his will that we should conform to the rules necessary for such a life; and we are unconditionally bound to obey them (2,3,20).

According to both authors, therefore, the law of nature is a kind of divine law. God alone has the power of putting that restriction on our inner freedom which is the essence of the binding force of the law. Positive human law is binding on the members of society because they have voluntarily submitted to the authority of the lawgiver by entering into the social contract; and the social contract is binding by virtue of the divine law of nature.

The difference between the law of nature and divine positive law

If the law of nature consists of commands issued by God, what then is the difference between the law of nature and divine positive law?

According to Grotius, the law of nature represents God's necessary will (1,1,10,2 and 15,1). He inevitably forbids that which is intrinsically evil and enjoins that which is good in itself. Evidently Grotius presupposes the theological position that the will of God is subordinate to his reason; he rejects the Ockhamist thesis that right and wrong depend on divine fiat alone. Divine positive law, on the contrary, is laid down by the *free* will of God. As Gronovius remarks, this is the reason why Grotius calls divine positive law *ius divinum voluntarium* (prol. 12, note 63). It refers to acts which are neither right nor wrong in themselves. The law of nature, Grotius says, is willed by God because it represents what is just; what is prescribed in divine positive law is just because this is the will of God.

Pufendorf disapproves the terminology of Grotius. All divine law is the will of God. It is therefore wrong to call a certain part of the divine law *ius voluntarium.* Pufendorf calls it *ius divinum positivum* because it has been ' posited ' by God.

The difference between the law of nature and divine positive law is that the latter has been specially promulgated by God; this is not, or need not, be the case with the law of nature (1,6,18). By promulgation he means God's declaring his will in some way. Such promulgation is necessary in cases where it would not be possible for us to know the will of God unless it has been signified to us. In the cases covered by the law of nature, the will of God is immediately manifest to us; it can be discovered by reason alone. Thus the law of nature and divine positive law are substantially of the same kind. The law is the will of God. The difference depends on the way in which His will becomes known to us: through reason alone or through revelation.

The reason for the binding force of divine law

The teachers of natural law are not satisfied to refer to the omnipotence of God in order to provide a ground for the binding force of the law of nature. They strive to establish a moral reason for our obligation to obey the commands of God. But there is considerable uncertainty on this point.

Both Grotius (prol. 11) and Pufendorf (1,6,12) invoke the many benefits conferred upon us by God. As Pufendorf's editor Hertius remarks (and Barbeyrac too), this argument is a weak one. Past favours are no sufficient reason for future obedience. But Pufendorf has a stronger argument. God has given us the capability of freedom of action. Nothing hindered him from taking away part of this freedom (*particula libertatis*) and making it subject to his own right. This is the source of God's moral power to impose obligations.

Pufendorf expressly co-ordinates God's power to impose obligations with the power of civil government to do so. The force of obligations, he says, which lays an inner bond (*intrinsecum velut vinculum*) on our will, follows from these two sources: (i) the power which God has reserved for himself in creating us and (ii) voluntary subjection to a ruler.

Pufendorf's statement in 1,6,12 runs as follows: *Qui homini dedit, ut libere posset agere, quare non is iure suo aliquam eius libertatis particulum circumscribere queat?* Barbeyrac translates: *Pourquoi celui qui nous a donné la Faculté d'agir librement, ne pourroit-il pas s'attribuer le droit d'y prescrire quelques bornes?* In this translation the essential expression *particula libertatis* is missing. This technical expression shows that Pufendorf has in mind the analogy of establishing obligations through promises. As was mentioned above, the essence of a promise, according to the teachers of natural law, was the alienation of a part of one's liberty. Pufendorf's view is that he who possesses *imperium* over somebody else (*i.e.* the power of imposing obligations) has the moral power over certain actions by the latter which have been removed from his sphere of liberty; part of his liberty (*particula libertatis*) belongs to the other party. In connection with Creation, God could reserve such a part of the liberty for himself. In the relation between man and man, *imperium* could only be established through voluntary submission, which meant voluntary transfer of part of the freedom. This idea will be further discussed in Chapter VI and Appendix I.

The commands of the lawgiver

To understand the teachers of natural law it is essential to obtain a clear view of their concept of a command.

In current usage a (verbal) command consists of some words uttered by one person to another with a view of prompting the latter to perform an action which he would not undertake by himself, or to refrain from doing something to which he might be inclined. In a typical command, the commander and the receiver are face to face. The words reach the mind of the receiver. There is a personal relationship, and the command is a transitory event. Usually the content of the command is rather simple; it refers to one action or to a sequence of actions that are intimately connected.

The provisions of a law do not easily fit into the category of commands in this every day sense. No personal relationship exists between lawgiver and addressee. A law may regulate a great many different actions with very little connection between them. It is not deemed necessary that a law should reach the consciousness of every addressee; according to a well-known maxim (*iuris ignorantia nocet*), the law is applied against persons who have no knowledge of its contents or even its existence.

The establishing of the law is a transitory event. But the law itself is intended to be in force for some period. If the provisions of the law are to be commands by the lawgiver, they cannot be commands only at the moment of laying down the law; the lawgiver must be represented as commanding the whole time. But how could that be maintained?

The teachers of natural law, however, had a concept of command which makes their theory comprehensible. They held the view that a command is a 'declaration of will' (*declaratio voluntatis*). This means that a (verbal) command is an utterance through which one person communicates the contents of his will to another. He makes his will known to the addressee.

There are several kinds of declarations of will in the doctrine of natural law. A promise, for instance, is a declaration of the will to be bound in relation to another person to perform some act or to refrain from doing something.[20] A command is a declaration of the will that the addressee should behave in a certain way. In both cases the most essential thing is the will itself. The declaration is an outward sign of the will (*signum voluntatis*). Its function is to give expression to the will so that others can know it; otherwise the will could not be relevant in social relations.

This concept of command was probably not invented by the teachers of natural law. It was highly important in their theory of law. But they apparently made use of a well-known concept which was common property in the seventeenth century. We find it, for instance, in Hobbes. He says that a command 'consisteth in declaration, or manifestation of the will of him who commandeth, by voice, writing, or some other sufficient argument of the same'.[21] Pufendorf has the same notion of a command.[22] Grotius no doubt entertained this notion too, though he makes no explicit statement on the subject.

In the case of a promise the declaration of will was a manifestation of the will of the individual, sovereign within his own sphere, to restrict that sphere himself in favour of another. In the law the declaration of will was the publication of the will of a superior concerning the behaviour of the subjects. In this sense the law consists of commands by the sovereign.

Pufendorf's account concerning the law of nature as a declaration of the will of God (1,6,4) is especially interesting. He

[20] Grotius 2,11; Pufendorf 3,5,4. *Cf.* Hägerström, *Recht, Pflicht* 70 ff. This will be further discussed in Chapter VI and Appendix I.

[21] Hobbes, *Leviathan* 2,26,8. *Cf. The Elements of Law* (ed. Tönnies 1889) 1,13,6: 'Commanding . . . is that speech by which we signify to another our appetite or desire to have anything done, or left undone, for reason contained in the will itself.'

[22] Pufendorf 1,6,1 and 4.

defines a law as a decree through which a superior imposes an obligation on a subject to adjust his actions to his own (the superior's) prescriptions. The term 'decree' (*decretum*) does not refer to the internal will but to that which has been communicated to another in such a way as to make him understand the necessity of obeying: which is the same as a command. But it is not necessary for a law that it be promulgated *viva voce* or in writing. It is sufficient that the legislator in some way or other communicates his will to the subjects; it may become known to them only through the internal, inborn light. Reason tells us not only that the laws of nature are beneficial to mankind but also that it is God's will and command that the mortals direct their actions according to them. This is sufficient for a law (*ad essentiam legis sufficit*). In a note it is added: God is understood to prescribe that which is His will (*cum Deus, quicquid vult; illud etiam praecipere intelligatur*). It is quite clear (i) that in its essence the law of nature is the will of God, and (ii) that a command by God only implies that His will is made known to us in some way or other. Perhaps the theory that a command is a declaration of will has its origin in such speculations.

The will of the lawgiver

The will theory of the teachers of natural law is not to be understood as implying that the will of the lawgiver is directed towards transforming a proposed text into law. If this were the case the theory would not purport to be an explanation of the nature of positive law. The concept of positive law would be presupposed. The theory would be a theory about the act of legislation. It would say nothing about what positive law is.

The aim of the theory is to explain the nature of positive law. It says that the law is the will of the sovereign made known to the subjects. His will is that they should behave in certain ways: they shall not commit such acts as are forbidden and made punishable, they shall respect the property of others, they shall fulfil their contracts, and so on. Properly speaking the law resides in the will of the sovereign: it is the contents of his will regarding the behaviour of the subjects. The written text has only the function of being a means of communicating the will to those concerned.

Pufendorf expressly states that it is not essential for law that it should be expressed and notified through words. It is sufficient that one knows the will of the superior (1,6,13; 2,3,20). Therefore, the law is what the superior wills. Positive law, whether divine or human, must be published because it cannot be discovered by reason alone. But only some sign of the will of the superior is needed.

The power of the sovereign to impose obligations belongs to his will. It is his will that affects the wills of the subjects. The relationship between sovereign and subjects is essentially a relationship between their respective wills, the one ruling over the others, who lack part of their freedom.

Once the will of the sovereign has been made known, it is supposed to remain the same until a change has been publicized. It exists by itself as an independent force. The will of the sovereign, therefore, in so far as its contents are the law, is not a transient, ever changing phenomenon like the ordinary human will. In some degree it is comparable to the will of God. The Decalogue was not only the expression of the momentary will of God several thousand years ago; it is His will today and every day. No more is the lawgiving will of the sovereign a passing event in his mind. The law is his until a new will has been declared.

Pufendorf tells us how the will of the sovereign is formed. The great diversity of inclinations and sentiments among people makes it necessary to unite the wills into one common will with regard to the purposes of the community. Such a union cannot be brought about in a natural, physical way. But several wills are held to be united when everybody has submitted himself to the will of one person or an assembly of persons; for one is thought to will what is willed by another, to whom one has submitted one's will. In other words, the will of the sovereign is the will of all the members of society because they have subjected their wills to his will.[23]

Pufendorf calls the supreme will, the will of the state. In a monarchy, it resides in the person of the monarch. Since the monarch also has his own will, two wills are present in him: the public will, or the will of the state, and the particular will. When the sovereign power belongs to an assembly, the will of the majority is held to be the will of all, because that is the only way of reaching decisions and getting anything done, even if it sometimes leads to the rejection of what is most honourable and beneficial to the state (7,2,14 and 15).

From all this it is abundantly clear that the will of the lawgiver is no will in a psychological sense. It is a fictitious, metaphysical

[23] Pufendorf 7,2,5. *Cf.* Welzel 59 f.

will, similar to the will of God. Positive human law is the content of this will just as divine law is the content of God's will.

The history of this idea of a lawgiving will cannot be pursued here. It was probably worked out during the Middle Ages in conjunction with theological speculations. *Cf.* Thomas E. Davitt, *The Nature of Law* (1951).

The power of the sovereign

The power of the sovereign is a power to impose obligations. Pufendorf defines *imperium* as *potestas obligationem alteri iniungendi* (1,6,11). It is for establishing such a power that voluntary submission is required. But an obligation is a bond on the interior will. The power to impose obligations, therefore, is a power over the will of each individual. The sovereign reaches into the minds of the subjects and puts fetters on their innermost freedom and will.

This power over the minds is not a factual power. As Pufendorf points out, the will is not bound in such a way as not to be able to depart from what is enjoined by the obligation (1,6,5). The bond is of a metaphysical nature as well as the will by which it is imposed.

As was mentioned before, Pufendorf tries to explain the nature of the bond by saying that one is forced to censure oneself and find oneself deserving of an evil if acting contrary to the obligation (1,6,5). But this reasoning is circular. The ground for censure is that an obligation has been set aside. Therefore the nature of the obligation cannot be explained by the censure.

But the sovereign needs another kind of power too. 'Whoever can be despised with impunity commands precariously among people of bad disposition,' Pufendorf says (1,6,12). To make his commands effective the sovereign must have means of visiting disobedient subjects with some evil. Then he will be feared by all the subjects. Pufendorf calls these evils 'sanctions' (1,6,14).

The power to impose sanctions is actual, physical power. It is used, or should at least be used, to support the power of imposing obligations. From the point of view of legal theory, this latter power is the primary and most essential thing. The social contract and the law of nature are constructed to explain it. The addition of physical power to the metaphysical power of imposing obligations is necessary because the inner bonds created by the will of the lawgiver are not effective on all persons. Fear must accompany the sentiment of being subject to obligations (1,6,12).

Despite its character of actual, physical power, the power of imposing sanctions is constituted in a way analogous to the formation of the will of the state. The sovereign is considered to have absolute disposal of the physical forces of all the subjects because they have engaged themselves not to use these forces except as it will please the sovereign (7,2,5). The physical power, too, is explained in a fictitious way.

Natural law and positive law

Since positive law is based on the law of nature, its contents must be in harmony with this law. But the lawgiver has got the right to supplement the law of nature in many ways according to the needs of the particular society. The right of property, for instance, has been introduced by positive law.[24] This is also the case with punishments. The precepts of the law of nature are not devoid of sanctions: their sanctions are the pangs of conscience.[25] But human punishments are a human invention, though the justification of punishment rests on the law of nature.[26]

The law of nature, therefore, gives wide scope to the activity of the sovereign as lawgiver. But he cannot do anything contrary to the law of nature.[27] If he did so, his precepts would lack binding force; they might create fear, but they could not impose obligations.

Positive law is entirely dependent on the will of the sovereign. But many cases occur for which there are no provisions in positive law. Then the solution is to be found in the law of nature.[28] In this way it becomes possible to decide every conceivable case according to the law. If positive law is deficient, the law of nature will fill the gap.

Thus the law of nature was always the background and complement of positive law. It therefore became important to show in detail what followed from the principles of natural law in particular cases. Another consideration gave an impetus in the same direction. This was the desire of laying down detailed rules of the law of nations.

The sovereigns had made no social contract between themselves; they had instituted no superior. They lived in the state of nature. Their relations were therefore governed by the law of nature (with the addition, according to Grotius but not according to Pufendorf, of

[24] Grotius 1,1,10,4; Pufendorf 4.4. [25] Pufendorf 2,3,21.
[26] Pufendorf 2,3,11.
[27] Grotius 2,3,6: *Nimirum humana iura multa constituere possunt praeter naturam: contra naturam nihil.* On Pufendorf *cf.* Welzel 57.
[28] Pufendorf 8,1,1.

rules based on the custom of nations, *ius gentium voluntarium* or *positivum*).

> Pufendorf maintains that only the sovereigns are living in the state of nature; isolated individuals never did. He points out that the first men were not living in the state of nature since Eve was subject to the authority of Adam. (*Adamo utique Eua sua maritali imperio fuit subiecta*, Gen. 3: 16.) But when their sons left home and created their own families, they entered into the state of nature and remained in that state (as heads of families) until they joined with others to form societies. Then the different societies came to live in the state of nature (2,2,4).

For Grotius the great problem is to make clear in which cases a war is just (*iustum bellum*). A just war requires a just cause; and this can only be an injury (*iniuria*) (2,1,1,4).

In the state of nature everybody has the right to seek redress by his own hand for injuries inflicted on himself. The social contract implies that this right has been transferred to the civil power acting through the courts on behalf of the injured person. Since the sovereigns are living in the state of nature they retain the original right to react against injuries. They are themselves the judges of their own cases, and their ultimate remedy is war: when there are no decisions by courts, war begins (2,1,2,1).

Grotius holds that only an injury is a cause of action in civil law. It is therefore an exact parallel between civil law and the law of nations as regards the causes which justify a reaction. There are as many causes of a just war as there are causes of action in civil law (2,1,2,1).

For this reason Grotius makes an exposition of the fundamental principles of civil law with a view to ascertaining the just causes of war. In the second and largest book of his great work he reviews the modes of acquisition of property, the binding force of promises and contracts, the principles of the law of torts and damages, and the justification of punishment. This provides the basis for drawing up a list of the just causes of war.

> The list was an extensive one. No seventeenth-century sovereign could have met with much difficulty in justifying, on the principles of Grotius, any war that he chose to undertake. If nothing else was available he could have recourse to that most fruitful cause of war—an anticipated injury, an injury that has not yet been committed, *iniuria nondum facta* (2,1,2). (As the authority for this, Grotius cites the possessory interdicts of the Roman praetor.) A preventive war could be justified by alleging the expectation of an imminent wrong. Grotius admonishes a

sovereign not to go to war rashly even if he has a just cause for it (2,24). But he also provides an excuse for a sovereign lacking a just cause. To act with injustice, one has to know it: many, however, are ignorant that they are doing something wrong. Both parties to a war might therefore be acting without injustice (2,23,13,2). Moreover, it has been established by the common consent of peoples that a war which is being waged by sovereigns after formal declaration—a solemn war, a *bellum solenne*—has to be considered just on both sides as regards its external effects, meaning, for instance, that there will be no (just) claim for recovery of what has been taken in such a war (1,3,4,1; 2,17,19; 3,3). So the just causes, after all, are significant for conscience only—the conscience of sovereigns.

The principles of the law of nature were still more elaborated by Pufendorf and his followers. A complete system of natural law as applied to the conditions of eighteenth-century European society was presented by Christian Wolff in his great work on the law of nature from the middle of the century.[29]

This doctrine of natural law has left its imprint both on laws and on legal science. It formed the basis of the great codes enacted in Prussia, France and Austria towards the end of the eighteenth and at the beginning of the nineteenth centuries, which have been called the natural law codes.[30] A new system of civil law was worked out by the teachers of natural law; and this system is still prevailing in continental Europe.[31] Last but not least, the conceptual framework of natural law doctrine was taken over by the legal writers of the nineteenth century, especially in Germany, and was transmitted by them to the twentieth century. The concept of a declaration of will in private law, for instance, was long thought to be a Roman concept but is actually a legacy of the seventeenth- and eighteenth-century natural law doctrine; it was in fact unknown to the Roman jurists and alien to their way of thinking.[32]

The Rise of Legal Positivism

The doctrine of natural law was open to criticism on many scores. Its weakness was especially apparent with regard to the assumption of a law of nature and a social contract as the basis of positive law.

[29] *Ius naturae methodo scientifica pertractatum* (1740–49).
[30] Wieacker, *Privatrechtsgeschichte der Neuzeit* 322.
[31] A. B. Schwarz, 1 *Politica* (1934/35) 185 f.; Thieme, *Das Naturrecht und die europäische Privatrechtsgeschichte* (1947) 42. *Cf.* Wieacker 309, 320; Koschaker, *Europa und das römische Recht* (1958) 279.
[32] Binder, 6 *Archiv für Rechts- und Wirtschaftsphilosophie* (1912–13) 102 ff.; Hägerström, *Inquiries into the Nature of Law and Morals* (1953) 299 ff. and *Recht, Pflicht* 67 ff.; Wieacker 293.

When these tenets were rejected by the critics, the obvious conclusion seemed to be that only positive law is real law, so-called natural law being some kind of ideal for lawgivers. The criticism did not necessarily entail a radical revision of the traditional concept of positive law. The idea that positive law is ' posited ' or laid down by a sovereign authority in society was thoroughly engrained in legal thinking and did not provoke criticism to the same degree as did the talk of a law of nature. The innovation therefore chiefly consisted in cutting out the law of nature and restricting the field of legal theory to ' positive ' law. The negation of a law of nature became the hallmark of legal positivism.[33] As Bergbohm remarks, the expression ' positive law ' became pleonastic when only positive law was held to be real law.[34]

When the notion of a natural law was rejected, much more attention was devoted to the structure and essence of positive law. These questions had presented no great problem to the teachers of natural law. They were interested in providing a secure foundation for positive law. But the nature of positive law itself was hardly subject to doubt. It was sufficient to state that positive law consisted of the commands of the sovereign. The implications of that thesis were not discussed at any length. With the rejection of the idea of a natural law, the position was radically altered. It now became the great problem of legal theory to elucidate the nature of positive law. A ' philosophy of positive law ' made its appearance.

> The term ' philosophy of positive law ' was first used, as it seems, by Gustav Hugo in a small work from the end of the eighteenth century (*Lehrbuch des Naturrechts als einer Philosophie des positiven Rechts*, 1798). Austin borrowed this expression and used it as a sub-title to his *Lectures on Jurisprudence* (see the note to his preliminary explanations I, 31 f.) because he found that it indicated ' the most significantly the subject and scope ' of his lectures. *Cf.* A. B. Schwarz, 1 *Politica*, 1934, 194 f. and G. Marini, *L'opera di Gustav Hugo nella crisi del giusnaturalismo tedesco* (1968) 164 ff. Characteristically Karl Bergbohm held the same opinion concerning his own work (35).

Philosophizing on the nature of positive law proceeded along several different lines. A common feature of most theories put for-

[33] *Cf.* Ago, *Annuaire français de droit international* (1957) 15 ff. (also in 51 *American Journal of International Law* 1957). As Bobbio points out, natural law doctrine is dualistic, legal positivism monistic. (*Guisnaturalismo e positivismo guiridico*, 1965, 128.)

[34] 1 *Jurisprudenz und Rechtsphilosophie* (1892) 49.

ward to supplant the doctrine of natural law was the voluntaristic approach which was, indeed, inherited from the teachers of natural law. Positive law, the one real law, was supposed to be the expression of the will of the supreme authority in society.

The term 'legal positivism' is here being used to designate theories comprising this fundamental tenet. In recent literature the term has many different connotations. Some remarks on this subject will be offered later. For the moment it is only required to make our own terminology clear.

Legal theory is always more or less closely connected with philosophical thinking, political conditions, and ideological currents. As these factors were vastly different in England, Germany and France during the nineteenth century, so legal theory took different directions in these three countries.

As has been noticed by some modern authors, there is no exhaustive history of legal positivism. (See Bobbio, 1 *Mélanges en l'honneur de P. Roubier*, 1961, 53; *Giusnaturalismo e positivismo*, 1965, 103; Henkel, *Einführung in die Rechtsphilosophie* 379.) The following survey is not intended to remedy this deficiency. Its purpose is to prepare the ground for the subsequent exposition of law as a factual social phenomenon.

English theory

The first great positivist was Jeremy Bentham. His whole outlook was determined by Hume's empiricism, which he enthusiastically embraced. The chimera of the social contract had been effectively annihilated by Hume, he thought, and he scorned Blackstone's attempt to find a basis for the common law in 'this formidable non-entity, the Law of Nature'.[35] His purpose was to build a theory of law on experience only. The great difficulty stemmed from the fact that 'the ingenuity of the first masters of language compelled by necessity has thrown a kind of veil of mystery over the face of every science, and over none a thicker than over that of jurisprudence'. It would not be 'practical or even expedient' altogether to remove this veil, but we must learn to 'pierce through it at pleasure' before we can obtain a clear perception of the real state of things.[36] This was what he tried to do. He wanted to penetrate the veil of words and grasp the realities of the law.

When Bentham sought to explain the law as an empirically given set of facts, he had the situation in contemporary England before his

[35] *A Fragment on Government* (ed. Harrison 1948) 1, 36. *A Comment on the Commentaries* (ed Everett 1928) 44.
[36] *The Limits of Jurisprudence Defined* (ed. Everett 1945) 57.

eyes. Supreme power there belonged to the King, Lords, and Commons. They issued commands and prohibitions which were habitually obeyed. To ensure obedience, punishments were attached to disobedience.

The person or assemblage of persons possessing supreme power in a political community Bentham called the sovereign.[37] For Bentham no question arose as to a moral ground for the power of the sovereign.[38] It rested on habitual obedience only.[39] No more was Bentham concerned with the question of the binding force of the law and its ground. He assumed no morally binding force of the law.

Thus the essential problems of natural law theory simply disappeared for Bentham when he tried to describe the law in terms of sociological facts. But in his interpretation of these facts the influence of traditional legal thinking is apparent.

By 'law' he understood what the teachers of natural law called positive law. As far as the present writer knows, he did not use the epithet 'positive', probably because he held the opinion that there was no other law.[40]

In Bentham's view every law consists of commands or prohibitions (and the repeal of such acts). Every statement about law can therefore be resolved into a statement about commands and prohibitions. In this way only the statements will be founded on experience.[41] To ensure obedience, threats of evil consequences must be attached to the commands and prohibitions. Without punishment, there could be no law.[42]

Now Bentham did not mean that English law was made up by commands and prohibitions issued during the centuries by a succession of different sovereigns. In that case there would not be a

[37] *The Limits of Jurisprudence Defined* 101.

[38] *Cf.* Harrison in his introduction to *A Fragment on Government* XXVIII.

[39] *The Limits of Jurisprudence Defined* 101: 'By a sovereign I mean any person or assemblage of persons to whose will a whole political community are (no matter on what account) supposed to be in a disposition to pay obedience: and that in preference to the will of any other person.'

[40] *Cf.* the utterance by Bergbohm cited above footnote 34.

[41] *The Limits of Jurisprudence Defined* 58: there can be no 'act of law which is not either a command or a prohibition, or the reverse of the one or the other of those operations'. Bentham continues to say that 'whatever words besides these may be made use of in expressing the matter of a law or body of laws and that are not names of real entities or of the sensible affections of determinable real entities, the import of the words just mentioned will serve as a key to the import of such other words'.

[42] *The Limits of Jurisprudence Defined* 53: 'In every law must be comprised two things: 1. a specification of the cases in which the punishment is to attach; 2. a specification of the punishment itself: without punishment, no such thing as law.'

single sovereign behind English law but a long row of persons acting as sovereigns for a period. Actual law consisted of the commands and prohibitions of one single sovereign, and this was the sovereign of the moment. He commanded, and he threatened with punishment.[43] Henry VIII could neither command nor threaten in 1780.

But how could it be explained that laws issued in the reign of Henry VIII were commands and prohibitions of George III and his Parliament? Bentham could not have recourse to such fictions as the immortality of the King. He held all fictions in contempt. Only an empirical explanation would be in accordance with his position.

The problem would seem to be insoluble. But Bentham found an explanation in the theory of adoption. The actual sovereign made the laws of preceding sovereigns his own. This he did as a matter of course; if he did not, the whole machinery of government would drop to pieces. No express declaration of the desire of the sovereign to continue established laws was needed. He manifested his intention by every act of government providing for the enforcement of those laws.[44]

This theory of adoption is connected with Bentham's view on the nature of a command. In this regard he followed traditional legal thinking. A command, he holds, is a declaration of will concerning the behaviour of another person; it communicates the content of the will to the addressee.[45] A law is an assemblage of signs declarative of the volition of the sovereign in a state concerning the conduct to be observed by a certain person or class of persons, connected with threats of some evil in case of disobedience.[46]

Strictly speaking the law is what the sovereign wills with regard to the conduct of the subjects. However, the will has to be made known to them. One way of making it known is legislation in the usual form. But the will can be signified in other ways too. Any indication of it is sufficient.[47]

The Limits of Jurisprudence Defined 243: 'A law is an expression of will: that is an assemblage of signs expressive of an act

[43] *The Limits of Jurisprudence Defined* 104: 'Whatever actual force there is in sovereignty rests in the sovereign for the time being: in the living, not in the dead.'

[44] *The Limits of Jurisprudence Defined* 105 f. *Cf.* Hobbes *Leviathan* 26,5: 'The legislator is he, not by whose authority the laws were first made, but by whose authority they now continue to be laws.'

[45] This is quite in accordance with the view of the teachers of natural law. On p. 245 a list of the principal forms of commands is drawn. The first form mentioned is this: 'It is my pleasure that you do not export any corn.'

[46] *The Limits of Jurisprudence Defined* 88 ff., 101, 243.

[47] This coincides with Pufendorf's view.

of the will. These signs may by possibility be any signs whatever which are capable of expressing such a will: the behaviour of him who instead of saying 'put to death the chief leaders of the people' smote off the tallest heads among a parcel of poppies, might instead of being an advice, have been a command.' Bentham alludes to the story told by Livy (1,54,6) of the response given by Tarquin Superbus to a messenger from his son Sextus asking for advice on how to deal with the citizens of Gabii. Tarquin, not trusting the messenger, said nothing but walked out into the garden. There, wandering about as if deep in thought and swinging his stick, he struck off the heads of the tallest poppies. The messenger found the behaviour of Tarquin very strange; but Sextus, a worthy son of such a father, understood the meaning.
The example clearly shows that the substance of a law is the will of the sovereign. Any sign of his will is sufficient. But Bentham adds that only 'those conventional signs the assemblage of which forms what is called *discourse*' is tolerably commodious.

The theory of adoption is based on the sign theory.[48] The adoption of laws issued by previous sovereigns takes place when the present sovereign tacitly shows that he continues to exercise the will of his predecessors. Customary law (judge-made law) is also explained by way of adoption. The sovereign 'pre-adopts' the acts of the judges; and their acts serve as signs to the people at large that similar acts of power will probably be exercised in the future in similar cases.

See *The Limits of Jurisprudence Defined* (243 f.). An example used here is particularly illuminating with regard to Bentham's conception of command as an act of will expressed in any suitable way. 'A Cadi comes by a Baker shop, and finds the bread short of weight: the baker is hanged in consequence. This, if it be part of the design that other bakers should take notice of it, is a sort of law forbidding the selling of bread short of weight under the pain of hanging. Whether the Cadi makes a record in writing attesting that the baker has sold bread short of weight, and issues an order to a public executioner to strangle him, or whether the Cadi himself without saying a word strangles him on the spot, is what to this purpose makes no difference. The silent act of hanging when thus made a consequence of the offence has as good a title in point of extent to the appellation of a law as anything that could be made out of a whole shelf full of pleadings put together.'

[48] As Hart points out (*The Concept of Law*, 1961, 62) Hobbes also has the theory of adoption. (*Leviathan* 26; *cf.* above note 44.) In Hobbes, too, the theory of adoption is connected with the sign of will theory.

Bentham gives the word 'law' a far wider field of application than it has in ordinary language. Every expression of will that is supported by the sovereign is a law, whether it be a judicial, military, or executive order. The same is the case with the most trivial order that a master may have occasion to give to his servant or a husband to his wife.[49] All these orders are adopted by the sovereign when not illegal; they are therefore signs of the will of the sovereign. 'Not a cook is bid to dress a dinner, a nurse to feed a child, an usher to whip a school boy, an executioner to hang a thief, an officer to drive the enemy from a post, but it is by his orders.' There is no fiction, 'the bane of science', in this. For the business of enforcing those orders rests ultimately with the sovereign. Covenants and conveyances also acquire 'all the validity they can possess' by being adopted by the sovereign.[50]

These are the principal features of Bentham's theory of law. He continues the voluntaristic tradition of natural law theory, but he scraps the law of nature and the social contract as well as the fictions belonging to the common law view. The law as an allegedly sociological fact is what the teachers of natural law called positive law or *ius voluntarium.* It consists of the commands and prohibitions of the sovereign. But the power of the sovereign is not of the double kind assumed in natural law theory. It is only an external power to inflict sanctions in case of disobedience.

Bentham enlarges on the will theory with regard to positive law far more than did the teachers of natural law. The law resides in the will of the sovereign. But as we have seen, it includes all kinds of orders or 'mandates' by subordinates which are not illegal (*i.e.* not contrary to the will of the sovereign); the sovereign adopts them and makes them his own. The will itself is the essential thing in the law. The ways in which it is manifested to the subjects is of secondary importance. No more consistent form of will theory could be imagined.

John Austin followed in the footsteps of his teacher and friend. His intention was to lay a scientific foundation for the study of law by fitting law into the world given to us in experience.

The divergencies from Bentham's position are of minor importance. Like Bentham, Austin defines law (positive law) as commands by a political superior (a monarch or a body of persons) to those who are in a state of subjection to him. A command is a declaration

[49] *The Limits of Jurisprudence Defined* 90 f.
[50] *The Limits of Jurisprudence Defined* 105 f.

of will. The commander gives an expression or signification of his desire concerning the conduct of the addressee; with that he combines a threat of some evil (sanctions) to be inflicted in case of non-compliance; and he must have the power of putting the threat into effect. The addressees are bound or obliged to compliance. But this only means that they are exposed to sanctions if they behave in a contrary way. The power of the sovereign is external only. It rests on habitual obedience on the part of the subjects. No moral ground for the authority of the sovereign is propounded.

> Austin, *The Province of Jurisprudence Determined* (ed. Hart 1954) 9: The matter of jurisprudence is positive law: law simply and strictly so called: or law set by political superiors to political inferiors. (*Cf.* 11: *positive* law = law existing by *position.*)
> 13: Every *law* or *rule* . . . is a *command*. Or, rather, laws or rules, properly so called, are a *species* of commands.
> 350: Every positive law . . . is set, directly or circuitously, by a sovereign individual or body, to a member or members of the independent political society wherein its author is supreme . . . It is set by a party armed with might, to a party or parties whom that might can reach.
> 193: The superiority which is styled sovereignty . . . is distinguished . . . by the following marks or characters:
> 1. The *bulk* of the given society are in a *habit* of obedience or submission to a *determinate* and *common* superior . . .
> 2. That certain individual, or that certain body of individuals, is *not* in the habit of obedience to a determinate human superior.
> 17: It is only by the chance of incurring *evil*, that I am *bound* or *obliged* to compliance.

From all this it is evident that legal relations, in Austin's view, are power relations. Legal rules as such are not moral rules even if they coincide with moral rules as they frequently do.

This 'separation of law and morals' is often regarded as the most prominent feature of Austin's doctrine.[51] It was a natural result of his empirical approach which led him to consider legal rules as commands by the actual power-holders in a political community supported by force.

> Julius Stone contends that Austin's theory is not a description of an actual state or of actual law. It is 'a formal theory, from which has been abstracted all reference either to actual political and social conditions or to desirable political and social conditions'. (*The Province and Function of Law*, 1946, 60 f.) Later this is further explained in the following way: '(Austin's)

[51] Positivism as such is often defined as a theory including the separation of law and morals.

main purpose and contribution, despite occasional lapses, appears to be to suggest a framework for viewing the propositions of a legal order as a logically self-consistent system, not to provide a theory of how power was or ought to be distributed in society.' (*Legal System and Lawyer's Reasoning,* 1964, 74 ff.) That Austin did not put forward a theory on how power ought to be distributed or concerning desirable social conditions in general is evident. It is also true that he did not propose to describe a particular legal system, though he usually had the English system in view. But his intention was to describe actual law, the general features of actual law. 'My design is', Austin says with a quotation from Hobbes, 'to show, not what is law here or there, but what is law.' (*Lectures on Jurisprudence,* ed. Campbell, 1929, 32.)

It might occur to an author of our day (with a certain philosophical leaning) to attempt 'viewing the propositions of a legal order as a logically self-consistent system'. This way of thinking—which is highly artificial—was undoubtedly alien to Austin's mind. As Morison points out in his article 'Some Myth about Positivism' (68 *Yale Law Journal* 1958/59) 'the definition of law as commands of the sovereign is presented (by Austin) . . . as a connotation of the word "law" in terms of empirical facts' (230). *Cf.* the quotations from Austin cited above. In the introduction to his edition of *The Province of Jurisprudence Determined* Hart underlines that Austin 'was determined to use in his analysis only clear, hard, empirical terms intelligible to common sense' (XI). It should also be borne in mind that Austin was a disciple of Bentham; and about his empiricism there can be no doubt.—*Cf.* on Bentham and Austin Mario Cattaneo, *Il positivismo giuridico inglese* (1962).

French theory

The great revolution was carried through under the banner of the law of nature. When the feudal order was swept away under the impact of the ideas of freedom and equality, the new legislation was to be based on a true appreciation of this law and of natural rights. Positive law was the expression of the general will (*la volonté générale*) in the sense of the will of all the members of society (*la volonté de tous*). But the general will was to be guided by reason, that is, by the law of nature. This was the position expressed in the declaration of rights of 1789.

During the time of revolution the work on a new civil code was begun.[52] In the draft of the year VIII it is said that there exists

[52] See especially Sagnac, *La législation civile de la révolution française* (1798–1804) 47 ff.; Bonnecase, 1 *La pensée juridique française de 1804 à l'heure présente* (1933) 207 ff.

a general and immutable law which is the source of all positive law; it is nothing but natural reason in so far as it governs all men.[53] The same opinion lay behind the *code civil* though the article was not included in it. In the famous *Discours préliminaire* by the minister of justice, Portalis, presenting the draft of the *code civil*, natural law is eloquently described as the foundation of legislation. Natural law (*le Droit*) is universal and supreme reason grounded on the very nature of things. Positive law (*la Loi*) is only, or should only be, natural law reduced to particular precepts.[54]

Since the legislation of Napoleon had such a background, it might have been expected that its interpretation and application would have been based on the doctrine of natural law. When the laws were obscure or deficient, one would have had recourse to the principles embodied in natural law doctrine. Portalis himself indicated this direction.[55] Some provisions of the *code civil* actually referred to the law of nature (arts. 565 and 1135).

Nevertheless another view concerning interpretation of laws became dominant. This was connected with a rationalistic belief in perfection. The revolutionary leaders were firmly convinced that the people, through its representatives (that is, through themselves), could give a correct expression to the principles of natural law. The laws, therefore, were not regarded solely as decrees by the legislators. They contained an authoritative expression of the law of nature as adapted to the conditions of French society.

Moreover, in accordance with Montesquieu the role of the judge was held to consist in a mechanical application of the laws; the judge was the mouth of the law and did not express any particular opinion.[56] The revolutionaries thought that the laws were so clear and complete that no interpretation would be needed. In a law of 1790 'interpretation' was actually forbidden. If there were any doubts as to the true meaning of the law, the question should be referred to the legislative authorities. This was called *le référé législatif*. The Court of Cassation was erected in 1790 with the purpose of keeping watch over the application of laws by the courts.[57]

The cumbersome *référé législatif* was dropped in the *code civil*. In its place a penalty was provided for a judge who refused to decide a case on the ground that the law was obscure or insufficient (art. 4).

[53] Bonnecase 224.

[54] Bonnecase 516.

[55] Bonnecase 515. *Cf. Le centenaire du Doyen François Gény* (1963) 69 f.

[56] Montesquieu, *De l'esprit des lois* 11,6. *Cf.* Gény, 1 *Méthode d'interprétation* 76 f.

[57] Gény, *Méthode d'interprétation* 77 ff.

This article presupposes that the law was clear and complete.[58] Napoleon himself seems to have entertained the same opinion, as is shown by his reported irritation on the publication of the first commentary to the *code civil* when he is said to have exclaimed: *mon code est perdu!*

It soon became the prevailing opinion that the laws were a complete and authoritative expression of the law of nature. This meant that the law of nature, for the purpose of French jurisprudence, was submerged in positive law.[59] One need not go behind the laws and speculate for oneself on the import of the law of nature. As being its purest expression, the *code civil* became the object of peculiar, almost religious veneration.[60]

In this way the difference between the law of nature (*le Droit*) and positive law (*la Loi*) disappeared. *La Loi, c'est le Droit,* was the maxim of the exegetical school, which was dominant throughout the greater part of the nineteenth century. Positive law was identified with legislation. All legal questions could be, and ought to be, answered on the basis of enacted law. Since the laws were expressions of the will of the legislator, interpretation consisted in ascertaining this will. Its expression could be obscure or deficient. Nevertheless, the will of the legislator could be found by means of the methods of jurisprudence.[61]

Legal positivism, in the sense we are using the term, appeared at a rather late date in French jurisprudence. Carré de Malberg has been called ' the father of legal positivism '.[62] His work *Contribution à la théorie générale de l'état* (1920–22) seems indeed to have been the first major exposition of a positivistic theory in France. The philosophical positivism of Auguste Comte is another matter, of which more will be said later.

German theory

The many-worded Friderician code of 1794 never gained anywhere near the same authority as the *code civil,* and since the

[58] Bonnecase 540. In art. 4 the same words (*sous prétexte de silence, d'obscurité ou d'insuffisance de la loi*) were used as in the decree concerning the *référé legislatif*. (The different interpretation by Koschaker, *Europa und das römische Recht* 186, does not seem convincing.)

[59] *Cf.* Charmont, *La renaissance du droit naturel* (1910) 177.

[60] *Cf.* Sagnac 395; Bonnecase 210 ff.; *Le centenaire du Doyen François Gény* 69.

[61] *Cf.* Bonnecase 234 ff.; *Le centenaire du Doyen François Gény* in several places; Gény in 1 *Archives de philosophie du droit* (1931); Germann, *Probleme und Methoden der Rechtsfindung* (1965) 280 ff.

[62] Héraud, ' Regards sur la philosophie du droit français contemporaine ' (2 *Le Droit Français,* ed. David, 1960, 546).

introduction of French legislation was restricted to the Rhineland, nineteenth-century German jurisprudence never stood under the influence of a code of universal application and the highest repute. Roman law as expounded in the Digests or *Pandekten* of Justinian was the law common to all German states. Its field of application was actually very restricted because it had been largely superseded in the various states by particular legislation. Nevertheless, it was the great, and almost the only, worthy object of jurisprudential research. But, in contrast to the *code civil,* it could not be regarded as an authoritative expression of the law of nature.

The conditions for the development of legal theory in Germany were thus entirely different from those obtaining in France. Nor were they similar to those prevailing in England. The jurists were not under the influence of empiricist philosophy. Their minds were dominated rather by the rationalistic philosophy of Kant and his successors, above all Hegel. No wonder, therefore, that German legal theory followed a third course, distinguished in character from both the English and the French.

Friedrich Carl von Savigny appears as the great figure in the opening stages of the nineteenth-century German *Rechtswissenschaft.*[63] It has been remarked that he never offered a direct criticism of the doctrine of a law of nature.[64] But it has not been sufficiently observed that his criticism was aimed at the natural law notion of positive law.

Savigny's celebrated pamphlet on the vocation of his time to legislation and jurisprudence (*Vom Beruf unserer Zeit für Gesetzgebung und Rechtswissenschaft,* 1814) was written to counteract the proposal of a common code for all German states in the manner of the French. He rejected the idea that perfection could be attained in a code and security established by making its application a mechanical business. This showed a lack of historical sense, he thought. But the proposal was also connected, he found, with the view on the origin of positive law traditionally entertained by most German jurists, namely that positive law is created through legislation or decrees by the supreme authority in the state (6 f.). This was precisely the opinion of the teachers of natural law.

Savigny rejects the unhistorical theory of a social contract. When

[63] The term *Rechtswissenschaft* seems to have been introduced by Savigny in 1814. *Cf.* Koschaker 265. The English translation ' legal science ' has come into use at a comparatively recent date.

[64] Bergbohm, 1 *Jurisprudenz und Rechtsphilosophie* 190; Koschaker 255[1].

history supported by written documents begins, he says, private law, like language, customs, and constitution, has already assumed a definite character peculiar to the people. All these phenomena are mingled with each other. They form a whole by being connected through the common convictions of the people, through the same feeling of inner necessity (8 f.).

The law exists in the common consciousness of the people. It grows with the people and is never static. The rules of civil law belong, indeed, to the folklore (*Volksglauben*). They are retained in the mind by being connected with symbolic, ritual acts which can be regarded as the grammar of the law in those ancient times. On a higher level of civilization the development of the law is taken over by the jurists as shown by the example of Rome (11 f.).

In this pamphlet Savigny is concerned with the *origin* of positive law. He does not raise the question what positive law is. A concept of positive law is presupposed. But when he rejects the theory that positive law has its origin in the decrees of the sovereign, he implicitly rejects the notion that positive law is the will of the sovereign as declared to his subjects. He does not, however, put another theory in place of this.

There is a lack of clarity about Savigny's exposition which is due to his talking of the origin of positive law while presupposing a never defined concept of positive law. But it is most remarkable that he resolutely discards the will theory of the teachers of natural law. In the pamphlet there is no trace of a supreme will whose declarations are law. The law is formed by ' inner, silent forces ', not through gratuitous acts by the legislator.

All this is very vague and it leaves many questions without an answer. But the break with the powerful voluntaristic tradition is unmistakable. This is the great importance of Savigny's pamphlet from the point of view of legal theory. We have before us the tentative beginnings of a non-voluntaristic theory of law.

In his work on Roman law Savigny reiterates the same statements about the origin of positive law and they are slightly more elaborated.[65] But he does not keep to the non-voluntaristic tendency. Now the ' spirit of the people ', the *Volksgeist*, is introduced.[66] The

[65] 1 *System des heutigen römischen Rechts* (1840) §§ 4 ff.

[66] The *Volksgeist* was not mentioned in the pamphlet. *Cf.* Brie, ' Der Volksgeist bei Hegel und in der historischen Rechtsschule ' in 2 *Archiv für Rechts- und Wirtschaftsphilosophie* (1908–09) 189, 193.

spirit of the people assumes the character of a supra-individual spiritual entity that pervades the minds of all who belong to the people (19). The law is created by, and resides in, the spirit of the people. Almost reluctantly, as it seems, the spirit of the people is endowed with a will. In this will, the law exists (20).

Moreover, paramount importance for the law is now ascribed to the state. The state is the corporeal form (*Gestalt*) of that spiritual entity, the people (22). Only through the state can the people become capable of acting. Without the state, civil law has an invisible existence in common sentiments, thoughts, and customs among the people. Through the state it acquires a form that is externally apprehensible (23). In legislation positive law is embodied and backed by irresistible might. But the contents of legislation are drawn from the law previously existing in the spirit of the people (39).

In contrast to the pamphlet this later exposition contains a strong element of voluntarism. Despite his original intentions Savigny returned to the will theory. But he tried to combine a voluntaristic and a non-voluntaristic theory. The bridge between the two theories is the idea that the law exists ' invisibly ' in the spirit of the people before being enacted by the state.

The shift in Savigny's position was probably due to influence from contemporary thinking. Savigny's friend Puchta, who shares with him the role of founder of the historical school in German jurisprudence, also emphasized the idea that the law had its origin in the mind of the people. He introduced the *Volksgeist* in jurisprudential writings. At the same time, however, his outlook was markedly voluntaristic.[67] Savigny was undoubtedly impressed by Puchta's ideas. The concept of the spirit of the people was taken over from Puchta, in whose theory it was fundamental.[68]

Puchta probably got his notion of the people as a supra-individual entity from Hegel.[69] It is also likely that the voluntaristic approach was largely due to Hegel's influence.

Great though the influence of Savigny and Puchta was, that of

[67] *Cf.* G. F. Puchta, *Das Gewohnheitsrecht* (1828) 141 f.: ' Ein dem Recht selbst entsprechender Rechtsschutz ist nur möglich durch ein Organ des allgemeinen Willens, also durch eine Verfassung und im Staate. Daher wird nur derjenige Wille, der die Verfassung hervorruft, auch die Quelle des Rechtes sein können; dieser gemeinsame Wille ist aber ursprünglich der des Volks.'—The voluntaristic view is strongly emphasized in the *Cursus der Institutionen* (1841) 11 f.: ' Wir gebrauchen das Wort Recht für den allgemeinen Willen, den Willen der Gesammtheit.'

[68] *Cf.* Brie 193.

[69] Brie 192.

Hegel was perhaps still more important in giving German jurisprudence its peculiar character. In Hegel's philosophy of law the will-theory reaches its apogee. The law is the will of the state.[70]

Superficially there is a certain similarity between Bentham's view and Hegel's in that the law is held to be the contents of a supreme will without having a foundation in a law of nature. But there is a fundamental difference. According to Bentham it is the actual holder of power who intimates his desire with regard to the conduct of the subjects, and threatens with evil if it is not complied with. The commands of the sovereign impose no real duties or obligations on the subject; to be under an obligation is only to be exposed to the likelihood of an evil.

For Hegel the lawgiving will does not belong to the state in the sense of the actual holder of power but to the state in a much more exalted sense. It would be impossible to render his ideas in a comprehensible language without entering on long explanations. Be it sufficient here to say that the individuals, in his view, are only elements (*Momente*) of the state. All worth and all spiritual reality that man possesses, he possesses through the state. The state embodies the ethical idea, it stands for the rational purpose of man, and therefore it is the highest duty of man to belong to the state and obey its laws. The idea of original freedom, which lay at the root of natural law thinking and suggested the fiction of a social contract, has no place in the philosophy of Hegel. The state assumes a divine character.

It became the general opinion in German jurisprudence during the nineteenth century that real law was positive law and positive law the will of the state.[71] The ultimate source, from which its contents were drawn, was the common consciousness of rights and duties (*das allgemeine Rechtsbewusstsein*). But the contents of this consciousness became law only through being enacted in some way by the lawgiving will. The 'material' source of the law was the *Rechtsbewusstsein*; but the will of the state was its 'formal' source.[72]

[70] For Hegel's philosophy of law see his *Grundlinien der Philosophie des Rechts* (1821, ed. J. Hoffmeister 1955). *Cf.* the account given by Verdross 151 ff.

[71] *Cf.* for instance Thon, *Rechtsnorm und subjektives Recht* (1878) 1: 'Seit Hegel ist es üblich, das Recht im objectiven Sinne als den allgemeinen Willen zu bestimmen'; Bergbohm 40; 'Ein Recht ist positiv, im Gegensatz zu einem bloss gedachten, . . . wenn und soweit er der "erklärte Rechtswille einer Rechtsquelle ist". . . . Nur die Erklärung . . . durch den competenten rechtsbildenden Willen macht es zum positiv geltenden.' *Cf.* Ago 21.

[72] *Cf.* Bergbohm 542 ff.

The prevailing opinion among the German jurists and legal philosophers differed essentially from the doctrine of Bentham and Austin, which was almost unknown in Germany until the end of the last century.[73] The most important difference concerned these two points:

(i) The lawgiving will was thought to be the general will or the will of the state, not the will of some actual power holders. The state was supposed to represent the whole community.[74]

(ii) Though the rules of law were described as commands or declarations of will, they were not represented as simply being power decrees supported by threats. To most German thinkers it was self-evident that the rules of law possessed obligatory force in the traditional sense.[75] Only rarely was the 'binding force' of the law reduced to mere compulsion.[76]

Two different types of legal positivism can therefore be discerned. The kind represented by Bentham and Austin may be called *naturalistic* legal positivism because it purports to give a purely factual, naturalistic explanation of the nature of the law. In contrast, the predominant German type may be called *idealistic* legal positivism. It contains an idealistic element in that the obligatory force is supposed to be a property of the law. This is connected with the

[73] The first German author to have taken notice of Austin's work seems to have been Bergbohm in the work just cited 13. *Cf.* A. B. Schwarz in 1 *Politica* (1934–35) 197 f.

[74] For a critical survey see Hägerström, *Inquiries* 17 ff.

[75] *Cf.* Bergbohm 49 f.: 'Wir sprechen von dem "geltenden" Recht, dem Recht, das "gilt" (oder "gegolten" hat), von seiner formellen "Giltigkeit", nach deren Gründen wir suchen. Wir meinen damit soviel wie Wirksamkeit, Verbindlichkeit, besonders geartete Verpflichtungskraft der als rechtliche bezeichneten Normen, kurz Dasjenige im Recht, was da macht, dass man ihm zu gehorchen verpflichtet ist. Das sind Anhäufungen von bloss erklärenden, nicht definierenden Worten, durch welche umschrieben werden soll das bisher undefinierte Etwas, um deswillen Recht eben rechtlich bindet.'—Referring to Bergbohm, Verdross says in *Abendländische Rechtsphilosophie* (1958) 252: 'Normalerweise versteht man [unter "rechtsverbindlich"] eine innere (sittliche) Verpflichtung, den Normen einer Gemeinschaft zu gehorchen.'

In his survey 'Zur Normentheorie' Affolter sums up the usual position of the German scholars in this way: 'Der Rechtssatz ist ein Satz, der Pflichten begründet, und wo wir eine Pflicht, sei es eine privatrechtliche oder eine öffentlich rechtliche annehmen, muss dieselbe auf einem Befehle beruhen.' (32 *Archiv für öffentliches Recht,* 1908, 362.)

Cf. Engisch, *Einführung in das juristische Denken* (1959) 22: 'Soweit die rechtlichen Imperative in Geltung stehen, haben sie verpflichtende Kraft.'

[76] Thus Julius Binder in an inaugural lecture from 1911 (*Rechtsnorm und Rechtspflicht*). *Cf.* Welzel, *Die Frage nach der Rechtsgeltung* (1966) 13 f., where the exceptional character of Binder's position is underlined.

strong idealistic current in German thinking as opposed to the empirist tradition in England.

The nature and basis of the binding force of the law were intensely discussed. It is not necessary here to go into the various theories. From about the end of the nineteenth century the so-called theory of recognition (*Anerkennungstheorie*) became the leading one. In one form or other it holds that the obligatory force of the law stems from its being recognized as binding.[77] In reality, this theory is akin to the old theory of a social contract since the binding force is supposed to derive from some sort of acceptance on the part of those who are to be bound.

The relationship between the 'historical school' of German jurisprudence, represented by Savigny, Puchta, and their adherents, on the one side, and the 'positivism' of the latter part of the century, on the other, is briefly as follows.

Both schools declined to accept the idea of a law of nature; positive law was the only real law and it always had an historical origin. But this origin was described in different ways. According to the historical school the law was primarily customary law (*Gewohnheitsrecht*). Enacted law was secondary.

Legislation was based on law already existing in the soul of the people. The positivists regarded positive law as the will of the state. If customary law was held to be real law at all, this was said to depend on its being recognized by the state. In this way the will of the state became the decisive element in customary law too. (*Cf.* Windscheid, *Reden und Abhandlungen*, 1904, 68 f.) But the distinction is by no means sharp and clear. Windscheid, for instance, called himself an historical jurist, out of veneration for Savigny perhaps, though he did not embrace the theory of the primacy of customary law (72 f.). For him the law was the will of the state. (*Lehrbuch des Pandektenrechts*, 9 Aufl. 1906, § 14.) He was an historical jurist in the sense that he always wanted to see existing law in an historical perspective. But he was a typical representative of German legal positivism in the sense that he regarded the law as state commands. (*Cf.* E. Wolf, *Grosse Rechtsdenker*, 1963, 591 ff.)

The Renaissance of Natural Law

Within the framework of legal positivism many different theories were put forward to explain the nature of the lawgiving will, the

[77] The theory of recognition was founded by Bierling in his work *Juristische Prinzipienlehre* (1894–1917, reprinted 1961). See the first volume 19, 41 ff. *Cf.* Henkel 442 f. and Welzel's essay *Die Frage nach der Rechtsgeltung,* where the literature on the *Anerkennungstheorie* is recorded and discussed. See further Hägerström, *Inquiries* 277, for a brief survey of the theories on the basis of the binding force of laws.

rules of law and their relationship to the concepts of rights and duties. But up to the year 1930 the prevalent opinion was that legal positivism provided the basis for a scientific theory of law. It was commonly regarded as the only conceivable alternative to the unscientific doctrine of natural law.

Morris R. Cohen writes for instance in his *Law and the Social Order* (1933) 249: 'In nearly all modern jural and political discussion that styles itself scientific, law is defined as the will of the sovereign.'

Welzel writes: 'Noch vor 20 Jahren (the beginning of the nineteen thirties) herrschte in der Wissenschaft und Praxis völlig unbestritten der Positivismus.' (In the *Naturrecht oder Rechtspositivismus*, ed. W. Maihofer, 1962, 322.) *Cf.* Kaufmann, *Naturrecht und Geschichtlichkeit* (1957) 6: 'Seit Menschengedenken war [about 1930] das Naturrecht aus den Hörsälen unserer Universitäten verschwunden, ganze Generationen von Juristen waren mit der Lehre des Positivismus grossgezogen geworden.' See also Larenz, *Methodenlehre der Rechtswissenschaft* (1960) 83.

The ideas underlying the doctrine of natural law were not, however, easily displaced. They had a strong hold on the human mind. It was not sufficient to proclaim that real law consisted of the commands of the sovereign or the state. Natural law concepts and views could nevertheless be retained; and this actually occurred on a large scale. Significantly, the first (and only) volume of Bergbohm's great work *Jurisprudenz und Rechtsphilosophie* from the year 1892 carries the sub-title: *Das Naturrecht der Gegenwart* (*Present Natural Law Doctrine*). The purpose of the author is to uncover elements of natural law thinking in the literature of legal positivism. In this he was undoubtedly successful. Other authors, too, have contributed to show how vast was the surreptitious influence of natural law views in positivistic literature.

For a large part Hägerström's principal work on legal philosophy was devoted to such criticism of legal positivism. (See *Inquiries* in many places, especially 48 ff., 74 ff., 201 ff.) Lundstedt followed up the criticism in several publications (*Die Unwissenschaftlichkeit der Rechtswissenschaft* 1932–36, *Legal Thinking Revised* 1956), and among other critics Kelsen should also be mentioned. In his work *The Revival of Natural Law Concepts* (1930), Haines showed the strong and persistent influence of natural law ideas in American jurisprudence.

It is, indeed, impossible to make a clear-cut distinction between authors who are positivists and those who embrace a natural law theory; so often are the views of authors who profess to be positivists permeated with natural law ideas and concepts. For this reason it would be impracticable to designate as positivists only those who are really positivists through and through. The term ' legal positivism ' will therefore be used here to denote theories which are *professedly* built on the basic assumption that real law is the expression of the will of a supreme authority in society, defined as the sovereign or the state or in some other way. It will not be implied that the theories are actually consistent with the basic tenets. Whether they are or not has to be decided separately in each case.

A resurrection of manifest natural law doctrine began about the turn of the century. It grew slowly in strength until the Second World War and culminated in the decade after the war. During recent years the movement seems to have abated to some degree.

The return to natural law had been prepared through the criticism directed against legal positivism on two important points: the principles of interpretation and the binding force of the law.

The principles of interpretation

According to classical natural law doctrine, positive law was based on the law of nature and included its principles. Positive law therefore had to be interpreted in the light of natural law. When positive law was obscure or deficient, natural law supplied a solution. From it an answer to every legal question could be deduced. Natural law thus became the basis of the administration of law.

The whole problem of so-called interpretation of law underwent a profound change when the law of nature was eliminated. Jurists were denied recourse to a never-failing fountain of justice. Since real law was nothing but the will of the supreme authority, the aim of interpretation could only be to ascertain the contents of this will. Such was the opinion prevailing among the German jurists. It led to the formation of ' conceptual jurisprudence ' (*Begriffsjurisprudenz*) in Germany, which was based on the supposition that every question could be answered by drawing the right inferences from the concepts of the law. The French jurists of the exegetical school came to much the same result through their identification of positive law with the will of the lawgiver as expressed in the codes.

For a succinct statement of the positivistic position, see Bergbohm 383 ff. Even if statutes and other ' indications of the law ' (*das Recht*) are lacking in clarity, completeness, and harmony, the law itself is always comprehensive, all-embracing, clear and harmonious to the judge at the moment when he has to give his decision. (*Cf.* Hägerström, *Inquiries* 74 ff.) Concerning the exegetical school in France, see Bonnecase 524 ff. *Cf.* Germann, *Methodische Grundfragen* 36.

The criticism of legal positivism began first with this point. Several authors showed that 'interpretation' could not consist in ascertaining 'the will of the lawgiver' only. Even if all possible material indicating the intentions of the 'lawgiver' were used, many questions would remain unanswered; moreover, the intentions of those engaged in drafting the law made no part of the law itself. A more general and satisfactory principle of interpretation was needed. But was it possible to attain such a principle on the basis of legal positivism?

In France the methods of the exegetical school were made the object of a penetrating and exhaustive criticism by Francois Gény in his great work *Méthode d'interprétation et sources en droit privé positif* (1899). He revealed the illusory nature of the principle of finding out the will of the lawgiver. The conclusion which he drew from his criticism was that one had to return to the doctrine of natural law.

The *code civil* was supposed to be an authoritative expression of the law of nature. The exegetical school interposed the will of the lawgiver between the law of nature and the interpreter. The authority of the lawgiver was held to be absolute. One had to take the law from him, and from him only; it was not permissible to go behind his will to seek out the ultimate source of justice. The criticism had the effect of removing this prohibition and establishing the opposite principle. Consequently, the law of nature regained its old place and importance.

Positive law, according to Gény, is an expression of the will of the state, embodying the nation. But positive law is based on an ideal of justice that is felt to be obligatory. Gény reversed the motto of the exegetical school and proclaimed: *le Droit, ce n'est pas la Loi*, 'le Droit' signifying the law of nature.

Gény avoids the term 'natural law' because it is connected with unclear ideas. He prefers the expression *le donné rationel*, about which he says: 'Il represente le fond essentiel du droit naturel classique nettement dégagé de tout alliage.' (2 *Science et technique en droit privé positif*, 1914–24, 380 f.) The natural law of Gény had a religious foundation. (See 1 *Méthode d'interprétation* 5.) The theory of Gény met with such success that Charmont already in 1910 could publish his book *La renaissance du droit naturel*. (*Cf.* Bonnecase 446.) On Gény, see further *Le centenaire du doyen Francois Gény* (1963). In the article

'La notion de droit en France' in 1 *Archives de philosophie du droit* (1931) Gény has summarized his position with regard to the concept of law.

From the first decade of the present century the German *Begriffsjurisprudenz* was under heavy fire. Jhering had started the criticism earlier. It was now pursued with great vigour by the 'free law movement' (*Freirechtsbewegung*), which was strongly tinged by natural law ideas. An element of such ideas was also present in the 'jurisprudence of interest' (*Interessenjurisprudenz*) of Philipp Heck and others. But these new tendencies did not gain as much influence as the teachings of Gény in France. German jurisprudence in general for a long time remained solidly positivistic.[78]

The criticism of the *Begriffsjurisprudenz* and similar methods did not necessarily lead to a renewal of natural law ideas. Other methods could be put in their place without reference to a supposed law of nature. In the U.S., for instance, both the sociological jurisprudence of Roscoe Pound and the American Realism are partly to be understood as resulting from the criticism of traditional, rigid methods in the administration of justice. V. Lundstedt vehemently attacked the *Begriffsjurisprudenz* and sought to replace it by his own 'method of social welfare' (*Legal Thinking Revised*, 1956).

The binding force of the law

With regard to the question of the binding force of the law, two different views, as we have seen, were represented within legal positivism.

In the naturalistic doctrine of Bentham and Austin the law was not invested with binding force in the usual sense. The law was only externally binding, as the teachers of natural law would have said: The commands of the sovereign were binding or obligatory in the sense only that the subjects were exposed to the threat of some evil (sanctions) in case of disobedience. The law of nature was eliminated. But the concept of positive law current in natural law doctrine was retained. This positive law now became the naked commands of a sovereign possessed with external power only, lacking the mystical power over the minds of the subjects.

The idealistic positivism of German jurists and philosophers expresses the opinion that the law has binding force in the traditional sense. It is not binding externally only. The binding force of the commands of the state is not identical with their being backed by

[78] *Cf.* Germann, *Methodische Grundfragen* (1946) 36.

force. To have a legal duty is not merely to be exposed to the risk of sanctions; on the contrary, sanctions are supposed to be applied as a consequence of the violation of a duty. The law, therefore, is not conceived as a sociological fact only; the concept contains an ideal element.

Idealistic positivism comes closest to the general, popular view. To the public the laws appear as commands or decrees of a supreme authority in society. But this authority is not regarded as possessing naked power only. It is supposed to have a right to legislate. Therefore it is held to be capable of imposing real duties. Generally speaking there is no doubt about that; even if one may be dissatisfied with some legislation, this is not held to affect the general duty of obeying the law.

In so far as idealistic positivism regards the law as commands of the state possessing binding force in the usual sense, it is therefore in accordance with the popular view. But legal positivism differs from the popular view if and when it holds the power of the state to be boundless. The idea that one would have a real duty to obey whatever the state authorities may decree is not acceptable to public opinion. Certain limits to the power of the state in creating duties are assumed, however vaguely they may be conceived. Legal positivism, however, defined the law as the will of the state, not relying on any superior law. At the same time it regarded law as binding in the usual sense. On these premises it became logically impossible to assume any bounds to the power of the state to create duties. As has often been pointed out, the state was, in fact, deified.

During the calm period of the latter part of the nineteenth and the beginning of the present century, the discrepancy between the popular view and idealistic positivism was probably not very acutely felt by the theorists. The state was supposed to be governed by considerations of justice and general welfare. If the state was a god, it was a righteous and protective, if sometimes stern, god.

As long as these views could be preserved as the background of legal thinking, the position of idealistic positivism was not really shaken. With emergence of the totalitarian states, the psychological situation was radically altered. Those natural rights that were believed to be secured as an integral part of our civilisation were trampled under foot by one regime after another. Now the cleavage between idealistic positivism and the popular view became apparent. The proposition that the decrees of the state, regardless of their contents, were capable of imposing real duties, came to be regarded as absurd. According to legal positivism, Jerome Hall says, the most outrageous enactment of a dictator must be recognized as law, *i.e.* recognized as obligatory.[79] Characteristically, it has been said that the doctrine of the legal omnipotence of the lawgiver was the Fall (*der Sündenfall*) of legal positivism and that the great task of the future would be to overcome this sin.[80]

The reproach that legal positivism made the state a god could only be directed against idealistic positivism. Naturalistic positivism implies no deification of the state, since it ascribes binding force to the commands of the sovereign in the sense only that the commands are accompanied by threats. But this distinction has often been overlooked; the same kind of criticism has been levelled against legal positivism in general. Some authors, however, have criticised naturalistic positivism precisely because it does not regard the rules of law as binding in the usual sense.[81]

It is important to keep these different kinds of criticism apart. To take exception to naturalistic positivism because it does not ascribe obligatory force (in the usual sense) to the rules of law is one thing; to belabour idealistic positivism for holding the state to have illimited power of laying down laws with obligatory force is another thing.[82]

From both kinds of criticism the same conclusion has been drawn. This is that the law cannot simply be an expression of the will of the state or of the holders of power. There must be something more in it. This line of thought has contributed more than anything else to the revival of natural law theories.

Modern Natural Law Theory

After the Second World War the theoretical considerations conducive to a revival of natural law theory were greatly reinforced by powerful waves of emotion. For obvious reasons, this was particularly so in Germany; but the general tendency was the same in many other

[79] *From Legal Theory to Integrative Jurisprudence* (1964) 24 (reprinted from 33 *Univ. of Cincinnati Law Review*, 1964). Also in 1 *Mélanges en l'honneur de Jean Dabin* (1963).

[80] Welzel in *Naturrecht oder Rechtspositivismus* 334.

[81] Salmond, *Jurisprudence* (9 ed., 1937) § 17; Fuller, *The Morality of Law* (1964) 147 ff.

[82] Cattaneo stresses the difference between English and German legal positivism (297 ff.).

countries.[83] An enormous amount of literature tending towards a natural law has been published during the last twenty-five years.[84]

Modern natural law theories may be divided into two categories, religious and secular. In 1962 a symposium was held at Vienna on the theme of the law of nature in political theory. All participants, with the exception of Professor Kelsen, expressed a natural law position; and all of them endorsed his thesis that there could be no foundation for a law of nature without God.[85]

Since the assumption of a divine law of nature is a matter of faith, it lies outside the boundaries of scientific discussion. But it may be pointed out that it seems to be questionable, from the point of view of the religious mind itself, whether a so-called law of nature could be based on divine fiat. Is murder, or rape, considered a wrong only because it is supposed to have been forbidden by God? It is hard to imagine a religious person really thinking that these actions could be turned into good through an arbitrary command by the divinity. Most likely, such commands would seem to be unthinkable. But if that is the case, some actions are held to be wrong in themselves, *mala per se*. As we have seen, this was the position of Grotius among others; the law of nature consisted of such precepts as were by necessity issued by God. This implies that the law of nature is actually independent of the will of God. To make the will of God, at the same time, the basis of the law of nature is self-contradictory. The religious foundation of the law of nature appears to be illusory from religion's own point of view.

In the secular theories of natural law there is no place for a lawgiver laying down the law of nature; and the classical method of deducing rules from actual tendencies of behaviour is patently obsolete. The result is that it becomes impossible to speak any more of a *law* of nature in the exact sense of the word. This seems to be the general standpoint of those authors who do not refer to the

[83] Gustav Radbruch's lecture in 1946 on '*Gesetzliches Unrecht und übergesetzliches Recht*' (printed in the fourth edition of his *Rechtsphilosophie,* 1950) is particularly expressive of this mood. Jerome Hall exempts, rightly I believe, England, Sweden and Denmark (44 *Virginia Law Review,* 1958, 321 f.)

[84] The collection *Naturrecht oder Rechtspositivismus,* edited by W. Maihofer 1962, contains a bibliography for the years 1945–60 running into 42 closely printed pages. Several surveys are available, as Henkel, *Einführung in die Rechtsphilosophie* (1964) 393 ff.; Julius Stone, *Human Law and Human Justice* (1965) 193 ff.; Jerome Hall, *From Legal Theory to Integrative Jurisprudence* 101 ff.; Erik Wolf, *Das Problem der Naturrechtslehre* (1964).

[85] *Das Naturrecht in der politischen Theorie,* hrsg. von Franz-Martin Schmölz (1963) 117.

divine will as the source of the law of nature. Many in fact prefer not to speak of a law of nature any more.[86]

What remains then as 'natural law'? There seems to be one common feature in the many divergent natural law theories of today. This is the assumption that the rules of law create rights and duties in the usual sense of the words. A right, in this sense, is not equated with naked, brutal power: right is not might. A duty to do something or forbear from something is not conceived as the situation of being exposed to the risk of sanctions in case of contrary behaviour. The sanction is held to be a reaction called forth by a breach of duty. The duty therefore is antecedent to the sanction; the sanction is justified through the violation of the duty.

Now it is evident that rights and duties in this sense are not held to be created at will through power decrees. No duty is believed to be imposed merely by a threat, no right conferred simply by giving somebody actual power over his fellow citizens. Something more is needed.

The fundamental problem is therefore the same as that which confronted the classical teachers of natural law. It is to find an explanation of the binding force of positive law. For what is meant by the binding force of positive law is its power to impose real duties and confer real rights, which cannot be done merely through actual power. But while the classical theorists sought the explanation either in the will of God or in some inborn social inclinations, modern theorists have recourse to ultimate values. Positive law, so the argument runs, assumes the character of real and true law only in so far as it possesses binding force; and binding force it can only have if and when it is inspired by certain fundamental values which compel the obedience of rational, civilized men.

The traditional dichotomy of 'law' into natural and positive law has been more or less definitely abandoned. It is being superseded by the idea that true law is to be distinguished from mere decrees of power through its intrinsic quality. Positive law is held to be really binding only in so far as it possesses this quality. The values in question afford a measure for judging positive law and a ground for rejecting enactments that violate the fundamental principles based on these values.

This modern view is enunciated by Professor Villey in the following words (*Archives de philosophie du droit*, 1957, 97,

[86] Thus for instance Henkel 415.

also in the *Leçons d'Histoire de la Philosophie du Droit* (1962) 282 f.):

'L'histoire a prouvé le caractère mouvant du droit, elle nous interdit le retour au rêve ancien des lois naturelles statiques. Cependant que la philosophie actuelle illustre l'idée de liberté. Point question de nier désormais toute compétence créatrice à la volonté. Mais nous sommes contraints de reconnaître des limites à cette compétence; tout convention en possède point de valeur juridique, et celle d'une bande de brigands ne crée pas du droit. Le droit nous paraît au contraire d'un second point de vue comme l'antithèse de l'arbitraire; il est un frein opposé aux initiatives de la volonté collective ou individuelle, il annule les contrats conclus contre l'ordre public ou les bonnes moeurs; il infirme des lois injustes. Il subordonne ces actes libres et volontaires au contrôle d'une certaine raison, d'une certaine idée de justice ou de moralité, à l'empire de certaines *valeurs*. . . . Le droit est l'invention de l'homme mais une fois constitué, restreint et contrôle sa volonté.'

The principles that are supposed to follow from the fundamental values are not said to be eternal and unchangeable. They must be adapted to circumstances of time and place. If a 'law of nature' is spoken of at all, it is therefore held to be variable. Many authors prefer to use Rudolf Stammler's expression 'right law' (*richtiges Recht*).[87] A scientific basis of the position is usually sought for in some objectivistic theory of value.[88]

An important question with regard to modern natural law theories is what conception of 'positive law' underlies these theories. It is difficult to generalize on this point since in most cases the writings contain no discussion of the concept of positive law. The traditional idea of law 'posited' by the state seems to be taken for granted; and the argument turns on the question of the conditions under which this positive law is real law, in the sense of being capable of conferring rights and imposing duties. There are, however, exceptions where this view concerning the nature of 'positive law' is subjected to direct criticism.[89]

Different Meanings of the Term 'Legal Positivism'

In the literature of the twentieth century the expression 'legal positivism' (*Rechtspositivismus, positivisme juridique, positivismo giuridico*) has become more and more frequently employed. At the beginning of the century it was only rarely used; now it is one of the

[87] Henkel 409 ff., 416.
[88] A critical survey by H.-U. Evers in 16 *Juristenzeitung* (1961) 241 ff.
[89] Thus Fuller in *The Morality of Law*.

most common terms in the vocabulary of legal theory. Unfortunately, it has no generally recognized meaning. Considerable confusion has ensued from its being used in several different senses and from lack of distinction between these.

To understand the present situation it is necessary to outline a historical background. I have therefore made an attempt to trace the origin of the term and the modifications in its meaning.[90]

To begin with it seems to be certain that legal positivism, or *Rechtspositivismus,* was first spoken of in German literature. Exactly when it was introduced is not known. A German author says that it was not in use until the latter part of the nineteenth century.[91] This is almost certainly correct.

It was the great ambition of the German jurists of that period to maintain a scientific standard in their work. As Gierke said, our legal science purports to, and ought to be, scientific through and through.[92] This entailed, first and foremost, the elimination of all speculations on a law of nature. The subject matter of legal science was to be positive law. The only true legal science was *die Wissenschaft vom positiven Recht*, or positive legal science (*positive Rechtswissenschaft*) as it was also called.

> *Cf.* Adolf Merkel in a famous article that has been considered as expressing the programme of legal positivism. (1 *Grünhut's Zeitschrift für das privat- und öffentliche Recht der Gegenwart,* 1874, 1 ff.; *cf.* Verdross 164.) Bergbohm remarks that the expression *positive Rechtswissenschaft* is current (*Jurisprudenz und Rechtsphilosophie* 52 f.). Like Austin he speaks of the philosophy of positive law (*Philosophie des positiven Rechts,* 27, 35). The expression *positive Rechtswissenschaft* had long been used in Germany. It occurs in the title of a book by Nettelbladt from 1772 (*Nova Introductio in Jurisprudentiam Positivam Germanorum Communem*); see A. B. Schwarz in 1 *Politica* (1934–35) 195. Feuerbach mentions *positive Rechtswissenschaft* in 1804, see Erik Wolf, *Grosse Rechtsdenker* 556.

Positive law signified law by position, *gesetztes Recht.* The subject matter of positive legal science was law in this sense, to the exclusion of the supposed law of nature. In the first place the contention that the subject matter of legal science was positive law merely said something negative: that the law of nature did not

[90] The following observations are far from complete. *Cf.* the article by Ago, cited above, footnote 33, and Cattaneo, *Il positivismo giuridico inglese* 2 ff.

[91] Herrfardt in 7 *Studium Generale* (1954) 88.

[92] 7 (Schmoller's) *Jahrbuch für Gesetzgebung, Verwaltung und Rechtspflege* (1883) 1112: Unsere Rechtswissenschaft will und soll ja doch durchweg Wissenschaft sein.

belong to its field of inquiry. But an affirmative assertion concerning the concept of law was involved too. 'Positive law' was thought to be posited in the sense of the will theory: it was the expression of the will of the lawgiving authority.

Despite many differences of opinion this view was common among those German jurists of the latter part of the nineteenth century who held positive law to be the one legitimate object of legal science—Windscheid, Jhering, Binding, Thon, Zitelmann, Adolf Merkel, Bergbohm, and many others. They have generally been called positivists, or legal positivists. I have not found the term *Rechtspositivismus* in their writings. But others called them positivists and designated their view on the nature of law as *Rechtspositivismus.* Probably these terms were first used by their adversaries.

In an inaugural lecture from 1882 (published in 1883 under the title *Naturrecht und deutsches Recht*) Otto von Gierke opposes 'the naked positivism' (*den kahlen Positivismus*) because it ultimately leads to the elimination of the idea of justice (*die Rechtsidee*). He characterizes 'positivism' in the following way (11): '*An die Stelle dieses in dem unzugänglichen Urgrunde unseres geistigen Wesens wurzelnden Etwas* [*die Rechtsidee*] *setzt er* [*der Positivismus*] *von der formellen Seite her die handgreifliche Thatsache der befehlenden und zwingenden Macht und von der materiellen Seite her die gemeinverständliche Vorstellung des bezweckten und erreichten Nutzens.*' Positivism easily engenders the belief '*es lasse sich alles, was sich in Gesetzesform befehlen lässt, dadurch auch in lebendiges Recht wandeln.*'

This is the first instance I have come across of the word *Positivismus* being used to designate a theory of law. A year later Gierke follows up the attack on 'positivistic formalism' (*positivistischer Formalismus*). He reproaches the positivists with resurrecting the whole apparatus of natural law doctrine—with the exception of its belief in the idea of justice: '*Dieselbe äusserliche, das Gesetz vergötternde, in das Zwangselement ausmündende Auffassung des Rechtes.*' ('Labands Staatsrecht und die deutsche Rechtswissenschaft' in 7 *Jahrbuch für Gesetzgebung* etc., 1883, 1191 f.) The theories which Gierke had in mind were those of his contemporaries Jhering, Thon, and Dernburg. In spite of all differences of opinion, Gierke says, they held Hegel's definition of law as 'general will' to be correct 'from a formal point of view' (*in formaler Hinsicht*). Therefore they represented the law as identical with the will of the community, especially of the state. (1 *Deutsches Privatrecht*, 1895, 116.) Gierke also refers to Merkel as being essentially a positivist.

From this it appears that what Gierke meant by *Positivismus* was the theory that all law is posited in the sense of being an expression of the will of the community or the state. According to his own view the rules of law were primarily rational propositions concerning the limitations on the several wills required for a just order of life (*Vernunftsaussagen über die zu einer gerechten Lebensordnung erforderlichen Willensabgrenzungen*). These propositions contain an element of will, too, because they have to be backed by external power. But this will content is a secondary element in the law; as to its innermost substance the law is not will. (*Ibid.*)

In its original and traditional connotation the term *Rechtspositivismus* primarily signifies a view *on the nature of law, viz.* that all law is positive in the sense of being the expression of the will of a supreme authority. A corollary to this view, also designated as *Rechtspositivismus,* is an opinion *on the object of legal science, viz.,* that its legitimate object can only be positive law in the same sense.

Cf. Ago 19 ff. with many quotations. In 1931 the prominent jurist Beling sums up on the *Rechtspositivismus* in the following manner:

'Vertiefen wir uns in die Gedankenwelt dieses heutigen Positivismus. Menschen haben im Namen eines Verbandes ein Machtwort gesprochen, lautend auf ein dem gesellschaftlichen Leben vorgezeichnetes " Soll ". Das is das " Recht ". Fügen wir diesem Bild einige Striche hinzu, nämlich dass nur das Gesetz Rechtsquelle ist; dass alles Gesetz bedingungslos Recht ist, und schliesslich, dass nur das Staatsgesetz in Betracht kommt, so haben wir den Positivismus im, wenn ich so sagen darf, orthodoxesten Sinne vor uns.' Beling goes on to say that, for rigid positivism, only the will of the historical legislator in the sense of the 'human' theory is 'the law' (*Recht*). (In the article 'Vom Positivismus zum Naturrecht und zurück', 133 *Archiv für die civilistische Praxis,* 1931, *Beilageheft, Festschrift für Heck, Rümelin und Schmidt,* 3 f.)

In his *Hauptprobleme der Staatsrechtslehre* (1911) Kelsen notes as self-evident that legal science can only be a science of positive law (6). In another work legal positivism is defined as a theory which earnestly refrains from every assumption of a law of nature and confines itself to being a theory of positive law. (*Die philosophischen Grundlagen der Naturrechtslehre und des Rechtspositivismus,* 1928, 7 f., 63.) Positive law, according to Kelsen, consists of norms posited (*gesetzt*) through acts of will. (*Reine Rechtslehre,* 2 Aufl., 1960, 205. See also the article '*Was ist Rechtspositivismus*?' in 20 *Juristenzeitung,* 1965, 465 ff.) Kelsen follows German tradition in his use of the term *Rechtspositivismus.* He set himself the task of constructing a legal science adapted to its object, positive law, with elimination of all foreign elements. This is what is meant by the 'Pure Theory of Law'.

In recent literature the *Rechtspositivismus* is often qualified as *Gesetzespositivismus.* This expression is hard to translate. One would have to say ' statutory legal positivism ' or something of the kind. The term is employed to designate the extreme form of legal positivism in which positive law is identified with enacted law, or statutory law. Usually the sense is pejorative.

Gesetzespositivismus is defined by Wieacker 431 as ' der immer wieder mit tiefem Recht bekämpften, aber in der Rechtspraxis bis heute vorherrschenden Überzeugung, dass *alles* Recht vom staatlichen Gesetzgeber erzeugt werde und sich in seinem Befehlen erschöpfe '. *Cf.* Verdross 168; Henkel 389.
In the article just quoted Beling speaks of the *Gesetzespositivismus* as opposed to the *Gewohnheitsrechts-Positivismus* (customary law positivism) of the historical school. This explains the origin of the term. Perhaps it was invented by Beling; I have found no earlier instance of its being used. (In his work *Studien zur Ideengeschichte der Gesetzgebung,* 1960, Sten Gagnér writes much about *Gesetzespositivismus,* which is, indeed, a central concept. But it is never defined, and it is being used in an inexplicable and most disconcerting way. *Cf.* W. Henke in 28 *Rabel's Zeitschrift für ausländisches und internationales Privatrecht,* 1964, 746; W. Ullman in 29 *Tijdschrift voor Rechtsgeschiedenis,* 1961, 123 ff.)

The traditional meaning of the word *Rechtspositivismus* is still common in German literature. But a new meaning has also been introduced. Several authors employ the word *Positivismus* in the sense of philosophical positivism. It then signifies the general view that science has to do with observable phenomena only. For positivism in this sense it is held to be characteristic that science should refrain from making valuations, should be *bewertungsfrei* or *wertblind.* The result is that *Rechtspositivismus* has come to be used as an appellation of theories of law declining valuation.[93] Many writers use the term *Rechtspositivismus* with pejorative implication. According to them the correct view is that the law must include an element of value, usually defined as justice. Without this element of value the law could not be obligatory and therefore not truly law. The positivistic theories are held to miss something essential in the law when they are ' blind to values '.

Larenz (67) finds both the psychological and the sociological approach of legal positivism to some extent justified. What is lacking is something essential to the law, its claim to possess validity (37).
Henkel (392) gives positivism credit for its interpretation of the

[93] Henkel 379; Welzel, *Naturrecht und materiale Gerechtigkeit* 182 f.; Larenz 35 ff.

‘ existential ’ side of the law. Its defect is said to be the lack of insight into the ‘ essential ’ quality of the law: ‘ Es mangelt hier an der Einsicht, dass im Recht zu der Existenz auch die Essenz, d.h. eine bestimmte Wesens-und Wertqualität, hinzugehört, die wir als “ Richtigkeit ” bezeichnen wollen.’

Legal positivism in this more recent sense does not comprise all forms of *Rechtspositivismus* in the traditional sense. It would not include the theories of the great German jurists of the nineteenth century usually called ‘ positivists ’. They evidently believed that they kept strictly to reality when they identified law with the commands of the state, discarding nebulous ideas of a law of nature. This, however, does not imply that, in their opinion, legal science should be non-valuating. No such question was raised in their time. Their philosophical master, Hegel, certainly had a valuating view of law. The principle of non-valuation in social sciences, including legal science, belongs to the present century. In fact, the nineteenth-century German jurists used valuation freely as a matter of course. It is therefore a mistake to include their theories under legal positivism in the new sense.

In his work *Grosse Rechtsdenker* Erik Wolf often speaks of positivism, always in a deprecatory sense, if sometimes tempered by some recognition of merit. See especially the essay on Jhering 622 ff. (Positivism is not only a phenomenon of decay, 623.) Since the term ‘ positivism ’ is never defined, its meaning can only be gathered from various utterances indicating that it signifies an empiricist, non-valuating, and morally indifferent philosophy. Positivism is said to rely on the factual, *i.e.* what is susceptible of proof (624). It has a negative character in that it is indifferent to values (622). Ultimately, positivism ends up in the personally irresponsible acquiescence with everything (623).

This unsavoury description of positivism and positivists (on which *cf.* Larenz 35) is obviously inadequate for the excellent German jurists of the nineteenth century. The author therefore adds that their purpose was entirely idealistic. They were not aware of the positivistic trend, but they collaborated to its furtherance, unconsciously as it were (627). This amounts to saying that they were not positivists in the author's sense though they contributed to the evil of positivism without being aware of the fact.

In referring to Gierke's attack on positivism—675 ff.—Wolf does not distinguish between positivism in his own sense and that of Gierke. Gierke did not, as Wolf does, take ‘ positivism ’ in the present philosophical sense. From his own exposition it is quite clear that by ‘ positivism ’ he meant a certain view on the nature of law, *viz.*, the view that all law is posited by a supreme authority in the community. It is inconceivable that he should have designated the followers of Hegel as positivists in the sense of adherents of Comte or of the small group of German philosophers now referred to as positivists in the history of philosophy.

The will-theory is not a characteristic of legal positivism in the new sense. There, the term comprises a number of theories which reject the will-theory, and which therefore do not belong to legal positivism in the traditional sense. Hägerström's theory of law, for instance, is a clear case of legal positivism in the new sense since it is definitely non-valuating. But it does not belong to legal positivism in the traditional sense because the will-theory of law is rejected. Another example is Ehrlich's sociological theory of law.

Evidently, therefore, *Rechtspositivismus* in the new sense is something other than *Rechtspositivismus* in the traditional sense. Both its connotation and its sphere of applicability are different. It is therefore confusing when *Rechtspositivismus* is spoken of without any distinction between the views covered by them.

In French literature the term *positivisme juridique* seems to be generally used in the same sense as *Rechtspositivismus* in the original meaning.[94] It is probably a translation of *Rechtspositivismus.* Several authors stress the distinction between *positivisme juridique* and philosophical positivism.[95]

In English and American literature the term 'legal positivism' seems to have been introduced quite recently, probably as a translation of the German expression. Austin's theory is a clear case of legal positivism in the traditional German sense. Until lately it has always carried the name of analytical jurisprudence. Now it is often referred to as a kind of legal positivism.[96]

I have not found the term 'legal positivism' in the writings of Holland or Pollock. Salmond speaks of 'positivist law (or jurisprudence)' meaning the interpretation of law by writers who have more or less accepted positivist philosophy derived from Comte; Duguit is mentioned as the chief exponent. (*Jurisprudence,* 9 ed., 1937, 46.) Allen seems to make use of the term only with regard to Kelsen, whose theory is called positivistic

[94] Virally, *La pensée juridique* (1960) VII; Héraud 522 f.; Cuche et Waline in the *Mélanges R. Carré de Malberg* (1933) 75 ff., 519 ff.

[95] Gény, 'La Notion du droit en France', 1 *Archives de Philosophie de droit et de Sociologie juridique* (1931) 26; Cuche, Waline and Héraud in the writings just cited; Battifol, 'Sur la positivité du droit' (1 *Mélanges en l'honneur de Jean Dabin,* 1963) 3 ff.

[96] Hart, *The Concept of Law* (1960) 7, 253; Friedmann, *Legal Theory* (4 ed. 1964) 209; H. F. Jolowicz, *Lectures on Jurisprudence* (1963) 101; Dias, *Jurisprudence* (1964) 351 ff.

because it is concerned exclusively with the actual and not with ideal law. (*Law in the Making,* 7 ed., 1964, 55.) In his work *Jurisprudence* (1959) Roscoe Pound mentions only the followers of Comte and Spencer as 'positivists'.

The use of the term 'legal positivism' in English and American literature has been strongly influenced by 'positivism' in the philosophical sense. This is especially apparent in Shuman's book *Legal Positivism* (1963) where it is taken for granted that 'positivism' means philosophical positivism. The author expressly makes a distinction between 'analytical jurisprudence' and 'legal positivism' and even reproaches Friedmann for creating confusion by calling Austin's theory 'positivistic'.[97]

Most often the characteristic feature of legal positivism is said to be that it separates law and morals, meaning that the rules of law are not fundamentally moral rules. This refers, in the first instance, to Austin's theory. Since he regarded the rules of law as commands by the actual holders of power, he could not reasonably maintain that they necessarily had a moral content. The heart of legal positivism and its great contribution to practical life, Jerome Hall says, is 'its separation of positive law from morals, mores, religion, fashion, the bye-laws of sub-groups, and so on', and its corollary is 'the sanctioned command of a determinate Sovereign or an equivalent formula'.[98] The same separation of law from other systems of rules is found in the present leader of legal positivism, Hans Kelsen. But the separation of law and morals is not bound up with either Austin's or Kelsen's view on the nature of law. An author who holds a different theory on the nature of law may very well be a positivist in the sense that he declines regarding a moral element as necessarily belonging to the concept of law.[99]

The confusion resulting from the different uses of the term 'legal positivism' has become embarrassing. Hart's enumeration of five separate meanings of the expression is well known.[1] At the Bellagio Conference on legal positivism in 1960 a great many meanings were

[97] *Legal Positivism* 11. (*Cf.* the review by Graham Hughes in 9 *Natural Law Forum* 1964, 164 f.) In the said connection Friedmann employs the term 'legal positivism' in the traditional German sense.

[98] *From Legal Theory to Integrative Jurisprudence* 29. *Cf.* Dias, *Jurisprudence* 351 ff., and his article 'Jurisprudence' in the *Encyclopaedia Britannica.*

[99] Thus Hart, who regards himself as a positivist, takes legal positivism to mean 'the simple contention that it is in no sense a necessary truth that laws reproduce or satisfy certain demands of morality, though in fact they have often done so'. (*The Concept of Law* 181 f., 253.) *Cf.* the article 'Criteria of Legal Positivism' in the *Archiv für Rechts- und Sozialphilosophie* 1969 by W. J. Uren.

[1] 71 *Harvard Law Review* (1957/58) 601 f. *Cf. The Concept of Law* 253 and *The Encyclopedia of Philosophy* (1968) v. Legal Positivism.

listed.[2] Among them was the view that only positive law in the sense of law laid down by a competent authority is real law. But this meaning of the term is seldom clearly distinguished from the meaning implying that legal positivism is characterized by the separation of law and morals. Moreover, this latter view is often held to be derived from the philosophical standpoint that no knowledge of values is possible. The criterion of legal positivism then amounts to its being based on a non-cognitive theory of value and ethics.[3] The terminological situation is not bettered because ‘ positivism ’ is employed by many authors as a term of abuse.[4] For others ‘ positivism ’ is clearly a mark of distinction.

The principal cause of the confusion is the circumstance that the word ‘ positivism ’ in ‘ legal positivism ’ stems from two different sources. In the traditional German meaning of *Rechtspositivismus,* as we have seen, *Positivismus* derives from *positives Recht,* law by position. In ‘ legal positivism ’ in the other sense, ‘ positivism ’ derives from philosophical positivism. Legal positivism in the former sense designates a certain theory on the nature of law (that all law is an expression of the will of supreme authority). In the latter sense legal positivism signifies a certain philosophical approach to the problems of law which has led to very different theories on the nature of law. These two meanings of the term ‘ legal positivism ’ are often confused.[5]

Moreover, in general philosophy the term ‘ positivism ’ carries different meanings. It was first applied to the philosophy of Auguste Comte. His fundamental principle was that science must be based on observation since observation is the source of knowledge. He seems not to have discussed legal science; probably he would not have regarded jurisprudence as a science at all. A science of law, according to his view, would rather have been what is now called sociology of law. But Comte sought to ascertain the laws for the development of society to greater and greater perfection, and here he

[2] 14 *Journal of Legal Education* (1961/62) 219 ff. contains a report on the conference.

[3] See the report on the Bellagio Conference and Shuman 15. If an author has a non-cognitive theory of value, his theory of law will, of course, be non-valuating. But the converse of this statement would not be true. It is possible to believe in the objectivity of values without necessarily maintaining that there is an element of value in the law.

[4] Almost a ‘ dirty ’ word in America though not in England according to Dennis Lloyd, *Introduction to Jurisprudence* (1959) XVI. In Scandanavia ‘ positivism ’ has no such disparaging sense as is now usually connected with the word in German literature.

[5] *Cf.* Wieacker 431 f.

touched problems of legal philosophy. He held the ideas of natural rights to be a hindrance to the achievement of perfection. On 'the positive stage'—when the theological and metaphysical stages have been left behind—these ideas would necessarily be dissolved. Everybody then has duties towards others; but nobody has any rights, properly speaking. The guarantees for the individual result from the universal reciprocity of obligations; nobody has any other right but that of always doing his duty.[6] This is evidently a kind of natural law doctrine.

The principal work of Comte carries the title *Cours de philosophie positive* (1830–42). He explains the meaning of the term *positif* by saying that it signifies *réel et utile*. (*La Grande Encyclopédie,* art. Comte.) According to Z. A. Jordan, *The Evolution of Dialectical Materialism,* (1967) 111, the expressions 'the positive sciences' and 'the philosophy of the positive science' were introduced by Mme de Staël 'in 1800'. This must refer to her work *De la littérature, considéré dans ses rapports avec les institutions sociales,* where the expression *les sciences positives* is employed in the preface and the expression *la philosophie des sciences positives* (co-ordinated with *la philosophie des idées intellectuelles*) in Part II, Chapter VI. There is no indication that she invented the term *sciences positives;* she seems to be making use of a current term.
The opposite to 'positivism' in philosophy is not, of course, 'negativism'. It is metaphysics.

German nineteenth-century *Rechtspositivismus* had no connection with the philosophy of Comte.[7] Bentham preceded Comte by half a century, and Austin shows no influence from him. It is therefore clear that legal positivism in the original sense must be sharply distinguished from the philosophical positivism of Comte.

The ideas of Comte were taken up by Léon Duguit and made the foundation of his great work. For that reason he has sometimes been called a positivist. But Duguit was no legal positivist in the original sense of that term. (*Cf.* Cuche and Waline in the *Mélanges Carré de Malberg* 73, 519.) Duguit expounded a sort of natural law doctrine based on the principle of social solidarity. (*Cf.* Allen, *Law in the Making* 39 f.)

Philosophical positivism in a more general sense is a vague appellation of empiricist philosophical theories averse to metaphysical speculations. As was already noted it is regarded as characteristic of these theories that valuation is excluded from science. The proper motivation for this standpoint is that no knowledge of values or of

[6] *Cf.* Roubier, *Théorie génerale du droit* (1946) 120.

[7] *Cf.* Bergbohm 51.

duty is possible; so-called value judgments and propositions about duties are then held to be emotive expressions. This is why legal positivism is sometimes defined as a theory of law based on ethical non-cognitivism.

> In his book *On Law and Justice* (1958) Alf Ross says that the term 'positivism' is ambiguous because it can mean both 'what builds on experience' and 'what is formally established' (100). He finds the modern reaction against positivism in the latter sense well founded. A realistic theory must recognize that not all law is positive in the sense of being 'formally established'. For his own part Ross embraces positivism in the former sense. In an article in Danish he defines legal positivism as a branch of positivism in the philosophical sense. This implies, he says, that the expression becomes a broad, indiscriminate designation of legal philosophy and legal theory based on empiricist and anti-metaphysical principles of epistemology. It therefore belongs to the kernel of legal positivism that no ethical knowledge (*i.e.* knowledge about right and wrong) and consequently no natural law is possible. (76 *Tidskrift for Rettsvitenskap,* 1963, 504.)
>
> In a review of a Swedish book by the present author, Ross modifies his position. Ethical non-cognitivism is no longer made an element in the definition. The term 'legal positivism' is taken to designate the view that the legal order is a 'social, empirical fact'. The proposition that a legal order including certain contents exists at a given time and place serves only as an expression of a complicated set of social facts. (80 *Tidskrift for Rettsvitenskap,* 1967, 290 f.)

The several meanings of 'legal positivism' can be understood as being derived either from 'positive' in 'positive law' or from positivism in philosophical positivism, or from a combination of positivism in both senses. In view of the prevailing confusion it is incumbent on an author to make clear in which sense he proposes to use the term 'legal positivism'. My choice has been based on the following considerations.

To make ethical non-cognitivism a criterion of 'legal positivism' is not very expedient. Bentham, Austin, the German nineteenth-century jurists, and others, who have generally been called positivists will all be excluded from the precincts of legal positivism. Very few authors, indeed, will find a place there. The non-cognitive theories of value and ethics are of recent date. As far as I know, a theory of this kind was first put forward between 1910 and 1920 (by Hägerström), but its influence was restricted to Scandinavia.[8] In the

[8] Hägerström, *Inquiries*, especially 127 ff.

twenties and thirties other non-cognitive theories began to appear.[9] It would be exceedingly difficult to say which writers from the period after 1920 would qualify for the honorific title of positivist. Their number would certainly be restricted.[10]

Nor would it be more practical to use the name of legal positivism for theories, whether based on ethical non-cognitivism or not, according to which no value element is ascribed to the law and the law therefore is held to be a complex of social facts. A value element may be surreptitiously introduced by an author who professes to be concerned with facts only. It would be very difficult to say which theories were to be classified as positivistic in this sense; very few theories would come into the category. Kelsen's theory, for instance, would not be among them though he regards his theory as *the* theory of positivism; for he holds that legal science is a value science (in the sense of understanding values) even though it is not establishing values itself.[11] The classification would be confusing.

When the term 'legal positivism' is used as a common designation for theories which are not natural law doctrines, its meaning depends on what is held to be characteristic of a natural law doctrine. This is by no means clear. Moreover, in this case too a penetrating analysis is needed in order to ascertain whether a theory belongs to the one class or the other. Many theories which profess to be anti-natural law are in reality permeated with natural law concepts and ideas. Finally, legal positivism in this sense will be a term embracing theories of the most diverse kinds, as those of Austin and Ehrlich, Kelsen and Hägerström, which have hardly anything in common beyond the rejection of the concept of a law of nature.

The best solution to the terminological problem seems to be simply to use the expression 'legal positivism' in accordance with the original and traditional sense of the German *Rechtspositivismus.* No confusion need arise from this, and the authors who have from the beginning been called positivists will still be called positivists.

In this usage the term 'positivism' is derived from positive law; it has no connection with philosophical positivism (which is, indeed, a term without precise meaning). 'Legal positivism' connotes the

[9] *Cf.* Giorgianni, *Neopositivismo e scienza del diritto* (1956); Warnock, *Contemporary Moral Philosophy* (1967) 18 f. and the review by Hare in 77 *Mind* (1968) 440; Urmson, *The Emotive Theory of Ethics* (1968) 15 ff.

[10] Though I believe I might aspire to membership of the club, I feel compelled to desist from using this classification.

[11] *Die philosophischen Grundlagen der Naturrechtslehre und des Rechtspositivismus* (1928) 70.

view that all law is positive in the sense of being an expression of the will of a supreme authority. As was previously remarked, however, a restriction has to be made. The term refers to theories which *professedly* include the said fundamental view on the nature of law. It can easily be ascertained which they are. But it is another question whether this view is consistently maintained without immixture of foreign elements.

Natural Law Theory and Legal Positivism as the Alternatives

We have now reached a point where the usual classification of legal theories as natural law theories or theories belonging to legal positivism has been more fully explained than could be done in the Introduction. It is generally supposed that existing theories of law can be exhaustively divided into those two categories, which might be called NL and LP. This opinion is based on the belief that a theory of law must necessarily pertain to the one or the other of these categories. They are supposed to be the alternatives that present themselves to legal theory. *Tertium non datur.*

Two questions should here be kept apart. One is whether every existing theory of law can be classified as either NL or LP. Another question is whether NL and LP are the alternatives between which legal theory has to make a choice, or whether there is a third possibility.[12]

As regards the first question, the classification of existing theories as either NL or LP is clearly exhaustive, provided that LP means every theory which is not NL. In this case NL and LP are contradictories. The import of the classification is dependent on what is meant by NL.

The classification is also exhaustive if LP means theories based on ethical non-cognitivism and NL all other theories. LP and NL then, too, are contradictories.

Finally, the classification is exhaustive if (i) NL means every theory which includes the tenet that the rules of law are essentially moral rules, or at least emanate from a lawgiver whose authority has a moral basis, and (ii) LP means every other theory. NL and LP are still contradictories.

The case will be different if NL signifies natural law theory, positively defined in one way or other, and LP legal positivism in

[12] *Cf.* to the following E. Pattaro's article ' Diritto, morale e concezione realistica del diritto ' in the *Rivista trimestrale di diritto e procedura civile* 1969.

the original sense of *Rechtspositivismus*. Then LP and NL are not contradictories. If nevertheless the classification is held to be exhaustive, an important assumption is surreptitiously made. This is the supposition that every non-natural law theory necessarily holds that all real law is an expression of the will of a supreme authority in society.

If this is the meaning, the standpoint is explicable as being based, more or less consciously, on the following reasoning. There always exists (in a developed society) a positive law in the sense of law given by a supreme authority expressing its will. As was pointed out above, this assumption is common to classical natural law doctrine and legal positivism in the original sense. (It is usually made in modern natural law doctrine too, but not always.) The assumption seems to be so self-evident that it is not discussed. A similar concept of positive law is supposed to belong to every theory of law. Next, the following question is raised: Is positive law sufficient in itself, or has it to be grounded on principles of higher quality in order to be real law? Legal theories are then classified according to their answers to this question. They either assume, or do not assume, a natural law basis of positive law. The classification seems to be exhaustive. Every theory of law is either LP or NL.

A fateful mistake is concealed in this reasoning. The assumption of a positive law in the traditional sense is not common to all theories of law. There are theories in which it is expressly rejected. To give some examples, the theories of Petrazycki and of Hägerström may be cited. These theories are dissimilar. But a common trait is that the traditional concept of positive law is subjected to penetrating criticism. Neither theory is a natural law theory. But neither, for that reason, belongs to legal positivism in the traditional sense. Consequently the classification of existing legal theories in NL and LP (in this sense) is not exhaustive. There are, indeed, a considerable number of theories outside these two categories, of which more will be said later.

As to the question of the *alternatives* for legal theory, it is evident that LP and NL are the only alternatives if the terms are used in a sense making LP and NL contradictory. But as was pointed out the situation is different if LP means legal positivism in the sense that has been adopted here, and the problem is held to be whether 'positive law' needs a basis in a natural law. Then the traditional concept of positive law is taken for granted. It is tacitly assumed that every theory of law must of necessity be based on this concept.

A positive law in the sense of expressions of the will of a supreme authority is supposed to exist.

The most usual course taken by legal theory has been to make this assumption and then proceed along the road of voluntarism (the will theory). But unfounded assumptions are dangerous things. Before going on we have to raise the question whether there really exists a positive law in the traditional sense. The answer is decisive for the direction that legal theory has to take.

CHAPTER 2

POSITIVE LAW

THE term 'positive law' has been used here in the original sense of law posited by a supreme authority in society expressing its own will. In recent literature other connotations have appeared. This is due partly to the view more and more common among modern authors that only a section of the law is ever laid down by a lawgiving authority. It is also partly due to criticism of the will-theory itself. Far from leading to the abandonment of the term 'positive law,' these tendencies have favoured the use of the term although its meaning has changed. 'Positive law' has come to signify law actually in force, law effectively applied, law 'factually valid', and the like.[1] The adjective 'positive' is being used in order to stress that one is concerned with 'real' law as opposed to an ideal law of nature without necessarily implying that the reality of law depends on its being laid down by a competent authority.

The ensuing terminology confusion is embarrassing.[2] It is necessary to make use of the expression 'positive law' in referring to theories including the traditional concept. But if this concept is eliminated, nothing is gained by giving the old expression a new connotation. It would always be difficult for readers to keep this connotation apart from the old one.

The question now before us is whether there really exists a 'positive' law in the traditional sense. The idea of such a law has been deeply engrained for centuries. In a society where legislation is the chief method of introducing rules called rules of law, it is quite natural to regard the lawgiving authority as the source of the law as a whole. The laws are issued from a power centre, consisting, in a Western democracy, of parliament, or diet, and government. The courts and the administrative agencies are connected with this power centre; and they apply, with irresistible force, the rules that are duly proclaimed. The individual citizen is subjected

[1] See the survey by Ago in the article 'Droit positif et droit international' in 3 *Annuaire français de droit international* 1957. As the author remarks (33 f.) with regard to recent literature, 'on demeure frappé du nombre de concepts differents de droit positif qui s'y trouvent adoptés'.

[2] I entirely agree with the opinion expressed by Professor Ago on this point (59).

to these rules whether he is willing or not. Thus there seems to exist a uniform, homogeneous authority that, so to speak, carries the social order on its shoulders. But the idea of such an authority entails the idea of its having a will of its own. The rules of law appear as the expression of this will. Ultimately the law is the will of the supreme authority.

On the basis of such more or less natural ideas the theories including the notion of positive law in the traditional sense have been constructed. Despite their being inconsistent, they have been maintained with amazing tenacity.

In the first place it is necessary to describe the nature of the supreme authority. This must be done in such a way that the authority appears to exist independently of the legal order. If the power of the supreme authority results from the functioning of the legal order, the legal order cannot be a creation of the supreme authority.

Secondly the following must be noted with regard to the will-theory. If the law is to reside in the will of the supreme authority, this will cannot be held to exist in the moment of legislative enactment only. Where, then, would the law be in the next moment, or after 10 or 100 years? If the law is to be an expression of the will of the supreme authority, the will must have a permanent character. But is such a will conceivable?

As was pointed out above, the teachers of natural law were not very much troubled with the problem of explaining the nature of 'positive law'. They held positive law to be commands by the sovereign in the sense of declarations of his will; and a permanent character of this will was assumed as a matter of course. The difficulties were more acutely felt when the law of nature was eliminated and the object of legal theory was reduced to positive law. A coherent and scientific explanation of its nature became a necessity.

In examining the theories it is advisable to keep apart the two questions whether (i) there can be a supreme power existing independently of the legal order, and (ii) how the will ascribed to the lawgiving authority is to be conceived.

From both points of view the positivistic theory has been criticized by a number of modern authors. The most comprehensive analysis is that offered by Hägerström, *Inquiries into the Nature of Law and Morals* (translation by C. D. Broad 1953). See also Lundstedt, *Die Unwissenschaftlichkeit der*

Rechtswissenschaft and *Legal Thinking Revised*; Kelsen, *Hauptprobleme der Staatsrechtslehre* (1911); Petrazycki, *Law and Morality* (1955); Hart, *The Concept of Law* (1961). Many other contributions could be cited.
With regard to the rich contents of the literature it should be sufficient here to restrict the following examination of the positivistic theory to the most essential points. There is not much to add with respect to criticism. The positivistic theories on the nature of rights and duties will be discussed at length later on.

The Lawgiving Authority

In positivistic theory the lawgiving authority has been represented in three different ways: (i) as an individual or a group of individuals possessing actual supreme power within a given community; (ii) as the state; and (iii) as the people itself. The first theory, which is that of naturalistic positivism, seems to come closest to reality. Our examination may therefore conveniently begin with this theory.

The lawgiving authority according to naturalistic positivism

In natural law doctrine the theory of the social contract as the basis of power of the lawgiving authority had a two-fold significance. The social contract was the source both of the actual power to govern and of the right of governing. These two points were not distinctly kept apart.

For Bentham, founder of naturalistic positivism, the social contract was a myth. It could not be the basis of the governing power. Moreover, he did not ask for a right of governing in the supreme power. He was exclusively concerned with the actual basis of its power. This, he believed, was habitual obedience. The sovereign was the person, or group of persons, whose orders are habitually complied with by the members of the community in general. This regular compliance is what Bentham puts in the place of the imaginary social contract.

Bentham fully realized that the lawgiving authority must exist and possess power independently of the legal order if the law is to be conceived as the expression of its will. But did the sovereign as represented by Bentham really have such a position? Was it independent of the existing legal order?

The sovereign was described as the sovereign *in a state*.[3] But a state presupposes the existence of a legal order. For how could we speak of a ' state ' in any conceivable sense of the word if there

[3] *The Limits of Jurisprudence* 88.

is not an organization of power? There can be no state in an unorganized mass of people. Organization implies, however, that there is a set of rules which the members of the organization feel bound to follow and actually follow more or less consistently. But the rules regulating the functioning of the state organization are precisely such rules as are called rules of law. When the sovereign is conceived as being sovereign in a state, a legal order is supposed to exist. The explanation is circular.

That Bentham's reasoning is circular can be shown in many other, less abstract ways. In England the sovereign was the King, Lords, and Commons in conjunction. But how had they reached their positions? The King had become King according to the rules of the English constitution. The Lords had inherited their peerages or been created by the monarch according to constitutional rules. The Commons had been elected, the procedure being governed by rules belonging to the constitution of England. It is therefore evident that those persons who made up the 'sovereign' in Bentham's sense had all arrived at their positions thanks to the existence of a system of rules which enjoyed general respect in the country. Moreover, they could exercise power only when acting in conformity with the constitution. Bentham says that, in Great Britain, 'the sovereignty is in the King, Lords, and Commons *in Parliament assembled*'.[4] This refers to the fact that laws were enacted by the King giving his assent, before the assembled Lords in the presence of the Commons, to bills approved by both Houses of Parliament. The constitutional forms were essential to the exercise of legislative power.

It is therefore obvious that the power of the so-called sovereign was not independent of the constitution as a living and working system of rules. The constitution could not be the expression of the will of persons who depended on constitutional rules for their ability to legislate with practical effect. The constitution existed as a working system of power and the holders of power changed according to its rules.

> To illustrate what is meant here by a 'working constitution' Karl Llewellyn's description of 'the Constitution as an Institution' might be quoted: 'An institution is in first instance a set of ways of living and doing. It is not, in first instance, a matter of words or rules. The existence of an institution lies first of all and last of all in the fact that people do behave in certain patterns *a, b,* and *c,* and do not behave in other conceivable

[4] *The Limits of Jurisprudence* 92. (My italics.)

patterns *d* to *w*. . . . As an institution of major size, then, our working Constitution embraces the interlocking ways and attitudes of different groups and classes in the community—different ways and attitudes of different groups and classes, but all cogging together into a fairly well organized whole.' (*Jurisprudence*, 1962, 233 f.)—I must make a reservation with regard to the assumption apparently made by Llewellyn that 'general behaviour in certain patterns' is prior to 'words or rules'. Surely, people would not be acting in patterns conforming to the rules of the constitution unless these rules had been enunciated in some way. But Llewellyn is evidently right in emphasizing that there is no 'working constitution' (but only a paper constitution) without the 'interlocking ways and attitudes of different groups and classes'.

We can proceed further in examining the conditions on which the power of the sovereign depended. The working constitution was one condition. But the constitution could not exist by itself. It presupposed a community regulated by rules. Amongst other things there must be a stable distribution of property. Neither the King and the Lords nor the Commons could hold their positions without the basis afforded through the existing distribution of property. But the distribution of property depended on the private and criminal law of England.

One can continue thus. The more one reflects on the power of the 'sovereign', the more it becomes clear that it is conditioned by the legal order as a whole. The supposition that the legal order rests on the will of a sovereign holding independent power is fictitious.

Bentham notes himself that the application of the existing system of rules goes on regardless of changes in the persons composing the sovereign. To explain how the enormous mass of rules stemming from bygone times are to be understood as the commands of the present sovereign, Bentham has recourse to the theory of adoption. Since no explicit adoption takes place in practice, the adoption is said to occur tacitly. As Sir Henry Maine interprets the theory, 'the Crown and Parliament command [the common law], because they permit it; and the proof that they permit it is that they could change it'; the formula is: 'whatever the Sovereign permits, is his command.' [5]

In actual fact the persons occupying positions as lawgivers have no thought of 'adopting' previous rules. If they really had such an idea, they would have to re-issue these rules; they can act in their capacity of lawgivers only through observance of the constitutional

[5] *The Early History of Institutions* (1874, new ed. 1890) 381, 374.

forms; tacit adoption, which is unknown to the constitution, would be of no avail.

The reason why previous rules are continuously applied regardless of changes among persons in 'the sovereign' is not that they have become, in some mysterious way, expressions of the will of new persons. It is due to those psychological factors which make for the application of legal rules in general. There is no difference in this respect between rules issued by the sovereign of the moment and those of earlier periods.

The argument that whatever the sovereign permits, he commands, is fallacious. Permitting is confused with not prohibiting and this with commanding. Thus the absence of a certain activity is identified with the activity of commanding: to say that the sovereign does not alter or abolish the law becomes the same thing as his commanding the contents of the law. This is like saying that the river flows in its bed because it is not diverted into another channel. The river follows its course from other reasons than the absence of a conceivable activity of men.

The prevalence of naturalistic positivism in England is due to the empiricist tradition. Nevertheless, it is somewhat surprising. The view that the law consists of the commands of the sovereign would be natural in a country where enacted law is dominant. It is much more difficult to understand how the common law could be conceived in that way.

In his critical appreciation of Austin's theory Sir Henry Maine clearly showed that it does not fit to the facts on early stages of civilization; and he adds (382 f.): 'The truth is that the one solvent of local and domestic usage in those parts of the world of which we have any real knowledge has not been the command of the sovereign but the supposed command of the Deity.' But the eminent author accepted Austin's theory as an accurate description of the law of a modern country (374 ff.). *Cf.* the remarks by Hägerström, *Inquiries* 73 f.

The criticism of the Bentham-Austin theory can be generalized. The same arguments are decisive against every form of naturalistic positivism. It is true that in every modern society there is always a group of power holders possessing the machinery of government and legislation. But their positions always rest on the existence of an actual order in society, governed by a set of rules which are more or less universally respected and followed. In general the power holders have attained their positions according to constitutional rules. They exercise power in the forms prescribed by the constitution. The general attitude of abiding by the law is not to be interpreted as a habit of obedience towards the temporary holders of power. We are not in the habit of obeying the politicians who fight for power among themselves. Our loyalty is to the institutions (monarchy, presidency, parliament, congress, etc.) and to 'the law'.[6] The occupants of the key positions are looked upon as wielding a power belonging to the institutions. This makes it possible for them to introduce limited alterations in the existing legal system. When they relinquish their positions, their peculiar power comes to an end; they are left with whatever influence they may have as private persons in the world of politics.

The fundamental error of naturalistic positivism is its misinterpretation of the relationship between legislative power and the existing legal order. The legal order is represented as being given and maintained by actual holders of independent power while in reality their power depends on the existing legal order as a functioning system. The legal order remains for generations, though subject to continuous change, partly through the lawgiving activities of the temporary holders of power, partly because of other factors.

The fact that legislative power rests on an existing legal order is emphasized by some authors, such as Hägerström, Fuller and Hart (71 *Harvard Law Review* 1957/58, 603 and 640) and others. This is one of those rare points where, by wide consent, definite and indubitable progress may be said to have been made in legal philosophy.

In a revolution the continuity of legal development is broken. But this is no argument against what has been said here. As will be pointed out at length below (ch. 4), a revolution implies a partial altering of the law in an unconstitutional way. The legal system as a whole survives.

The state as the fountain of law

Since legislation in a modern community is carried on through agencies belonging to the state organization, 'the state' can be said to be the lawgiving authority. But this is true only in the limited sense that new rules, which are generally recognized as rules of law, are regularly issued by those agencies. It would not be correct to say, for that reason, that 'the law' is the creation of the state, or that the state is the fountain of the law. Two arguments are decisive against this view. (i) The law comprises much more than enacted law (judge-made law, customary law). (ii) The state presupposes the law.

[6] *Cf.* Hart in 71 *HLR* (1957/58) 603.

(i) The state makes its appearance in history much later than the law.[7] During the earliest stages of civilization known to us, we find men living in communities governed by rules determining their 'rights' and 'duties'. Family relations are strictly regulated, a distribution of property is maintained, and so on. Very slowly an organization is evolved which ultimately grows into the organization of the modern state. It is a matter of dispute at what point the state shall be said to have come into existence; the answer is a matter of taste. Be it enough here to remark that the state is younger than the law in the sense of generally respected rules about rights and duties.

The laws enacted by the organs of the state were for a long time usually held to be supplementary to the old law, regarded as being of divine origin or simply inherited from time immemorial. To this day statutory law takes the second place in relation to the common law, or customary law, of England. But even when legislation is considered to be the primary source of law, as is the case in continental Europe, it is always supplemented by a vast mass of rules generated in other ways.

(ii) Historically speaking, the state presupposes the law. It is created on the basis provided by the respect for the law that is held to exist. At higher stages of civilization the state and the law are always co-existent. They are mutually interdependent. On the one hand, the state organization is regulated through rules of law, determining its composition, the competence of various organs, and the forms of their activities. On the other hand, the rules of law must be backed by state power to achieve efficacy.

The legislative machinery functions within the framework of a legal system. The organs of legislation are defined in the constitution. Their power can only be exercised in constitutional forms. The whole machinery is a device for bringing about peaceful change in the law according to rules of law. It presupposes a community where there is a stable distribution of property, security to life and limb, and many other things dependent on a working law. The state is no power outside the law which could be its fountain.

The people as the fountain of the law

Since the emergence of the idea of popular sovereignty in the latter part of the Middle Ages the view that the people itself is the

[7] *Cf.* Ehrlich, *Fundamental Principles of the Sociology of Law* (1936) ch. VII.

ultimate and legitimate source of the law has become more and more prevalent. But how can it be maintained that the people gives the law unto itself?

In order to be the lawgiving authority, the people has to be organized. It is said to act through its representatives. But organization and representation presuppose rules that are universally respected. There must be rules about the selection of representatives and about the forms of their activities as representatives. In other words, some sort of constitution is needed. But as we have seen, the functioning of a constitution presupposes a working law regulating the distribution of property, etc. The idea of the people being the ultimate lawgiver is based on the assumption of conditions which can only be present when there is a working law in the community.

Moreover, if the people is to be regarded as the fountain of the law, the people must be supposed to exist independently of its law and prior to it. But this is impossible. The people cannot exist without the law. It cannot even be nourished and protected against the weather without a system of efficient rules assuring security to life and limb, a stable distribution of property, reliability of contracts, an administrative apparatus, and so on. The fact is that the people develops with its law and the law with the people. The law is as essential to the very existence of the people as the skeleton to the human body.

The people is no more an authority existing prior to the law than the state is. It cannot, therefore, be the source of the law.

The Will of the Lawgiver

When the law is held to be posited by a supreme authority in society, it is being regarded as the expression of that authority's will. In legal positivism the rules of law are usually interpreted as imperatives issued by the lawgiving authority; and an imperative is defined as a declaration of will by the commanding person concerning the behaviour of the addressee. The will of the supreme authority is the substance of the law; printed legal texts are a means of making the will known. The law exists as the contents of the will of the lawgiver, and this will is a force maintaining the whole legal system.

> In an essay on Austin's theory, C. A. Manning sums up the gist of the theory in these words: 'As the lighting system lives by reason of the power station in the background, so the system of law is kept in operation by the always imperative aspect of the sovereign in the background. The Statute of Frauds has its

place in the system because enacted by Parliament in 1677, but it is binding because commanded by the sovereign number here and now.' (*Modern Theories of Law*, ed. W. I. Jennings, 1933, 198 f.)

The will of the lawgiver is conceived as being directed towards the behaviour of the citizens. It is the will of the lawgiver that one should refrain from such acts as are defined as crimes; that buyer and seller should fulfil their mutual undertakings in certain ways; that married people should behave in certain ways towards each other, and so on.

Bentham says for instance, *The Limits of Jurisprudence* 88: 'A law may be defined as an assemblage of signs declarative of a volition conceived or adopted by the *sovereign* in a state, concerning the conduct to be observed in a certain *case* by a certain person or class of persons.'

There is some difficulty in fitting all legal rules into this scheme; see for instance Larenz 152 ff. These difficulties have induced several authors to reject the imperative theory more or less completely. The rules of private law are conceived by some as declarations of will directed towards the creation, alteration, or extinction of rights and duties. (More on this theory below 159 ff.)

After a criticism of the imperative theory, Kelsen in his first work came to the conclusion that the rules of law are propositions concerning future actions of the state itself. (*Hauptprobleme der Staatsrechtslehre* 1911, 251 f.)

Holland takes an intermediate position. He holds that 'every law is a proposition announcing the will of the State, and implying, if not expressing, that the State will give effect only to acts which are in accordance with its will, so announced, while it will punish, or at least visit with nullity, any acts of contrary character.' (*The Elements of Jurisprudence*, 4 ed., 1888, 75.) In the first place, the will of the state is directing the behaviour of the citizens; in the second it is concerned with the activities of the state if its primary will is not complied with.

The will of the lawgiver must be the will of the present lawgiver. If the law is to be the will of a supreme authority, it cannot be the will of a long succession of people who are for the most part dead or out of office. Bentham and Austin sought to solve this difficulty by their theory of adoption. Most authors pass it over lightly. The law is the will of the state, and the state is a permanent body; its existence is not bound up with the existence of those individuals who for the time being act as its organs.

Evidently, the lawgiving will is supposed to exist not only in the moment of legislative enactment. The law is the will of the supreme authority as long as it remains 'in force'. This will appears to be fixed for indefinite periods, which may stretch over centuries. It is susceptible of alteration, in principle at least, but only in the forms prescribed by the constitution.

The history of this will-theory—which has taken many different forms in the course of the years—has not yet been written.[8] The modern will-theory is a heritage from classical natural law doctrine. But the great teachers of natural law drew upon older sources. As was pointed out before, the origin of the theory is probably to be found in legal and theological speculations of the Middle Ages.[9] In the beginning the idea cannot have been that the lawgiving will was the will of 'the state'. Most likely, it was first held to be the will of the ruling prince, acting as the representative of God on earth, whose decrees supplemented the old customary law. When opposition to princely power arose and gathered momentum, it was suggested that the lawgiving will was, or should be, the will of the people, considered as a collective of originally free individuals. The view that the lawgiving will is the will of the state seems to belong to a third stage in the development of the will-theory. At a fourth stage the will-theory is more or less completely dissolved. It is expressly asserted that the lawgiving will is no real will. Only the ghost of the will remains in the shape of a 'fictitious' will or as a figure of speech.

> Radbruch says that the will of the lawgiver is not the collective will of those who take part in the legislative process, but the will of the state. The will of the lawgiver coincides with the will of the law; and the will of the law is only the personification of the contents of the law as reflected in a unitary, fictitious mind. (*Rechtsphilosophie* 211.) There remains not even a fictitious will but only a fictitious consciousness. Furthermore, it seems impossible to imagine a conscience embracing the enormously vast and complicated legal system of a modern state.

[8] *Cf.* Villey, 'Essor et décadence du volontarisme juridique' (*Archives de Philosophie du Droit* 1957).

[9] No will theory seems to have been developed during Antiquity. As regards the view of the Romans in Republican times, see Hägerström, 1 *Der römische Obligationsbegriff* 540 ff. The Roman people itself was bound by the law though it could alter the law by a certain procedure which could only take place under favourable auspices. The famous dictum of Ulpianus: *Quod principi placuit, legis habet vigorem* (D 1,4,1) does not imply that the law was the will of the princeps; it only says that the princeps could lay down new laws at will, this power being derived from the *lex regia*. Some roots of the will-theory are probably to be found in the ideology of the Byzantine empire. *Cf.* on this point Francis Dvornik, *Early Christian and Byzantine Political Philosophy. Origins and Background* (1966).

The fiction itself is impossible. Nothing remains but some traditional words which have been deprived of their original meaning without acquiring any new, comprehensible sense.

In his first work, *Hauptprobleme der Staatsrechtslehre* (1911), Kelsen strongly emphasizes that the law is the will of the state. But this will is no will in a psychological sense. It does not belong to the sphere of nature at all. The will of the state is a juridical fiction, giving expression to the unity of the legal system. (*Hauptprobleme* 183 f.) In later works much less is made of the will of the state. In the *General Theory of Law and State* (1946) it is said that the will of the state must be understood as a figurative mode of speech (35). In the *Reine Rechtslehre* (2. ed. 1960) the will of the state is a metaphor; the state is the personification of the legal order constituting a community. ('Dass das Recht der "Wille" des Staates, vom Staate "gewollt" ist, ist eine Metaphor, mit der nichts anderes gesagt wird, als dass die durch die Rechtsordnung konstituierte Gemeinschaft der Staat und die Personifikation dieser Rechtsordnung die Person des Staates ist', 307.) In whatever manner these difficult statements are to be interpreted, it is evident that the expression 'the will of the state' has lost its original connection with a real or imaginary will. The author seems to have become less and less inclined to use the expression even metaphorically. But it is to be noted that a real act of will is supposed to be essential to the process of legislation. (*Reine Rechtslehre* 4 ff.) In the *Hauptprobleme* Kelsen acutely criticized the will-theory in so far as it referred to the will of the state as a real will. (*Cf.* the summary of this criticism made by Hägerström, *Inquiries* 259 f.)

In a review of a Swedish book (80 *Tidskrift for Rettsvitenskap,* 1967, 284) Alf Ross reproaches me for paying so little attention to the statements of Radbruch and Kelsen on the so-called 'will'. He defends their use of the term 'will' as a means of 'figuratively personifying the systematic unity of the legal order'. In his view it serves to emphasize that the legal order is 'an order, a unity, and not only a conglomerate of rules'.

I cannot agree with this opinion. Think of the English common law. Is it anything but a conglomerate of rules? What exists is a vast bulk of records of decisions by the courts during several hundred years, plus the general opinion among both jurists and the public that the courts ought to seek guidance in these records for deciding new cases (in so far as statutes do not prescribe anything else), plus the fact that the courts generally act in conformity with this opinion. As everybody knows the precedents are subject to many different interpretations. It seems to be not only useless, but highly misleading, to ascribe a fictitious unity to the mass of precedents by means of the figurative talk of a will.

Ross goes on to say that the many holders of official positions are regarded as organs of a single power, 'the state', which is an expression of their being co-ordinated to a systematic unity; he thinks it natural to use the term 'will' to designate their unity in an activity. I must reiterate that I find the figurative talk of a will useless and misleading. To ascribe, even in a figurative way, the activities of thousands, or hundreds of thousands of state officials, to a single 'will' is to give a wrong impression of the facts.

The surprising capacity of the will-theory to survive may be explained partly by our natural inclination to find single causes for complex phenomena. The idea of a will at the centre of the legal order satisfies this desire. The will serves as a homogeneous source of the vast multitude of rules; it invests the system with an apparent unity and is supposed to act as its driving force. All this is only vaguely represented, of course, and innumerable difficulties arise as soon as more specific information is asked for. But that does not seem to matter. On the basis of the fundamental ideas, certain combinations of words have been evolved, on which our thoughts may tread, so to speak, through the bewildering maze of social facts.

In reality there is no homogeneous source of the rules reckoned as legal. The origin of the core of ancient rules is lost in the mists of history; and new rules flow to the common pool through several different channels. The relative unity of the legal system results from the stability of certain ideas of rights and duties, from the durable existence of institutions (legislative, judicial, and administrative), and from the continued application of a vast body of rules connected with these institutions. There is no single driving force to the system; the regular application of the rules and their efficacy in governing the life of society depend on a network of psychological and material factors (ideas of rights and duties, habit, belief in authority, fear of sanctions, and so on). The will-theory substitutes an imaginary will for this infinitely complicated reality.

Good-bye to 'Positive' Law

As we have now seen, there is no 'positive' law in the sense of the term as used in legal positivism. No rules of law at all are the expression of the will of an authority existing prior to the law itself. What we have before us is a body of rules that has been slowly changing and growing during the centuries. It would be no use to call this body of rules positive law. The adjective 'positive' is entirely superfluous; it might be misleading because it is connected with the idea that the law is ' posited ' in the sense of being the expression of the will of a lawgiver.

The term ' positive ' law may therefore conveniently be dropped as a term for an objectively existing phenomenon. It is necessary to make use of it only in referring to the will-theory. When speaking of the law itself it is much better simply to say ' the law ' without the adjective ' positive '.

CHAPTER 3

LEGAL THEORY AT THE CROSSROADS

LEGAL positivism, for so long considered the scientific theory of law, is an offspring of classical natural law doctrine. Its conceptual framework, first and foremost the concept of positive law, was taken over from the great teachers of natural law. The difference lay chiefly in the rejection of the idea of a law of nature being the foundation of society and of positive law.

The great problem of the teachers of natural law was how to explain the binding force of positive law. It was in order to solve this problem that a law of nature was constructed with the help of stoic philosophy, theological speculations, and the writings of the Roman jurists. When the positivists eliminated (or sought to eliminate) this foundation of positive law, two different courses were open to them. (i) They could waive the idea of the binding force of the law; the rules of law were then reduced to commands by the actual holders of power; to be under legal duty became only an expression for the fact that one is threatened by some evil in case of contrary behaviour. (ii) The idea of the binding force of the law could be retained but grounded without recourse to a law of nature; the people or the state was then held to be endowed with a mystical power of imposing real obligations.

Both courses were tried—the first one by Bentham and Austin, the second one by Hegel, Savigny, and the German positivists in general. The revival of natural law theory is the outcome of a readily explicable dissatisfaction with theories of both kinds. The binding force is regarded as being essential to the law; and it must be derived, so it seems, from a law of nature or from ultimate values. As regards the principles of interpretation the positivistic tenet (that interpretation consists in ascertaining the will of the lawgiver) is clearly unworkable.

The common element in legal positivism and most of such theories as are called theories of natural law is the *voluntaristic* approach. The concept of positive law remains fundamentally the same; the law is held to be the expression of the will of a supreme authority. The difference between nineteenth-century legal positivism and classical natural law doctrine was a difference of opinion within the framework of voluntarism. On the whole the same framework is common to present legal positivism and modern natural law theory. This is the reason why legal positivism and natural law doctrine still are so often held to be the alternatives open to legal theory. The assumption that there is a 'positive' law in the traditional sense seems to be self-evident; and the great problem appears to be whether this positive law needs a basis other than the will of the lawgiver.

The whole position undergoes a radical change when the error of the voluntaristic approach is realized. No longer then is legal theory reduced to the choice between legal positivism and natural law doctrine. The great crossroads of legal theory is the point where a distinction is made between voluntarism and non-voluntarism and one or other direction is taken.

The voluntaristic assumption, which seemed so natural, has been like a signpost through which generations of philosophers and jurists have been induced to take the wrong road. This was a road that led to an impasse. In most cases it was not even noticed that there was another road which took off from the main thoroughfare of legal theory at an earlier stage. This road was far less conspicuous and it was seldom taken.

Some Non-Voluntaristic Theories

The conscious distinction between voluntarism and non-voluntarism in legal theory is of comparatively recent date.[1] But the crucial importance of this distinction is still far from being generally realized. It is seldom mentioned at all. Instead, interest is usually focused on the opposition between legal positivism and natural law doctrine.

The will-theory has, perhaps, the psychological advantage of affording a seemingly clear and comprehensible definition of law. A non-voluntaristic theory cannot offer a comparable definition. The reality of law as fact is too vast and complicated to be seized in a brief formula.

In the beginning the non-voluntaristic theories were put forward in a tentative way and were lacking in clarity. I will not try to give a complete survey of them, but a few examples may be briefly mentioned.

As we have seen, Savigny's theory in its original form was non-

[1] *Cf.* Battifol, 'Sur la positivité du droit' in the *Mélanges en l'honneur de Jean Dabin* (1963).

voluntaristic. But it was too vague to withstand the impact of the powerful voluntaristic tradition and Savigny subsequently introduced a will as the source of the law.

Gierke, who was undoubtedly strongly influenced by Savigny, vacillated between voluntarism and non-voluntarism. On the one hand, the law represents the declared *convictions* of the community; the rules of law are rational propositions concerning a just order in society. On the other hand, the convictions of the community are accompanied by its *will*; the publication of the convictions entails publication of the will; there is, therefore, an element of will in the law though it is secondary to the convictions concerning justice.[2]

In his *Fundamental Principles of the Sociology of Law* (1936) Eugen Ehrlich refutes with many valid arguments 'the prevailing concept on the nature of law', *viz.*, 'that a norm is a legal norm only if it has been posited by the state as a legal norm' (159). It is difficult to give a brief and accurate rendering of his own view on the nature of law. The tendency is manifestly non-voluntaristic. But it is not easy to get a clear notion from the author's definition of the legal norm (169):

> Legal norms are those norms that flow from the facts of the law, to wit from usages, which assign to each member of the social association his position and function, from the relations of domination and subjection, from the relations arising from possession, from articles of association, from contracts, from testamentary and other dispositions; furthermore, those norms are legal norms that arise from the legal propositions of state and of juristic law (*i.e.* legal propositions created by the jurists, 175).

The vagueness of the definition is characteristic of the emerging non-voluntaristic theories. It illustrates the difficulty of giving a definition of 'the law' on a non-voluntaristic basis.[3]

American Realism had a non-voluntaristic tendency. Oliver Wendell Holmes' classical definition of law as prophecies of what the courts will do in fact served as a sort of banner to the movement. Though the definition was patently inadequate—as is now universally recognised—the liberation from voluntaristic doctrinairism had a profound effect in letting loose a stream of investigations into the facts of law.[4]

[2] *Deutsches Privatrecht* 116. *Cf.* above 52 f.

[3] Ehrlich's definition is circular since the law is defined by means of 'the facts of the law'. A number of legal concepts, such as possession, contracts, and the state, are presupposed.

[4] A non-voluntaristic approach is emphasized by E. A. Hoebel, *The Law of Primitive Man* (1954) 22 f.

The remarkable Polish-Russian philosopher Leon Petrazycki (or Petrazhitsky in the Russian form) strove to elaborate a complete non-voluntaristic theory on the nature of the law. He pointed out that the state cannot be the source of the law since the state is conditioned by the law. The reality of law, according to Petrazycki, is psychological. The law exists as a certain kind of experiences in the mind of the individual which are called ' imperative-attributive experiences ' or ' law-convictions '. By this Petrazycki means ideas of rights and duties. Enactments, precedents, and other so-called sources of law are ' normative facts ' (facts giving rise to ideas of rights and duties). Petrazycki offers a long list of such facts including, besides written laws, summaries of usages, opinions of prominent jurists, pronouncements by religious and political leaders, and so on. The scope of the law, as defined by Petrazycki, is very extended since it includes much of what is generally referred to as rules of morals and custom.

Petrazycki's chief writings on legal philosophy were published in 1955 in the *20th Century Legal Philosophy Series* under the title *Law and Morality*: *Leon Petrazycki*. Previously good accounts of his main ideas were given by a number of scholars of Polish or Russian origin—N. S. Timasheff in his *Introduction to the Sociology of Law* (1939), Pitirim Sorokin in his *Contemporary Sociological Theories* (1928), G. Gurvitch in his *L'idée du droit social* (1932), and some of the authors in the *Interpretations of Modern Legal Philosophies, Essays in Honor of Roscoe Pound* (1947). In 1948 the present writer published a critical appreciation of Petrazycki's theory in an article in the philosophical journal *Theoria.* After studying the English edition I have found no occasion to retract or modify anything that was said in the article.

The view of law which Hart expounds in his book *The Concept of Law* (1961) is to be seen against the background of naturalistic positivism. In the preface to this edition of Austin's work *The Province of Jurisprudence Determined,* Hart suggests that Austin's doctrine could be amended by the introduction of ' the notion of a rule ' at the appropriate places instead of the notion of a command.

In *The Concept of Law* Hart criticizes naturalistic positivism principally on two points: (i) regarding the notion of a sovereign behind the law, and (ii) regarding the notion of legal rules as commands or coercive orders. The simple model of law as the sovereign's coercive orders is replaced by another model.

The notion of ' a rule ' is put in the place of the notion of a command as the basis of legal theory. The reason for this is that the command theory cannot explain how human conduct is made obligatory through the law. A simple command, accompanied by threats, represents 'the gunman situation'; but no obligation is created when the gunman points his pistol at your head and demands your wallet. Obligations (what ought to be done) are dependent on rules. Besides these 'primary rules of obligation' there is a secondary set of rules which are called rules of recognition, change, and adjudication. They provide that new rules of the primary type may be introduced, old rules removed or modified, and the operations of the primary rules controlled. The secondary rules are, therefore, the rules of legislation and jurisdiction in the widest sense. These secondary rules are put in the place of the sovereign in Austin's system.

The claim of the author is that 'the key to the science of jurisprudence', which Austin proposed to have found in the notion of coercive orders, lies in the combination of those two types of rules. The will-theory is never referred to under that name, but in its Austinian form it is rejected. Hart's own model is an example of non-voluntaristic theory. The rules of obligation are substituted for the commands of the sovereign and the rules of recognition for the sovereign himself.

> The theory suffers from lack of clarity in that the notion of a rule is never defined or explained. Hart evidently accepts the traditional assumption that the binding force or obligatory character is essential to the law. He says that the theory of law as coercive orders 'started from the perfectly correct appreciation of the fact that where there is law, there human conduct is made in some sense non-optional or obligatory' (79 f.). In what sense? Hart rejects the notion that an obligation consists in the being exposed to evil consequences in case of contrary behaviour. What else, then, can an obligation signify but an inner bond in the traditional sense?
>
> The principal gain is the demonstration of the inadequacy of the Austinian theory regarding the role of the sovereign. But it is not sufficient to replace the sovereign by a set of rules existing, as it were, by themselves. In the place of the sovereign we find what may appropriately be called 'a political command structure'. (S. J. Stoljar in *Current Legal Problems*, 1961, 148.) This implies much more than a set of 'rules of recognition'. (The many reviews of Professor Hart's book are recorded by R. Sartorius in 52 *Archiv für Rechts- und Sozialphilosophie* 1966, 161 ff.)

Hägerström's writings on legal philosophy are for the most part devoted to criticism of the will-theory and to the analysis of legal concepts. But he also laid the foundations of a non-voluntaristic theory of law.[5] Lundstedt's work too was mainly critical. The reader may perhaps be confused by his repeated assertions that there are no rules of law. As far as I can understand he meant by this that there are no rules of law in the sense of commands by a mythical lawgiver. Lundstedt emphasized that what we call the law is a vast and complicated working machinery in a society. But he hardly ever made any attempt to describe this machinery. His interest became more and more absorbed in the endeavour to replace 'the method of justice' in solving legal problems by 'the method of social welfare'.[6]

The theory of Alf Ross (*On Law and Justice*) may also be regarded as non-voluntaristic. In so far as Ross interprets 'statements concerning valid law at the present time' as referring to 'hypothetical future decisions under certain conditions' (41), his position is akin to that of the American Realists.

The Approach to the Problem

The principal advantage of the preceding discussion is that the voluntaristic fallacy can be avoided. There will be no need to take sides in the dispute between legal positivism and natural law theories as far as they represent different views based on voluntarism. The task will be to elaborate a realistic, non-voluntaristic view concerning the nature of law.

In the introduction a circuitous approach to this problem was indicated. We have travelled rapidly through three centuries of legal thinking and the time has come to begin the direct investigation of the facts covered by the term law.

As was said in the introduction, the starting point for this investigation might be taken almost anywhere in the vast material before us. We could for instance begin by asking what a policeman is. The answer to this question would lead to new questions, and in this way we would soon arrive at the problem of how the organization of the force, to which a policeman belongs, is functioning, how its rules are established, what its effects on the community

[5] *Inquiries* 14 ff., 37 ff., 315 ff. Some series of lectures by Hägerström, posthumously published by Martin Fries under the title *Rätten och staten* (1963), contain additional contributions to a non-voluntaristic theory.

[6] In my opinion Lundstedt's best work is his book *Die Unwissenschaftlichkeit der Rechtswissenschaft* (1932–36). His posthumous work *Legal Thinking Revised* (1956) suffers from unsatisfactory translation.

are, and so on. It seems more appropriate, however, to start immediately with the rules generally called legal.

As everybody knows 'laws' are issued by a central authority after a more or less complicated legislative process. We may begin by asking what really takes place when laws are resolved upon and promulgated. Thereafter, we may go on to ask in what way other rules reckoned as legal are established.

Chapter 4

THE FORMATION OF RULES

The problem now before us is to explain how new rules are introduced into an existing legal system and how old rules are eliminated from it. This is done on a vast scale through the procedure called legislation. But rules are also evolved through imitation of the behaviour and the pronouncements of people who are regarded as legal authorities.

Since legislation through parliamentary acts plays such a prominent part in our present society, it seems suitable to study this way of establishing rules first. It is a process which takes place according to a working constitution. The founding of a constitution presents peculiar problems which have to be discussed separately.

Legislation at Parliamentary Level

Since an example is necessary, I shall use the legislative process in my own country—a typical constitutional monarchy with parliamentary government.

The process is started by a desire in some quarters for a change in some branch of the law. To avoid complications we may think of some rules of a technical character without political importance.

In the opinion of jurists and bankers the law of mortgages has come to be regarded as being out of date; it is unnecessarily complicated and makes no use of modern technology in the registration of mortgages. In due course some minister of justice becomes sufficiently interested in the matter to appoint a committee of able jurists to draft a new law of mortgages. The jurists study the present situation carefully, discuss it with the authorities keeping the mortgage register and with representatives from the lending institutions. Draft upon draft is made and discussed with these people until at last a final draft is submitted to the minister. He now sends it out to the lending institutions, to unions of real estate owners, and to a number of state officials, inviting them to offer their criticism and submit their own views as to possible amendments. When the answers have accumulated in the ministry, a couple of junior departmental officials are set to work on them to see what changes in the draft may be advisable. A new draft is submitted to the scrutiny of a committee consisting of a few members of the supreme courts. After that the final draft is submitted by the government to the Diet.

At last the matter has reached the stage where the legislative acts are beginning to take place. According to the constitution laws are enacted by the King and the Diet in conjunction, the King being advised by his ministers.

In the Diet a parliamentary committee is entrusted with the study of the governmental proposal. In cases like this they often recommend to the Diet to accept it as it is. Sometimes they propose a few alterations, usually of minor importance. It seldom occurs that the proposal is altogether rejected, and major alterations are very rare. The question is not of political importance, and nobody claims to be able to devise anything better than what the jurists have worked out. The proposal is passed in a session of the Diet, usually without a vote being required.

The decision of the Diet is officially reported to the King in a Council of State, and he gives his formal assent which is recorded in a protocol. The King also signs a copy of the text (in practice the final proof for printing the text in the official collection of laws). This is called the promulgation of the law.

The promulgation is the final stage in the legislative process. Until the promulgation has taken place, there is no new law. With the promulgation a new law has been enacted.[1]

The three phases in the legislative process

In this legislative process three phases are to be distinguished: (i) the drafting of the text; (ii) the decision to transform the draft into a law; and (iii) the acts through which this transformation is effected.

The *drafting* was carried out by the jurists in the legislative committee and worked through by the jurists in the ministry and by the members of the committee of the Diet. In this case it might be supposed that the jurists of the first committee had no specified

[1] A law need not necessarily come into force immediately after promulgation. Often a law provides that it is to come into force at some future date, for instance January 1 the following year. There may be a constitutional rule saying for instance that a new rule shall come into force some specified time after promulgation or publication, if nothing else is said in the law itself. See on different rules in this respect, *La promulgation, la signature et la publication des textes législatifs en droit comparé*, ed. by J. B. Herzog, G. Vlachos & M. Waline (1961), here cited *La promulgation*.

directives as to the contents of the future law; it was left to their good judgment to find out what improvements could be made in the mortgage system. The contents of the law were therefore, practically speaking, determined by the jurists. In other cases the minister of justice will lay down the principles on which the law is to be constructed; the committee will be charged with the task of putting these principles in a legal form and of filling in the details. Sometimes a draft is submitted to the Diet by one of its members. It is very rare that such attempts are successful, but amendments to a governmental proposal introduced by members of the Diet are often included in the final law.

The *decision* to transform the final draft into a law is taken by a great many people. Everyone who participates in the legislative acts has to choose for himself whether or not he will contribute in making the draft into law. But these decisions are far from free. In a constitutional government the King will not personally take any position with regard to the merits of the draft. He will sign the text because he regards this as belonging to his function in the government of the country. If an exceptional occasion were to arise where a revolutionary minded government was proposing legislation absolutely contrary to his beliefs, he would be compelled to make a real choice and would have to face a constitutional crisis if he refused to co-operate.

The members of the Diet also have to decide for themselves how to vote if a vote is called for. In questions that are not politically important they will probably be guided by the recommendations of the parliamentary committee; only in cases of special interest to themselves will they take a personal position regarding the proposed law. When the question is of political consequence the members will usually follow party lines; if they do not, they will damage their political career and perhaps put an end to it.

The most important decisions are taken outside the deliberations of the Diet. In political matters, the party line is fixed in councils of the inner circles of the respective parties. The government always holds a key position. But the decisions require much preparatory work by subordinate agencies which therefore obtain considerable influence on the contents of laws. The contributions actually made by the different groups that take part in reaching decisions vary from one case to another—there are no rules for that.

On the other hand, the right to take part in the *legislative* acts and the role to be played by each individual is strictly determined by constitutional rules, as is the whole procedure. In the Diet formal deliberations are held. When they are declared closed, the speaker asks whether the recommendations of the parliamentary committee will be followed by the chamber. If he pronounces that the 'ayes' have it and nobody asks for a vote, he declares that this is the decision of the chamber. On demand by any member a vote is taken, usually by means of an electric signal system, and the votes are duly counted. According to the result of the count, the speaker declares that the proposal has been passed or defeated. This is regarded as being the decision of the chamber.

The whole procedure consists of a series of formal acts prescribed by the constitution: convocation of the Diet, closing the deliberations, asking of questions by the speaker, his pronouncements on the nature of the answers, the decision to take a vote, counting the votes, pronouncing the results, convocation of the council of state, reporting to the King, the assent of the King, and his signature. These acts must be distinguished from the decisions to make a law of the draft: they are the means by which these decisions are put into effect.

The effect of legislative acts

The effect of the legislative acts is that a draft, or bill, becomes law. What does this imply?

If we keep to the facts, we find the following. According to fixed use of language, the word 'law' instead of that of 'draft', or 'bill', is now applied to the text. But the word 'law', supposing the law to be 'in force', is a solemn word. It commands respect. What is prescribed in a law should be followed by everybody concerned. State officials immediately feel obligated to apply the rules of the new law in so far as it concerns them. When the provisions of the law become known to the general public, the law will influence their conduct. The new law causes a change in ideas about what one should do and should not do, about what is permitted and prohibited. Depending on the degree of respect for laws and many other factors, these ideas will be more or less decisive for people's behaviour.

How is this effect of the legislative acts to be explained? Any group of individuals could take it into their heads to form a sort of assembly and produce texts under the name of laws. But these people would be thought mad and their declarations would be of no avail; they would have no effect on the general behaviour of society.

What makes legislative acts by King and Diet effective is, in the first place, the engrained respect for the constitution. In the constitution the right of making laws is conferred on King and Diet; the formalities to be observed are described. The respect for these rules is so universal and so powerful that a text promulgated as law after due procedure is automatically accepted by everybody as being a law; and this implies the idea of duty to follow its prescriptions.

Thus the ability to make laws with practical effect results from the general attitude among the population with regard to the constitution, this attitude being the immediate source of the law-making 'power' of the legislators. They are in a position to invest a text with the quality of law, in the eye of the public; when it has become a law, it belongs to a great body of rules commanding universal respect.

This is the effect of the legislative acts. It is an effect on the psychological level.

Two objections against this reasoning may be expected. (i) A poll would probably show that the general public has very hazy notions regarding the constitution. (ii) Even if they know something about the constitutional forms of legislation, they can hardly know that this text has really gone through the requisite formalities.

To the first objection the answer is that rather hazy notions of the constitution are sufficient; it is enough that people have the idea that the power of issuing laws belongs to certain authorities in the capital, known as King and Diet. To the second objection the answer is the following. It is quite true, of course, that very few people see for themselves that the constitutional formalities have been observed with regard to a text that is published as a law. But there are a number of technical links between the legislative authorities and the public. Officials take care that the text signed by the King is the same as that which has been passed by the Diet. They then see to it that this same text is published without alteration in the official collection of laws. The texts in this collection are read by few people outside the bureaucracy. But for the use of the public private editions are printed with commentaries, and these have to be reliable if they are to be sold at all. The press, the radio, and the TV help in spreading knowledge of new laws; organizations of different kinds distribute information to their members, and so on. This activity refers only to texts that have really gone through the constitutional formalities.

Legislation according to the will-theory

According to the will-theory the law consists of the contents of the will of the sovereign. But people cannot know his will unless it has got some outward expression; they cannot therefore be required to obey it until such expression has been given to it. This is done primarily through legislation. In its essence legislation is a declaration of will (*declaratio voluntatis*) on the part of the sovereign. Its purpose is to make his will known to the subjects.

Pufendorf holds that a law may be made known to the subjects in any suitable way. In general this is true of the laws of God too. But an exception is made. The law of nature need not be specially publicized by God because it can be discovered by reason unaided (1, 6, §§ 4, 13, 18).

The teachings of Jean-Jacques Rousseau represent the purest form of will-theory. In his view the 'legislator' is a wise man who guides the people. (*Cf*. Gagnebin, 'Le role du législateur dans les conceptions politiques de Rousseau,' in *Etudes sur le contrat social de Jean-Jacques Rousseau,* 1964.) The legislator cannot impose any law on the people because only the general will can bind the individuals. (*Du contrat social* 2, 7: *Il n'y a que la volonté générale qui oblige les particuliers.*) The contents of the general will can only be ascertained through a free vote (*ibid.*). The essence of legislation therefore consists in discovering, through a vote, the general will. When a law is proposed in the assembly of the people, what is demanded of them is not exactly that they say if they approve the proposed law or not; the question is whether the proposition conforms to the general will or not; everybody has to give his opinion on this point. According to the social contract the declaration of the general will is made through the counting of the votes. (*Du calcul des voix se tire la déclaration de la volonté générale*, 4, 2.) If the opinion contrary to my own has prevailed, this only proves that I was mistaken as to the contents of the general will. (Simple majority should not suffice in matters of grave importance.)

Rousseau is evidently familiar with the traditional view that legislation has the character of a *declaratio voluntatis* on the part of the sovereign. But the declaration almost fades away. The sovereign is no longer a king but the people. The people cannot, like the king, immediately give expression to its will. First of all the contents of its will must be found out. To this end a certain procedure, the vote, is required. As soon as the votes have been counted, the general will is known. No additional

declaration is needed. The *declaratio voluntatis* becomes submerged in the procedure for ascertaining the will of the people. This means carrying the will-theory to its extreme length as Rousseau does in other respects too.
A very clear example of undaunted will-theory is what Georg Jellinek says on legislation in his work *Gesetz und Verordnung* (1887) 312 ff. In a monarchical government the decisive act takes place in the mind of the monarch (the act is *ein innerer Vorgang in der Monarchenpersönlichkeit*). It consists in his willing the contents of the law and the resolve to require obedience to it (*Wollen des Gesetzesinhalts und Entschluss denselben anzubefehlen*). But the will has to be proclaimed in order to attain juridical relevancy.

The role of the legislators

The will-theory implies minimizing the importance of the formalities in the process of legislation. From its point of view the essential thing is the publication, in one way or other, of the will of the lawgiver. The formalities are only of outward, secondary significance.

This means turning the realities upside down. The legislative acts are no declarations of will; their import is not to give expression to the 'will of the lawgiver'; this pretended will is a myth. In actual fact the legislative acts are a series of formal acts described in the constitution and depending for their practical efficacy on the universal respect for the constitution. The formalities may seem trifling when they are regarded in isolation. They are nevertheless essential. They may consist of this or that according to the historical circumstances in the country; the important thing is that the forms of the existing constitution are observed.

The motivation for performing the legislative formalities varies greatly among the participants in the procedure. They rank from the conviction that the proposed law would be good for the country, to expectation of reaping political profit from it or mere following of routine as a matter of course. For the efficacy of the legislative acts, the various motives are irrelevant. The participants need not even have any knowledge of the contents of the proposed law; in general only a few of them are really familiar with the proposal except in matters arousing great political interest. The one important thing in transforming the draft into a law is the correct performance of the formalities.

The personal influence of the several legislators (persons taking part in the formal legislative process) is also subject to great variations; it may be anything from null to decisive. Individuals or groups outside the legislative bodies may possess far more influence than the legislators themselves; it depends on the power structure of the country.

The essential characteristic of the legislators is their occupying the positions required for correct performance of the constitutional formalities. The respect for the constitution is the great source of power for governing the country. Like an electric current, the flow of this power is directed through legislative acts according to the constitution. The political struggle is primarily a struggle for the key positions from which the switchboard is being operated. Those who have reached these positions are necessarily subject to the influence of a great many forces in deciding how to make use of the formalities of legislation. The laws that emerge from the process are no declarations of their ' will ', but the outcome of a long series of ideas concerning desirable novelties, opposition to such ideas, persuasion, propaganda, governmental and private initiatives, discussions, propaganda, and compromises ultimately leading to the passing of a set of rules through the sequence of formalities ending with the act of promulgation.

The growing complexity of modern society has led to a marked increase in the influence of the experts. *Cf.* the account given and the question posed by René Savatier in his article ' Observations sur les modes contemporains de formation du droit positif ' (1 *Mélanges en l'honneur de Jean Dabin,* 1963, 293 ff.). Réalise-t-on combien difficilement le député et le sénateur élus, entre les mains desquels le peuple souverain remet, théoriquement encore, le pouvoir législatif, s'adaptent aux éxigences nouvelles? (those posed by the rapid changes in technology and social structure).

The example of legislation cited above represents the case where *tardivement, des lois, préparées par l'évolution de la jurisprudence et les contrats, s'imposent pour ainsi dire, du dehors* (299).

Promulgation

The word ' promulgation ' comes from the latin word *promulgare,* which means publicize, make known to the people. (The etymology is uncertain.) In the time of the Roman Republic, the initiative for legislation belonged to the magistrates who submitted their proposals to the people's assembly. A proposal had to be publicized at a certain time before the day when the assembly was to be held. This was called to promulgate the law (*legem promulgare*). After the assembly had passed the law by answering in the affirmative, when the presiding magistrate asked whether they would accept the law, the result was proclaimed through a *renuntiatio* by a herald. From that moment the law was in force; no other form of publication was needed, though in practice it was usual to put the law down in writing on tables of wood or copper.[2]

In modern terminology the term 'promulgation' has another meaning. The change began to take place in mediaeval doctrine, where the need for promulgation seems to have been the subject of much discussion.[3]

From the point of view of the will-theory promulgation came to signify the publication of the will of the sovereign. This was the idea behind a number of similar promulgation formulae used in the monarchies of Europe.[4] It is apparent in the celebrated English ceremony for the passing of a law. The monarch proceeded in state to the House of Lords; and in the presence of the Commons the royal assent was given to a public bill with the words 'Le Roy (la Reyne) le veult'. Through these words the bill was transformed into a law.[5] This is what was called promulgation. The law was afterwards published in certain ways. But the publication was not needed to give it the force of law. According to constitutional theory everybody was deemed to have knowledge of the law, since Parliament represented the whole body of the realm.[6] By means of this fiction the requirements of the will-theory of legislation that the will of the sovereign should be made known to the subjects was satisfied.

In modern constitutions the old promulgation formulae have disappeared. The sovereign will is the will of the people, and it is

[2] See 3: 1 Mommsen, *Römisches Staatsrecht* (3. Aufl. 1887) 370 f., 413 ff.

[3] On promulgation according to St. Thomas, see Jacques Leclercq in 2 *Natural Law Forum* (1957) 78 ff.

[4] *Cf.* Waline in *La promulgation* 5 and Kelsen, *Hauptprobleme der Staatsrechtslehre* 413, 547 with literature on the 'sacramental' promulgation formulae.

[5] In his diary for March 2, 1665, John Evelyn relates the procedure in the following way: When the Commons had come to the House of Lords, the Speaker made an oration 'after which he presented divers bills, read by the Cleark, the King by a nod only passing them, the Cleark saying *le Roy le veult*'. Samuel Pepys gives a similar account in his diary. Since 1855 the royal assent has been given through a commission. *Cf.* Neville Brown in *La promulgation* 98; Jennings, *The Law and the Constitution* (5 ed. 1959).

[6] The authority for this is a precedent from 1365. *Cf.* Brown in *La promulgation* 99. The doctrine is stated by Coke in the following words (4 Inst. 26): 'Although proclamation be not made in the county, every one is bound to take notice of that which is done in parliament: for as soon as the parliament hath concluded any thing, the law intends, that every person hath notice thereof, for the parliament represents the body of the whole realm: and therefore it is not requisite that any proclamation be made, seeing the statute took effect before.' (Cited from Jellinek, *Gesetz und Verordnung* 19.)

supposed to be expressed through the vote of the Diet. Usually the laws passed by the Diet have to be promulgated by the head of state, a monarch or president. But the significance of the act of promulgation has been altered since it cannot be considered as a declaration of the will of a ruler concerning the conduct of his subjects. It has become a routine business that is no longer shrouded in the ancient mysteries of kingship.

Like the preceding stages in the legislative process promulgation is a formal act. It marks the end of the process. Its import is to attach, so to speak, the designation of 'law' to the text. This fixing becomes effective thanks to the habits of thought and speech generated through the universal respect of the constitution. In private as well as official language the text now represents a law.

The act of promulgation is generally interpreted in a different way by writers on constitutional law. It is said to be an official declaration to the effect that the constitutional forms of legislation have been observed. (See Waline in *La promulgation* 5.) But this cannot be the import of promulgation when the act is an element in the legislative process. There is no law until the text has been promulgated. The promulgation cannot be a declaration saying that it has taken place itself. It is true that in an orderly government the head of state is not required to promulgate a text unless the preceding formalities have been gone through according to the constitution. From the fact that the text has been promulgated one may therefore infer that the constitutional formalities have been observed with regard to the text. But the sense of the act is not, for that reason, to proclaim this fact. Every preceding step in the legislative process presupposes that the earlier steps have been taken in due order. The vote in the Diet, for instance, shall not take place unless a proposal has been submitted as required by the constitution; from the fact that a vote has been taken, one may therefore infer that a proposal has been submitted in due form. But the sense of the vote is not, of course, to make an official declaration concerning this fact. The several steps in the process of legislation have their sense or import as meeting the requirements of different provisions of the constitution. The final step is the promulgation.

There is a need for some sort of promulgation. The moment in which a draft shall be held to be transformed into a law is evidently of great importance. It is therefore required that this moment be exactly fixed. The act of promulgation in its present shape serves this purpose as well as did promulgation in the sense of publicizing the will of the sovereign. Publication (in the official collection of laws and perhaps in other ways) follows upon promulgation. It now means publication of a law that has been duly enacted; therefore it is not part of the legislative process proper.

Establishing a Constitution

The preceding discussion referred to the legislative process in a modern country with a parliamentary government regulated by a working constitution. A constitution, however, is also a kind of law. It may have been enacted according to a previous constitution. But this regress cannot go on for ever. Sooner or later we arrive at a point where a constitution has been established in an illegal, or shall we say extra-legal, way. The argument, therefore, would not give us a final explanation of how legal rules are established. It presupposes the existence of a working constitution, *i.e.*, of a kind of law. Thus it would perhaps be said that the explanation is circular.

This is not, however, the case. The purport of the exposition was not to afford a 'final' explanation of how laws are established. It was a description of how alterations in a system of rules referred to as 'the law' are introduced by means of a procedure called legislation. The existence of the system, in which the alterations take place, is, of course, presupposed. But the alterations can be described without entering on the question of how the system came into being. To describe the human body it is not necessary to explain the origin of man.

Thus the exposition was limited in scope. It gives a partial answer only to the question of how laws are established. The inquiry must now proceed to a new phase in discussing the question of how constitutions are founded.

This is an historical problem. No general answer is possible. The origin of each constitution has to be investigated separately. But some common features in the process are clear enough.

A modern written constitution is a law containing the rules about the organization of the government, the composition of a representative assembly, the mode of election of its members, the powers of the assembly and of the government, and so on. Such constitutions are a relatively recent phenomenon; they presuppose a highly developed community. The oldest written constitution now in force is said to be that of the U.S.A. from the year 1787. Next in order of seniority comes the Swedish constitution from 1809. Earlier examples are Oliver Cromwell's short-lived constitution from 1653 and a Swedish constitution from 1634. But such instances of old constitutions embodied in enacted laws are very rare. Written, systematical constitutions became common only during the nineteenth century.

Long before that time, however, there was some constitution in every European country. Usually it had grown around the kingship. The British constitution is of this older type; it has slowly evolved during struggles between kings, feudal lords, and rising sections of the population, with occasional legislative acts covering parts of the field each time. Written constitutions of the modern type came into fashion through the influence of eighteenth-century natural law doctrine.

In tracing the history of constitutions we finally reach the most remote ages about which records have been preserved. Even there we find working constitutions, as for instance in the Greek states and in Rome. Their origin is not known and can presumably never be known to us. It is only possible to study the facts as they appear from the sources and draw some conclusions from them.

A working constitution implies that some men have power over others, that there are rules defining their powers, and that there is some established mode of succession to the positions of power. How are we to understand in what way this originally came about?

In trying to find some answer to this question we must avoid the pitfall of anachronism. For us it seems self-evident that there must be some central authorities endowed with the power of government and legislation. When this opinion is held and the existing authorities are considered legitimate, the legislative process functions smoothly and forthcoming products are automatically included in the body of 'the law in force'. But it has certainly taken a long time to reach this situation. The modern mind has been formed under the influence of hundreds of years of orderly government. Our views cannot be ascribed to people living under primitive conditions in ancient times simply because they are natural to us.[7]

There must always have been some men with a special gift for leadership, who were capable of co-ordinating activities in the bitter struggle for survival. But leadership alone cannot explain the establishment of permanent organizations based on fixed rules. Something more was needed for the creation of archaic constitutions.

The evidence of the oldest sources unmistakably points to one

[7] In a great work on the archaic order in Rome called *Primordia civitatis* (1959), De Francisci stresses the necessity of freeing oneself from dependence on all expositions that are the fruits of conventional doctrinal speculation and of our spiritual environment. *Cf.* Orestano, *I fatti di normazione nell' esperienza romana arcaica* (1967) 102 ff.

factor of paramount importance in establishing early constitutions. This was religion, which made obedience to fixed rules natural and regular.

In ancient times religion and law were not separated into different spheres. They formed an entity. If social rules evolved in connection with religious rites and beliefs, we can understand how they could obtain enduring respect. They were then supported by reverence and fear of superhuman powers. With the backing of such powers government could be established.[8]

The Roman Republic is an example of a constitution originally founded on magico-religious beliefs. Of the preceding kingship we know very little; no doubt it was sacral.[9] But the constitution of the Republic is well known and there are obvious traces of its religious foundation.

De Francisci devotes a large part of his *Primordia civitatis* to the study of the magico-animistic origins of the concept of power among the Romans (199 ff.). Orestano's work *I fatti di normazioni nell'esperienze romana arcaica* is also concerned with the connection between the legal ideas of the Romans and their religion. Wagenwoort contends that *imperium* originally meant 'chief's mana', *imperare* 'to transfer mana' and *imperator* 'the chief who transfers mana' (*Roman Dynamism,* 1947, 66). This is an example of the direction of modern research. (*Cf.* on Wagenwoort's hypothesis De Francisci 367 ff.)

In a series of works on the legal ideas of the Romans, Hägerström presented an elaborate argument to show the magical nature of the ancient legal acts (*mancipatio, sponsio,* etc.) and the origin in magic of fundamental legal concepts. But he met with little comprehension when in 1927 he published the first volume of *Der römische Obligationsbegriff* and two years later *Das magistratische Ius in seinem Zusammenhang mit dem römischen Sacralrechte*. De Francisci notes (363) that Hägerström's views were too revolutionary at that time; and his insistence, as De Francisci puts it, on the superstitious basis of Roman law created resentment among scholars. The result was that his expositions were not even seriously discussed; they were, in fact, for a time completely forgotten. (It is significant that a learned scholar like Wagenwoort is apparently unaware of Hägerström's work.) The second volume of *Der römische Obligationsbegriff,* posthumously published in 1941, seems never to have been reviewed, partly owing to war conditions. It was Hägerström's intention to devote a second half of this second volume to the

[8] It is not necessary to discuss here the question of the relationship between religion and magic. Even if a distinction is possible at such early stages, it is in any case evident that religion and magic were closely connected.

[9] So it was also in ancient Greece. A summary of the facts in Hägerström, 1 *Der römische Obligationsbegriff* (1927) 303 [1].

question of the basis of the binding force of consensual contracts according to the Roman jurists; but he was unable to complete this work before his death in 1939. A summary of his results has, however, been published in the essay *Recht, Pflicht und bindende Kraft des Vertrages nach römischer und naturrechtlicher Anschauung* (*Skrifter utgivna av k. humanistiska vetenskapssamfundet i Upsala* 44: 3, 1965). In the intervening time the climate of opinion has changed, and it would be difficult now to understand how serious scholars could recoil before the assertion that legal acts like the *mancipatio* or the *sponsio* were magical. (*Cf.* below 227 ff.) In a paper with the title 'Zur *Frage des magischen Charakters der älteren Rechtsvorstellungen*' (*Bulletin de la société royale des lettres de Lund* 1956–57 I) I have tried to clear up some misconceptions concerning Hägerström's theories. The most essential novelty in his method is the application of philosophical analysis to the concepts of the Romans. This has not yet been appreciated.

For the Romans, surrounded by enemies and almost constantly engaged in war, the protection of the gods was of the utmost importance. Jupiter had empowered Romulus to found the city and conferred kingship on him. The welfare of the city was dependent on the continued favour of the gods and especially that of Jupiter.

The will of Jupiter was revealed through the auspices (*auspicia*), which were certain natural occurrences, such as the flight of birds, lightning, and thunder. Such signs could be offered spontaneously by the gods (*auspicia oblativa*). But for the preparation of state actions auspices were demanded (*auspicia impetrativa*). This was not done by the priests but by the magistrates (consuls, praetors, and others). Before the creation of a magistrate, before holding a people's assembly, and before the departure for war of the commander-in-chief, the taking of auspices was obligatory. In many other cases, auspices were to be taken, if possible.[10] Cicero tells us that the ancestors did hardly anything, even of a private nature, without taking auspices. According to Livy, the decemvir Appius Claudius Crassus (about 450 B.C.) said: 'Who does not know that this city has been founded under auspices, and that everything in war and peace, at home and during campaigns, is conducted under auspices?'[11]

Not everybody could take auspices; a certain power (*potestas*) was needed. This was acquired by a magistrate through his being

[10] For the Roman auspices, see Mommsen, 2 *Römisches Staatsrecht* (3. Aufl. 1887) 76 ff.: Catalano, 1 *Contributi allo studio del diritto augurale* (1960). The augurs could announce the appearance of *auspicia oblativa*. They also cultivated the science of auspices. But it was the exclusive privilege of the magistrates to manage the *auspicia impetrativa*. See Mommsen 81^1, 109^3.

[11] Cicero, *De divinatione* 1,16,28; Livy 6,41,4. *Cf.* Orestano 117.

elected during an assembly held under the auspices of a preceding magistrate. Ultimately this mystical power rested with the patricians. Therefore it ' returned ' to them when there was a vacancy and there was no competent magistrate to take the auspices. The members of the senate—the patricians—then chose an ' intermediate king ' (*interrex*) from among themselves to fill the gap. In this way the auspicial power could always, when required, be replenished from its source.

The power (*potestas*) of a magistrate was the ability to perform the acts belonging to his office. In the first place, it was a power to take auspices. The power over other men followed from this mystical ability. In the case of the highest magistrates this *potestas* was called *imperium*. Usually the empire and the auspicial power are mentioned in conjunction—*auspicia imperiumque.*[12] In inscriptions commemorating a victory the formula is that the victory was won under the leadership, auspices, and empire of somebody (*ductu, auspicio, imperioque*). But possession of the supreme command could also be expressed simply through the words *meis auspiciis*.

The primary factor in magisterial power was the auspicial power.[13] It is related by Cicero and many other authors that the city was founded by Romulus through auspices, his auspices being stronger than those of Remus since he had seen twelve vultures while Remus had only seen six.[14] As the strength and welfare of the city derived from the auspices of Romulus, so governmental power flowed from the auspices taken by the magistrates.

In opposition to Hägerström and De Francisci, Catalano maintains that the ' human magisterial power ' was the primary thing; the auspicial power is said to be a projection of the magisterial power on the level of sacral law. (' L'*auspicium* (come potere auspicale) è proiezione sul piano del diritto divino dei singoli potere magistratuali: potere di consultare il Dio circa il *dies* degli atti che ciascun magistrato ha il potere di compiere ', 445. ' Il *prius* erano praticamente i poteri umani ', 449. *Cf*. 365.) Without doubt, this view is mistaken. It is not possible to discuss this at length, but it should be sufficient to refer to the chief document of the case, an extract from a textbook by the augur Messala, preserved by Aulus Gellius in his *Noctes Atticae* (13,15,4). Messala says that the auspices of the patricians

[12] Sometimes the locution *imperium auspiciumque* is used. But the correct expression was *auspicium imperiumque*, see Mommsen 76[1].

[13] See Hägerström, *Das magistratische Ius* 10 ff. and De Francisci, *Primordia civitatis* 364 ff. Already Mommsen calls the auspices the ultimate source of magisterial power though this is done in passing only (91).

[14] See the numerous quotations collected by Catalano 577 ff.

(meaning their auspicial powers) are divided into two kinds of powers. The major ones are those of the consuls, praetors, and censors. The auspices of the other magistrates are minor. Therefore, these latter magistrates are called minor, the former major. (*Patriciorum auspicia in duas sunt divisa potestates. Maxima sunt consulum, praetorum, censorum. — Reliquorum magistratuum minora sunt auspicia. Ideo illi minores, hi maiores appellantur.*) The consuls etc. are major magistrates because their auspicial powers are greater than those of the other magistrates. This implies that the source of magisterial power is the auspicial power.

Catalano contends that the word *potestas* in the first sentence does not mean 'auspicial powers' but '(human) magisterial power'. (P.444 [17]: 'con potestas nel passo si intenda il potere magistratuale.') But it is impossible that Messala, in his strict language, could have divided the *auspices* of the patricians into two kinds of *human magisterial powers.* This would have been like dividing apples (*auspicia*) into two kinds of pears ('human magisterial powers'). According to Catalano, Messala is saying: 'Massima è la potestas e il correspondente potere auspiciale dei consoli, dei pretori, dei censori, minore la potestas e il potere auspicale degli alteri magistrati' (445). If Messala had wanted to say this, he would have expressed himself in another way. As Hägerström remarks, the word *potestas* twice refers to the auspices (in the sense of auspicial power): 'Es handelt sich um die dem Staate glückbringende Kraft der verschiedenen Auspizien' (*Das magistratische Ius* 10 [1]). De Francisci concurs, *Primordia civitatis* 367; *cf.* 372: the position of the augurs, of the *rex,* of the magistrates derived from the auspices; the patricians tried to defend their privileges against the plebeians with the argument that they possessed the auspices (Livy 4,2,5).

Legislation was enacted by the people's assembly on the proposal of a magistrate. The right auspices were required and the day must not be religiously unsuitable. The legislative power of the people was not unlimited; the people could not, for instance, deprive anybody of his citizenship. The people was bound by its own laws. A higher power was engaged when a law had been rightly (*iure*) proposed and rightly decided on by the people. If the college of augurs pronounced that the auspices had not been right, the law had been wrongly carried (*vitio lata*); it then lacked validity and the senate had to issue a decree to that effect to make it possible for the magistrates to set the law aside as void. The decree said that the people were not bound by the law in question (*populum ea lege non videri teneri*).[15]

[15] See Hägerström, 1 *Der römische Obligationsbegriff* 539 ff. and *Das magistratische Ius* 5 f.

In time the taking of auspices became a mere formality. According to Roman principles the declaration of a magistrate as to the flight of the birds or the occurrence of lightning and thunder could not be called in doubt by anybody. The magistrate's declaration was valid. Originally it must have seemed dangerous to make a false statement. Livy relates a story indicating that the auspices at one time were regarded with real awe. For military purposes the Romans used hens which were carried with the army under the care of special hen-keepers (*pullarii*). Once before a battle a hen-keeper wrongly reported to the consul in command that the hens had behaved in a way indicating the pleasure of the gods. The gods instantly punished him.[16] But nothing more is heard of calamities like this; and the practice of proclaiming the appearance of such portents as were wanted became general. It was not considered necessary for the sign to have really appeared. It was sufficient that the magistrate declared that it had been perceived. This was evidently expedient from the point of view of conducting business, since the holding of people's assemblies and other state acts would have been greatly hampered had authentic signs been required.[17]

What popular beliefs may have remained in the late republic is doubtful.[18] But originally such beliefs must have been strong.[19] The rules concerning the powers of magistrates and succession in office gained psychological effectiveness and permanency through them.

This is not to say that the same causes supported the constitution of the Roman Republic the whole time. Over a period of several hundred years great changes in the psychological basis of the constitution necessarily took place. When government has been carried

[16] He was accidentally killed by a spear thrown by a soldier. The incident took place in the year 293 B.C. See Mommsen 80[4] with Livy 10,40,11. The theory was that a false announcement called down the wrath of the gods on him who made it, but not on the Roman people; and the sign was valid if accepted by the magistrate. *Cf.* Hägerström, *Das magistratische Ius* 78 f. Pompey, as consul, once broke up an assembly by announcing that he had heard the rumblings of thunder. See Mommsen 106[4]. (No assembly could be held on a day when thunder occurred.)

[17] On taking office a consul first of all asked Jupiter for a sign of his favour; and it was invariably reported to him that a stroke of lightning had been observed travelling from the left to the right, which indicated the pleasure of Jupiter. See Mommsen 81, 609.

[18] At the time of Cicero the taking of military auspices was neglected. See Mommsen 97.

[19] It is attested by several authors from Antiquity that the Romans were extremely religious. *Pietate ac religione . . . omnes gentes nationesque superavimus,* Cicero says (*de haruspicum responso* 9,19). See Orestano 108 f. with many quotations. Orestano remarks that according to Polybius, writing in the second century B.C., the Romans even at that time exalted religion and introduced it into private and public life to an extent that could not be surpassed.

on for a long time according to a set of rules, such rules are supported by habits of thought and many other factors. The old creed may be undermined and the ritual acts reduced to mere formalities; but for numerous reasons respect for the rules may nevertheless be upheld and the forms reverently observed.

For the purpose of the present argument it is sufficient to state that the power of the Roman magistrates was primarily a mystical power of taking auspices. This seems to be an indubitable fact. It is not necessary to go into the details of the curious science of auspices. Hägerström gives a fascinating exposition of its principles in his essay *Das magistratische Ius,* especially in the chapter on the will of the gods with the characteristic philosophical rubric *Über die Natur des Willens einer römischen Gottheit.*

I should like to add that the social importance of magical and religious beliefs cannot be measured by the percentage of individuals within the population who believe in the literal truth of official dogmas. Still less can any conclusion be drawn from the fact that an outside observer can attach no belief to the rites and tenets of more than two thousand years ago.

The Roman example is particularly valuable because the ancient forms were preserved down to the time when literary sources became numerous. We have therefore plenty of material for studying the views of the Romans, even those belonging to the early period of the Republic. But the examples could easily be multiplied. In the European countries the old creeds were superseded by Christianity before the peoples had any literature of their own. The sources are therefore meagre with regard to the oldest, pre-Christian institutions. But enough traces are left to indicate that the forms of society were intimately connected with magico-religious beliefs.

Archaic constitutions are found in societies where a large number of rules belonging to 'private law' are firmly established—rules about property, marriage, etc.—and there are rules about reactions against wrongdoers. These rules are also intimately connected with religion in the widest sense. Law and religion were interdependent, and they must be supposed to have grown together from beginnings far beyond the horizon of history.

This is what we can surmise regarding the 'ultimate' origin of constitutions and of rules of law in general. In historical times we can only witness changes in the law and additions to the law being made. Perhaps it would be more correct to say that we can witness how the body of rules, now called the law, has grown out of the customary, magico-religious rules found in ancient societies.

A great step forward was made when the legislative process became accepted as a regular phenomenon. It is a device for introducing new rules into a given system in a peaceful and psychologically effective way. Usually legislation takes place according to the rules of a working constitution. But history affords many examples of laws becoming effective though they have been enacted in a more or less irregular way. In some cases, perhaps, minor faults are overlooked. In other cases the imperative needs of the moment make it seem necessary to dispense with some formalities; if this feeling is sufficiently widespread, the new law is accepted despite the irregularity. There are many variations on this theme.

Most conspicuous among the irregular acts of legislation are those which occur in connection with a revolution. A monarch has fled the country after an unsuccessful war; or a government has been overthrown through violent action. The seat of power is for the moment vacant, and the old constitutional order has lost its hold on the minds of the people. New leaders step in and proclaim that they have 'assumed power', which is an empty phrase unless they are successful. They begin to issue laws and administrative decrees. To succeed they need, of course, organization and a special political and psychological situation in the country. The ordinary source of strength for a government and a legislature, the respect for the existing constitution, is supplanted by a momentary gathering of diverse forces. But in actual fact, the revolutionaries make use of much of the foundations of the old order. Most of the law is left as it is; only the constitution is put aside. People are, however, familiar with the idea that there must always be a government and a legislature; the necessity for this is obvious. Therefore the respect for the previous constitution may easily be transferred to the new one.

To make the transition more painless and success more certain, the traditional forms are often followed or imitated as far as possible. The combinations of revolutionary novelty with actual or pretended observance of constitutional rules are infinitely varied.

Still more important, however, is the ideological ground for the legitimacy of the new order that is generally invoked. This is that the new order is based on the will of the people. The idea is that the will of the people is the ultimate source of the law. A new constitution, enacted without reference to an old constitution, therefore, needs no other justification than its being willed by the people. The idea of popular sovereignty is, so to speak, the constitutional principle on which constitutions are founded.

This has been the prevalent idea since the doctrine of the divine right of kings went out of fashion. But it is far from universal. Marxist ideology is different. The communist party is not held forth as the bearer of the will of the people. It acts as the leadership of the proletariat in effecting the inevitable overthrow of capitalist society. After the revolution it carries on the dictatorship of the proletariat, which is justified, in all its harshness, as an unavoidable phase that has to be passed on the road to communist society with its perfect freedom and equality. The ideological basis of the government is not the natural law ideas of the sovereignty of the people and of natural rights. It is the supposed historical necessity of the evolution of society from primitive communism via feudalism and capitalism to socialism and ultimate communism. The communist party is represented as the agent of the historical necessity itself. This is its super-human source of strength.

Imitation

Though legislation is nowadays the most important way of introducing new rules into the legal system and eliminating others, it is by no means the only one. Legislation implies the conscious and deliberate laying down of rules through a formal procedure. But rules that are reckoned as belonging to the legal system may also be established in other ways. This is the case in the fields usually spoken of as customary law and judge-made law.

The concepts of customary law and judge-made law are not always kept apart. But it is advisable to do so. The concept of customary law, as presented in the literature, is difficult to grasp, whereas that of judge-made law offers no special difficulty.

For the purpose of showing how new rules are introduced into the legal system outside formal legislation, only a few remarks on customary law and judge-made law are necessary.

Customary law

A custom as such is a certain manner of acting, regularly observed within a community. In a primitive society there are always a lot of such ways of acting. When a man wants to marry, he proceeds in a certain way to obtain the consent of the relations of the prospective bride; gifts are exchanged, and the marriage is concluded in a ritual form. When a member of the family has been slain, retaliation is made by slaying a kinsman of the offender. In a village each family cultivates its own parcel of land; but certain grazing grounds are common to all.

Thus the life of the community follows a regular pattern. The same ways of acting are invariably observed by all. But to the members of the community the customs are not only what actually and regularly takes place. For everyone who grows up within the community it is natural to look upon the customs as representing what ought to be done in certain situations; and he is taught so by his elders. A custom becomes a *rule* of behaviour that one is considered bound to follow; and one feels entitled to claim that others follow it too.

Moreover, the customs are intertwined with beliefs pertaining to a primitive people. The marriage ritual is designed to ensure fertility. The spirit of the dead man will harass his descendants forever if he is not revenged. By magical means making intrusion dangerous, the parcel of land is protected. Thus the rules of custom are not only rules for the behaviour of men to men. They are also rules for the functioning and manipulation of occult forces.

These customary rules of primitive societies are often spoken of as their customary law. It is a question of terminology whether one should apply the term ' law ' to the rules obtaining before the emergence of a state organization capable of wielding superior force. In any case it is evident that the whole situation is changed with the appearance of the state.

Now organized force is beginning to be applied as a means of creating respect for the fundamental rules of social life and bringing redress to those who suffer from transgressions. The fatal custom of revenge is suppressed and the assassin is brought to punishment by the authorities. If the parcel of land is taken from the rightful occupant, the intruder is penalized and the parcel is restored to the owner.

The courts set up to direct the use of state power in such matters take their guidance from the old customs and such legislation as there may be. In the course of time the relative importance of custom and enacted law is slowly reversed. As the fields covered by legislation are extended, the need for having recourse to custom is diminished. Furthermore, a stock of precedents is being accumulated. Instead of looking for rules of custom that are supposed to exist within the community but which are difficult to ascertain, the courts are inclined to imitate previous decisions on similar cases. Precedents are interposed between the rules of custom and the actions of the courts.

Under modern conditions the importance of customary rules as guides of actions for the courts has dwindled to insignificance. Actual customs—in business for instance—may be taken into consideration by the courts in framing their decisions as one element among others that may have a bearing on the question. But it seems hardly well grounded to speak any more of a customary law as existing beside enacted law and judge-made law. For these two kinds of 'law' it is characteristic that they are intimately connected with the state organization. Customs and ideas about rights and duties and correct behaviour exist to a large extent without any such connection. In so far as they are taken into consideration by the courts among the reasons for their decisions they contribute to the development of judge-made law. This is their true role in the formation of legal rules.[20]

Judge-made law

Courts are naturally inclined to constancy in their decisions. When a similar case has previously been adjudged, they are wont to take the same course unless there are strong arguments against it. In this way new rules are continuously formed within the judiciary. Rules of custom are gaining the support of state power. Questions of interpretation regarding enacted laws are settled as far as the courts are concerned. In countless details the laws are supplemented by court decisions that are followed in the future as diligently as the provisions of the laws themselves. In areas not covered by enacted law decisions are made by the courts on the basis of natural law ideas, supposed customs, expediency, or other reasons; and as a decision once made is likely to be imitated the next time, the bulk of precedents is steadily growing.

The practice of the courts as such is only a series of actual decisions. Rules are built on these decisions in so far as the idea prevails that precedents should be followed.

The idea of an obligation to follow precedents is, however, in conflict with the idea that the courts only have to apply the law as it is, not to make law. But this old idea in its turn is in conflict with reality. It presupposes a comprehensive law from which all decisions could be deduced. Since this is an illusion, the courts necessarily have to make decisions on many cases where there is no pre-existing law or where the law is open to different interpretations. To say that no decision can be given because there is

[20] *Cf.* Battifol, 'Sur la positivité du droit' (1 *Mélanges en l'honneur de Jean Dabin,* 1963, 7 f.).

no law would run counter to an imperative need for decisions in legal disputes. The demands of practical life prevail over an unrealistic idea. Decisions are made without the supposed basis of an existing law. Since a principle once adopted is likely to be followed in the future, the courts, after all, 'make law'.

But there is a connecting idea by which the conflict between unrealistic assumptions and practical needs is obscured. This is the idea that the courts are authoritative interpreters of the existing law. The law is supposed to contain principles according to which every conceivable case can be decided. The courts are held to know this law and to be able to say what it means as applied to a particular case. They are the highest authority on such questions and their pronouncements may not be called in doubt. In this way the actual innovations necessarily made by the courts are covered up as merely being authoritative interpretations and applications of an existing law. The result is the same when the idea is that 'the law' in a mysterious fashion speaks through the mouth of the judge.

These fictitious ideas may have had their historical importance. There is no need for them now, and they have been dispelled in modern theory. The power entrusted to the courts must of necessity include a certain law-making capacity. In vain have rulers like Justinian and Napoleon tried to reserve the formation of legal rules for the 'sovereign'. Rules have always, and on a large scale, been introduced into the legal system through the work of the courts. There is no reason why the facts should not be recognized as they stand.[21]

Theoretically the relationship between judge-made law and enacted law is different in the common law countries and in continental Europe. In the former countries the common law consisting chiefly of precedents is regarded as the basic law; legislation is viewed as codifying, supplementing, or abrogating the common law. In continental Europe enacted law is held to be the basic law to which addition is made through judge-made law (if judge-made law is at all recognized). In practice, however, the difference is not so great as might be supposed. Precedents have nearly the same importance on the continent of Europe as in England or the U.S.A., and legislation plays the same role within both systems.[22]

[21] On judge-made law recently O. A. Germann in his work *Probleme und Methoden der Rechtsfindung* (Bern 1965) 228 ff.

[22] *Cf.* Esser, *Grundsatz und Norm in der richterlichen Fortbildung des Privatrechts* (1956) and Germann, *loc. cit.*

Acts of legislation differ as to their content and meaning from the acts through which judge-made law evolves. In legislation general rules are purposely laid down in a formal way designed to this end. The act of promulgation together with reliable official publication in print supplies an easily identified criterion on the texts that have passed the procedure. Precedents are decisions on individual cases. The decision itself is a decree allowing or rejecting the claim of the plaintiff (to mention civil cases only). In the reasons given for the decision, the court sets forth its opinion on the facts of the case, on applicable legal rules, on arguments for or against certain interpretations of statutes or precedents, and perhaps other points of view that have induced the judges to decide the case as they have done. In this there is no formal laying down of general rules. But when the judge knows that his reasons will be regarded as authoritative interpretations of an existing law (or that they are anyhow likely to be used as grounds for decisions in future cases), his position is similar to that of the lawgivers. He actually lays down general rules in speaking of a single case.

Legislation at Lower Levels

The discussion on legislation in this chapter was carried on with regard to parliamentary enactments. But rules are laid down in similar ways by other agencies both within the state organization and outside it. This formation of rules may appropriately be included under the term ' legislation ' in a wider sense.

According to most constitutions the government is empowered to issue rules on many subjects without the co-operation of the Diet. This is a practical necessity since parliamentary procedure is too cumbersome and slow for dealing with every detail. Under various appellations a stream of general directives emanates from the government and from the ministries.

Supplementary legislation is not, however, confined to the government. At lower levels, too, authorities are often entrusted with rule-making power in their respective areas. This may also be the case with the courts. In England, for instance, rules of court make up a large part of the rules of procedure that are established through parliamentary or governmental legislation in several other countries.

This legislation by government and subordinate authorities is much greater in volume than parliamentary legislation. Still larger is the production of rules outside the state organization. It takes different forms.

Most similar to state legislation is the establishing of rules for associations of different kinds (business companies, trade unions, cultural societies, etc.). The procedure is similar to the procedure of parliaments in that the vote of an assembly is formally decisive. The rules are also moulded into a form borrowed from ordinary laws; and they are intended to govern the life of an association just as the constitution and the administrative regulations govern the activities of the state.

Besides statutes for associations, contracts are the most important form of legislation outside the state organization. Every contract may be viewed as an act of legislation for the parties concerned: it lays down rules for their behaviour in certain respects, as concerning the delivery of and payment for some goods, or concerning some work to be done by the one party and remunerated by the other. The scope of contractual legislation is widened when the contract is concluded between associations representing opposing groups with the intention of binding their members. The most prominent example is collective bargaining between trade unions and employers' associations through which laws are effectively established for the industry.

Statutes and contracts are incorporated into the legal system in so far as they are held to be legally binding. The practical significance of the legal recognition may, however, be variable. In many cases people never think of applying for legal redress if contracts or statutes are violated. But these are not for that reason meaningless. Besides ethical considerations long-term interest and social sanctions against rule-breakers are powerful inducements to follow the rules. For the same causes rules that are considered devoid of 'legal validity' may also have great importance as guides to action. Indeed, with regard to practical efficiency no clear dividing line can be drawn between such contracts and statutes as are deemed legally valid and those that are not.

Actual Formation and Validity

The contention of the positivists that every legal rule must have a historical origin is, of course, perfectly sound. But the positivists were mistaken in thinking that the origin could, in every case, be ascertained. This is not possible. In many cases the origin is lost in the mists of history. We can only study the alterations that have taken place within the framework of an existing system through the elimination of some rules and the introduction of others; and this can only be done to a limited extent since the sources are necessarily more or less deficient.

The legislative process is a method for introducing new rules in a peaceful and psychologically effective way. In the will-theory this process was misinterpreted since the legislative act was conceived as a declaration of will on the part of a supreme authority in society. Moreover, the positivists generalized this supposition as to how a legal rule is established. It came to be regarded as a fact that all sorts of legal rules, even those belonging to 'customary law' and judge-made law, were expressions of the will of the supreme authority. To give the theory some semblance of fitting the facts, the facts had to be torn and twisted to fit the theory.

Legislation according to the constitution is only one way among several of effecting changes in the legal system. Sometimes a similar procedure is used without being in accordance with a working constitution; and it may become effective owing to a special psychological situation, as in a revolution. Judge-made law always grows side by side with enacted law supplementing and altering it. Legislation through contracts and rule-making for associations goes on continually.

Again, the sense of an enacted law is not absolutely fixed. It is subject to subtle modifications through the changes that are always taking place in the meaning of words, in the actual conditions to which the laws refer, in the social structure of the country, in prevailing views as to what is right and wrong, and in the general cultural atmosphere. The words of the *Code Civil* of France have not the same meaning to the present generation of Frenchmen as to those living in the eighteen-twenties or in the first decade of the present century. The black figures on paper representing letters remain the same; but the ideas evoked in the minds of readers are conditioned by the vastly different situations at different times.

The legal system is never static. The formation and transformation of rules continue. Innumerable agencies are at work proposing new rules or modifications to old ones, making propaganda for their views, pushing texts through the legislative machinery, pronouncing decisions in courts of law, laying down statutes for associations, concluding contracts, and so on.

Each generation takes over a body of rules from the preceding one and leaves it in a more or less different state to the next generation. Some rules are formally abrogated, others are modified, still others fall into oblivion, new rules are produced through legislation in several forms and through imitation; and an altered body of rules is left to the next generation to be changed in similar ways. There is no single 'will' behind all this activity. It results from the efforts, struggles, and co-operation of millions of people.

Thus it appears that the formation of rules is a continuous process. Acts of legislation are only its most conspicuous parts. Less perceptible changes are always going on as in the living organism.

In legal theory the greatest and most controversial problem with regard to the formation of rules has not been how to explain the actual process of formation. This problem has been overshadowed by another which has attracted much more interest.

It is usually regarded as an essential property of legal rules that they are 'valid.' This means that they are 'obligatory' or have 'binding force.' The great problem is then to show the reason for this binding force and find a criterion by which it would be possible to ascertain whether a rule possesses the property of being binding.

This problem is of another order than the question how the formation of rules actually takes place. It is obviously no empirical problem. Ascribing binding force to a rule means proclaiming that it ought to be followed, objectively speaking. This is a value judgment. It has the linguistic form of a proposition concerning a property in the rule. But the 'oughtness' is no conceivable property. To discuss whether certain rules possess oughtness or not is therefore useless. This is no scientific problem.

Nobody cares to raise the question whether Greek law, or Persian law, or Roman law was binding some thousands of years ago. What we find in history is a mass of material concerning systems of government, decisions rendered by persons acting as judges, legislative acts, opinions of jurists, etc. We can get a more or less detailed picture of what rules were considered binding, to what extent they were actually followed, how and why new rules were introduced, and why old rules were discarded, etc. But to ask whether a certain system of rules at this or that time was really binding would seem very strange. Indeed, no answer could be given to such a question.

It is no more possible to give an answer to a question of the same type if it refers to the situation ten or twenty years ago or to the present day. Nevertheless the validity problem is the subject of much discussion in current literature. This is to be explained partly because it has been a standard problem ever since the time of classical natural law doctrine, and partly because opinions on questions of validity have considerable bearing on political issues. In a study devoted to law as fact we have to go on to an investigation of the actual nature of legal rules.

It would carry us too far to discuss at length the various theories on the 'validity' of law. I do not think that such a digression would be necessary for the purpose of this investigation. (For recent surveys of the literature, see H. Welzel, *Die Frage nach der Rechtsgeltung*, 1966, and Rupert Schreiber, *Die Geltung von Rechtsnormen*, 1966.)

Kelsen's well-known theory of the basic norm illustrates the hopelessness of the attempts to give a rational account of the concept of validity. In conformity with the traditional view Kelsen regards 'validity' as a property in the law. ('A quality of law', *General Theory of Law and State* 39 f.) Without validity there is no law. 'The existence of a legal norm is its validity' (48).

The validity of a norm (its 'oughtness') cannot be derived from any facts but only from a higher norm empowering some authority to create the norm. The higher norm derives its validity from a still higher norm, etc. The judge lays down a norm for the case submitted to him. This he does by virtue of a norm empowering him to do so. The legislator who has issued this norm has been empowered by the constitution to legislate. The regress is to be terminated by a basic norm, from which the validity of the constitution is derived. Behind the basic norm there is no other norm.

Finally, the basic norm turns out to be an ultimate hypothesis of legal positivism. This is the hypothesis that the historically first legislator was authorized to create the original constitution. Such an hypothesis is not needed for those who think that God empowered the fathers of the first constitution to lay it down. But it is necessary from the point of view of legal positivism because this theory dispenses with a religious justification of the legal order (116):

'The whole function of this basic norm is to confer law-creating power on the act of the first legislator and on all other acts based on the first act. To interpret these acts of human beings as legal acts and their products as binding norms, and that means to interpret the empirical material which presents itself as a law as such, is possible only on condition that the basic norm is presupposed as a valid norm. The basic norm is only the necessary presupposition of any positivistic interpretation of the legal material.'

Thus the reason to be given for the supposed validity of the basic norm itself is that the validity is a postulate necessary from the point of view of a certain legal theory, the theory of legal positivism (116):

'The basic norm is not created in a legal procedure by a law-creating organ. It is not—as a positive legal norm is—valid because it is created in a certain way by a legal act, but it is valid because it is presupposed to be valid; and it is presupposed to be valid because without this presupposition no human act could be interpreted as a legal, especially as a norm-creating, act.'

The basic norm is valid because it is presupposed to be valid. This amounts to stating that no reason can be given for the validity of the basic norm. Consequently, no reason is given for the validity of the norms that are supposed to derive their validity from the basic norm. The whole edifice of the theory crumbles because there is no basis for it. The obvious conclusion would seem to be that one has to raise the question of what is wrong with legal positivism.

Lately Kelsen has altered his conception of the basic norm. The reason is that the original conception is not consistent with his concept of a norm. Every norm, he thinks, presupposes an act of will by which a certain act is 'commanded, prohibited, or authorized'. The norm is the meaning (*der Sinn*) of such an act of will. (*Pure Theory of Law* 5.) But previously this did not refer to the basic norm, which was not described as the meaning of any act of will. On this point Kelsen corrected himself during the Vienna discussion of 1962. Now Kelsen said that the basic norm is a *fictitious norm* presupposing a *fictitious act of will* that lays down this norm:

'Ich habe in meinen früheren Schriften von Normen gesprochen, die nicht der Sinn von Willensakten sind. Meine ganze Lehre von der Grundnorm habe ich dargestellt als eine Norm, die nicht der Sinn eines Willensaktes ist, sondern im Denken vorausgesetzt wird. Nun muss ich Ihnen leider gestehen, meine Herren, dass ich diese Lehre aufgeben musste. . . . Ich habe sie aufgegeben in der Erkenntnis, dass ein Sollen das Korrelat eines Wollens sein muss. Meine Grundnorm ist eine *fiktive* Norm, die einen *fiktiven* Willensakt voraussetzt, der diese Norm setzt. Es ist eine Fiktion, dass irgendeine Autorität will, dass dies sein soll. . . . Was man sich bei der Grundnorm denkt, ist die Fiktion eines Willensaktes, der realiter nicht besteht.' (*Das Naturrecht in der politischen Theorie,* hrsg. von F. M. Schmöltz, 1963, 119.)

A realistic account of how a new constitution comes to be regarded as binding is offered by Hamao Abe in the paper 'Feeling of Being Bound and Role of State Organs' in *Festskrift til Alf Ross* (1969).

CHAPTER 5

THE NATURE OF LEGAL RULES

IN the preceding chapter we have studied the formation of rules called legal through legislation and imitation. The next step in our inquiry will be to clear up the import of these ' rules '. It is suitable to begin with the rules of enacted law since they are most easily grasped.

Rules of Enacted Law

Enacting and proclaiming a text as a law according to the constitution is used as a means of exerting influence on the minds of people and thereby on their behaviour. The purpose is to restrain certain kinds of activity and to promote others. What else could be the meaning of legislation?

To achieve its purpose the text must be able to call forth certain ideas concerning human conduct in the mind of a reader; a pattern of behaviour has to be placed before his eyes. But something more is needed. It is not enough that people form abstract ideas of certain actions. If I simply imagine the situation of two drivers going in opposite directions, each of them keeping to the right, I have no rule in mind. A rule says that people shall behave in accordance with a pattern. A traffic rule, for instance, says that drivers shall keep to the right on the roads. In a typical rule of enacted law expression is given to an idea of a pattern of conduct in such a way as to impress people with the feeling that the pattern ought to be followed when occasion arises.

Consequently, we can discern two elements in such a legal rule. On the one hand we have an imagined pattern of conduct, on the other hand the particular form in which expression is given to it. We shall now study these two elements separately.

The pattern of behaviour

A committee charged with the task of drafting a set of regulations proceeds roughly in the following way. After making an inquiry into the existing situation and forming an opinion on its defects, the committee draws a mental picture of a new state of things. This implies devising certain patterns of conduct to be observed in certain circumstances. Next comes the question of supplying a motive for people to behave in accordance with those patterns. This is usually done by attaching unpleasant consequences to contrary behaviour.

In the simple case of traffic regulations the committee seeks to visualize a desirable order on the roads in which drivers and pedestrians consistently act in certain definite ways in various situations so as to make the traffic flow smoothly with as little danger to the participants as possible. On the basis of these considerations a series of patterns of conduct for drivers and pedestrians are worked out. These patterns are put forward in the text which, after due procedure, becomes a law.

The pattern of conduct is the *ideational element*, or the *ideatum*, of a rule. It makes up the content of the rule as opposed to the form of expression.

In order to supply a motive for people to conform to the patterns of conduct in the traffic regulations penalties are attached to deviations from these patterns. This implies setting up patterns of conduct for other people: the police, the public prosecutors, and the judges. (For the sake of brevity, the jury may be disregarded.) For the judge the *ideatum* of such a rule consists in a certain action on his part taken in a certain situation: according to the rules of procedure, a person has been legally charged with causing a collision through turning to the left without making a sign, and it has been convincingly shown that he has really done so; in this situation the judge metes out a penalty.

The content of legal rules like these, therefore, is an idea of a certain conduct as being observed in a certain situation. For the driver it is the idea of his making a sign when he is going to make a turn on a road; for the judge it is the idea of his pronouncing, in due form, a decree concerning a penalty to be exacted from a driver who has been shown not to have made a sign when this was required by the first rule.

From this it appears that two elements can be distinguished in the *ideatum* of a rule. On the one hand, there is the situation of the driver on the road when he is going to make the turn and the situation of the judge when he is to make his decision. On the other hand, we have a certain action to be taken by a person in this situation: for the driver to make a sign, for the judge to give a sentence of a certain kind. The first element may be called the *requisitum* because it represents the requirements that should be present when the action is to be taken. The other element, the action itself, may be called the *agendum.* To apply a rule means acting according to the *agendum* in a situation corresponding to the *requisitum.*

In the example, the rules are as little complicated as one could think. Yet, even here neither the *requisitum* nor the *agendum* is as simple as may be supposed at first sight. This is especially true of the rule for the judge. To get a full picture of the *requisitum* it is not enough to know the traffic regulations alone. In addition, a great many rules of procedure and evidence have to be taken into consideration. One must know the constitution of the courts: how they are to hold their sessions, how an indictment is to be made, how evidence is to be produced, and so on. All these rules and many more are needed for the description of the situation in which sentence is to be given. As regards the *agendum* of the judge, many rules besides the traffic regulations have also to be taken into account. The driver must for instance be old enough to be liable to punishment. In many cases both the *requisitum* and the *agendum* will be infinitely complicated.

There is, indeed, no case where a single legal provision can be regarded in isolation by the judge or by any other person called upon to decide what sort of action conforms to the law in a given situation. Each provision is like a piece in a puzzle. Many pieces have to be put together before one can say whether an actual situation corresponds to any legal *requisitum* and, if this is the case, what sort of *agendum* is applicable. The *requisitum* and the *agendum* of the respective legal provisions are the material out of which the final *requisitum* and *agendum* are built. In many cases the purpose of the pieces is to contribute to determining the *requisitum* or the *agendum* laid down in a number of other rules. An example of this is a provision offering a definition of words used in the law. In a law on the sale of goods such terms as 'current price', 'promptly', etc., may be defined. These definitions form part of the *requisitum* of several rules. Other definitions may refer to words used to express the *agendum* of a rule.

The composition of the *ideatum* of legal rules raises many questions. Different techniques are used in different ages and different countries; and it might be discussed whether they could not be improved on the basis of scientific analysis. But these problems need not detain us now. For the present it is sufficient to point out that every legal rule must be conceived as a means of directing human behaviour. Therefore, a rule must depict a situation in which an action is to be performed. Only two remarks should be added here:

(i) In the example from the traffic regulations the assumption was made that the legal text expressed separate rules for the people on the roads and for the authorities charged with the application of sanctions. In many cases, especially in criminal law, we find only rules of the latter kind. The law says, for instance, that larceny is to be punished in this or that way. This is a rule for the courts. But the rule for the courts is used as a means of directing the behaviour of the general public; it is not necessary to give a separate rule stating that larceny must not be committed.

(ii) Considerable complications arise out of the use of the fundamental legal concepts, such as the concepts of rights and duties, in expressing legal rules. On the face of it, such rules are concerned with the creation, alteration, transference, and extinction of rights and duties. We may assume that their ultimate purpose is to direct human behaviour. But how this is done is an intricate problem that needs elaborate treatment. This question must now be postponed for discussion in a later part of the book.

The form of expression

The form of expression is determined by the purpose of legislation: to direct the conduct of people. But the text is not an expression of a wish on the part of the lawgiving authorities that people should behave in this or that way. Nor does it contain advice to people as to what is prudent to do in order to gain certain advantages and avoid unpleasant consequences. It is quite true, of course, that one can draw inferences in this respect from the contents of a law; but the meaning of the law is not to say that you ought to do so-and-so if you want to reap such and such benefits, or that you ought to abstain from certain kinds of actions if you do not want to expose yourself to sanctions. The law says directly that you *shall* do this or that, you *shall not* do such and such. The traffic regulations do not tell people that it will be expedient to keep to the right. They say that you shall keep to the right. The form of expression is therefore the imperative.

It is characteristic of the imperative that it does not refer to any values for the addressee. The imperative is unconditional. It may refer to a hypothetical situation: if this or that happens, do such and such. But no advantage is given as the reason why one should act in the way prescribed. In this sense the imperative is unconditional.

Often a 'shall' or some word to the same effect is employed in the formulation of a rule. ('The seller shall effect delivery of the goods as required by the contract and the law.') But this is not necessary. The indicative mood may as well be used. The essential thing is that the law as a whole is put forward in an imperative sense. The text is published in a form known to be effective in making people feel obliged to behave in accordance with the patterns enunciated. It is only a matter of style if the patterns of behaviour are expressed in the indicative form or as imperatives. Different traditions exist in this respect.

On the face of it some legal provisions contain no imperative at all since they only 'empower' somebody to do something. The law may say, for instance, that the buyer, in case of the seller's failure to deliver the goods, 'may either require performance by the seller or declare the contract avoided'. This, of course, is no imperative to the buyer. But it indirectly entails an imperative to the seller, conditioned by the request of the buyer: if it is required by the buyer, the seller shall still perform delivery. Furthermore, the provision contains certain elements of imperatives for the judge as to how he is to decide a case arising out of a contract for sale of goods. Another example of seemingly non-imperative provisions are those which contain legal definitions given in the indicative mood. They serve to fix the meaning of imperatives contained in other provisions.

Now if laws consist of imperatives, it seems natural to reason in the following way. An imperative is a command. But a command presupposes someone who issues it. Therefore one has to seek for a commanding authority. This can only be some supreme power in society. The question will therefore be how that power is to be conceived.

So we seem to be back at the will-theory again. But then all the difficulties previously exhibited will arise. As was shown, it is impossible to find any power in society, existing independently of a working law, whose commands could be the law; and the legislative process does not result in the issuing of commands by the lawgivers.

We are apparently faced by a dilemma. On the one hand, the imperative character of the laws is evident. They say what people shall or shall not do. On the other hand, no commanding authority can be said to exist and no commands are given through legislation.

In order to eliminate this ostensible dilemma, we have to investigate the nature of the imperatives. In a famous passage Austin says that the concept of a command is the key to the science of jurisprudence and morals.[1] There is much truth in this. The imperatives are essential both in law and in morals. As Austin insists, their meaning should be analysed as carefully as possible.

The Imperatives

Under the term 'imperative' are here comprised all sorts of verbal expressions containing an unconditional 'shall'. In the first place, we think of imperatives as referring to the behaviour of people: you shall do this or you shall abstain from doing that. As was said above, the imperatives are unconditional in the sense that they make no appeal to any values on the part of the addressee.

The imperatives form a large category within which certain distinctions have to be made. The prototype is an imperative given by one person face to face with somebody else. I propose to reserve the term command for imperatives of this kind. It is suitable to begin with an analysis of these.[2]

Commands

Commands refer to a future conduct of the addressee. They therefore give expression to an idea of his behaving in a certain way: doing or abstaining from doing something. This is the *ideatum* of the command. In the simple command: 'Shut the door!' the *ideatum* is an action by the addressee resulting in the shutting of the door.

According to an old and still quite common theory of commands, the commander gives expression to his wish that the addressee should behave in a certain way. He desires him to behave in this or that way, and he makes this wish known to him. The command is therefore said to be a declaration of will, a *declaratio voluntatis* (*Willenserklärung*).

This was the theory of the teachers of natural law.[3] It was also

[1] *The Province of Jurisprudence Determined* 13.

[2] For the following *cf.* Hägerström's analysis of the psychological content of a command in his *Inquiries into the Nature of Law and Morals* 116 ff. *Cf.* C. D. Broad's article 'Hägerström's account of the sense of duty and certain allied experiences' in 26 *Philosophy* (1951) 99 ff.

[3] See above 19 f.

the theory of Bentham. In his view every law consisted of commands and prohibitions. But a law is also defined as 'an assemblage of signs declarative of a volition conceived or adopted by the sovereign in a state'.[4] The expression 'signs declarative of a volition' is a translation of the latin *signum voluntatis* and *declaratio voluntatis.*

It has often been added that a declaration of will, in order to be a command, must be accompanied by a threat of some evil consequences in case of contrary behaviour. This view on the nature of a command has been expounded in a classical way by Austin. It forms the basis of his theory of law.

The command as a declaration of will

Austin defines a command in the following way:

> If you express or intimate a wish that I shall do or forbear from some act, and if you will visit me with an evil in case I comply not with your wish, the *expression* or *intimation* of your wish is a *command.* A command is distinguished from other significations of desire, not by the style in which the desire is signified, but by the power and the purpose of the party commanding to inflict an evil or pain in case the desire be disregarded. If you cannot and will not harm me in case I comply not with your wish, the expression of your wish is not a command, although you utter your wish in imperative phrase. If you are able and willing to harm me in case I comply not with your wish, the expression of your wish amounts to a command, although you are prompted by a spirit of courtesy to utter it in the shape of request.[5]

The definition refers to verbal commands. Other commands need not be considered.

The 'wish' that is the first element in a command might be expressed 'in imperative phrase', by which Austin obviously means that the grammatical imperative is being employed. The speaker says for instance: 'Shut the door!'. But the form of expression is irrelevant according to Austin. The essential thing is that a wish is communicated to the addressee.

This can be interpreted in two different ways: (i) The words used by the speaker amount to a statement of the fact that he harbours a certain wish. (ii) The words are a direct expression of a wish.

In the first case the phrase 'Shut the door!' would be equivalent to saying: 'It is my desire that the door should be shut'. Such a

[4] *The Limits of Jurisprudence Defined* 88.
[5] *The Province of Jurisprudence Determined* 13 f.

phrase may have the same effect as the phrase 'Shut the door!' if the addressee is intent on complying with the wishes of the speaker. But the meaning is not the same. An officer commanding the company to turn to the right does not inform them of the fact that he wants them to turn to the right. He makes use of an impressive form of speech ('right wheel') in order to make the company march in a new direction.

In the second case—if the imperative phrase is interpreted as a direct expression of a wish—the phrase would have the character of an exclamation. Saying 'Shut the door!' would be equivalent to saying: 'Oh, I wish that the door would be shut', or 'Oh, I wish Peter would shut the door'. The meaning is clearly not the same.

The relationship between a wish and such verbal expressions as Austin has in mind is misunderstood when an imperative phrase is interpreted either as a statement concerning the existence of a wish or as a direct expression of a wish. A wish may be a motive for uttering an imperative phrase. Such a phrase is a means employed by the speaker to realize the wish. I say, for instance, 'Shut the door!' because I want the door to be shut; and I use this phrase because such language is a verbal instrument for inciting people to perform actions.

It should be added that a wish is a common motive for issuing a command, but by no means the only possible one. In many situations commands are given for other reasons. People in a hierarchical organization, for instance, often have to give commands to their subordinates because they feel obliged to do so. Giving a certain command can even be utterly distasteful to him who has to give it. We may think of a company commander in the First World War who had to order his men to go over the top in face of the machine-guns, though he personally held this particular offensive action to be senseless from a military point of view.

Austin takes it for granted that an imperative phrase could have no effect unless it be accompanied by a threat which is serious because the speaker has the power of carrying it out. This is also a misconception. It is true that the chance of a command being obeyed is enhanced if the commander is in a position to inflict an evil on a recalcitrant addressee (or if sanctions are inflicted by an organization). But situations occur in which a command may take effect without being backed by any power or any threats. Some people have the capability of impressing others in such a way that their commands are complied with. To take a somewhat extreme example, we may think of the case of a small group finding itself in a dangerous situation in the mountains; a forceful personality may very well assume command and give orders that are obeyed.

Austin's theory of commands derives from the natural law theory that a command is a sort of declaration of will, a *declaratio voluntatis.* It is similar to the theory of Bentham.

> The declaration of will-theory is apparently still prevalent. It is put forward by Kelsen without any indication of its being controversial. In his *General Theory of Law and State* (31) he says: 'A command is the expression of an individual's will (or wish) the object of which is another individual's behaviour. If I want (or wish) somebody else to conduct himself in a certain way and if I express this my will (or wish) to the other in a particular way, then this expression of my will (or wish) constitutes a command. A command differs from a request, from a mere "entreaty", by its form. A command is the expression in an imperative form of the will that somebody else shall behave in a certain manner.' Earlier this view on the nature of a command was expounded in the *Hauptprobleme der Staatsrechtslehre* 202 ff. It was an essential part of the foundations of Kelsen's theory of law. His theory of command is not identical with Austin's. Kelsen regards the form of expression as being essential, which Austin denies; and a threat is not said to be an element in a command. In his work *Norm and Action* (1963) von Wright puts forward essentially the same theory of commands as Austin, also without reference to any other opinion. To the question as to what the agent does who issues a command the following answer is given: 'He promulgates the norm and attaches to it an effective sanction or threat of punishment for disobedience' (126). The promulgation consists in 'making known to the norm-subjects, by means of language or other symbols, *what* the norm-authority wants them to do or to forbear' (124). Like Austin, von Wright holds it to be necessary for a command that the commander possesses power. 'Ability to command is . . . logically founded on a superior strength of the commander over the commanded' (though it is sufficient that the subject mistakenly believes in the superior strength of the authority, 127).

The requirement of authority

In modern literature the requirement of power in the commander appears in the form that it is said to be essential that he has a right to command. The concept of command is then presupposed. Since commands can actually be given without any pretension of a right to do it, the meaning must be that a command can have no effect unless the commander possesses the right to command.[6]

This might seem plausible. People are apt to react negatively to a command given by somebody in whom no right to command is recognized; active opposition is rather natural. But there are weighty reasons against the theory.

First, existence of a right to command could be of significance only if the right were a mystical force compelling obedience. But this would be an absurd supposition. Speaking rationally, there can only be a question of the psychological requirement for the efficacy of a command. From a psychological point of view, however, only the idea in the mind of the addressee, concerning the right to command, can be of importance. The right itself as really existing (if a right may at all be said really to exist) can exert no influence on the behaviour of the addressee except through the mediation of his idea of its existence: and if the addressee has got this idea, it is irrelevant whether the right really exists.

Secondly, it is true that the idea of a right in the commander is of great importance in causing the recipient to obey. But a command may be obeyed for other reasons. Fear, habit, personal respect for the commander, pure suggestion, etc., or a combination of such factors, may be decisive. The idea of a right to command is only a contingent element in a complicated psychological situation.

> In *The Concept of Law* (19 f.) Hart criticizes Austin's definition of the notion of a command as referring to 'the gunman situation', *i.e.,* to the situation where an order is supported by threats only. (*Cf.* above 83.) This, Hart suggests, is not the situation where we naturally speak of 'commands', since this word carries with it very strong implications that there is a relatively stable hierarchical organization, such as an army. Where a command is given, there need not be any latent threat of harm in the event of disobedience. To command is characteristically to exercise authority over men, not power to inflict harm. Though it may be combined with threats of harm, 'a command is primarily an appeal not to fear but to respect for authority'.
>
> This argument is of great importance in Hart's work. He draws the conclusion that the notion of authority is involved in the

[6] See for instance Paul W. Taylor, *Normative Discourse* (1961) 61 f.: 'One person can issue an order, command, or directive to another only if he has authority over the other. Such a practice is understandable only in a social context of authority and subordination. . . . The command comes from an authority having the right to command, as defined by established rules, and these rules can be applied to enforce obedience.' *Cf.* 209, 220.

notion of a command. But in the notion of authority, he says, the notion of law is involved (evidently because the hierarchical organization presupposes a law). For this reason 'we cannot profitably use, in the elucidation of law, the notion of a command': the notion of command involves the notion of law. Consequently, Hart rejects Austin's contention that the notion of a command is 'the key to the science of jurisprudence'. (*Cf.* 71 *Harvard Law Review*, 1957/58, 602 ff.)

What is meant here by 'authority' is not clear. I suppose 'authority' signifies 'right to command'. In any case it seems to be a mistake to say that the concept of a command involves the concept of law (as involving the concept of authority). As was pointed out, many commands are given, and obeyed, without the commander occupying a position in a hierarchical organization. (Hart mentions an example of this himself: Christ commanding his disciples.) The concept of a command is surely most important for the elucidation of the concept of law. It has to be defined without reference to the law. Therefore, there is no circularity (as Hart seems to suggest) in explaining the nature of the law by means of the concept of commands (and of imperatives in general). In another place Hart stresses the importance of the study of imperatives for the study of law, morals, and sociology (p. 235).

The constative fallacy

As Hare points out, there is a strong temptation to reduce imperatives to indicatives.[7] This may be called the constative fallacy.

If the imperatives are reduced to indicatives, they will be interpreted in one or other of the following ways: (i) As statements about the mind of the speaker; (ii) As statements about future occurrences implying that something unpleasant will take place unless the addressee behaves in a certain manner.[8] In the view of John Austin, a command is a combination of statements of both kinds: first a statement about the mind of the speaker, then a statement about sanctions to follow in case of disobedience.

The underlying psychological assumptions are clearly stated by Kelsen. If a person is to be induced to behave in a certain way, Kelsen says, this can only be effected by causing him to regard this behaviour as a means of acquiring some benefit or avoiding some

[7] *The Language of Morals* (1952) 8. This is an instance of the 'descriptive fallacy' pointed out by J. L. Austin, *How to Do Things with Words* (1962) 3. For an account of various attempts to interpret imperatives as declarative statements see Sforza, 'Sul significato degli imperativi giuridici', *Rivista Italiana per le scienze giuridici* (1957/58) 7 ff.

[8] Hare 5.

prejudice. The mere declaration by A that he wants B to behave in this or that way can never call forth a will in B to do so. The declaration is aimed at the intellect of B. It evokes the idea that A entertains a certain wish. But this idea cannot act as a motive for B. His will can be brought into conformity with the will of A only through his getting the idea that it is in his own interest to act according to the wish of A.[9]

If this strangely rationalistic view of the causes of men's behaviour were correct, it would be impossible to understand how any legal order could exist; for a legal order could surely never have been established had the actions of men been exclusively determined by their ideas of what is beneficial and disadvantageous to them. There must be other currents in their minds that have enabled them to build societies. In this connection it is only necessary to point to one factor of great importance: the forces of suggestion acting upon the individuals making up a human community. It is evident that each one among us is continuously subjected to numerous influences of this kind. Here we have to seek a good deal of the explanation of how societies have been formed and are being kept together.

If a command as such takes effect, this is a case of suggestion. The addressee is made to behave in a certain way precisely without reference to what is valuable to him. The 'shall' works directly.

The constative fallacy is connected with the disregard for the suggestive function of commands. Indeed, the essential characteristic of commands is overlooked when they are interpreted as constative utterances.[10]

The imperantum

Besides the *ideatum*—the behaviour put before the mind of the recipient—a command contains another element. This is something conveying the impression that the behaviour in question shall be

[9] *Hauptprobleme der Staatsrechtslehre* 202 f. Similarly H. G. Bohnert in the article 'The Semiotic Status of Commands' (12 *Philosophy of Science*, 1945) 303: 'Living organisms . . . are motivated characteristically (except for involuntary and reflex action) by situations which promise or threaten to have physiological or psychological consequences of greater or less desirability than those possible if the individual's behaviour causally intervenes.' The author suggests that commands are declarative sentences pointing out a motivating situation (the house is on fire), an appropriate reaction (you run), and the penalty for not reacting appropriately (you burn) though the form is often truncated owing to conditions of urgency.

[10] The term 'constative utterances' was introduced by J. L. Austin, *How to Do Things with Words* 3.

observed. For the sake of brevity this element may be called *imperantum.*[11]

When the imperative mood is used, it serves as an *imperantum.* It is a way of speaking calculated to incite another person to an action or to inhibit an action by him. The imperative mood, however, is no exclusive form for giving a verbal command. An *imperantum* may as well be adjoined to a sentence in the indicative mood. If I say to a child: 'You shut the door', this is a command if the words are uttered in a certain way with the intention of causing the child to shut the door. Though the indicative mood is used, the sentence does not serve to convey information. It is a suggestive sentence. The *imperantum* is the tone and bearing of the speaker. In some languages the imperative mood does not even differ from an infinitive. The way of using the words decides whether a phrase is an imperative or a constative sentence.

Even when the imperative mood is employed, the expression and the carriage of the speaker are of great importance. They belong to the *imperantum* and serve to strengthen the effect of the imperative mood. Indeed, no mere words as such constitute a command. Even a sentence in the imperative mood must be pronounced in a certain way if it is to be a real command. The *imperantum* may be more or less striking. Sometimes it includes a forceful display of personality; at other times it is hardly noticeable, and the command becomes similar to a courteous request.

To make commands effective on a large scale the recipients have to be inured to receiving commands from the speaker. Preparation on the part of the recipients is therefore of the utmost importance if lines of command are to function reliably. In every hierarchical organization the subordinates are trained to respond to commands from above, and sanctions are enforced in case of disobedience. The extreme form of such training is military drill, which tends to make obedience instant and automatic.

The amount of personal effort needed to ensure obedience is chiefly dependent on the degree of preparation in the recipient. If he is well conditioned to respond to commands from a person who is supposed to be his superior, no special effort at all is required; it may be sufficient to put before his eyes what he is to do. The contention that 'authority' or 'right to command' is needed for a command to be effective stems from the experience that some preparation in

[11] The use of the home-made latin words '*ideatum*' and '*imperantum*' may be excused on account of their practicability.

the recipient is generally required. But the legal or moral relationship expressed by words like 'authority' and 'right' is substituted for the actual psychological factors that cause one man's behaviour to be directed through the commands of another.

The *imperantum* is aimed at the volitional side of the recipient's mind, not at the intellectual side. The idea of the behaviour to be observed is aroused by the ideational element in the command. The echo of the *imperantum* in the mind of the addressee is 'I must' or something similar. But no idea besides the mental image of the words themselves is evoked. Nothing is signified by the 'must' or its equivalents.

In its simplest form the *imperantum* is the form of language, the manner of speaking, and the bearing of the speaker. Such forms of the *imperantum* are spontaneous. Other forms are conventional or standardized. The officer's uniform and the word signifying his grade belong to the *imperantum* in his case. In a business firm an executive's title and the designation of his place in the organization are elements in the *imperantum*. Innumerable contrivances are used to build up an *imperantum* according to the needs of the circumstances. They serve to make it a matter of course that persons in certain positions should follow orders from persons in other positions.

Among the means of standardization the most important are perhaps the formalities that are to be used in making certain pronouncements. The distinction between private utterances and official orders depends on the circumstances in which the pronouncements are made and on the form that is employed. To be an official order, an utterance has to be made in a special context and in a certain way. The same distinction is maintained in business life; a bank clerk is acting 'on behalf of the bank' only when certain formalities are observed.

Nowadays forms are far less rigorous than in ancient times. There is so much informality that we are inclined to think that formalities are no longer of any importance. This is, however, a mistake. The formalities have become looser, but they are as prevalent as ever. Forms are necessary in every society as a means of signalling what pronouncements are to be taken as guides to action and, above all, taken as legally relevant.

Independent imperatives

A face-to-face command implies a personal relationship between two individuals. But imperative phrases are widely used outside such relationships. The sentence: 'You shall speak the truth' may be uttered as a command; but it may be uttered in giving instructions concerning right behaviour.

Such imperative phrases may conveniently be called independent imperatives since they are independent of the personal relationship characteristic of a command. They are similar to commands in the proper sense in that they serve as means of inculcating a certain behaviour in a categorical way. For this reason it seems legitimate to classify them as a kind of imperatives side by side with commands.[12]

No clean-cut distinction can be made between commands and independent imperatives. The personal relationship pertaining to a command may be more or less close. As the distance between the persons grows, the commands assume the character of independent imperatives. A mediating form is that which obtains when a person or a god is represented in imagination as issuing commands.

Habits of language make us prone to think of 'imperatives' as identical with commands in the strict sense of the word. There even seems to be some psychological difficulty in conceiving imperatives without referring them to an *imperator* addressing somebody else. The matter is, however, very simple. Imperative sentences may be put forward in many ways and disseminated through many channels. No *imperator* is needed. The addressee may be an audience of millions.

The category of independent imperatives is very large. It comprises ethical sentences as well as legislative enactments. But why should only verbal pronouncement be included in this category? It seems correct to include a number of mute signs, as for instance traffic lights. Even a fence around a garden or the lock to one's door may be said to have the function of an independent imperative. Usually neither the fence nor the lock is a physical obstacle of importance to an intruder. But both of them are signs to stop and keep hands off. If one looks at things in this way, independent imperatives of divergent kinds will be encountered at almost every step.[13]

[12] On the concept of independent imperatives *cf.* I. Tammelo in 49 *Archiv für Rechts- und Wirtschaftsphilosophie* (1963) 257 ff.; J. Stone, *Legal System and Lawyers' Reasoning* (1964) 93. Alf Ross adopts the concept though he prefers to use the more general term 'directive'. (*On Law and Justice*, 1958, 8.) Recently the independent imperatives have been discussed in a clarifying way by Enrico Pattaro in a long article in the *Rivista trimestrale di diritto e procedura civile* 1968.

[13] *Cf.* E. Bucher, *Das subjektive Rechts als Normsetzungsbefugnis* (1965) 69.

Rules of Law Independent Imperatives

The imperative theory as found in classical natural law doctrine and continued by great teachers of law until our day was led astray by the tenet that the rules of law were imperatives in the sense of declarations of will by an *imperator*. When a divine law was held to exist, this law was the will of God. Human law was the will of the sovereign, the people, or the state, as explained in many different ways.

Every attempt to identify the lawgiving will with a real human will necessarily failed. The will was a mythical will, created in imagination to meet the requirements of preconceived ideas.

The clue to the riddle of the nature of the rules called legal is the concept of independent imperatives. The imperative character of those rules is evident. But an imperative is no declaration of will. It is a mode of expression used in a suggestive way in order to influence the behaviour of people. The rules of law form a vast complex of such expressions containing patterns of conduct that are more or less universally followed within a group of people. Their efficacy depends on a set of relatively firm attitudes among the people which in their turn have manifold and deep-seated causes.

The *ideatum* of legal rules has been briefly discussed above. But what is the *imperantum*? Of what does it consist?

It cannot be taken for granted that the *imperantum* is the same in all cases. Enacted law, ancient customary law, and judge-made law have to be considered separately with regard to the question of the *imperantum*.

Rules of enacted law are independent imperatives that have passed through a series of formal acts. The *imperantum* is the whole setting in which the enactment takes place: the working constitution, the organization functioning according to its rules, the familiar designations of parliamentary bodies and state officials, etc. Once a constitution has been firmly established, the people respond automatically by accepting as binding the texts proclaimed as laws through the act of promulgation. Thanks to this attitude among the addressees the *imperantum* becomes effective.

The fulcrum is the act of promulgation. It is immediately decisive for the officials charged with the publication of new laws. Other officials rely on the publication being conscientiously performed according to constitutional rules, so that only texts that have been rightly promulgated—but all such texts—are printed in the official collection of laws. Only very rarely do courts or other state authorities have occasion to ascertain for themselves whether a text has been promulgated in proper form.

The general public knows nothing of such formalities as promulgation. The texts reach them under the official appellation of law and that is enough. The appellation of law, when presumed to be correctly applied, carries with it the implication that the rules of conduct contained in the text are binding on everybody.

As regards ancient customary law, nothing can be said of general application concerning the *imperantum*. Conditions have differed widely. An example may suffice to illustrate how we have to conceive the *imperantum* in remote, primitive times.

In my own country it is recorded in the oldest sources that the law was authoritatively preserved in the memory of wise men ('men of young memory') before the time when it was written down. The 'lawman' (*lagman*) had to recite the law at the *ting*, the assembly of free men. The text was rhythmical and alliterative, which made it impressive (the language was beautiful) and easily remembered. Probably the men acclaimed the recitation by the clang of arms. This procedure corresponded to the modern act of promulgation, though it had to be often repeated. The law was what the lawman had said it to be. Those who were present had to repeat it to their homefolk. This presupposes that they had learnt the law by heart. To do so must have been highly important to every free man; it was an essential part of his education. One can imagine how long, dark winter evenings in the huts were spent in teaching the young people the law with an occasional saga as a reward for good results. At the *ting* one had occasion to refresh one's memory, fill up gaps, and correct errors.

The law was couched in strongly imperative language. But the *imperantum* was not made up solely by the imperative form of speech. To it also belonged the solemnity of the *ting* (held on holy ground), the position of the lawman, the acclamation by the assembly, the authority of parents, etc., in short everything that contributed to create the feeling that these rules were sacred and should be unconditional guides for conduct.

Judge-made law is not identical with the pronouncements of the courts. Each decision is a decision on an individual case. It differs from the act of legislation in that it is not a proclamation of general rules. According to the traditional view, the courts are the authoritative interpreters of the law. For that reason it is supposed to be possible to infer the contents of the law from the decisions of the courts: since the decision in the case A versus B has been based on the rule X, this rule belongs to the law of the land.

To be valid, such inferences are supposed to be made according to certain traditional rules. *Obiter dicta* are not to serve as a basis for inferences. Courts of different degrees possess different grades of authority. Some decisions are entirely rejected as a basis for inferences concerning the law, etc.

Inferences from decisions can actually be drawn by lawyers and laymen alike. But the practical importance of the inferences varies with the status of the persons drawing them. When a court, on the basis of previous decisions, declares that rule X belongs to the law, this is generally accepted. Rule X is then firmly established as a rule of law. The opinions expressed by renowned writers may have the same effect. Between themselves these authorities, practically speaking, decide what is to be regarded as the law and therefore applied by the courts in the future.

In actual fact, however, the ' inferences ' are not real inferences. From the pronouncement of a court nothing can be inferred concerning the content of a pre-existing law. One may perhaps conclude that the court was of the opinion that there was a pre-existing law of this or that content. Not even this, however, is necessarily true. A modern judge may very well be conscious of the fact that he is not merely applying a pre-existing law in making this particular decision.

When a court accepts or rejects a previous ruling of a court as a guide for its own action, it really draws no inference. It makes a decision. It decides to regard this ruling as representing the law, or, from a more modern point of view, it decides that this is the most reasonable solution to the legal problem raised by the case before it. The decision usually entails that the rule which the court has embraced will be placed, in the opinion of lawyers, within the body of rules designated as ' the law '. Likewise, a writer on law decides to accept or reject the rulings of courts as representing the law. Depending on his renown, and possibly on his arguments, his decision will be followed by legal opinion. The law will be what he declares it to be.

These decisions by courts and writers are the nearest counterpart, in the field of judge-made law, to promulgation in the field of legislation. The body of texts officially designated as enacted laws is exactly defined through a series of acts of promulgation. General opinion relies, without hesitation or doubt, on this formal criterion. (Exceptions, as for instance the situation after an abrupt change in the system of government, may here be disregarded.) The decisions to accept or reject rulings of courts as expressing the law are not formalized in the same way. Therefore the body of rules regarded as belonging to judge-made law is not as exactly circumscribed. Its compass can only be more or less vaguely defined and is often the subject of controversy.

Particular Imperatives

In the general discussion of the nature of legal rules a certain objection against the imperative theory has played an important part. Conceding that rules prescribing some conduct may be viewed as imperatives, it has been pointed out that there are other rules besides the rules of conduct, such as the rules concerning the acquisition, import, transference, and loss of rights. The right of ownership is acquired in certain ways; it is transferred through such and such acts; and it may be lost in other ways. It has been suggested that the rules governing these legal questions are not imperatives because they do not say that you shall behave in this or that way. Instead, they regulate the legal effects of so-called operative facts. The case is the same with rules regulating the acquisition, import, and loss of legal qualities, such as being king or president, judge or member of the Diet, married or guardian of a minor. It will seem that such rules are not imperatives.[14]

The importance of the objection is evident since a very considerable part of legal rules is of this kind: most of private law and large sections of public law. If valid, the objection would also be an argument against the view here expounded of legal rules as independent imperatives.

The objection rests on the assumption that imperatives are necessarily imperatives of conduct. What else but a conduct could be imperatively prescribed? But if imperatives are always directed towards the conduct of an addressee, it is really difficult to fit the legal rules about rights and legal qualities into the category of imperatives.

The basic assumption, however, is unfounded. It may seem obvious that imperatives must always refer to other people's conduct. But our actual language does not conform to this preconceived idea. If I hand over a watch to my son saying: 'This shall be your

[14] This objection is clearly stated by Larenz, *Methodenlehre der Rechtswissenschaft* (1960) 152 ff.

property ', I am using an imperative form of speech. But I am not commanding him to do anything. The imperative is directed towards his acquiring the ownership of the watch.

This sort of language may, upon reflection, seem strange. But it is a fact that we have it; and it is a most important part of our legal language. We constantly use it in legal transactions. It is employed in legislation in laying down that a person shall acquire ownership of a piece of land through certain formalities; that he shall lose it when certain things happen, etc.

These imperatives are obviously of a peculiar kind. In a previous work I called them ' imperatives of existence ' because they refer to the coming into existence of rights and legal qualities.[15] The choice of expression was not a particularly happy one. It is much better to adopt the term ' performatory ' or ' performative ' expressions introduced by J. L. Austin.

The imperatives in question will here be called *performatory imperatives.* Their meaning is that something should come to pass: a right should be created or transferred; a person should acquire a legal quality. This effect is held to be brought about through these imperatives.

> Originally Austin used the expression ' performatory utterances '. But soon he changed it to ' performative utterances ' or simply ' performatives '. (*How to Do Things with Words* 6, footnote 3.) For my own part I find the term ' performatory imperatives ' appropriate. As will be seen in Chapter VIII, my view is not the same as Austin's.

The performatory imperatives have been a source of great difficulty to legal theory. What is performed through them? This is a perplexing question when one comes to think about it. No satisfactory answer can be given immediately. To clear up the problem, an analysis of our fundamental legal concepts is necessary. This will be the subject of the next chapter.

[15] *Judgments in civil cases* (Swedish 1943) 69.

Chapter 6

THE CONCEPT OF A RIGHT IN LEGAL THEORY

The fundamental legal concepts are not exclusive professional tools for the jurists. They belong to the common stock of concepts that everybody needs for his contacts with his fellow-men. Expressly or implicitly we are using them in everyday life, buying things, taking a room in an hotel, or paying debts. In this connection they are vehicles for attaining practical ends. But they are also essential ingredients in our view of the community in which we are living, and of the world at large. When we speak of governments, of elections, of state officials, of new laws and new taxes, of trials and punishment, of peace and war, we are using legal concepts. We could not, for instance, understand a newspaper without being familiar with them. They determine our whole outlook on society. Therefore they are necessary means of conveying information as to what is going on in the world.

These legal concepts are as natural to us as are concepts of time, space, movement, etc. But just as these concepts have posed grave problems to philosophers who have begun to reflect upon them, so is the case with legal concepts. An enormous literature has been produced on the subject. But the discussion has not led to any generally accepted solution. The divergence of opinion is perhaps greater than ever in our own time.

Most fundamental, and most discussed of all, are the concepts of rights and duties. Seemingly, they are very simple. But they are amazingly difficult to pin down, and so it seems advisable to concentrate on them in the analysis of legal concepts.

But how is the inquiry to proceed? Usually the question has been supposed to be: what *is* a right or a (legal) duty? When the discussion starts from this question, it is being presupposed that there are some realities denoted by the terms right and duty. This, however, implies the avoidance of a vital question. It is by no means certain from the beginning that precisely these two words signify any realities at all. Whether this is the case is an open question. It cannot be taken for granted that every substantive has, so to speak, an object in reality attached to itself. A substantive may, for instance, be used as an expression of feeling or in a purely exhortative sense.

In order to avoid by-passing relevant questions, the inquiry has to be conducted on the lines indicated in the introduction above. We have to start from some given facts and search for further information without any preconceived ideas concerning the result.

Given facts are here the actual use of the words right and duty. To begin with, one can ask how the words are employed in ordinary language and in professional legal language. Certain meanings are bound to appear from the actual usage.

Next comes the question as to how the meaning of the words has been defined in the literature of jurisprudence and legal philosophy. After stating the import of the various definitions, certain questions may be raised concerning them. One may ask, for instance, whether a certain definition really gives expression to the sense in which the word defined is employed in ordinary discourse or in jurisprudence. It may be that this is not the case. Further, one may ask whether the definition is logically consistent, whether the author of the definition adheres to it himself in his use of the word, etc.

The object of the first part of the inquiry may be said to be 'the living concepts', the concepts living in actual usage. The second part is concerned with the definitions.

In the discussion of the fundamental legal concepts an essentially new method was introduced by Hägerström. See especially the introduction to *Der römische Obligationsbegriff* and the essay on the concept of a declaration of intention, both in *Inquiries into the Nature of Law and Morals* (1953). Lundstedt pursued the analysis in several writings, most recently in *Legal Thinking Revised* (1957). Hohfeld's purpose was to create a new system of legal concepts. This was an entirely different matter.

The Living Concepts

In technical legal language as well as in common parlance rights and duties are spoken of as being created through so-called operative facts. A contract for sale and purchase is held to give rise to certain rights and duties: for the seller the obligation to deliver the goods and the right to receive payment, for the buyer obversely the obligation to pay the price and the right to receive the goods. These rights and duties are the 'legal effects' of the contract. The idea is that they are brought into being through the declarations of will made by the parties. Rights of property, money claims, and other rights are also transferred from one person to another through declarations of will, though something more may also be needed, as for instance transference of possession of an object or certain formalities. Rights and duties are also thought to be modified or extinguished through declarations of will. These are the principal operative facts in the field of private law. But there are many other operative facts besides these, for instance the lapse of a certain period of time.

This view is to be found in every textbook on private law. The subject-matter of the exposition is the creation of rights and duties, their content, their transference, their fulfilment and extinction. The great German scholar Ernst Zitelmann coined the expression 'juridical causality' for the relationship between the operative facts and their legal effects.[1] In doing so he did not introduce a new outlook. He only gave a succinct formulation for the general view of his time—a view that is still fundamental despite all criticism and discussion that has taken place since the 1870s.

The 'juridical causality' differs from natural causality. It has nothing to do with the chain of cause and effect in the usual sense.

Let us take a contract for sale and purchase as an example. The contract initiates a sequence of activities by the parties and other persons. In most cases the parties carry out the terms of the contract: the seller delivers the goods and the buyer pays the price. The seller then considers himself entitled to use the money as belonging to him, and he can do so without incurring any risk. The buyer on his side considers himself owner of the goods, and this view is accepted by those around him. This means that he is in fact able to make dispositions with regard to the goods. His subordinates find it legitimate that he does so and nobody interferes from the outside. Like a ship that has entered a harbour, the goods have come within a sphere that seems to be somehow protected. Within this sphere the buyer is supreme. He can use the goods for his personal needs, he can sell them, give them away, etc., just as he likes. His dispositions will in general be respected by everybody concerned.

This is what happens in the ordinary course of things. But events sometimes take another turn. Perhaps the seller fails to deliver the goods, or he offers faulty goods which the buyer feels unable to accept in fulfilment of the contract. The buyer may then let the matter rest and supply his needs from another source. But he may also insist on getting what has been promised. If he does not succeed in

[1] *Irrthum und Rechtsgeschäft* (1879) 200 ff.

inducing the seller to perform the contract as desired, he may eventually claim damages. First, there will be some discussions with a view to settling the dispute; if negotiations are successful the buyer will perhaps receive a sum of money to compensate him for the loss, and there will be an end to the whole affair. But if no settlement is reached, the buyer will consider taking the matter to court to claim damages; if he is a prudent man, he will carefully weigh the chances of success against the heavy costs involved in litigation. Suppose he goes to court; if a judgment for damages is given, a sum of money may be extracted from the seller if he is solvent; otherwise the buyer ends up with a loss.

Many other variations of the theme are possible. The contract is an item in the infinitely complicated chain of causes and effects. The effects are, indeed, never exactly the same in two different cases.

There can be no doubt that the 'legal effects' are conceived as being something other than the manifold actual consequences of the contract. The following two points of difference may be noted. (i) The 'legal effects' (*die Rechtswirkungen*) are not held to be what the parties actually do with reference to the contract; they are believed to consist in certain rights and duties created by the contract. (ii) The actual consequences of the contract are conditioned by the sense of duty of the parties, their interest in maintaining good business relations, their economic situation, their energy in defending their interests, the skill of their advocates, the insight and impartiality of the members of courts, etc. The legal effects are not regarded as being subject to any such conditions. They are held to follow with absolute certainty from the contract.

Such is the general view in jurisprudence, as well as in daily life. We reckon with a separate legal chain of events apart from the chain of natural events. The creation, modification, transference, and extinction of rights and duties are no natural, observable phenomena. They are occurrences on another level, in another sphere of reality. This has been quite clear to a long succession of philosophers and jurists. But how to fix this sphere of reality conceptually and how to explain its relation to what happens in the spatio-temporal world of nature has been the great problem.

It is in fact perplexing. There is a natural temptation to try to avoid it by showing that rights and duties are, after all, only abbreviated expressions for complicated actual situations. The reasoning would be as follows.

Through the contract of sale and purchase the buyer puts himself in a situation of constraint. If he receives the goods, he has got to pay the price, or else he will expose himself to very disagreeable consequences, ultimately distraint for debt, not to speak of loss of reputation and credit. On the part of the seller a position of power corresponds to the buyer's situation of constraint. But the seller also puts himself in a situation of constraint since he must deliver the goods if he wants to avoid unpleasant consequences of the same sort. The buyer has a position of power corresponding to the seller's position of constraint.

Now it might be said that a legal duty is only an expression of the situation of constraint in which each party to the contract has been placed. A right would be an expression for the corresponding position of power for each party.

If this were a correct explanation of the meaning of the words as used in ordinary language and in jurisprudence, the problem would disappear. Rights and duties would not belong to another sphere of reality. These words would simply connote actual situations.

But such is not the case. According to current usage the words right and duty signify no actual situations of constraint with corresponding actual positions of power. Whether or not any real situation of constraint for either party will arise from the contract depends on various conditions. In the first place the resolution and resources of the opposite party are of decisive importance. If this party from whatever cause (laxity, lack of money, etc.) does not react against a breach of contract, the supposed situation of constraint comes to nothing. When a party wants to make use of the legal remedies available, there may be many difficulties. Unless the contract can be proved to the satisfaction of a court, the party supposed to be bound can extricate himself and there will be no real situation of constraint. Doubts concerning the validity of the contract or concerning its interpretation may be so grave that the party pretending to have a right under it finds it too risky to submit the question to a court. Many, many different circumstances may lead to the result that there will be no real situation of constraint and consequently no real power on the other side.

Evidently the existence of the rights and duties arising from the contract is not held to be dependent on circumstances like those just mentioned. The rights and duties are exclusively determined by the operative facts according to the law. If a valid contract has been concluded, the parties to it are believed to have certain rights and duties towards one another. It is another question whether these rights and duties can be ' enforced '. As was just mentioned, this depends on many circumstances, such as the energy and resources of the parties, the availability of proof, the skill of advocates, etc. Existence of a right and possibility of enforcement are different things.

It is therefore a mistake to identify the rights and duties arising out of a contract with the actual, normal consequences of the contract. The rights and duties are not actual powers and bonds.

Similar reasoning applies to the right of property. Ownership is acquired through a ' legal title ', for instance a purchase. The right is held to exist when the legal title is perfect. The normal consequence is that other people refrain from touching the object and one is left free to use it for one's own purposes without being disturbed. The result is an actual domination over the object. But the right of ownership is evidently not identical with this actual domination. It is by no means certain that one ever acquires such actual domination over the object by getting a title to it; when it has been acquired it may be lost. The existence of the right of property is held to manifest its importance especially when the actual possession of the object has been lost because it then entails the right of recovery. The right of property is said to be created through certain operative facts and to remain in existence until certain other operative facts have occurred.

Further reflection on these concepts shows that the right is conceived as a power and the legal duty as a corresponding bond on the freedom of the other party. The creditor has a ' claim ' against the debtor, and the debtor is liable to fulfil the claim. But what is this ' claim '? Anybody can actually raise a claim against somebody else in the sense of making a demand on him. But the claim of the creditor is not identical with such an actual demand. The claim is of a higher quality grounded in the law. It is a demand that ought to be complied with by the debtor. In that sense it is a powerful demand.

But what is the meaning of this? The powerful claim of the creditor is not identical with his actual position of power in relation to the debtor. It is not certain that he has got any actual position of power. There may be no power at all if it is impossible to prove the facts on which the claim is supposed to be grounded. Nevertheless, the ' claim ' is supposed to exist.

Moreover, the following point is important. The actual power of the creditor consists in his ability to exert pressure on the debtor by raising a claim in court. But if the claim is allowed by the court, this is said to be because the party really 'has' the pretended right. The existence of the claim is supposed to be the reason why judgment is given against the debtor and put into execution if he does not satisfy the claim. Therefore, it is evident that the 'claim' precedes the power that accrues to the creditor from the regular functioning of the court. State power is put at his service by the court because he has a claim.

The right of property is also conceived as a kind of power. But it is not identical with actual power over the object. The existence of the right of property depends exclusively on the law and operative facts. Actual control follows partly from such facts but it depends on innumerable other circumstances too. If the right of property is infringed, this gives rise to a 'claim' analogous to the claim of a creditor.

We seem to be faced with a riddle. The right is supposed to be a power of some kind. But it is not an actual power. On the contrary, there is a distinct opposition between actual power and rights. Naked power and rights are different things. Conversely, the bond corresponding to the duty is not identical with actually being bound. It is a bond belonging to the same sphere as the right.

These non-factual powers and bonds are difficult to grasp. They slip away when we seek to get hold of them. No wonder, therefore, that the concepts of rights and duties have been a headache for legal theory.

The concept of a right has usually been conceived as being the primary one. For this reason I propose to concentrate the review of theories to the theories of the concept of a right. This will also simplify the exposition. The concept of a legal duty is evidently of the same general character as that of a right. No separate treatment is therefore necessary for our purpose.

The Theories

When the positivists of the nineteenth century wanted to make a clean break with natural law doctrine, they ceased to cite the old authorities. But as a matter of course they took over their fundamental concepts.[2] To understand the modern discussion concerning legal concepts it is therefore essential to go back to the teachers of natural law.

[2] *Cf.* references in ch. 1, footnotes 30–32.

In its turn natural law doctrine drew for its concepts on the heritage from the Roman jurists, stoic philosophy, and mediaeval jurisprudence. But it can be understood without delving into this enormous material and, since some limitation is imperative, the historical exposition may start from classical natural law doctrine.

Natural law doctrine

Grotius and Pufendorf defined a right (*ius*) as a moral quality or faculty (*qualitas* or *facultas moralis*).[3] They also used expressions like *potestas* and *imperium* to signify rights. Clearly, a right was conceived as a power.

But what was meant by qualifying a right as a 'moral' power or faculty? Pufendorf explains that a right implies the power of raising a claim against another person with the effect that the addressee becomes obligated to do as required. A creditor, he says, has an *imperium* over the debtor. The will of the debtor is subject to the domination of the creditor in the sense that he is under an obligation to fulfil a demand falling within the sphere of the right. The creditor commands for instance the debtor to pay a sum of money according to a promise. It then becomes morally necessary for the debtor to perform this action. He is not free to do as he likes. He must obey. The obligation 'imbues' his will. He is not internally free but bound.[4]

This will be best understood by considering the origin of rights as described by the teachers of natural law.

In the state of nature everybody is free. Nobody is under the dominion of anyone else. There is no moral power for any man over another.

Through the social contract and the institution of a civil power, the members of society desist from their natural liberty. They make it morally necessary for themselves to obey the commands of the sovereign. This is the source of the moral power to govern the state (*facultas moralis civitatem gubernandi*).

Still, no private individual has any moral power over another. To establish such a power a joint act of will is required. The one party renounces a part of his liberty and the other party assumes a corresponding power. The debtor promises to pay a sum of money. By accepting the promise, the creditor assumes the power of claiming payment with the effect that the debtor is under obligation to pay.

[3] Grotius 1,1,4; Pufendorf 1,1,19; 3,5,1 and 3.
[4] *Cf.* ch. 1 at footnote 14.

Thus a *facultas moralis* for one man over another is established through an act of will on the part of the latter, accepted by the former. But the internal act of will is not sufficient by itself because it cannot be known to others. For practical reasons the will has to be declared or signified in some suitable way.

A promise is a declaration of will through which the declarer alienates a part of his liberty, or his right to decide over his own actions, to the other party, the promisee. He loses the power of decision over a particular action, as this power (right) is transferred to the promisee.[5]

Curiously enough, therefore, a promise is viewed as causing the transfer of a right. This no doubt seems odd to a modern jurist. Nowadays a new right is held to be created through a promise. There is no right to be transferred. But the teachers of natural law saw the matter in another light. For them the starting point was the original liberty of Man, his right to decide over his own actions. There was only one way of establishing a right against oneself for somebody else. This was to carve out some part of the liberty—the right to decide over a particular action, or over a series of actions—and confer it on another person who, through his acceptance, assumed the power, or right, to decide concerning this action.

Even when the promise has been extracted by coercion, the alienation of part of the liberty has taken place (Grotius 2,11,7). The promisee therefore acquires a right through such a promise, and the promisor is bound. If the promisee has exercised coercion himself, and done so unjustly, he is bound to liberate the promisor if the latter asks for it. The promise is not void. It has its usual effect. But the promisee has done an injury which he is bound to repair. If the coercion was exercised by a third party, there is no remedy in the law of nature but only in civil law.

> Pufendorf differs from Grotius in the treatment of coercion. His reason is not that the will of the promisor is inefficient in this case. In the person of the promisor everything required for the transference of a right is present. But the promisee is prohibited from accepting it. Therefore the obligation of the promisor becomes void (3,6,12). In this ingenious way Pufendorf avoids the conclusion drawn by Grotius. But the premises of the argument are the same.

In the explanation of the nature of a promise and its ability to confer a right on the promisee, neither the maxims of natural law

[5] Grotius 2,11; Pufendorf 3,5,2. Pufendorf says that this theory was generally accepted.

nor the social nature of man or the commands of God are relevant. The promise becomes so to speak self-sufficient. It is conceived as an act of will through which the promisor, in an almost mechanical way, transfers part of his liberty, in the sense of his power to decide over his own actions, to the promisee. The effect is caused by the will itself, though the will has to be signified in some adequate way, through words or gestures.

The moral power of imposing an obligation can only be a power over a person. The right of property was therefore interpreted in terms of obligations for other persons in general to restore the object if it had come into their possession, etc. But this view could not be consistently upheld. In conformity with common legal language the teachers of natural law also spoke of *dominium* as a *potestas* over the object. This *potestas* was, however, thought automatically to engender obligations in all others. No actual claim or command on the part of the owner was required. Had this been the case, Grotius says, the 'force' of the *dominium* would have been too weak (2,10,1,2).

Every *facultas moralis*, therefore, implied an obligation in another person, or in an indefinite number of persons. Directly or indirectly every such right derived from an act of will by the obligated party through which he had alienated a bit of his liberty and transferred it to the opposite party.[6] There was only one exception to this rule. This was the right of parents to claim obedience from their children, which according to Grotius was grounded on generation (2,5,1).[7]

But the moral faculty needed a complement. The duty it imposed could be disregarded. In this case the possessor of the right had a secondary right—the right to use force. He was entitled to employ such force against the other party as was necessary to compel fulfilment of the duty or payment of damages.

This secondary right was not of the same nature as the primary one, the *facultas moralis*. It was not power to make a demand with the effect of imposing an obligation. A new demand would have been without purpose if the first one had proved inefficient. Now the time had come to use force in support of the primary right.

How, then, is this secondary right to be characterized? According

[6] The right of property, and consequently other rights over things, had been introduced through the human will.

[7] Pufendorf expresses another opinion on this point. He suggests that the consent of the children to the domination of the parents may be presumed (6,2,4).

to Grotius, it existed before the introduction of laws, that is, before the formation of society.[8] Already in the state of nature there was something which belonged to each person, the *suum* as Grotius says. This was his life, limb, and liberty. But even before the introduction of property the *suum* could be enlarged through the 'appropriation' of things for one's own use. The *suum* constituted a sphere that was protected by the law of nature in the sense that every infringement on it entailed an injury. The offended person then had the right of employing force to protect himself and recover what he had lost. This was called private war, *bellum privatum*. The import of this right was that no injury was done to the offender if force was used against him. Through committing an injury he had lost the protection of the law of nature and exposed himself to the just violence of the offended person.

With the formation of society the right of employing force was transferred to the civil power. It was exercised through the courts acting in the interest of the offended person and using his right. But the individual retained the right of having recourse to force himself in so far as the delay caused by an appeal to court would entail danger or loss, and in places where no community exists, as in uninhabited islands (Grotius 1,3,1 & 2). Since the sovereigns live in the state of nature with regard to each other, they possess the right of vindicating their rights through force, that is, through war (*bellum publicum*).

Such was, in brief, the view of the teachers of natural law. It appears that they employed the word 'right', or *ius*, in two different senses: one positive and one negative. In the positive sense the word signified a *facultas moralis*, a moral faculty of imposing an obligation on another person. In the negative sense it implied absence of injury in vindicating the *suum* or one's primary rights. The purpose of the secondary right was to give substance to the primary one.

The mysterious *facultas moralis* is a part of the power of the obligated person over his own actions as transferred to another person, who has thereby acquired the power of decision with regard to this action. It is a moral power which involves the moral necessity of the obligated party to conform to the claim or command; and it is supported by the capability of using force without committing any injury to the party obligated.

[8] *Ius suum per vim consequendi ante positas leges* (1,1,10,7).

There is an obvious psychological basis for this theory. When one has made a promise, it is natural to feel bound. I regard my liberty as being circumscribed through the promise. I must do as I have promised, at least if the other party insists upon it. This is a feeling of being under a moral necessity or having a duty. Correspondingly, the promisee is regarded as possessing some sort of power over me. By making a demand, he actualizes my obligation; he can let it drop, if he so wishes.

In natural law theory these subjective views are made objective and their contents transformed into entities belonging to a supersensible sphere. Pufendorf called it the sphere of moral entities, *entia moralia*. One can also easily understand the idea that no injury is done to an offender in using force against him to vindicate a right.[9]

There were two lines of thought in natural law doctrine respecting the reason for the binding force of the social contract: (i) Its binding force was derived from the law of nature, which was therefore the 'grandmother' of positive law. (See above 13.) (ii) The binding force of the social contract was established independently of the law of nature through the theory that an obligation was created by means of transferring a part of one's liberty to another person. This latter line of thought was the most important. It would be an interesting task to try to ascertain what significance 'the law of nature' really had in classical natural law doctrine.

Legal positivism

In natural law doctrine the concept of a right was not dependent on positive law. It was antecedent to it; positive law was based on the social contract. As we have seen, the origin of all rights was the transfer of parts of the individual's sovereignty within his own sphere. Positive law could prescribe formalities for the creation of rights, it could put limits on their use, and regulate people's rights in many other ways with regard to the conditions prevailing in a given community. But the substance of rights did not stem from positive law.

With the rise of legal positivism, this position was bound to be subject to doubt and criticism. There began a long and laborious

[9] The above exposition is a summary of the article 'The concept of a right according to Grotius and Pufendorf' in the *Festschrift für O. A. Germann* (1969), reprinted here in an enlarged form as Appendix 1. *Cf.* Hägerström, *Recht, Pflicht und bindende Kraft des Vertrages nach römischer und naturrechtlicher Anschauung* (1965), which is devoted to showing the difference between natural law doctrine and the view of the Roman jurists.

argument about the concept of a right, a conflict which is still going on.

The history of this discussion is extremely complicated. To disentangle the principal lines of thought I propose to arrange the matter in the following way. First, the chief theories linked to the imperative theory are reviewed. Secondly, the difficulties of the imperative theory are systematically set forth and the attempts to overcome them explained. Thirdly, we arrive at the final stage in the discussion on the concept of a right: the negation of the reality of rights.

The will-power theory

The will-power theory is best known under the German appellation of the theory of the *Willensmacht*.

We find it in Savigny. A right, according to Savigny, is a power belonging to a person. It is a sphere wherein his will is ruling with our consent. The right as such is a spiritual phenomenon. But it appears in apprehensible form when, being doubted or opposed, it is recognized by a court decision.[10]

In a less-known work on the law of obligations, Savigny gives a particularly illuminating account of his view. An obligation means that the action of one party has been dissevered from his sphere of liberty and put under the domination of the will of another party. In this way the action of the obligated party becomes necessary and certain. Fulfilment of the obligation is the natural thing. Compulsion through action in court only implies the elimination of an unnatural state of affairs. The right of property is the illimited and exclusive domination over a material object. Its appearing in the form of court action is contingent.[11]

It is plain that the view of Savigny is very closely related to that of Grotius and Pufendorf. Even the wording is partly identical. Thus important parts of natural law doctrine are preserved, while the ideas of original liberty and social contract are repudiated.

Savigny has also taken over the concept of a declaration of will. The creative force is the will, he says; strictly speaking, only the

[10] 1 *System des heutigen römischen Rechts* 7: '[Die der einzelnen Person zustehende Macht ist] ein Gebiet, worin [der Wille der einzelnen Person] herrscht, und mit unsrer Einstimmung herrscht. Diese Macht nennen wir ein Recht dieser Person, gleichbedeutend mit Befugniss: Manche nennen es das Recht im subjektiven Sinne. Ein solches Recht erscheint vorzugsweise in sichtbarer Gestalt, wenn es bezweifelt oder bestritten, und nun das Dasein und der Umfang desselben durch ein richterliches Urtheil anerkannt wird.'

[11] *Das Obligationenrecht* (1851) 4 ff.

will itself is important and operative. An outward sign is required solely to make the will known to others.[12]

The most noted proponent of the *Willensmacht* theory was Bernard Windscheid (1817–92). In his view a right (*subjektives Recht*) is a power exerted by the will of one person over that of another. A money claim, for instance, implies that the will of the creditor is determinant (*massgebend*) for the will of the debtor with respect to a certain action: that of paying off the debt. The creditor is able to command the debtor to perform this action.

So far the theory continues the natural law tradition. But the power of the creditor is no longer a part of the debtor's power over his own actions which has been transferred to the creditor. Instead, it is the power of the legal order itself. The legal order commands the debtor to fulfil his obligation. But it has put this command at the disposal of the creditor; the right of the creditor is so to speak merged with a state imperative. By being put at his disposal the imperative of the state becomes his imperative. As wielding this imperative he has the power of commanding.[13]

In this way the concept of a right was fitted into the system of legal positivism. The right derives from the commands of the state. It is an ideal power in the individual. But this power is the power of the state as delegated to him.

According to Windscheid's definition, a thing (*eine Sache*) could never be the object of a right. Since a right means the domination of one will over another, a right is always directed towards another person. This causes considerable embarrassment with regard to the

[12] *System* III § 134: 'Eigentlich muss der Wille an sich als das einzig Wichtige und Wirksame gedacht werden, und nur weil er ein inneres, unsichtbares Ereigniss ist, bedürfen wir eines Zeichens, woran er von Anderen erkannt werden könne, und dieses Zeichen, wodurch sich der Wille offenbart, ist eben die Erklärung.'

[13] Windscheid, *Lehrbuch des Pandektenrechts* (9. Aufl. 1906) § 37: 'Das Recht . . . hat auf Grund eines konkreten Tatbestandes einen Befehl (Norm, Imperativ) zu einem Verhalten bestimmter Art erlassen und diesen Befehl demjenigen, zu Gunsten dessen sie ihn erlassen hat, zur freien Verfügung hingegeben . . . Die Rechtsordnung hat sich des von ihr erlassenen Befehls zu seiner Gunst entäussert, sie hat ihren Befehl zu seinem Befehl gemacht . . . Auszugehen ist davon, dass der im subjektiven Recht gebietende Wille der Wille der Rechtsordnung ist, nicht der Wille des Berechtigten.' Binding explains the theory (which he embraces himself) in the following way: '(Das Recht) auf Befolgung der Normen kann allein ihrem Urheber zustehen. Regelmässig . . . ist dies der Staat. . . . Dieses Recht kann vom Staate an Private übertragen werden, und das übertragene Recht auf Befolgung der Normen zum Schutze des Eigentums würde dann zum Rechte des Eigentümers, das Recht auf Erfüllung der Schuldnormen zum Gläubigerrecht usw. Berechtigt sein hiesse: mit Normen zu seinem Gunste bewaffnet sein!' (2 *Strafrechtliche und strafprozessuale Abhandlungen,* 1915, 538 f.)

rights of property and other rights over things. Windscheid tries to explain such rights as implying a power to dominate (through commands) the will of everybody else. But despite his own proclamation Windscheid actually spoke of the right of property as a power over a thing.

Windscheid himself points out a difficulty in the theory. The owner of an object need not issue any commands. Other people are nevertheless subject to the domination of his will. If I trespass on the property of somebody else, I violate his right even if he has not commanded me to abstain; he need not even be aware of my activity (§ 38). The power to command exists whether the possessor of a right is asleep or awake, whether he knows anything about his rights or not, whether he is a grown-up person with full mental faculties, a baby or a lunatic. Evidently, the power in question is represented as a mysterious force in the will which is active irrespective of the psychological situation.
This is strikingly evident in the exposition on the concept of right by James Goldschmidt in his great work *Der Prozess als Rechtslage* (1925). Goldschmidt keeps strictly to the imperative theory of law. A right, he says, is the power of letting the imperatives of the law become effective (*die Macht, die Imperative des Rechts wirksam werden zu lassen*, 232 f.). This refers to the primary imperative. The possessor of a right has a state command at his disposal. It becomes effective only if this is his will. (*Die Auslösung des das subjektive Recht begründenden rechtlichen Imperativs* depends on the will of the possessor of the right.) When the possessor of the right makes use of the imperative, an obligation for the opposite party is created. But the will to 'release' the imperative need not be manifested in any way. It is presumed that this will exists. Indeed, it may even happen that an express declaration of the will to the contrary is void. ('Eine dem Wirksamwerden des rechtlichen Imperativs entgegenstehende Willenserklärung des Berechtigten [kann] nichtig sein,' 233 footnote 1279).

As will easily be seen, the theory is wholly fictitious. A creditor does not direct a command to his debtor in claiming payment; he makes a request with reference to the obligation of the debtor which is supposed to exist independently of his will. The owner of an object does not issue imperatives to the whole world to abstain from interfering with his use of it. The right is held to exist by virtue of the law and certain operative facts; and its possessor need not issue any commands.

E. Bucher, *Das subjektive Recht als Normsetzungsbefugnis* (1965) embraces the imperative theory but also holds the concept of a right to be indispensable for the exposition of private law (7). This concept is to be made consonant with the imperative theory. The solution proposed is that the law delegates to the individual the competence of 'positing' a norm. This is the essence of a right. As Bucher himself remarks, his theory comes close to Windscheid's. (See especially 16,20.)

In addition to what has been said previously the following might be remarked with regard to this theory. Suppose I am the owner of a house where I am living. In what sense am I positing norms for others? I have no thought of doing such a thing; and it would be useless for me to try doing it. Most probably I shall live undisturbed in the house. Other people refrain from interfering simply because they have the idea that the house is 'not theirs'. No activity on my part that could be qualified as positing of norms is required or even possible. In the unlikely event that I feel compelled to bring a law suit against somebody for infringing my property rights, I shall not be laying down any norms for him; I shall only make use of the facilities offered to me by the state organization through the courts and rely on them to apply correctly certain norms to my advantage. When I receive notice from the bank that interests on the mortgage are due, the bank lays down no norm for me; the notice is a reminder of what I have to do in order to avoid forcing the bank to seek the help of the courts for extracting the money from me according to norms laid down through legislation and precedents. Nowhere do we find any *Normsetzung* by the supposed possessor of a right.

Innumerable authors have adopted the theory of the *Willensmacht*, sometimes in a more or less varied form. To this day, the theory remains influential, especially in German jurisprudence.

In his work *Das Markenrecht als subjektives Recht* (1964) W. Schluep records a number of definitions of the concept of a right. He concludes that the element of a *Willensmacht* is to be found in the majority of definitions (270). See also Bucher's work.

In his book *Rechtsnorm und subjektives Recht* (1878) August Thon sought to improve on Windscheid's theory. What the state puts at the disposal of the individual, he says, is not the primary imperative establishing an obligation; it is only the secondary imperative addressed to the state organs ordering them to give the possessor of a right protection in case the primary imperative is not obeyed. (See especially 175 ff., 202 ff. *Cf.* Windscheid, Anm. 3 to § 37.) In Thon's theory the primary right is actually dissolved; only the secondary right remains (*cf.* 218). The theory did not meet with much approval.

On French jurisprudence see Rieg, *Le rôle de la volonté dans l'acte juridique en droit civil français et allemand*. Diss. Strasbourg 1958. (Also 3 *Archives de Philosophie du Droit*, 1958.)

Though Kelsen does not regard legal rules as imperatives in his earlier writings, his view on the concept of a right is similar to Windscheid's. The essential thing is the merging of rights and norms. But Kelsen is more consistent than Windscheid since he expressly denies that the right is something beside the norms: 'Das subjektive Recht ist kein vom Objektiven Recht verschiedenes, es ist das objektive Recht selbst, nur sofern es sich mit der von ihm statuirten Unrechtsfolge gegen ein konkretes Subjekt richtet (Pflicht) oder einem solchen zur Verfügung steht (Berechtigung).' (*Reine Rechtslehre*, 1. Aufl., 1934, 43 f. Vgl. Dubischar, *Grundbegriffe des Rechts*, 1968, 32.) As Dubischar points out, this view is in accordance with Kelsen's avowed purpose of only drawing the final conclusions from certain fundamental propositions of nineteenth-century legal positivism. One conclusion must indeed be that legal positivism has no room for the concept of a right. (*Cf.* below 156 ff.)

The right as a legally protected interest

The next phase in the discussion on the concept of a right was inaugurated by Jhering's vigorous criticism of the *Willensmacht* theory and his definition of a right as a legally protected interest. This definition has met with much favour. But there is really less difference between Jhering's view and the *Willensmacht* theory than his language and the vehemence of his attack may suggest.

As we have seen before, Jhering held the will-theory of law. Positive law—the only real law—was the will of the state. He had no intention of rejecting this fundamental tenet. But he strongly insisted that the content of the law was determined by its purpose. (*Der Zweck ist der Schöpfer des ganzen Rechts.*) Jhering also accepts the view that a right is a compound of state will and individual will.[14] His criticism is directed against a certain form of the *Willensmacht* theory: the view ascribed to Hegel and his followers that the will-power is an end in itself. This opinion he rejects. A right, Jhering holds, is not bestowed upon an individual in order that he should experience the satisfaction of the feeling of power; it is given to him to serve the interests, requirements, and

[14] He agrees with the Hegelian jurist Kierulff who characterizes a right as *concrete Einheit des Staats- und Einzelwillens.* In this sense, Jhering says, a right is 'ein in der Privatperson concret und lebendig gewordenes Stück des allgemeinen Willens'. (3:1 *Geist des römischen Rechts*, 4. Aufl. 1888, 329.) *Cf.* 2:1, 4. Aufl. 1880, 140: 'Der Inhalt eines jeden Rechtsverhältnisses, wenn man dasselbe des Beiwerks entkleidet und auf seinen juristischen Kern zurückführt, ist Willensmacht, Herrschaft, die Unterschiede der Rechtsverhältnisse sind Unterschiede der Herrschaft.'

purposes of social exchange and intercourse. This end puts restrictions on the will.

If the law treated the will-power as an end in itself, Jhering says, all agreements, if not immoral or forbidden, would have binding force. A contract would be valid even if it entailed serious restrictions on the one party without any corresponding gain on the other side. As an example Jhering mentions the case that A has promised B not to exercise a certain profession though his abstaining from doing so is of no interest whatever to B. If such promises were valid, meaningless restrictions would multiply; real liberty would be destroyed under the banner of the false one.

Jhering's attack is actually aimed at the principle of unfettered 'liberty of contract' (the principle that every agreement is binding regardless of content). He advocates the principle that rights should be, and are, accorded only to protect interests worthy of protection. This is done in the oblique form of launching a new definition of the concept of a right. Incidentally, Jhering also thinks that the definition makes it possible to explain how lunatics, babies, and juristic persons can possess rights, which was regarded as a thorny problem. A right, he says, belongs to the person, or persons, to whom its benefits are destined, not to the person who exercises the will-power.

The definition says that a right consists of two elements: the substance and the protection. The substance is the use, advantage, and profit which the possessor of a right is to enjoy. The protection is provided by the right of raising a claim in a civil court if the need arises.

The first element, Jhering explains, is, in itself, an actual situation. In the case of my right of property it is the fact that I am using the object for my own purposes. As long as this situation remains purely factual, it is insecure; it can be done away with by anybody for whom this is physically possible. The situation loses its contingent character by being accorded the protection of the law. It then becomes secure: it becomes a right.

This is what Jhering means by saying that a right is a legally protected interest. The essence of a right is the legal security in enjoying certain advantages. The security is established through the right of bringing an action in a civil court, which is under the obligation of affording protection.[15]

[15] 'Der Begriff des Rechts beruht auf der rechtlichen Sicherheit des Genusses, Rechte sind rechtlich geschützte Interessen' (3:1 *Geist* 339).

This is not very clear. The actual insecurity in the enjoyment of the advantages is not removed through the possibility of bringing actions in court. The security that is said to be brought about is only 'legal'. Actually, the owner can of course be deprived of the object. But from a legal point of view his security is absolute. What Jhering means is that the owner has got an ideal power over the object which cannot be disturbed by any factual actions of other people. He wants to say that this ideal power is not accorded to the owner for its own sake but for certain social purposes.[16]

In the concept of 'protection' through the right of bringing action in court, the ideal power is presupposed. Jhering never thought of challenging the view that in bringing an action in court, the claimant pretends that he possesses a right. This was self-evident for him. He therefore expresses himself illogically in saying that the actual enjoyment of an advantage is elevated to the rank of a right through the right of bringing action in court.[17] There is a jump in the argument. What Jhering really thinks, is that the actual enjoyment of an object is transformed, in some unexplained way, into an ideal power, or a right, by being taken under the wings of the law. Then the possessor of the right is in a position to go to court if anybody infringes his right; and the court has to give him protection. The primary and the secondary rights reappear in a new clothing and with some modification.

Jhering had a visionary feeling of the inadequacy of contemporary jurisprudence. But he was unable to free himself from the fetters imposed by centuries of legal teaching on the fundamental legal concepts.

In classical natural law doctrine, as we have seen, the right of a creditor was a particle of the liberty of the debtor, or of his power over himself, as transferred through an act of will. The transference was represented as analogous to the handing over of a physical object. All rights stemmed from such transfers. In Savigny's theory this mode of thinking is still evident. Windscheid has dropped the idea that rights derive from the original freedom of the individual. Instead, they derive from the will of the state.

[16] Wieacker, *Privatrechtsgeschichte der Neuzeit* (2. Aufl. 1967) 451, relates Jhering as defining a right as *zur Befriedigung schutzwürdiger Interessen eingeräumte Willensmacht*.

[17] Jhering felt that he came close to the position that rights are only actual consequences of the legal system. He tried to forestall this conclusion by elaborating the difference between rights and 'reflexes' of legal rules (*Reflexwirkungen*). See 10 *Jherings Jahrbücher* (1871) 245 ff.

The *Willensmacht* of the individual possessing a right is confounded with the power of the state; and yet it is a power of his own. The theory has become more abstract and difficult to grasp. Jhering's theory, though sounding less metaphysical, is more involved and still more obscure.[18]

The right as the reverse of a duty

Before Windscheid and Jhering had put forward their views, Austin had propounded a different theory. As in other matters of importance, he took his cue from Bentham. In *The Limits of Jurisprudence* (55) Bentham says:

> It is by creating duties and by nothing else that the law can create rights. When the law gives you a right, what does it do? it makes me liable to punishment in case of my doing any of those acts which would have the effect of disturbing you in the exercise of that right.

This definition is obviously circular. The law creates rights by creating duties. But the duties are duties to refrain from disturbing rights. Thus the concept of a right is presupposed in the concept of a duty.[19]

Austin avoids the circularity. He explains the meaning of a right in the following way. A person is commanded by the sovereign to do something or forbear something with respect to another person. Thereby a duty is established. The person towards whom the duty is to be observed is invested with a right. His view is 'compressed into the following propositions' (1 *Lectures on Jurisprudence* 396 f.):

> Right, like Duty, is the Creature of Law, or arises from the command of the Sovereign in a given independent society.
> Every right is created or conferred in the following manner.
> A person or persons are commanded to do or forbear *towards* or with regard to, *another* and a *determinate* party.
> The person or persons to whom the command is directed, are said to be *obliged*, or to lie under a *duty*.
> the party *towards* whom the duty is to be observed, is said to have a *right*, or to be invested with a right.

Austin differs from Bentham in not defining the concept of a duty by means of the concept of a right. A right, he holds, i

[18] As Dubischer points out (32) 'heutige Standarddefinitionen (des subjektive Rechts) bewegen sich meist auf der Linie eines " milden Kompromisses " zwische den Definitionen Windscheids und Jherings'.

[19] Bentham's contention that rights and duties are mere imaginations is mor interesting. See below 168 f.

simply the reverse of a duty; and a duty only means that a command by the sovereign is directed towards a person.

This implies that rights and duties are not separate entities existing alongside the commands of the sovereign. A 'duty' is only an expression for the situation that a command is directed towards a person; and a 'right' is an expression for this situation as looked upon from the point of view of the person towards whom a behaviour is to be observed.

This might have been a stipulative definition. Austin could have said that he chose to employ the words 'duty' and 'right' in the said sense. He would of course have been free to do so; and there would have arisen no question about the correctness of the definition.

But such was not his intention. He expressly states that his purpose is to explain the import of the term 'right' (396, *cf.* 343, 393). It is also 'to explain the nature or essence which is common to *all* rights' (393). What Austin wants to do is therefore both to give a lexical definition (stating the meaning in which the word is actually being used in jurisprudence) and a real definition (explaining the nature of that which is denoted by the word).

Actually, Austin is giving a new meaning to the term. In common parlance and in legal language, which Austin himself employs, rights and duties are powers and bonds, created through operative facts, transferred through other facts, and extinguished through a third class of facts. A right cannot be identified with the fact that commands are addressed to one or more persons. The right of property, for instance, as the word is being used, does not signify that millions of people are being commanded to abstain from interfering with an object. The rules of law themselves refer to the concept of the right of property. People are held to be obliged to abstain from violating the right of property of others.

Austin's influence is apparent in many English and American writings. Max Radin says for instance that 'rights and duties are not correlative, but identical' (51 *Harvard Law Review*, 1938, 1163, *cf.* 59 *Yale Law Journal*, 1950, 214). A right is the same thing as a duty, looked at from another point of view. Kelsen takes the same position in the 2nd ed. of the *Reine Rechtslehre* (1960) 130 ff. Hart's elucidation of the expression 'a legal right' (*Definition and Theory in Jurisprudence*, 1953, 16 f.) is strongly reminiscent of Austin's though Hart does not embrace the imperative theory.

The difficulties encountered by the imperative theory with

regard to the concept of a right were brought out with special clarity in Austin's exposition. They deserve separate treatment.

Difficulties of the imperative theory

As the positivists tried to free themselves from the heritage of natural law doctrine, the implications of their imperative theory of law became more and more apparent. The imperative theory poses, indeed, a serious problem with regard to the concept of a right.

From the point of view of the imperative theory a money claim, for instance, seems to involve the following: when A has borrowed a sum of money from B, a general state command becomes applicable. This is the command that borrowed money shall be paid back as promised. A is now the addressee of this state command. If he does not obey, the state further orders that judgment shall be given against him on the application of B; eventually, execution of the judgment shall take place. Since courts and officials charged with the execution of judgments can be relied on to obey the commands addressed to them, a palpable advantage accrues for B in that he can usually secure state support for extracting from A the sum of money the latter has promised to pay. This is, so to speak, a *reflex* of the state commands and of certain regular activities by state organs. But it is by no means certain that B will get the money. State support may fail for lack of proof or other circumstances; and if the debtor is insolvent, the support offered by the state is of no avail.

The reasoning leads, indeed, to the elimination of the traditional concept of a right. There is no place for it in the system based on the imperative theory. Instead of the rights that are supposed to be created, modified, and extinguished through the operative facts, we have the 'reflexes' of the imperatives. The old view is turned upside down. The possessor of a right who imposes obligations on others by virtue of the right is replaced by the recipient of certain relative advantages that result for him from the imperatives of the lawgiver. Gone is the image of the sovereign individual whose sphere of mysterious power has been extended through the transfer from others of parts of their original liberty. The citizen living under the wings of the state has no such powers; but he enjoys relatively secure benefits that are consequences of the powerful activities of the state.

In the case of the right of property the situation will be the following from the point of view of the imperative theory. If A is 'owner' of an object, this means that a great many commands forbidding the use of the object are directed to everybody except himself. There is a 'gap' in the system of norms (commands) which the owner fills. Because everybody else is commanded to abstain from interfering with his use of the object, he has got it for himself; he can make use of it for his own purposes as he likes. If he sells the object to X, an alteration in the application of the norms takes place. The prohibiting norms no more refer to X. He now fills the gap, and A is now placed among the addressees of the prohibiting norms. There are also positive norms commanding state organs to give the owner support against encroachments. From all these norms the owner reaps considerable advantages—not with absolute certainty, but in the general course of things. Here, too, the advantages are a reflex of the state commands and of the regular function of the courts and executive organs.

In both cases the important advantages accruing to individuals are of a factual and relative nature. They are not what is meant by a right. But they are held to be the consequences of one's having a right, though these consequences may not always materialize.

The unavoidable conclusion would seem to be that the traditional concept of a right had to be discarded along with the other foundations of natural law thinking. The imperative theory leads to negating the existence of rights; the concept of a right cannot be assimilated to it.

This was realized by Zitelmann. (*Cf.* below 160 on his theory.) See also W. Sjögren, 'Die Formen des Unrechts' (35 *Iherings Jahrbücher*, 1896) and Larenz, *Methodenlehre der Rechtswissenschaft* 150 ff.

The argument was forcefully put by Theodor Kipp in his often cited article 'Über Doppelwirkungen im Recht' (in the *Festschrift für von Martitz*, 1911). Kipp embraces the imperative theory. The law, he says, is the general will as expressed in rules (*in Regeln gefasster Gemeinwille*, 212). So-called operative facts are only conditions for the hypothetical imperatives of the law; if the facts a, b, c . . . have occurred, the will of the law is . . . ('Etwas anders als Bedingungen für Imperative oder Befreiungen von solchen können die juristischen Tatsachen schlechterdings nicht sein,' 220.) The general will directs both private individuals and state organs to act in a certain way. For both of them the operative facts are motives for a certain behaviour. If the facts a, b, c . . . have occurred,

this is a ground for me to perform action X because that is the will of the lawgiver. When I have borrowed a sum of money from A it is the will of the lawgiver that I pay it back as promised; and therefore I ought to do so. This is the whole significance of the operative facts. That they give rise to rights and duties is a misleading, allegorical language.
Hägerström remarks (*Inquiries* 217): 'The whole theory of the subjective rights of private individuals as corresponding to duties in others, and of duties existing towards private individuals as possessed of rights, and with it the distinction in principle between private and public law, is incompatible with the imperative-theory.' *Cf.* James Goldschmidt, *Der Prozess als Rechtslage* (1925) 230, where critical authors are quoted as saying that no bridge leads from the legal imperative to the right.
The impossibility of bringing the concept of a right into accordance with the imperative theory is clearly enunciated in Bucher's work *Das subjektive Recht als Normsetzungsbefugnis.* The concept of a right, Bucher remarks (4 ff.), was until lately the pivot of the doctrine of private law. In practical questions this is still so. ('Wie sollen zentrale Vorstellungen des Privatrechts wie Verzicht, Abtretung, Verwirkung und Verrechnung anders verstanden werden denn bezogen auf subjektive Rechte?') Nevertheless, the concept of a right has become more and more doubtful during the last decades—not because of any reservations on the part of practical jurists against legal theory, but because doubts have arisen in legal theory against a mode of thinking familiar to practical jurists. The author looks upon this theoretical attitude as a consequence of the increasingly 'normative' thinking. The opinion that the law consists of nothing but precepts for behaviour is now the prevailing one, he says; and he thinks that no other view is defensible. But it seems to be impossible to assimilate the concept of a right into a system of norms. The right is therefore (7) being reduced to a mere reflex of the law. ('So wird das subjektive Recht zum "Reflex" objektiven Rechts, dazu bestimmt, "den Inhalt des objektiven Rechts subjektbezogen auszudrücken".') Bucher himself takes exception to this view. As already mentioned, he propounds a modernized version of the will-power theory.

Although it was impossible to fit the concept of a right into a system of legal norms, it was also difficult to expel it from jurisprudence. For how could one avoid talking about rights? How would it be possible to describe legal situations and transactions without talking of rights as being created through certain operative facts, as being transferred through certain means, as being violated, etc.? But all this would seem to be nonsense if the only realities were the norms and their actual 'reflexes'. One could not, for instance, seriously say that the right of property is infringed if what happens is only that certain imperatives are actualized, causing the advantage to the 'owner' of being able to extract damages from the culprit. It would also be strange to talk about the transference of the right of property if it is only a matter of altered application of certain norms.

These difficulties might have been disregarded had it only been a question of a form of speech without special significance. But the language we use is the natural expression for deeply rooted views. Legal theory itself was built on them. The theorists did not, so to speak, stand apart, looking on these views as matters for inquiry. They took up the living concept of a right and wanted to give it a scientific character.

The result was an impasse. On the one hand, the law was conceived as a system of state commands. On the other hand, the legal situation obtaining at a given moment was conceived as a system of rights and duties. But it seemed to be impossible to deduce any rights in the traditional sense from the commands of the state. By giving the term 'right' a new meaning the difficulty was only glossed over.

To find a way out of the dilemma, theories of two different kinds were put forward. The one implied abandoning the imperative theory of law and replacing it by the 'declaration' theory; the other consisted of depriving the 'right' concept of its substance, reducing the rights to mere convenient representations.

Austin's position implied that there was no room for the concept of a right within the imperative theory of law. This was pointed out by Salmond (*Jurisprudence*, 1893, 97 f.; *cf.* Hart, 71 *Harvard Law Review*, 1958, 605). Austin himself was content to define a right as the reverse of a duty. The authors now cited have gone a step further. They have expressly contended that the concept of a right is not compatible with the imperative theory.

The declaration theory

When it was realized that there was no place for the concept of a right within the imperative theory, some authors drew the conclusion that the fault lay with the imperative theory. The fixed point for them was the concept of a right. The nature of the legal rules had to be explained in such a way as to be brought into harmony with it.

Such was the view of Zitelmann. He rejected the imperative theory because it was incompatible with the necessity of thinking and speaking in terms of rights being created, transferred, and extinguished through operative facts. But Zitelmann was a rigorous positivist. The creation, etc., of rights had to be determined by the will of the lawgiver.

If we ask how a legal effect can be recognized by the judge, Zitelmann says, we are referred to the law. In the abstract, the law says that the right of property is created through certain facts. In a concrete case the judge says: the right of property has been created here because those facts have occurred; the law has established a causal connection between them and the right of property.[20] In the world of law this connection is the counterpart to causality in the world of nature.

Legal norms are not imperatives, Zitelmann contends. They are propositions (*Urteile*) stating a connection between certain facts (operative facts) and certain rights and duties. This connection is actually established by being stated by the lawgiver. It is valid only because it is willed by him.[21]

This may be called the declarative theory of legal norms since it says that legal norms are declarations concerning connections between facts and legal effects in the shape of rights and duties. The theory is not at all a theory of the concept of a right. The purpose is to show how the concept of a right can be made consonant with legal positivism by referring the creation of rights to the will of the lawgiver. In the argument the concept of a right is presupposed.

The theory amounts to a clear and unequivocal statement of the general view. We undoubtedly think and speak in terms of rights as being created, transferred, and extinguished through certain facts that are called operative facts. The problem is precisely to explain this language and the ideas behind it. But this problem is left as it stands. It is not brought nearer a solution by the assertion that the mythical will of the lawgiver possesses the power of establishing connections analogous to natural causality between operative facts and rights and duties.

[20] *Irrthum und Rechtsgeschäft* 220.

[21] 'Jede Rechtsnorm ist ein Urteil, und nur das Eigenthümliche hat dieses Urteil, dass die Synthese der Begriffe in ihm bloss deshalb giltig ist, weil der Gesetzgeber es will. . . . in dem Aussprechen der Norm vollzieht der Gesetzgeber zu gleicher Zeit die Verknüpfung der Thatsachen in Wirklichkeit, welche er zugleich im Urteil als verknüpft ausspricht. . . . Der Rechtssatz besteht also darin, dass eine Rechtsfolge als Wirkung an eine Thatsache . . . als Ursache angeknüpft ist.' (*Irrthum und Rechtsgeschäft* 223, 225.)

The theory of Zitelmann gained considerable influence in German jurisprudence. See A. von Tuhr, *Der allgemeine Teil des bürgerlichen Rechts* II:1 (1914) 5 f. (*Cf.* Engisch, *Einführung in das juristische Denken*, 1959, 35 f., 195.) Rudolf Henle expresses himself very clearly in his *Lehrbuch des bürgerlichen Rechts* (1, 1926) 29 f.: 'Das Verhältnis der vorausgesetzten Rechtstatsachen zur Rechtsfolge kann man unter dem Gesichtspunkt von Ursache und Wirkung auffassen. Zwar haben die Rechtstatsachen ihre rechtserzeugende Kraft nicht aus sich selbst, sondern durch Gesetz oder Gewohnheit: die rechtliche Kausalität ist von der obersten Gesamtheit, dem Staate, einge richtet worden.' The declarative theory of legal norms was also adopted by W. Sjögren in the essay cited above.

A modern version of the theory is presented by Larenz in his *Methodenlehre der Rechtswissenschaft* (1960). Since the legal norm generally prescribes a certain conduct in case of a certain state of affairs, it is usually defined as a conditional imperative: when F has occurred, A should observe behaviour B. But there is a difficulty with regard to norms according rights, modifying, limiting, or extinguishing rights, such as norms about the acquisition and loss of the right of property, the transfer of a claim by virtue of the law, the creation of a mortgage, etc. Windscheid's theory is unsatisfactory. The right of property has a positive content; it is not only a 'reflex' of the injunctions against all others. The positive element implies that the legal order acknowledges the will of the owner as determinant, within certain bounds, for the object. When a norm ordains that in a certain case the right of property to an object shall pass from A to B, the meaning of this is not only that the commands to abstain from interfering with A's use of the object are replaced by commands to abstain from interfering with B's use of it. The legal effect of the transaction is first and foremost a change in the division of property: what belonged to A now belongs to B. (See 152 f.) The author's idea is that the transference of the right is the primary thing; the obligations imposed by the legal norms refer to the existence of a right for this or that person.

Larenz concludes that the legal norm cannot be described as a hypothetical imperative. It says that the legal effect E is valid in every case where facts F are present. He rejects the view that there is a causal relationship between a state of affairs (*Tatbestand*) and a legal effect. The norm conditionally establishes a *connection of validity* between F and E, not one of causality. It is not an imperative but a *Geltungsanordnung*. What, then, is the meaning of 'validity'? It is explained as implying the inner, spiritual power of the law, by virtue of which a legal relationship or a legal norm is held by all concerned to be determinant or obligatory. ('"Geltung" bezeichnet hier soviel wie die "innere", geistige Macht des Rechts, vermöge derer ein Rechtsverhältnis oder eine Rechtsnorm von allen, die es " angeht ", als massgeblich oder verbindlich betrachtet wird,' 151.)

This is perhaps the best expression possible of the view of rights based on the living concept and the long tradition of legal and philosophical teaching. It is more refined than the theory of causality. But its weakness is apparent. The concept of ' validity ' that has been substituted for ' causality ' is defined in terms of psychological facts. The meaning of the statement that the right of property to an object has been transferred from A to B would be: it is now recognized by all concerned that the object belongs to B, not to A. The ' validity ' of an act of transference would then be dependent on the opinion of A and B (and perhaps others ' concerned '). If A (or somebody else ' concerned ') held the opinion that A is still the owner of the object (perhaps on the ground that he never had the intention of alienating it), no transfer would have taken place. No jurist would concur in this. It is not possible to interpret the usual juridical statements about the creation, transference, etc., of rights as statements about psychological facts. They refer to effects of operative facts in the supposed ' world of law '.

In the second edition of the *Methodenlehre* (1968) the same statements recur (181). But in the article ' Der Rechtssatz als Bestimmungssatz ' (*Festschrift für Karl Engisch zum 70. Geburtstag*, 1969) the psychological explanation of the *Geltung* is omitted. Instead Larenz refers to the phenomenological explanation offered by Adolf Reinach (*Die apriorischen Grundlagen des bürgerlichen Rechts,* 1913, reprinted 1953 under the title *Zur Phänomenologie des Rechts*).

Reinach distinguishes between imperatives and *Bestimmungssätze.* The latter do not directly refer to the behaviour of persons. They regulate rights, duties, and legal qualities. If a *Bestimmung* is issued in such a way as to be legally valid, its intended effect is realized through the *Bestimmung* itself. The first paragraph of the *Bürgerliches Gesetzbuch* says that the legal capacity of a human being commences with the completion of its birth. Consequently, when a human being has been born, it really has legal capacity. This effect does not belong to the sphere of facts but to the sphere of legal validity, which consists of supersensible but real states of things and relationships. The *Bestimmung* creates *die Existenz des als sein sollend Gesetzten.* (*Cf.* Larenz' article 156 ff.)

What Reinach says amounts to a very clear restatement, in a philosophical language, of the common view. It is particularly valuable because it brings out the difference between rules of conduct and rules of rights and duties and legal qualities. But I cannot see that it is anything more than a restatement. It seems impossible to understand how the supposed supersensible effects could be created by provisions in a text that has passed

certain formalities and is therefore called a law. The contention that the Ought 'exists' seems to be contradictory.
Henkel professes the same view as Larenz and Reinach (*Einführung in die Rechtsphilosophie* 67 f.)

The representation theory

In connection with replacing the imperative theory of law by the declaration theory, Zitelmann also launched a theory that is really a theory on the concept of a right. He felt called upon to do so because Siegmund Schlossmann had denied the reality of rights in a remarkable work. Schlossmann regarded rights and duties as products of the imagination. He conceded that it might be to some advantage to use these concepts as we habitually do. But he maintained that they lacked scientific character.[22]

Zitelmann was in accord with Schlossmann's thesis that rights and duties are not objective realities. They do not exist outside the human mind, he says. But he holds them to be a necessary form of thought. They are required in order to make it possible to survey and master the complex material of the law.

The argument is as follows: The law is a spiritual phenomenon created by men. It appears primarily in the form of norms. But we cannot cope with the law in this form. It would lead to an insupportable clumsiness if we always had to enumerate all relevant norms. How difficult it would then be, to understand the law, to retain its content, and to express oneself! It is necessary to mould the law in another form. This is done by analogy to our way of looking at the physical world. A part of the external world is conceived by us as a thing. In like manner the legal position of a person as governed by a set of interconnected norms is condensed into a right (*subjektives Recht*). We think of rights as coming into being, disappearing, and changing just as we think of things. These entities are created by us. The cumbersome expression that the norms a, b, c . . . are applicable with regard to a person (X) is avoided and we say instead that X has a right. The eminent practical and theoretical value of such compressions must be obvious

[22] *Der Vertrag* (1876) 247: 'Gibt es . . . in Wirklichkeit ein Etwas, welches wir als Recht bezeichnen, und wie ist dieses Etwas im Allgemeinen beschaffen? Es ist ausser allem Zweifel, dass wir mit "Recht" kein körperliches, greifbares Ding bezeichnen, dass jenes Etwas ein Abstractum, ein Gebilde unserer Vorstellung ist, und dass die übliche Redeweise, in welcher wir von Entstehung, Untergang, Übertragung, Verletzung, Einschränkung der Rechte sprechen, lediglich eine bildliche ist, welche im eigentlichen Sinne nur auf körperliche Dinge passt.'

to the most insensitive person. They are constantly employed in jurisprudence.[23]

So far legal rights and duties seem to be of an entirely subjective nature: images or representations that we use as vehicles of thought for practical purposes.[24] But then Zitelmann glides over to another view. If rights and duties were entirely subjective representations, it would evidently follow that everybody could make these representations according to his own needs and fancies. But this is not Zitelmann's meaning; and it would not be in accordance with the actual mode of thinking and speaking about rights and duties. The images are created by the *lawgiver*. In the world of law his will is supreme. Through his pronouncements he really establishes the causal connection between states of affairs (*Tatbestände*) and rights and duties.

> Sometimes Zitelmann speaks of legal duties, sometimes of rights. But this makes no difference. As 'legal effects', rights and duties are on the same level. Zitelmann says expressly of the legal effects (221):
> Es ist nicht wie bei der natürlichen Causalität unsere Erfahrung, welche uns auf dem Wege der Induktion das Bestehen dieses Causalzusammenhanges gelehrt hat, sondern der Zusammenhang zwischen beiden [facts and legal effects] ist gleichsam vor unseren Augen durch den Gesetzgeber selbst hergestellt worden: weil das Verpflichtetsein eine rein ideale Folge ist, so unterstand sie seiner Disposition, und so schuf er jene Verbindung.

So, after all, rights and duties are made objective. This is in accordance with the general outlook. In the common view rights and duties are certainly not subjective representations. They are somehow objective entities. Zitelmann hovers between this view and the critical view that rights and duties are images created by the mind.

Since Zitelmann, and often apparently independently of him, the representation theory has been reiterated. Few authors have combined it with the declarative theory of legal norms. The essential thing has been the idea that rights and duties are subjective representations used in order to master the infinite complexity of legal norms. They are held to be necessary for this purpose. It has often been repeated that we need short expressions for whole

[23] *Irrthum und Rechtsgeschäft* 201 ff. 212 ff.

[24] 'Es kommt [den von uns geschaffenen gedachten Objecten] keine Wahrheit an sich zu, sie sind subjective Zuthat von uns—aber eben die Zuthat, durch welche die Speise selbst erst geniessbar wird' (209).

groups of norms. The terms 'right' and 'duty' are believed to fill this function. Instead of talking of a situation where facts a, b, c, etc., are present and where norms x, y, z, etc., are therefore applicable, we say that A has a right and B a corresponding duty. Without this expedient it would be almost impossible to give brief and succinct accounts of legal relationships. This is the usual form of the representation theory.

A few examples of this view may be cited. In his *Allgemeine Staatslehre* (1914) George Jellinek says (162):
'Den Rechtsbegriffen als solchen entspricht keine Realität ausser uns. Ausser uns gibt es nur materielle Körper, aber keine Sachen im Rechtssinne, kein Eigentum, keinen Besitz. . . . Wenn wir von Rechten als Wesenheiten sprechen, so sind das nur Abkürzungen für einen höchst komkomplizierten Prozess.'
James Goldschmidt, *Der Prozess als Rechtslage* 225: 'Das Recht ist doch etwas Gedachtes. Entstehung, Untergang von Rechten, Rückwirkung usw. sind nur Bilder.'
A particularly good account is given by Leo Rosenberg in the work *Die Beweislast* (3. Aufl. 1953) 111: 'Das Dasein eines Rechts ist nicht Bestandteil der körperlichen Aussenwelt und nicht Gegenstand sinnlicher Wahrnehmung. Wenn wir von einem Rechte wie von einem lebenden Wesen sprechen, das entstehe, sich verändere, übertragen werde, untergehe usw., so fassen wir, um unserem Denken eine sinnliche Grundlage, unserer Vorstellungs und Ausdrucksweise Anschaulichkeit zu geben, die Wirkungen von Rechtssätzen zu einem Bilde zusammen. Wir personifizieren ein Produkt unseres Denkens und hauchen ihm Leben und Seele ein. . . . Diese oft beobachtete und besprochene Übertragung körperweltlicher Anschauungen auf die bloss in unserer Gedankenwelt existierenden Rechte mag zweckmässig, ja notwendig sein, weil anders wir die Fülle der Rechtsvorschriften in ihrem Ineinandergreifen, Ergänzen, Entgegenwirken usf. nicht beherrschen und ausdrücken könnten.'
According to Engisch, *Einführung in das juristische Denken* (1959) to talk of 'legal effects', especially the creation, etc. of rights, is only a metaphorical *façon de parler* (41 f.).
A prominent Swedish adherent of the representation theory is Östen Undén. He says that the legal concepts are 'artificial' concepts, freely constructed in order to facilitate the conception of the system of legal rules. Their value depends on their practicability only. A legal concept should, of course, be some 'unity of meaning'; but this requirement should not be too rigorously stressed. (*Festskrift tillägnad Axel Hägerström*, 1928, 171. My own translation.)

It seems obvious that we cannot, as things are, speak about legal matters without using the terms ' right ' and ' duty ' or ' obligation '. If we make an attempt to do without them, speaking only in terms of norms, the difficulties of expression really become insurmountable.

As an example, let us take the assertion that A is owner of a piece of land. How is this simple phrase to be replaced by statements about norms? Reflecting on this problem we soon detect that the right of property appears as an element in the *requisitum* of a great many norms. Because A is owner of this piece of land he can mortgage it, sell it, and dispose of it in other ways; because he is owner he has a lot of obligations; because he is owner he can claim damages in certain situations, etc. All these norms—which are indeed innumerable—have to be reformulated. The right of property as an element in their *requisitum* has to be replaced by a group of facts. The norms will then say that when facts a, b, c, etc., are present, A can dispose of the piece of land with legal effect, etc.

This is the first step in the replacement operation. But here we meet with a difficulty. How are the facts in question to be described? If we say that they consist of A having bought the piece of land or inherited it, an objection will immediately be made. Buying means acquiring the right of property through a contract; inheriting means acquiring it by virtue of being a relation of a deceased person. The ' facts ' that are substituted for the right of property are described by means of this very concept.

The replacement has therefore failed. To be successful, ' pure ' facts have to be substituted for the right of property. This is not easily done. A purchase cannot be described as uttering certain words or writing them down on paper; only if they are uttered under certain conditions is a purchase perfect according to the rules of law. To include all these facts in the description would be very, very difficult. In the case of inheritance, it would not be sufficient to refer to the consanguinity existing between the deceased and the heir. Physiological consanguinity is not the relevant fact because it cannot be proven. Instead we have to say that the heir was born of a woman who was married to the deceased. The concept of marriage therefore becomes involved; and to describe it without using legal terms would entail great difficulty.

If all these difficulties were overcome, an important obstacle would still remain. How are we to describe the norms applicable to the facts that have been substituted for the right of property?

They must be singled out from the mass of legal norms. But how can this be done without referring to them as the norms concerning the acquisition of the right of property? With unfailing persistency the concept of the right of property reappears as an element in the description supposed to replace the expression that A is the owner of a piece of land.

The proponents of the representation theory are right in their contention that the concepts, or at least the expressions, of right and duty are necessary elements in our legal language. But this is not enough to substantiate the theory. Having conceded that the expressions are unavoidable, the question remains as to what they signify and how their use is to be explained.

In the representation theory of rights two contentions are included: (i) that rights are images or representations, and (ii) that these representations are substituted for legal norms. But is this really so?

Regarding the first contention, it is never made clear of what the image or representation consists. In the representation of a tree, a centaur, or a ghost, we have a picture in our mind. What corresponds to this in the representation of a right? In the case of the right of property, we may represent to our mind the person of the owner, the object of the right, certain consequences that are supposed to follow from his having this right, and some norms that are relevant for those questions. But where is the right itself? No proponent of the representation theory seems to have made any attempt to give an answer to this question; and it is very difficult to see how it could be answered. We have the word 'right' in our mind; but we find no image or representation designated by this word.

The second contention implies that we first have the norms; these are the reality of the law. Then the 'representations' of rights are used for convenience to replace the norms; the metaphorical talk of rights is substituted for the cumbersome talk of norms.

In this argument the norms are evidently supposed to be given independently of the concept of a right. But then it is being overlooked that the norms are very largely norms about the creation, modification, transfer, and extinction of rights. Moreover, as was just pointed out, in many cases a person's possession of a right appears as an element in the *requisitum* of a norm. But under such circumstances the concept of a right cannot be a representation employed to facilitate the talk of legal situations as governed by legal norms; for it is the language of the legal norms themselves.

Negating the reality of rights

Surveying the history of the concept of a right we can discern how legal theory has long been moving towards negating the reality of rights. In the imperative theory, there was really no place for the concept of a right; in their endeavours to preserve it, the adherents of the theory were forced to employ unnatural constructions. The representation theory implies, without directly stating it, the non-reality of rights. But there are also theories in which the central contention is that rights are not realities but products of imagination.

The first philosopher to take this position was Bentham. But he was followed by many others who hit on similar ideas independently.

Bentham

'Real entities' in the field of law, Bentham holds, are commands by the sovereign on the one hand and acts by real persons on the other hand. Rights and duties are 'fictitious entities' which the law is said to create. The law is full of them. 'Not an operation does it [the law] ever perform, but it is considered as creating or in some manner or other disposing of these imaginary productions.' But all this is 'the mere work of the fancy; a kind of allegory'.

To know what the law implies in a given case, Bentham continues to say, we must know the persons, the acts, and the things, if such are in question; further, we must know if the acts are prohibited or permitted, commanded or left uncommanded. 'Knowing thus much, we shall have ideas to our words: not knowing it, we shall have none.' [25]

When speaking of rights and obligations as fictitious entities, Bentham undoubtedly had Pufendorf's theory in mind. Those entities are Pufendorf's *entia moralia.*[26] Bentham called them fictitious because they cannot be empirically ascertained. The ideas connected with the words 'right' and 'obligation', he says (58), are not names of 'real entities or of the sensible affections of determinable real entities'.

[25] *The Limits of Jurisprudence Defined* 57.

[26] In one place, at least, Bentham makes use of the expression 'fictitious moral entities' (58). Pufendorf was much studied in England. Welzel relates that six English editions of his principal work (*De jure naturae et gentium*) were published until 1763 (*Die Naturrechtslehre Samuel Pufendorfs,* 1958, 2).

But though the moral entities are the products of imagination, Bentham is not inclined to deny that there is some reason for them. Somewhat tentatively, he advances the opinion that they are practical, and perhaps necessary, for the purpose of expression (57). As was mentioned before, he says that 'the first masters of language compelled by necessity have thrown a kind of veil of mystery over the face of every science, and over none a thicker than over that of jurisprudence'. To remove this veil altogether 'will not be practicable perhaps not even expedient'. But to obtain 'a clear perception of the real state of things' we must learn 'upon every occasion how to pierce through it [the veil] at pleasure'. Finally: 'These phantastic denominations are a sort of paper currency: if we know how at any time to change them and get sterling in their room, it is well: if not, we are deceived, and instead of being masters of so much real knowledge as by the help of them we mean to supply ourselves with, we possess nothing but nonsense.'

Bentham seems to have had no interest in the legal ideas themselves. He contemptuously discards them as fictitious without attempting to analyse them and show what the ideas contained, what was imagined in speaking of rights and duties, or how the 'allegories' were conceived. This is an important restriction.

Instead of inquiring into the contents of the fictitious ideas, Bentham wants to 'pierce the veil of language'. He makes no attempt to define 'the names of fictitious entities' in the usual way *per genus et differentiam.* This method, he thinks, is applicable to real entities only. Instead he employs a method which he calls 'the method of paraphrases'. It is based on the assumption that our ideas 'are derived all of them from our senses'. The only way of rendering them clear and determinate is to trace each idea 'up to the sensible objects in which it originates' (317).

The paraphrasing consists in describing the sensory objects which have given rise to the fictitious ideas.[27] In the case of rights and duties the description runs as follows (316):

> An act is a real entity; a law is another. A duty or obligation is a fictitious entity conceived as resulting from the union of the two former. A law commanding or forbidding an act thereby

[27] In his *Theory of Fictions* Bentham describes the method of paraphrase in the following way: 'By the word *paraphrasis* may be designated that sort of exposition which may be afforded by transmuting into a proposition, having for its subject some real entity, a proposition which has not for its subject any other than a fictitious entity.' (C. K. Ogden, *Bentham's Theory of Fictions,* 1932, 86.)

> creates a duty or obligation. A right is another fictitious entity, resulting out of a duty.

To pierce the veil of language means keeping in mind that the real, sensory facts in the field of law are the commands of the sovereign and the persons and acts to which they refer. The rights and duties are some undefined (and perhaps indescribable) fictitious entities created in our imagination on the basis of our sensory perceptions. But Bentham also uses expressions implying that rights and duties are really created through the ' union ' of commands and acts. He seems not to have succeeded in freeing himself completely from the common view concerning rights and duties.

Austin never said that rights and duties are fictitious entities. On this point, therefore, he differs from Bentham. But he evidently had some qualms about the concept of a right. He says that an adequate definition of a right as signifying ' faculty ' cannot be rendered easily (*The Province of Jurisprudence* 287). Obviously he had the *facultas moralis* in mind. Especially interesting is the following observation (*Lectures on Jurisprudence* 396):

> It is difficult to indicate the import of the term ' right ' (considered as an abstract expression embracing *all* rights). For right (as thus considered) is so extremely abstract—is so extremely remote from the particulars which are comprised in its extension—that its meaning or import is, as it were, a shadow, and closely verges upon the confines of *no*-meaning.

One hundred years later, views on the concept of a right similar to Bentham's were enunciated by adherents of the representation theory in Germany. Examples have already been cited. An outspoken champion of this theory was Julius Binder. Rights, he said, are only representations of the mind (*Gedankendinge*) which lack objective reality. It is sheer nonsense when jurists speak of ' legal effects ' (*Rechtswirkungen*). In talking about the creation, alteration, and extinction of rights we are using an allegorical language which is highly improper if taken seriously.[28] Without being aware of it, Binder was using almost the same language as Bentham.

In trying to make clear how the concepts of rights and duties, despite their ' imaginary ' character, can be employed with such apparent success, the adherents of the representation theory went beyond Bentham. But their explanations were brief and tentative. As we have seen, they remained unsatisfactory.

[28] 6 *Archiv für Rechts- und Wirtschaftsphilosophie* (1912/13) 290; *Philosophie des Rechts* (1925) 904.

Petrazycki

The reality of rights was emphatically negated by Petrazycki. He derides the idea that the right of property consists of an 'invisible' bond between an individual and a thing, the essence of which is the complete and exclusive domination of the individual over the thing. It remains unexplained, he says, how the law is able to create these bonds; and the 'complete and exclusive dominion' is supposed to exist even if the owner has no real power at all over the thing; he takes the striking example of the proprietor of a menagerie finding himself in the embarrassing position of being held in the paws of his own tiger. Petrazycki also takes objection to the theory that the right of property consists of prohibitions addressed to all persons, except the owner himself, against encroachments on a particular thing. It is 'a strange logical sequel', he says, that if anyone buys a pin in a store, 'all other persons alive come to be in a peculiar relationship as regards the purchaser: prohibitions arise with regard to them, and the like'.

Rights and obligations, Petrazycki holds, are purely psychological phenomena: they exist only in the mind. He calls them 'phantasmata'. But they are of great psychological and social importance.

If I ascribe the right of property to somebody else, I consider myself bound to tolerate his use of the object and to abstain from using it without the permission of the owner. When I ascribe the right of property to myself, the converse situation obtains: I consider myself entitled to do what I like with the object and regard others as bound to tolerate my dispositions. These 'imperative-attributive experiences', as Petrazycki calls them, create a pressure on the minds of those who ascribe the right of property to themselves or to others, and this results in individual and mass conduct. The character of a thing as 'belonging' to an 'owner' is an 'impulsive projection of phantasm' comparable to 'attractiveness' or 'ugliness'.[29]

American Realism

The American Realists argued in a way similar to that of Bentham. They shared his empiricist basis. Like Bentham they

[29] *Law and Morality*: *Leon Petrazycki* (1955) 123 ff. Less clear is Petrazycki's theory of the possibility and usefulness, 'for the technical ends of practical jurisprudence' (126), of defining property from the projection point of view. For a discussion of Petrazycki's work I refer to my paper in 14 *Theoria* (1948) 168 ff.

recognized that our legal language is loaded with a heavy burden of metaphysical notions. They wanted to get rid of these in order to put legal science on a really scientific basis. It had to concern itself with facts, not with metaphysical entities.

In a language strangely reminiscent of Bentham (of whose corresponding utterances he could not be aware since they had not yet been published) Felix S. Cohen says:

> Our legal system is filled with supernatural concepts, that is to say, concepts which cannot be defined in terms of experience, and from which all sorts of empirical decisions are supposed to flow. Against these unverifiable concepts modern jurisprudence presents an ultimatum. Any word that cannot pay up in the currency of fact, upon demand, is to be declared bankrupt.[30]

In contradistinction to Bentham the American Realists did not embrace the will-theory of law. For them the reality of law consisted in legal decisions. Current legal concepts were a superstructure built on actual occurrences. In legal science they had to be removed. Since it was deemed necessary to employ such terms as 'right' and 'duty', they had to be redefined in terms of realities. This meant that they had to signify the likelihood of certain court actions in specific situations. The theory may therefore be called the predictive theory of legal concepts.

As is well known the Realist movement was inspired by some famous dicta by Mr. Justice Holmes:

> [We must not be content] with hollow forms of words merely because they have been used very often and have been repeated from one end of the Union to the other. We must think things not words, or at least we must constantly translate our words into the facts for which they stand, if we are to keep to the real and the true.[31]

With regard to the concepts of rights and duties Holmes says:

> The primary rights and duties with which jurisprudence busies itself . . . are nothing but prophecies. One of the many evil effects of the confusion between legal and moral ideas . . . is that theory is apt to get the cart before the horse, and to consider the right or the duty as something existing apart from and independent of the consequences of its breach, to which certain sanctions are added afterwards. But . . . a legal duty so called is nothing but a prediction that if a man does or

[30] 'Transcendental Nonsense and the Functional Approach', 35 *Columbia Law Review* (1935) 823. Also in Morris and Felix Cohen's *Readings in Jurisprudence and Legal Philosophy* (1953) 572. Similarly Llewellyn in 44 *Harvard Law Review* (1930–31) 1223 (= *Jurisprudence* 43).

[31] *Collected Legal Papers* (1920) 238.

> omits certain things he will be made to suffer in this or that way by judgment of the court; and so of a legal right.[32]

An empirical basis for legal science is thus to be gained by substituting statements concerning judicial action for statements about rights and duties in the traditional sense. As Cohen puts it:

> Holmes and Hohfeld have offered a logical basis for the redefinition of every legal definition in empirical terms, *i.e.* in terms of judicial decisions. The ghost-world of supernatural legal entities to whom our courts delegate the moral responsibility of deciding cases vanishes; in its place we see legal concepts as patterns of judicial behavior; behavior which affects human lives for better or worse and is therefore subject to moral criticism.

A redefinition of juridical concepts in the spirit of Holmes has been attempted by A. L. Corbin in his article 'Legal analysis and terminology' (29 *Yale Law Journal,* 1919). The general view is clearly set forth in this way (164):

> When we state that some particular legal relation exists we are impliedly asserting the existence of certain facts, and we are expressing our present mental concept of the societal consequences that will normally follow in the future. A statement that a legal relation exists between A and B is a *prediction* as to what society, acting through its courts or executive agents, will do or not do for one and against the other.[33]

In the Realist view rights in the traditional sense are chimeras. Nevertheless, Karl Llewellyn says, it would be flying in the face of fact 'to attempt their excision from the field of law'. Real rights, as distinguished from 'paper rights', are but convenient shorthand symbols for the actions of the courts. For a legal scientist a right exists '*to the extent that* a likelihood exists that *A* can induce a court to squeeze, out of *B*, *A*'s damages; more: *to the extent that* the likely collections will cover *A*'s damage'. In this aspect, Llewellyn adds, *substantive* rights (meaning rights in the traditional sense) 'simply disappear—on the descriptive level'. In 'the realm of description' there remain at the one end 'the facts, the groupings of conduct' which may be claimed to constitute an interest, and at the other the practices of courts in their effects upon the conduct and expectations of the laymen.[34]

[32] *Loc. cit.* 168 f.

[33] 29 *Yale Law Journal* (1919) 163 ff. *Cf.* 1 Corbin, *Contracts* 4: 'Legal relations are merely existing facts of life viewed in the light of a past uniformity of societal action, that enable us to predict similar action in the future with respect to two or more persons.'

[34] *Jurisprudence* (1962) 21 f. (from an article in *Columbia Law Review* 1930).

The position implies (i) that the current legal concepts are chimerical; (ii) that it is necessary to continue to employ the usual words for these concepts; (iii) that the sense of the words has to be redefined in terms of realities; and (iv) that this means in terms of court actions.[35]

Jaehner

In 1933, in an essay which is remarkable for its originality, Theodor Jaehner, a retired Prussian official, says that the concept of a right is the product of imagination. It is a psychological consequence of the activities of the courts. The measures consistently applied by them exert an influence on the behaviour of people; the owner of an object, for instance, is usually left in peace with it. The function of the courts is decisive for the general attitudes of society. But on the basis of these attitudes the idea is formed that there are ' rights ' and that they are decisive for the actions of the courts. In the popular view the relationship between the general attitudes and the actions of the courts is therefore turned upside down. A myth is engendered, from which legal science has to free itself.[36]

Scandinavian Realism

The term ' Scandinavian Realism ' applies to a group of authors who have all been strongly influenced by Axel Hägerström. In many ways their views are divergent; but for all of them Hägerström's critical examination of legal concepts has been of decisive importance.[37]

Hägerström had a consistently anti-metaphysical tendency. Much of his work was devoted to sorting out metaphysical concepts (as being pseudo-concepts) from scientific thinking. But he did not stop at rejecting them. He also had a keen interest in metaphysical ideas as psychological facts. This is apparent not least in his discussion of the concept of a right.

With regard to this concept he raised a number of questions. First he took up the ' living ' concept as found in common parlance and in the language of jurisprudence. He asked whether the word,

[35] Some comments on the views of the American Realists are offered in my article ' Legal Language and Reality ' in the *Essays in Jurisprudence in Honor of Roscoe Pound* (1962) 158 ff.

[36] Theodor Jaehner, *Der Mythos vom Recht und seine empirischen Grundlagen* (1933) 2,203.

[37] In 13 *Natural Law Forum* (1968) Nils Kr. Sundby has published an article with the title ' Legal Right in Scandinavian Analyses '. It covers only the discussion from the year 1945 onwards. The analysis of Hägerström and Lundstedt, from which this discussion started, is only very briefly referred to.

as actually employed, could denote empirical facts. The attempts that have been made to discover such facts were reviewed and found unsuccessful. Every conceivable possibility of identifying a right with empirical facts was examined with negative result. The upshot was that we had here to deal with an unrealistic idea:

> The factual basis which we are seeking cannot be found, then, either in *protection guaranteed* or *commands issued* by an external authority. But, on the other hand, we cannot find any other fact of which it could be said that it corresponds to our idea of a right of property or a rightful claim. This insuperable difficulty in finding the facts which correspond to our ideas of such rights forces us to suppose that there are no such facts and that we are here concerned with ideas which have nothing to do with reality.[38]

Next came the question of fixing the content of the idea of a right. After thorough analysis, Hägerström came to the conclusion that this is the idea of a supernatural power with regard to things and persons. He searched for a psychological explanation of the idea and found it in the feeling of strength and power associated with the conviction of possessing a right. The following statement is a characteristic expression of his view (5 f.):

> It seems . . . that we mean, both by rights of property and rightful claims, certain forces, which exist quite apart from our natural powers; forces which belong to another world than that of nature, and which legislation or other forms of law-giving merely liberate. The authority of the state merely lends its help to carry these forces, so far as may be, over into reality. But they exist before such help is given. So we can understand why one fights better if one believes that one has right on one's side. We feel that here there are mysterious forces in the background from which we can derive support. Modern jurisprudence, under the sway of the universal demand which is now made upon science, seeks to discover facts corresponding to these supposed mysterious forces, and it lands in hopeless difficulties because there are no such facts.

Hägerström also investigated the historical roots of the idea of a right. To this purpose he made extensive studies of Greek and Roman law. The results regarding Roman law were published in the great work *Der römische Obligationsbegriff* (I, 1927, II: 1, 1941). Hägerström wants to show that the law proper of the Roman citizens, the *ius civile,* was conceived as a system of rules for acquiring and exercising supernatural powers. The ancient legal

[38] *Inquiries into the Nature of Law and Morals* (1953) 4 (from the introduction to *Der römische Obligationsbegriff*).

acts, such as the *mancipatio,* the *stipulatio,* etc., were magical acts. He also studied the transformation that the Roman ideas underwent in classical natural law doctrine.[39]

Hägerström's friend, Vilhelm Lundstedt, followed up his criticism of juridical concepts. Lundstedt insisted that rights and duties are chimeras. He repeatedly expresses himself to the effect that they are imaginary entities interposed between legally relevant facts (operative facts), as for instance a contract, and the legal consequences attached to them, as the enforced paying of damages for breach of contract. He fought for the elimination of these 'superstitious phantasms' from jurisprudence; this was necessary in order to give jurisprudence a scientific character:

> The chimera, against which we have above all to fight, consists in interposing this imaginary something, a right, between the facts and the possible legal consequences. Nobody has ever been able to give real grounds for the existence of this something.[40]

The quotation sums up Lundstedt's view on the fundamental legal concepts. He drew the conclusion that all talk of rights and duties should be banished from jurisprudence, at least from scientific writings. The discussion ought to be concerned with relevant facts and actual legal consequences only.

Nevertheless, Lundstedt found it difficult to avoid speaking of rights and duties. He tried to explain his use of language, which seemed to be at variance with his theory. In his Swedish works he sometimes said that a right in a realistic sense could be nothing but a favourable position which ensues for a person by virtue of the psychological pressure exerted on other people through the maintenance of the legal machinery; a duty in a realistic sense was the corresponding situation of constraint. He was of course aware that these factual positions are not what we mean by rights and duties; in one place he expressly says that he radically twists the language in using the terms 'right' and 'duty' to denote such factual situations.[41] In his last work he went further and contended that these terms ought to be altogether avoided in scientific discourse:

> The expressions legal rights, duties, obligations, relationships, claims and demands, properly speaking, should not be used, not even as terms or labels [for certain realities]. But I think it will be impossible in the common practice of law (be it outside

[39] In the essay *Recht, Pflicht und bindende Kraft des Vertrages.*
[40] 1 *Die Unwissenschaftlichkeit der Rechtswissenschaft* (1932) 268, *cf.* 74.
[41] *Grundlinjer i skadeståndsrätten* (1944) 523.

or before the courts of law) to eradicate them. If legal writers use such a term and if they are afraid thereby to be misunderstood they may place the term in question between quotation marks.[42]

In the Scandinavian countries Hägerström's and Lundstedt's criticism of the legal concepts provoked much discussion during the nineteen-twenties and -thirties. Everybody was anxious to refute the charge of superstition. Lundstedt's chief opponent during that period was his colleague in the law faculty of Uppsala, Östen Undén. Undén conceded that the criticism had some foundation in so far as the concept of a right was used as a 'substance' concept (meaning, if I understand him correctly, that the word was used as denoting an entity of some sort). Traces of this usage could be found in jurisprudential literature. But Undén suggested that modern writers on law generally had a more rational approach in that they largely employed the concept of a right as a 'functional' concept freely constructed for the purpose of facilitating the description of legal rules and legal situations. As already mentioned, his view was a variety of the representation theory.

Lundstedt's criticism of jurisprudence and its concepts made a deep impression on many jurists of a younger generation. They wanted, of course, to escape criticism; strictly scientific methods were to be employed. But Lundstedt's proposal to banish the concept of a right, and even the word 'right', from jurisprudence did not meet with approval. The Hägerström-Lundstedt analysis itself was not much discussed. Instead interest was focused on the question of how the indispensable concept of a right could and should be used in a realistic, non-metaphysical way.[43]

Among the authors pursuing this line of thought, Alf Ross took a prominent place with his article 'Tû-tû'.[44] Ross apparently accepts Hägerström's analysis of the concept of a right. (There is no independent argument on this point.) He holds that current terminology is 'associated for us with more or less indefinite ideas that a right is a power of an incorporeal nature'; he thinks that

[42] *Legal Thinking Revised* (1956) 17.

[43] This is the background of the discussion related by Sundby in the article mentioned above in footnote 37.

[44] The article was first published in Danish in the *Festskrift til Professor Henry Ussing* (1951). An abbreviated English version appeared in 70 *Harvard Law Review* (1956/57) 812 ff. It was re-published in 5 *Scandinavian Studies in Law* (1961). *On Law and Justice,* § 35, contains a summary of the article. There is another summary in *Svensk Juristtidning* (*Swedish Law Journal*) 1953. Here the article in the *Harvard Law Review* is cited when no other source is mentioned.

these ideas ' bear a considerable structural resemblance to magic thought ' (818). Ross expressly endorses Lundstedt's contention that ' the only demonstrable reality in the so-called situations of rights consists in the function of the machinery of the law ' (817 footnote). In words reminiscent of Lundstedt's, Ross emphasizes that nothing intervenes between the conditioning facts and the legal consequences (the acts of judges and other state organs) that are to follow upon them. The supersensible power supposedly ' created ' by ' juristic facts ' is purely imaginary. It is nonsense, for instance, to say that between the purchase of an object and access to recovery ' something was created that could be designated as ownership ' (820 f.).

Ross concludes that words like ' right ' and ' ownership ' denote nothing. They are ' meaningless words ', ' words without semantic reference '. Nevertheless he holds that *statements about rights,* as made in current legal language (the language used in legislation and the administration of justice), may very well be interpreted in such a way that they get a realistic content.[45] His main purpose is to show how this is done.

Lundstedt's position with regard to the question how the terms ' right ', ' duty ', and other legal expressions should be used seems to me untenable. I can see no need to avoid these terms or to give them a new meaning and ' twist the language '. Even if it were feasible (from a practical point of view) to do so, nothing would be gained.

Obviously the terms ' right ', ' duty ', etc. have important functions in existing legal systems. If the critical analysis of the concepts ostensibly expressed by these words is in the main correct, the practical conclusion should not be to throw the terms overboard but to study their functions. In so far as Ross sets out to do so, he is, I believe, on the right track. But his brief argument tells us nothing about the vast and complicated problem of the role of the basic terms in a legal system.

It is necessary to substantiate this proposition at some length. To begin with a few preliminary remarks are required.

First, an observation has to be made on the identification of ' meaninglessness ' and ' lack of semantic reference ' (which came about because Ross adopted a certain definition of the concept of meaning). Ross actually talks about the meaning of words like ' right ' in a manner which is not consistent with

[45] Explicitly so in the article in the *Svensk Juristtidning* 540.

the contention that such words are meaningless. (*Cf.* A. W. B. Simpson, 'The Analysis of Legal Concepts' in 80 *Law Quarterly Review,* 1964, 537.) In a later article Ross says that his original mode of expression was 'unsuitable'. He thinks it more correct to say that the word 'right' does not 'stand for anything' in the sense 'that its meaning can be defined by the substitution method'. (5 *Scandinavian Studies in Law,* 1961, 124.)

Secondly, it must be kept in mind that the explanation refers to the terms 'right', 'ownership', etc., as used in 'practical legal language', *i.e.,* in legislation and the administration of justice. (Danish article 474, 478.)

Thirdly, a certain concept of 'legal rules', defined by Ross in another context, is presupposed. The 'real content' of a rule of law, according to Ross, is a directive to the judge concerning the use of force; the instructions for the private citizens are 'derived and figurative' legal rules deduced from the real norms. 'A national law system is an integrated body of rules, determining the conditions under which physical force shall be exercised against a person'. (*On Law and Justice* 33 f.)

Ross gives different answers to the question how the word 'right', though signifying nothing, can be used (i) in expressing rules of law (particularly legislative rules) and (ii) in assertions concerning the existence of rights.

(i) In expressing legal rules the word 'right' is used 'solely as a tool of presentation' (820). The 'real rules', we must remember, are rules directing the judge to apply force in certain circumstances. In the case of ownership a great many conditioning facts (a purchase, a gift, etc.) entail similar directives to the judge (to give judgment for recovery, for damages, etc.). But it would be very unwieldy to express the rules by directly connecting the conditioning facts with the directives to the judge. Instead the empty word 'right' is inserted between the conditioning facts and these directives. In one series of rules the facts that 'create ownership' are expressed and in another series the 'legal consequences' that 'ownership' entails. This is 'a simple example of reduction by reason to systematic order'. To accomplish it is ultimately the task of legal science; but it has largely been anticipated by prescientific thought (821).

It is, of course, an obvious fact that the rules of private (civil) law are, on the whole, expressed as rules about rights and duties. It is also obvious that the legal system would be extremely complicated if legislative rules were expressed in terms of what Ross calls 'real rules' (supposing this could be done at all). But these circumstances do not warrant the conclusion that the word 'right' is used in legislation 'as a tool of presentation', *i.e.,* as a means of presenting, in a simplified way, the rules directing the use of force.

The argument implies that the rules of private law are *primarily* conceived as rules about the use of state force and that they are then expressed in a more simple and practical way by inserting the word 'right'. There is no historical foundation for this assumption. The rules of the *code civil* or the *Bürgerliches Gesetzbuch,* for instance, were certainly not conceived in this way. No more can it be said that lawgivers of our own time proceed according to the method suggested by Ross.

According to the general view, on which current legal language is based, the rules of private law are conceived as rules regulating people's rights and duties. This is what is called 'substantive law'. People are supposed to get, in the ordinary course of things, that to which they have a right and to fulfil their duties. Procedural law, which is a sort of 'adjective' law, regulates the settlement of disputes about rights and duties. The judge is supposed to give judgment for the plaintiff when, and only when, he is satisfied that the plaintiff really has the right which he pretends to have.

The structure of the system of private law, conceived as a system of rules about rights and duties, entails many difficult problems. (*Cf.* below 199 ff.) Among other things the role of such words as 'right' and 'duty' has to be explained in a realistic way. But this cannot be done by saying that the words are tools for presenting, in a simplified manner, underlying rules about the use of force. Ross himself presupposes indeed that these words have another function. As Simpson points out (552) Ross is forced to use the concept of ownership already to identify the rules that are said to be expressed in a simple way by interposing the word 'ownership'. He must do so. We cannot take a single step in describing private law without making use of the words 'right' and 'duty'.

(ii) Though the word 'right' or 'ownership' stands for nothing, the *whole sentence* that somebody possesses the right of ownership to an object has semantic reference to a complex actual situation, Ross contends. In the book *On Law and Justice* he says (174):

'The statement that A owns a certain object refers not only to the purely factual circumstance that A has either purchased the object, inherited it, acquired a prescriptive right to it, and so on; but also to the legal circumstance that, according to the law in force, these happenings entail specific legal consequences and therefore are said to "create ownership".'

In order to explain what it means that A is the owner of an object Ross here makes use of the concept of ownership. For this concept is included in the concepts of purchase and inheritance as well as in 'acquiring a prescriptive right'. To purchase a thing is to acquire the right of ownership to it.

Therefore, what Ross says is that A possesses the right of ownership to an object when he has acquired the right of ownership to this object.

The legal consequences entailed by the acquisition of property are described as being that A 'can obtain recovery, claim damages, etc.' (822). But what does it mean that I 'can' obtain recovery if I have lost something belonging to me? Suppose a thief snatches my wallet from my pocket and carries it away in a crowd. In what sense 'can' I obtain recovery? My chances of ever seeing the wallet again are very slender indeed if the thief is not immediately arrested by the police.

Ross does not speak of what I actually can obtain. He talks of what I have a *right* to: the right to obtain recovery, etc. So the concept of a right is introduced in this connection too. That A possesses the right of ownership to an object refers to the 'actual situation' that he has acquired the right of ownership to it and therefore has some rights concerning recovery, etc., which follow from the right of ownership.

The only argument adduced by Ross to show that the word 'right' has no semantic reference was the contention that nothing is created as the result of A and B exchanging a few sentences 'legally interpreted as a contract of purchase' (821). This argument in itself is insufficient. To be sure, no tangible, immediate effects are brought about through the exchange of words. But nothing of the sort is intended when jurists say that rights and duties are created by the contract. The meaning is that the relations between the parties (perhaps their relations to other people also) undergo a change; and this change is characterized by saying that the parties have acquired certain rights and assumed certain duties. Ross, too, holds this view. Though he maintains that nothing is created by the contract, he nevertheless assumes that the purchase gives rise to certain rights for the buyer (the right of recovery, of obtaining damages, etc.).

Ross started by accepting the analysis purporting to show that the creation of rights by contracts and other 'operative facts' cannot be identified with any real consequences of a contract. This is why he says that 'nothing is created' by the contract. Then the initial argument seems to have been forgotten and it is taken for granted that rights in the usual sense of the word are acquired by the buyer.

Ross is not aware of the fact that he simply reverts to the standpoint which he begins by refuting. The discussion leads nowhere. This is quite natural because the essential argument contains two propositions that cannot be reconciled. As we have seen, Ross maintains: (i) that the word 'right', contrary to what is generally taken for granted, stands for nothing, has no semantic reference, and (ii) that nevertheless whole sentences concerning people having rights refer to actual situations. But if the word 'right' signifies nothing, the statement that A possesses the right of ownership to a thing cannot refer to any real situation. A final remark: The assertion that the word 'right' has no semantic reference cannot be substantiated by pondering over the isolated word alone. If the assertion is true, this can only be demonstrated through an analysis of *sentences* about rights and duties as they occur in legal language and common parlance. Since Ross affirms that such sentences have semantic reference to actual situations, he makes it impossible for himself to give any reason at all for the first and fundamental assertion: that the word 'right', as used in legal language, has no semantic reference.

Conclusion

The survey is far from complete.[46] But it covers the principal attempts to solve the riddle of the concept of a right; and it shows the direction in which legal theory has been moving.

From the beginning the task was to fit a presupposed concept into the scientific view of the world. The teachers of natural law apparently had no feeling of any special difficulty on this point. They explained the concept of a right by means of the idea of original freedom which was fundamental for them. All human rights derived from the voluntary transference of parts of this original freedom. Through a declaration of will, a moral power over a certain action was alienated by the individual and conferred on somebody else. The recipient became possessed of the moral power over this action. He could command its performance with the consequence that a duty was imposed on the addressee. It became morally necessary for him to perform the action; in his innermost mind he was compelled to do so. Actually, he could disobey; but in that case he exposed himself to coercion against which there was no moral obstacle.

This theory did not conflict with the general scientific view of the time. The situation changed when the basis of the natural law doctrine began to crumble under the impact of critical philosophical reasoning. Grave difficulties then began to appear.

From the point of view of legal positivism rights had to be derived from the sole real law, the commands of the lawgiving authority. But this was not easily done. It is, indeed, impossible to explain how rights in the traditional sense can be generated by

[46] Among authors negating the realities of right Duguit, Max Weber, and others could also be cited.

the commands of the lawgiver. Already Bentham perceived that there was no room for the concept of a right as an ideal power within the imperative theory. The *Willensmacht* theorists tried to fit the ideal power into the legal system by letting the state delegate its power of command to the individual; in this way he became endowed with a power to command, the effect of the command being the imposition of a duty. This is the natural law concept modified in order to conform to the imperative theory. The theory that a right is a legally protected interest entailed a further modification of the same basic view.

Gradually legal theory receded more and more from the position of natural law doctrine. In the representation theory the ideal power faded away, though it was still spoken of in the traditional form of language; the theory was an attempt to explain how this could be done while upholding the principles of strict scientific thinking. The predictive theory, though more radical, aimed at the same goal.

These two theories implied the negation of the reality of rights. Several authors with other theories have overtly proclaimed this conclusion, having reached it by different paths.

The reality of rights can be negated in two different senses. (i) It can be said that the *facultas moralis* of natural law doctrine or the *Willensmacht* of the imperative theory does not exist. This language was consistently used by Lundstedt. It is like saying that centaurs or ghosts do not exist. (ii) The meaning can also be that the word right, as commonly employed, does not signify anything at all; it does not even refer to something existing in imagination only, as the centaurs. The word lacks semantic reference in this sense.

This latter position seems to be the correct one. Obviously the word right is not used to denote any objects. If the word has got semantic reference, it can only refer to some sort of relationship between persons, or between persons and things. But it is quite evident that the supposed relationships called rights are not actual relationships. The actual situation in the world cuts across the system of rights. If the word right signifies a relationship, this will be a relationship of a supersensible kind. But what is such a relationship? It can only be negatively defined as a relationship not belonging to the sensible world, the empirical world in which we live. It is a relationship, though no actual relationship.

The mental content behind our talk of rights seems to be as

follows: We have *a presentation of the object of a right*—usually a physical object or the action of a person. To this we have a right, as we say. The word ' right ' stands for nothing, it designates nothing. But the word itself is *visually or auditively passed on to the mind*. These two presentations—the word and the object—make up the idea of a right.

We have, however, the illusion that the word ' right ' signifies a power over the object, though a power which we can never grasp. The illusion stems from the emotional background. Under certain circumstances, especially in situations of conflict, the idea of possessing a right gives rise to a feeling of strength. When I am convinced of having a right, I am in some way more powerful than my opponent, even if he be actually stronger. My power is not an actual power but a ' must-be power '. This means that the feeling of strength is ' objectivated '. It produces a floating idea that I possess some kind of power which is independent of, and elevated above, the actual power-situation. So the word ' right ' seems to signify an unseizable power. It is used in this sense even when no emotions are actually engaged.

Like many others we have reached the conclusion that the word ' right ', as used in jurisprudence as well as in common discourse, lacks semantic reference. It does not even denote something existing in imagination only.

But this conclusion is bound to meet with much opposition. People generally find it impossible to admit that rights are not realities. The following objection is therefore to be expected.

Whatever arguments are adduced to show that the word ' right ' denotes nothing they must contain some fault. It seems incontestable that rights somehow are a basic element in the existing legal order. Indeed, the proposition that there is a law without rights and duties seems to be contradictory since it belongs to the very essence of the law that it regulates people's rights and duties. Is it not therefore to ' fly in the face of fact ' to deny the reality of rights? But if this is so, we have to start anew the search for a definition of the concept of a right in terms of hard facts.

This search would, however, lead to the same conclusion. It would be found impossible to identify the right with any factual situation. It is essential for the meaning of the word ' right ', as we use it, that it does not signify a situation which actually obtains.

But the subjective *ideas of rights* are facts. They cannot be 'excised' from the law in the sense of law as fact. What is to be done is to study these ideas as elements in a working legal system. This will be considered next.

Chapter 7

THE IDEA OF A RIGHT IN A WORKING LEGAL SYSTEM

When rights are taken to be objective entities, they are usually divided into legal and natural. Legal rights are defined as rights conferred by positive law.[1] Natural rights are not so grounded. They are held to exist independently of positive law. Their basis is supposed to be the law of nature; or they are immediately derived from the absolute value of human personality.

Correspondingly, ideas of rights can be divided into ideas of legal rights and ideas of natural rights. The latter are certainly not without bearing on the legal system. But for our subject the ideas of legal rights are much more important. Since some limitations are necessary, the discussion will be confined to ideas of legal rights.

These ideas may be studied in different connections. They are obviously of great importance in legislation and in the administration of justice. But these official functions take place in a community where some general, if more or less vague, ideas of legal rights and duties are current. Therefore it is advisable to reflect on the role of such ideas in the general commerce of men before investigating their use in legislation and the administration of justice.

Ideas of Rights in General Commerce

The ideas of our own rights and of the rights of others normally act as guides for our behaviour. It is natural for us to regulate our activities so that we may make use of, and guard, our own rights and respect the rights of other people. But it is also evident that we employ the word 'right' in order to convey information. In many ways knowledge seems to be imparted through statements referring to a person's rights of property, his monetary claims, etc.

Two different functions of the idea of a right in general commerce can therefore be discerned. They may conveniently be called the directive and the informative function.

[1] Austin, *The Province of Jurisprudence* 159: 'Rights conferred by positive law, or rights existing through duties imposed by positive law, may be styled, emphatically, *legal*.'

The directive function

From early childhood we have been taught to distinguish between what belongs to us and what belongs to others. To learn this is most important. I may do what I like with my own things; but I am bound to run into trouble if I take things belonging to others or use them without permission.

Most things I see about me are not 'mine'. They belong to others. The criterion for a thing's being mine is that I have 'acquired' it in some way or other: usually by having received it as a gift or having bought it with my money. My rights are identified through their origin.

I feel sure of the existence of my rights when I know how I have got them; and I feel equally sure of the consequences of my having the right to an object: I may use it according to my own pleasure, and others have to leave it alone.

This sequence of ideas is firmly established at a very early age. Certain transactions, such as a giving or a purchase, are held to give rise to a right for me over a thing. From the existence of the right, certain consequences are held to follow with regard to correct behaviour: my freedom to use the object and the prohibition for others to use it without my permission.

The child is well acquainted with the origin of its supposed rights over things and with the effects of those rights. It would be at a loss if asked to describe what a right itself is. The question would not be understood. But this is irrelevant from the point of view of behaviour. The attitude of the child will be largely determined by the connection between ideas of having acquired things in the proper way, of therefore possessing them as its own, and of the consequences of ownership. The child will use the object freely and defend it against others as best it can using words like: 'It's my ball' in order to impress its playmates; eventually the child may appeal to grown-ups for help because somebody has taken away its belongings. Conversely, with regard to objects not identified as the child's own there will be a connection between the ideas: not mine—not take it. Even if deviations are fairly common, the behaviour of the child with regard to objects within its range of activity will, on the whole, be regulated by these two sets of inter-connected ideas.

In order for this effect to take place, is it required that the word 'right' and its equivalents (being 'mine' etc.) have any semantic reference? Obviously not. It is sufficient that the words 'this is mine ' or something of the kind are connected on the one hand with the idea of having acquired the object in a proper way and, on the other hand, with sentences saying that only I myself may meddle with it but nobody else. The words ' it is mine ' will serve as a permissive sign for the child itself, while the words ' not mine ' or something to the same effect will act as a prohibitive sign with respect to objects not included within the sphere of ' mine '.

No exact demarcation line separates the adult world from that of the children. The principles for distinguishing ' my ' property from the property of others are similar among adults though they are infinitely more exact and complicated. The consequences for correct behaviour are also similar.

Suppose I have bought a piece of land from a person identifying himself as owner to it by showing a ' title '. I am then convinced of being the owner myself now, that is, of having the right of property to the land. What the right ' is ', what semantic reference the word has got, will seem to be a strange and perhaps incomprehensible question. But this will not bother me at all. I am only interested in the familiar consequences of ' being owner '. I know that I can build a house on the plot if there are no building regulations to the contrary, I can cultivate the garden, put up a fence around it, and so on. If any problems arise as to what I may do, I can consult a lawyer for advice. With regard to others, I have firm-set ideas. Other people must not in any way interfere with my use of the ground or the house. Relying on my right I ward off intruders in good conscience. Phrases like ' I am the owner ', ' this is not your property ', and others, are employed as psychological weapons in my struggle to be left in undisturbed possession. But I am careful not to extend my activities as proprietor to land beyond the confines of my own lot. That other land does not belong to me, it is not ' mine '. Therefore I abstain from using it except in so far as it is allowed for everybody to walk on it, etc.

The chain of ideas is basically the same as that in the children. The sphere of ' mine ' is supposed to be defined by means of certain recognized modes of acquisition. To the idea that this is ' mine ' and ' not mine ' certain ' consequential ' ideas are attached. Our behaviour with regard to handling things is largely conditioned by these ideas.

The consequential ideas will not, of course, be evoked by every use of the word ' ownership ' or ' right of property '. If somebody asserts without reason that he is the owner of an object and the arbitrariness of his pretensions is apparent, he will meet resistance and resentment. Only if the right of property is believed to be correctly ascribed to somebody, will the consequential ideas be called forth. ' Correctness ' means ' according to the law '. The statement that A is the owner of an object is held to be correct when A has ' acquired ' it in a lawful way, which means that he has a ' legal title ' to it, as a purchase from a previous owner.

The ideas about acquisition of property and the consequences of one's own and other people's right of property are instilled into the minds of the young to prepare them for adult life. It is essential for their adaptation to society that the chain of ideas between acquisition, right, and proper behaviour is firmly established. Nobody can live as a recognized member of his community if these associations are wholly lacking or without influence on his conduct; in all probability he would be treated as insane.

For every human society some distribution of property (in the sense of actual command over things) is a necessity. To achieve it the general behaviour among the population must be effectively regulated by rules. But abstract rules are not enough, especially as they have become extremely complicated. For the public, signs that can be easily understood are required. They need not always be of a material kind. Words and phrases can also be used as signs. This is what happens in adult life as well as in the world of children. Expressions like ' right of property ', ' ownership ', ' mine ', ' not mine ', and the like are signs with consequential ideas attached to them. Everybody has a more or less clearly defined sphere of things identified as being ' his ' because he has acquired them in some approved way. These he might use for his own purposes. The use of other objects is forbidden for him unless there is some special reason for an exception (such as being employed by the owner).

In order to illustrate the sign function of the word ' right ' (and connected words) we may imagine that the following situation obtains in a primitive community.

There are no words corresponding to our ' right ', ' ownership ', or ' property '. But the land is not indiscriminately used by all the members of the community. It has been cut up in a number of pieces enclosed with fences. On each piece a family is living. Every family has got a mark which is put up along the fences. The children are taught that we, in our family, cultivate the ground set apart by the fence with this special mark. It is strictly forbidden to pick bananas on trees beyond that fence. To do so is dishonourable and will expose you to the wrath of the neighbours. But on their part they must keep away from the ground within the fence. To delete or alter the marks of others will be a serious crime.

Suppose these ideas are firmly established. In the minds of the people there will then be fixed associations between the fences, with their markings on the one hand, and consequential ideas concerning correct behaviour on the other hand. The result will be that every family lives peacefully within its fence.

How the land was originally divided in pieces will not be known. The families have been living in this way since time immemorial. But it may happen that a man decides to move his family to another island, where there is vacant land of a promising nature. He will then make an agreement with a neighbour to the effect that he will take his markings away and leave his lot in exchange for a number of cowrie shells. Thereafter, the neighbour pulls down the fence between the two lots and puts up his own marks along his new boundaries. With his family he will now cultivate the enlarged piece of land; and the neighbours will silently acquiesce in his so doing.

The marks will not be psychologically effective if put up in a haphazard way. People have only been taught to respect marks that have stood of old as they are standing now and marks which have been put up according to agreement.

In a more sophisticated community there are also boundary marks. But the ideas of correct behaviour are not directly and exclusively attached to them. Instead, these ideas are associated with words and phrases like 'this is mine' or 'not mine'. The idea of the right of property has been formed. The right is regarded as the essential thing. The boundary marks are of secondary importance. They are supposed to refer to the right of property; and they may be replaced by lines drawn on a map by a competent authority. The actual point of reference for the consequential ideas will be the word 'right' and its equivalents, as used according to certain rules. A regulated use of language has taken the place of physical marks for providing the signs with which the ideas concerning proper behaviour are connected.

> The example from a primitive society is, of course, purely imaginary. It has been constructed for an illustrative purpose only. It is not an expression of my view on the real situation in such societies. The taboo signs used to mark the boundary lines evidently have magical significance. The situation is therefore much more complicated than in the example.

Corresponding reasoning can be applied to other rights. Suppose

I pretend to have a monetary claim against another person. The reason for this is that he has borrowed some money from me on the promise of paying it back on June 1st, 19—. What is present in my mind is the representation of a certain action of the debtor—the paying of a sum of money on the day in question—in connection with the words that 'I have a right' to claim the performance of this action. I cannot describe what the right is; I can only indicate its 'object', the action by the debtor. When asked what the right is I will probably repeat that I have the right to get payment because the other man has borrowed money from me and promised to pay it back. He is under an obligation to pay the debt. If he is a normal and conscientious person, he will share the same idea. He will feel himself obligated to pay me back what he borrowed from me; and this opinion will influence his behaviour.

We find here a sequence of ideas similiar to that described in the case of ownership. A right is supposed to have been created through an agreement. The right itself is unseizable. But there is a consequential idea attached to the idea of my having a certain right: the idea that the borrowing party has assumed an obligation which he must fulfil.

As in the case of ownership the word 'right' need not have any semantic reference in order to exert a directive function. When used according to certain legal rules it acts as an imperative sign for the debtor: he shall or must pay. The idea of his being obligated to pay is firmly connected with the idea of the lender's right. This will entail psychological pressure on him.

The psychological effect of the chain of ideas is partly dependent on knowing that the power of the state is standing behind the possessor of a right. He can normally apply to the courts for help to get what is supposed to be his due. In addition there are the penal sanctions for larceny, etc.

In the first place, however, the ideas of having rights and duties and the consequential ideas attached to them are immediately decisive. We regard it as self-evident that we respect the rights of others and fulfil our legal obligations. The threat of sanctions looms in the background only. It would become inefficient if people paid regard to the supposed rights of others only out of fear of punishment, and if they implemented their legal obligations only under the immediate threat of sanctions. If such attitudes were general, chaos would ensue and the machinery of justice could not operate.

The directive function of the ideas of rights and duties on the one hand and the working of the machinery of justice on the other are mutually interdependent. These ideas would lose their sway over human minds if there were no real power behind the rights and duties. But the power of the state can be exerted through courts and executive organs on a relatively small scale only. The system presupposes that people's behaviour is largely determined by general ideas of rights and obligations so that the authorities have only to deal with marginal cases.

This may sound over-optimistic in view of the increasing rate of crime and the frequency of defaults on debt. But it still holds. The division of property would obviously break down without the engrained habit of respecting what belongs to others. The area where the threat of legal action presents itself most immediately to people's minds is probably that of debt relations.

Our original stock of ideas concerning the acquisition of rights and the consequences of rights was implanted at a very early age. Subsequently it was enlarged through the teachings we receive and the experiences we have as we proceed through life. We learn a lot more about the modes of acquiring rights; and we are taught that they are regulated by law. Our ideas concerning the acquisition of rights become more or less clear and faithful reproductions of the contents of the law in this respect. In everyday life we can usually get on with such knowledge as we possess ourselves; but in matters of importance we often have to rely on professional assistance to make sure that a transaction is performed in the proper way; a business enterprise employs its own jurists for this purpose. The consequential ideas also become moulded on the rules of law. The psychological effect of the prohibitive sign 'not mine' is enhanced by the knowledge that punishment is meted out according to rules of criminal law for those who disregard this sign and appropriate things belonging to others. Our ideas about what we may do with our own property have to conform to the law; there are many restrictions with which we must be familiar if we are to avoid unpleasantness. In countless instances ideas about what is prohibited or permitted are formed on the basis of law; this is how the law becomes effective.

It must be kept in mind that the directive function of the word 'right' can be exerted within a social context only. As an isolated phenomenon the word is nothing but some sounds produced by a human being or some letters on paper. It becomes an element in the system of rules regulating the intercourse of men when it is being constantly used in certain routine fashions. Since we have been effectively taught how to use the word and how to respond to its use by others, everybody is familiar with the general practice; and we know that it is backed by the power of the state. If this is taken into consideration, it will cause no surprise that certain forms of language are successfully employed for directing human behaviour though the words used possess no semantic reference. Words with consequential ideas attached to them may be used as signs as well as material objects. Language is, indeed, a most convenient tool for putting up the signposts which are needed to guide human conduct in a complicated society.

The informative function

That a noun like ' right ' can be used in a directive sense without possessing semantic reference should be clear enough. It seems far more difficult to understand how the word, under such circumstances, can be employed for conveying information. This would seem to be information concerning the existence of concrete rights. But if the word ' right ' denotes nothing, how could any information be gathered from the statement that A or B possesses a certain right? Suppose the word ' watch ' had no semantic reference; how could the statement that A has a watch in his hand tell us anything?

Yet it seems incontestable that information of some kind is imparted through statements that people possess rights. Are we not receiving some useful knowledge by learning that A owns a certain house or that B has got a monetary claim against C? Such communications are made every day in millions of cases. Apparently, we understand them very well. They form the basis of countless decisions on important matters. Indeed, it seems impossible to comprehend how we could go on without information about people's rights.

There seems to be a dilemma. Analysis shows that the word ' right ', as commonly used, lacks semantic reference. Nevertheless, it is constantly used to convey information; and this is done in such manner as to imply that the word has got some semantic reference.

To find a way out of the difficulty, let us see what kind of information we receive through statements that certain rights exist. Suppose X tells me that A is the owner of this house in front of which we are standing. It appears that I get some information from this statement; but wherein does it actually consist?

The statement tells me that the house ' belongs ' to A. We are familiar with the idea that everybody has a sphere of objects belonging to himself. I have a number of things that are 'mine'. Others are supposed to have corresponding spheres of what is 'theirs'. But saying that a thing 'belongs' to me does not explain what 'I am its owner' means. Both expressions have the same meaning. Among adults, a thing is 'mine' when I possess the right of ownership to it.

So we have come no further. Indeed, it seems impossible to explain what it means that the house 'belongs' to A without using the concept of the right of property.

As we have seen before, the right of ownership cannot be identified with any factual situation. The statement that A is the owner of this house tells me nothing about the actual relationship between A and the house. It does not say that A is living in the house, that he takes care of it, or draws an income from it. He need not have it in his power to make any decisions concerning the use of the house; the house may be so heavily mortgaged that the power of decision has passed to the creditors. The owner may, indeed, be ignorant of the existence of the house.

Nevertheless, it seems that I receive some information through the statement that A owns the house. Suppose I am asking about the ownership out of sheer curiosity. If I regard my interlocutor as a reliable person and he tells me with certainty that A is the owner, I will usually be content with this. On the face of it, the phrase tells me an ostensible fact: that A is the owner of the house, that it 'belongs' to him, or however else one would like to circumscribe the phrase. But I know that, *in the usual course of things*, a person to whom the ownership of a house is correctly ascribed exercises some control over it. Therefore I assume that this is the case here, too, unless I know something to the contrary. This is an inference which I draw from the fact that the phrase has been uttered to me by a person considered reliable. I cannot conclude what kind of control A is exercising; only a very vague idea of control is associated with the phrase that A is the owner of the house. If I want precise information on this point, further questions will be asked.

One conclusion can be drawn with certainty from the statement that A is the owner of the house, supposing it to be correct. This is that the co-operation of A (or of a representative for him) is required for a legal transaction concerning the house. The statement will therefore be useful because it shows with whom one has to make contact if some legal transaction with regard to the house is contemplated. Whether the statement itself will be sufficient as a prerequisite for entering into an agreement is another question; in many cases something more will be needed.

Suppose I want to rent a flat in the house. In this case I shall probably be content with the information that A owns the house. It points to the person with whom I have to make a contract. Most probably I will not think it necessary to ask how A has acquired the right of ownership; it is very unlikely that somebody who has not got a legal title to the house will pretend to let lodgings in it. I sign a contract with A, or with his representative, and everything will be all right.

If I am intent on buying the house, the statement about A's ownership will also lead me to the person with whom I have to open negotiations. But in this case I will not be content with the simple statement that ' A is the owner ' even if I regard my interlocutor as reliable. Before signing a contract and paying out money, I shall want to ascertain that A has a ' legal title ' to the house. This is the important thing. To make sure I shall also want to know that A has not already sold the house to somebody else, or given it away, etc. This is difficult to ascertain. If there is a land register, it will be sufficient that A is noted as the present owner. Otherwise, I shall have to rely on the honesty of A and the improbability of his trying to sell the house to me if he has already disposed of it in some other way.

These simple examples show how serviceable information is conveyed through statements about ownership of things. Immediately, the statement that ' A is the owner of this house ' tells us nothing more than that—' A is the owner of the house '. This phrase will be repeated in the mind of the addressee. But if he takes the statement to be correct, he usually makes certain assumptions. (i) He supposes that A is in some way or other connected with the house, ordinarily as the person in actual control. The reason for this assumption is that a person to whom ownership is correctly ascribed generally is in a position to make effective decisions with regard to the object. (ii) The addressee assumes that A has a legal title to the house. If the statement is correct, there must be some title. The statement does not say which title A has got—whether he has bought the house, inherited it, or received it as a gift. But some title there must be unless the statement is incorrect. Therefore, legal transactions concerning the house have to be made with A or his representative.

In this way we indirectly get useful information through statements concerning a person's right of ownership to things. Strictly speaking, however, the word 'information' is not exact. What has been provisionally called 'information' actually consists of certain assumptions made on the basis of statements concerning a person's rights when the statements are supposed to be reliable. To be precise, the explanation should be given in the following way.

On the face of it, the phrase that 'A is the owner of this house' conveys information concerning the relation of A to the house. But every attempt to describe the import of this information results in circularity. What the addressee immediately gets through the communication is only the phrase itself. He believes that he has been informed of a fact: that A is the owner of the house. In reality, the phrase itself has been presented to his mind; and he probably repeats it if he is asked about the ownership of the house.

But when the statement is supposed to be correct, it may give rise to certain assumptions. This is not always the case. As was noted, one may be content simply with the phrase that 'A is the owner of the house'. When assumptions are made, they may vary widely as to their content. The same statement may cause two different persons to make more or less different assumptions concerning the actual situation, because, for instance, the one has more knowledge than the other of the affairs of the owner. Generally speaking, however, it will be vaguely assumed that the owner, in some way or other, is in actual control of the house. To be in actual control is not the same thing as 'being owner'; but it is the usual corollary to 'ownership'. If the questioner is interested in knowing who is in actual control, his curiosity will therefore ordinarily be satisfied through the statement that A is the owner; for he will assume that in this case, as usual, actual control is concomitant with ownership. This will suffice as a basis for a number of simple transactions with the person designated as owner. Furthermore, since objects are identified as belonging to a person's sphere of 'his' through their having been 'acquired' by him in some lawful way, the assumption will be made that the 'owner' will have some legal title to the object; and the title can be ascertained in case of need. Thus one has got a firm basis for important business regarding the object.

The essential thing is to distinguish between the statement about a person's right of ownership to an object and the assumptions made by a person to whom this statement is addressed. The apparently informative function of statements about the existence of concrete rights actually consists in their giving rise to such assumptions as have been mentioned.

The difference between statements concerning the existence of rights, on the one hand, and the assumptions made on the basis of such statements, on the other hand, may be illustrated by the following example. After a long period of unconsciousness a person wakes up in a hospital and is informed that the date is April 1. If he comes to think of the weather, he will probably assume that there is no snow now on the ground as there was when he fell ill; in the district where he is living the snow has usually melted away before the month of April. The assumption may be correct; but it may also be mistaken since snow sometimes falls at a later time of the year. The information concerning the date and the assumption made concerning the snow are obviously different things.

The assumptions based on ostensible information concerning people's rights are made only when the information is supposed to be correct; if the statement that A possesses a certain right of ownership is not really correct, it will be misleading and therefore useless from a practical point of view. But what does 'correctness' mean here?

Obviously, it cannot be the same thing as truth regarding assertions concerning physical properties. Suppose somebody tells me that this house is made of bricks; the truth or falsity of this statement can be ascertained by inspecting the house. The same method cannot be used for deciding whether the statement that A owns the house is correct. The law must always be taken into consideration. A is supposed to be owner if he has acquired the house in a legal way and has not subsequently parted with the right of ownership. Correctness means being correct according to the law.

It should always be kept in mind that the assumptions we make on the basis of statements concerning people's rights are made within the framework of a legal system. Outside a working legal system there would be no grounds for them. They presuppose that there are rules for the acquisition of property which are generally respected, that therefore the legal, or ideal, distribution of property has an actual counterpart in the distribution of the actual control over things, etc. Only when a great number of such conditions are realized, will the assumptions be fairly well founded; only then will they serve practical purposes.

Ideas of Rights in Legislation

For the most part the rules of private law are conceived as rules about rights and corresponding duties. They are supposed to regulate the creation, acquisition, transference, modification, and extinction of rights and duties. The textbooks purport to give information on such matters. But the legal texts themselves have no informative function. Their purpose is to influence behaviour. The provisions of a law about rights have a directive function only.

How it has come about that private law acquired the form of prescriptions concerning rights and duties is a question for legal theory. Most probably ideas of rights and duties—or, to be more exact, historical precursors to the ideas of the present age—were established long before formal legislation became an instrument of social control. From the beginning it must have seemed quite natural to relate enacted rules to existing ideas of rights and duties. The object of a law could, for instance, be to put limitations on the exercise of rights; new kinds of rights could be introduced. In historical times, legislation has proceeded in this way.

To be effective among the general public, legislation on rights presupposes that people are familiar with the notion that rights are created through such-and-such occurrences; it is also required that people attach consequential ideas concerning their own behaviour to the supposed existence of rights. People must further entertain the idea that it is within the power of the legislative authorities to alter the conditions for the acquisition of rights, to modify the consequences of old, well-known rights, and to introduce new rights.

It is evident that these conditions are fulfilled. To all of us it seems to be the most natural thing in the world that the legislative authorities can regulate people's rights (even if there are supposed to be some limits to their powers in this respect). The sequence of ideas about the acquisition of a right, the existence of a right, and the consequences thereof for behaviour, is firmly established with regard to the old, well-known rights. When new rights are introduced through legislation the same scheme of thought is automatically applied to them. Therefore, to legislate in the form of issuing prescriptions for the acquisition, transference, etc., of rights is a suitable means of directing behaviour among the general public.

In the field of private law the ideas of rights of property and of monetary claims with corresponding debts are of course fundamental. The silent assumption that they are generally entertained by people and guide their behaviour belongs to the background of almost all private law legislation. No fundamental changes in the rules concerning these two kinds of rights are contemplated. The business of new laws is only to introduce modifications such as restrictions on the use of property, changes in the rules for recovery of debts, etc.

An instance of the creation of a new kind of rights was the introduction of patent rights. In such a case the law has to contain the whole series of rules concerning the mode of acquisition, the content of the right, and the sanctions for non-compliance with these rules. On the basis of the law ideas of new rights and consequential ideas connected with them are formed among the general public. The inveterate habit of taking one's own right as a green light and that of others as a red light is applied to the ideas of the new rights.

Since a right, according to the law, can often be acquired in several different ways and a great many rules can refer to the situation where a person is in the possession of a right, the supposed right becomes a link between two sets of rules: the rules about the acquisition of the right and the rules referring to the existence of the right. The right of property may be acquired through a purchase, through receiving a gift, through a will, etc.; and innumerable rules of private, criminal and public law refer to the right of property.

This is the 'connecting' function of the notion, or word, 'right' which has often been pointed out since the latter part of the nineteenth century, especially by adherents of the representation theory. Its significance can hardly be overrated; how a legal system could be constructed without the connecting function of 'rights' is difficult to understand. But we must not think that the technique has been deliberately created as a device for expressing rules primarily conceived as rules of conduct. This is a great mistake. The technique has come about quite naturally, without such premeditation. The rules have not been first conceived as rules of actions to be thereafter, for the sake of convenience, transformed into rules about rights. They were rules about rights from the beginning; and from the rules about rights, rules of action are supposed to follow.[2]

Ideas of Rights in the Administration of Justice

We now turn to the third great question concerning ideas of rights in a working legal system: their role in the administration of justice. This problem must be discussed at some length.

[2] *Cf. Law as Fact* (1939) 110 ff. Things are turned upside down when the concept (or word) 'right' is said to be a technical device for conveniently expressing pre-existing rules. *Cf.* above 167 f., 178 ff.

The focal point is the nature of a judgment in a civil case. In the traditional view, still upheld by most writers on the subject, the judgment is essentially a declaration concerning a pretended right affirming or negating its existence. The first thing to do is to examine this declaration theory of judgments.[3]

The declaration theory of judgments

The declaration theory of judgments is the natural outcome of the traditional view concerning private or substantive law as regulating the existence of rights and duties. When according to these rules a right has been duly 'created' and no facts entailing its 'extinction' have occurred, the right is held to exist. Normally the possessor of a right peacefully enjoys the resulting benefits. But when this is not the case and the right is violated, it has to be enforced if it is not to be annihilated. Since self-help is forbidden by law, enforcement is the task of organs of the state.

First the existence of the pretended right has to be ascertained. To do this is the principal business of the courts. An action has to be brought. Facts supporting the contentions of the plaintiff have to be alleged and proved to the satisfaction of the court. In allowing the claim of the plaintiff, the court declares that he really possesses the right in question; in rejecting the claim, the court denies the existence of the right.

On the basis of this view judgments in civil cases are divided into three categories: declaratory, executory, and constitutive judgments.

A *declarative* judgment is defined as a pure determination of right. If the judgment is in favour of the plaintiff, it merely asserts that he possesses a certain right. He has not contended that the right has been infringed; the purpose of the action was only to have the existence of the right put beyond doubt. No question of awarding relief arose.

Such declaratory judgments have won official recognition only in comparatively recent times. Previously the general principle was (both in continental and English law) that no action of a court was called for unless a right had been violated. In order to obtain a court decision the plaintiff therefore had to allege that some violation had taken place and seek relief for it. Consequently every judgment was supposed to be executory.

[3] The following is based on a Swedish work on right and judgment (*Rätt och dom*, 1960, 410 pp., 2nd ed. 1966).

An *executory* judgment is described as containing, first, a determination of the contested right and, secondly, an award of relief. The first element is considered the most essential. Relief is awarded because a right has been infringed. The executory judgments are regarded as the normal ones, though there has been a marked increase in the use of declaratory judgments.

The category of *constitutive* judgments comprises judgments which are obviously intended to alter the legal situation. Examples are judgments for divorce or dissolution of partnership. Sometimes these judgments are called 'investitive'. The most consistent theorists maintain that these judgments, too, contain a determination of a right, that is, the right to have a change brought about in the legal situation.

The declaration theory of judgments has been especially developed and discussed in German jurisprudence. The principal writings are recorded in Leo Rosenberg's *Lehrbuch des deutschen Zivilprozessrechts* (8. Aufl. 1960) §§ 84–7. But the theory is also prevalent in Anglo-American as well as in continental European jurisprudence in general. A couple of examples may be sufficient to illustrate the theory.

In his work *Civil Procedure of the Trial Court in Historical Perspective* (1952) R. W. Millar sums up the usual position in the following words (380 f.):

'The ordinary judgment or decree, rendered in favour of a plaintiff, embodies essentially two elements, first, a determination of right, . . . and, secondly, an award, effectuable by state-provided means, of the relief to which the verified right entitles. The declaratory judgment, on the other hand, concerns itself only with the determination of right and is in order where the situation is not ripe for anything more than that determination.'

In the work *Declaratory Judgments* (2nd ed. 1941), where abundant references to the literature are to be found, Edwin Borchard stresses that the declaration concerning a right is the essential element in a judgment (10):

'The court's function is completely performed by determining and deciding the case in a form binding upon the parties; and it is the judgment, and not the execution, which establishes their rights and constitutes the essence of judicial power. A judgment, as Mr. Black points out, has in general "nothing whatever to do with the means of enforcing the liability which it declares". Its declaratory, determinative, and adjudicatory function is its distinctive characteristic. While it must be given final effect by all officials of the state and cannot be reviewed or revised by administrative or executive authorities, it is the fact that it constitutes an official, final, binding, and unchallengeable declaration of the rights of the parties, constituting *res judicata*, which gives it its character in the judicial process.'

As Borchard points out (137) the rendering of declaratory judgments is, in fact, an old-established institution called forth by the necessities of organized communal life. 'All that is new about the declaratory judgment is its name and its broad scope —the phenomenon itself is as old as judicial history,' he says.

The category of constitutive judgments was introduced into German literature toward the end of the nineteenth century. But it had been used in French jurisprudence since the early part of the century. (See Mazeaud in the *Revue trimestrielle de droit civil*, 1929, 18.)

Often the judgments are divided into two chief categories: declarative and constitutive judgments, the former category being subdivided into purely declaratory judgments and executory judgments. (Thus for instance Rosenberg, *loc. cit.*) The French *court de cassation* has made this distinction: declarative judgments are *ceux qui se bornent à reconnaitre des droits préexistants*, constitutive *ceux qui ont pour objet de créer un droit nouveau ou de modifier un état de choses légalement existant*. (See Mazeaud, *loc. cit.*)

The constitutive judgments will not be considered at this point.

Difficulties of the declaration theory

The tenet that a judgment in a civil case is a pronouncement by a court on the existing rights of the parties seems so natural because it is the necessary complement to the view that we really possess juridical rights accorded to us by the law. The declaration theory is the very keystone in the traditional conception of private law as an order for the distribution of rights and duties.

Nevertheless, it is difficult to fit the theory into a coherent, non-contradictory view of a working legal system. An instance of this is the doctrine of *res iudicata* as we find it in the literature.

According to the theory the courts have no creative function with regard to the rights of the parties (constitutive judgments excepted). The rights exist prior to, and independently of, the relatively rare cases of litigation. Since the courts only make pronouncements on the existence or non-existence of rights, it follows that the judgment does not affect the rights of the parties. But is this consequence compatible with the principle of *res iudicata*, the finality of judgments?

No trouble arises if the judgment can be regarded as being a correct statement concerning the legal situation. But the judgment cannot always be correct: judges are not infallible beings. Sometimes a judgment will be based on a wrong or incomplete conception of the facts of the case or on a mistaken interpretation of the law. What happens in such a case? According to the theory a plaintiff who has lost his case for want of proof must still be in possession of his right. But this makes no sense: when the claim has been dismissed by the court, the 'right' seems to amount to nothing. It may also occur that the plaintiff puts forward a claim for money though the debt has actually been paid off; the defendant loses the case because he is unable to prove that payment has been made. If the theory be true, the winning party still has no real right and the defendant is under no obligation to pay the debt a second time; but he has got to pay in order to avoid distraint for debt. He is under no obligation to do what he must do. This also seems to be very strange.

In every tangible sense the legal relationship between the parties seems to be determined by the judgment. To maintain that their respective rights and duties are the same as before the decision of the court therefore appears to be senseless. So the incorrect judgment seems to have a constitutive effect. But how to distinguish between correct and incorrect judgments? Any judgment may be incorrect. Whether this is the case in a particular instance is an open question; and no legal decision can be obtained on that point.

From a conceptual point of view it is obviously very difficult to reconcile the rule of *res iudicata* with the declaration theory of judgments. In the doctrine on the subject prevailing from the Middle Ages until the end of the nineteenth century the problem was slurred over by invoking the Roman adage *res iudicata pro veritate accipitur*. The judgment was held to be necessarily true—in the eye of the law. From a legal point of view there could never be a discrepancy between the rights of the parties and the judgment. The pronouncement of the court should be regarded as always coinciding with the rights as they stood. The judgment was final and irreversible as being an authoritative, and therefore always correct, statement concerning the rights of the parties. The rule of *res iudicata* was embodied in the principle *res iudicata pro veritate accipitur*.

This adage stems from Justinian's Digesta. As in so many other cases an utterance by a Roman jurist was misinterpreted. The principle *res iudicata pro veritate accipitur* referred only to decisions concerning the status of a person. The meaning was that the pronouncement of a court in these cases should obtain instead of his real status. Thus if a court declared a man to have been born free (*ingenuus*), he should be held to be *ingenuus* even if he was really a liberated slave. This is what Ulpian says in D 1,5,25: *Ingenuum accipere debemus etiam eum, de quo sententia lata est, quamvis fuerit libertinus: quia res iudicata pro veritate accipitur.* In D 50, 17, 207 the phrase *res iudicata pro veritate accipitur* (by Ulpian) has been taken out of its setting and rendered in a catalogue of *diversae regulae iuris antiqui,* which gives the impression that it enunciates a general rule. (See Hägerström, 1 *Der römische Obligationsbegriff* 520 ff.) In the Middle Ages the statements of Ulpian were interpreted as saying that the judgment is always true.

In more recent jurisprudence great efforts have been made to reconcile the rule of *res iudicata* to the declaration theory of judgments. But every attempt in this direction is doomed to failure. When judgment has been rendered, the legal relations of the parties are determined by the judgment. The facts on which it was grounded are no longer relevant. In so far as they are covered by the judgment, they have, so to speak, been replaced by the judgment: one has no longer to go back to those facts. The judgment is now the relevant fact. In no sense can it be maintained that the rights of the parties are not affected by the judgment.

The fiction *res iudicata pro veritate accipitur* was still generally accepted during the nineteenth century. When Savigny said that the right appeared in apprehensible form in the judgment, this is to be seen in conjunction with his assertion that the judgment is necessarily true and therefore elevates the right to the level of certainty (6 *System* 265 ff.). Like many other authors of the same period, when treating the law of procedure he had in mind the case where the claimant really has the right for which he asks protection and where this right is correctly recognized by the court. (*Cf.* Otto Bülow, 27 *Zeitschrift für deutschen Zivilprozess*, 1900, 217: 31, 1903, 191 f.)

After a vigorous criticism initiated by Bülow the use of fictions in jurisprudence fell into disrepute towards the end of the nineteenth century. The possibility of a discrepancy between the judgment and the rights of the parties could then no longer be covered up by the fiction *res iudicata pro veritate accipitur.* In order to explain how the legal situation obtaining after the judgment was to be described two principal theories were put forward in German jurisprudence.

The one theory came relatively close to the old fiction. It said that the judgment, though being a declaration concerning existing rights and duties, *made itself true* if it were at variance with the real situation: after the judgment the parties had those rights and duties which the court declared them to have. (Pagenstecher, *Zur Lehre von der materiellen Rechtskraft,* 1905,

304 f.) The problem was solved by ascribing to the judgment the surprising capacity of making itself true.
Another theory, which became more influential, preserved the fundamental tenet that the judgment exerted no influence on the rights of the parties. These remained as they were even if they were not recognized by the court. But in that case they could no longer be enforced. Eventually they 'withered away'. (Hellwig, *System des deutschen Zivilprozessrechts*, 1912, 776 f.) The meaning was as follows: A judgment which wrongly denied the existence of the claimant's right left him in undisturbed possession of his *Willensmacht* over the other party. But this was a pure *Willensmacht* lacking the support of the state. For the rule of *res iudicata* imposed on the courts an obligation, pertaining to public law, of not rendering a different judgment on the same case. Rosenberg, who is an adherent of the Hellwig theory, explains the matter in this way. (*Lehrbuch* § 148 II 2): 'Die prozessuale Rechtskrafttheorie, von Stein und Hellwig begründet und jetzt vielfach von den Prozessualisten vertreten, verneint allen Einfluss des rechtskräftigen Urteils auf das materielle Recht und sieht das Wesen der Rechtskraft darin, dass jeder künftige Richter an die urteilsgemässe Feststellung gebunden und verpflichtet ist, dieselbe Sache in gleichem Sinn zu entscheiden.' (*Cf.* Hellwig 780.) The long discussion on the subject, often carried on with great acumen, lays bare the difficulties of the declaration theory. (A survey of the discussion is offered by Rudolf Bruns in his *Zivilprozessrecht*, 1968, § 43 V.)

The difficulty caused to the declaration theory by the principle of *res iudicata* is only one among many. The following instances may be pointed out.

First, the facts alleged and proved may be insufficient to warrant either asserting or negating the existence of a pretended right. Suppose the plaintiff has succeeded in establishing some probability for his version of the facts. But it is by no means certain that his story is the true one. If the essence of the judgment were really a declaration as to the existence or non-existence of the plaintiff's right, no judgment at all could be given in such a case. The court would have to state that the case could not be decided: *non liquet*. But this is not permitted. The court is not allowed to refrain from rendering judgment because the facts are obscure. Consequently, a decision has to be given even if it cannot be a declaration concerning the existence or non-existence of the pretended right.

A judgment by default may be rendered on the ground that the defendant has failed to appear after having been duly summoned. Such a judgment obviously cannot be a declaration concerning the existence of the claimant's right.

These are cases where there is no sufficient factual basis for a conclusion concerning the existence or non existence of a pretended right.

Secondly, the law may be insufficient. The declaration theory presupposes that there is always a legal rule applicable to the case from which a conclusion concerning the rights of the parties could be drawn. As is now universally recognized, this cannot be the case. There is no 'complete' system of legal rules covering all situations that may occur in life. It cannot be objected that a court has to reject a claim when there is no legal rule to support it. In many cases claims are allowed by the courts though it cannot really be argued that there was previously an existing rule on which the decision is grounded. One need only think of the long succession of precedents by means of which the law of torts has been developed in most countries. Each time a novelty has been introduced, a judgment has been given without the support of an established rule. But this is no rare and exceptional happening. When a court takes its guidance from a number of precedents, which are more or less conflicting, it has no hard and fast rule from which a conclusion could be drawn. There is always something new in the case.

Thirdly, the rules of law, when such can be said to exist, often leave a wide margin to the discretion of the court. This is usually the case in the law of torts. We are told by an adherent of the declaration theory that even then the judgment merely recognizes the existence of a right:

> Even in the cases where there is involved a right to unliquidated damages, so called, it is, after all, the substantive law which measures the right, rather than the procedural law. The amount is in fact fixed by the law of damages, which is substantive law, and again the court merely recognizes the existence of the right so measured.[4]

Surely, this is to stretch the facts in order to meet the requirements of the theory. Suppose A has suffered an injury which he imputes to the negligence of B. Through his lawyer he addresses to B a demand for compensation. In the first place, the law of torts (that is, a vast amount of precedents) supplies a basis for a settlement of the matter out of court. If no agreement can be reached and A carries the matter to a court, the court does not ascertain the existence of a right in A to damages amounting to this or that sum of money; it *awards* damages according to certain general principles established in judicial practice and its own estimation.

[4] Bernhard C. Gavit, 30 *Columbia Law Review* (1930) 811.

Ascertaining the existence of a right

The arguments now put forward against the declaration theory are valid even under the assumption that it is at all possible to ascertain the existence of a right. But is this really possible?

If a question arises as to the material from which a house is built, the question can be decided by inspection. But this method does not apply to the question of the right of ownership to the house. It is generally recognized that there is no possibility of directly ascertaining the existence of a right. Our knowledge concerning concrete rights is supposed to derive from *inferences* drawn from certain operative facts in conjunction with the content of the law. The major premise is a rule of law (or a complex of rules) saying that a person shall acquire a certain right under certain circumstances; the minor premise is that circumstances answering to those described in the law have actually occurred with regard to A; the conclusion is that A has acquired the right in question. The law says, for instance, that ownership to real property shall be acquired through a deed of conveyance. When it is known that A has got a deed of conveyance concerning a certain piece of real estate from B, who was its owner, the conclusion is drawn that A has acquired the right of ownership to this piece of real estate. He therefore is its owner as long as he has not transferred his right to somebody else or lost it in some other way.

The inference is based on the assumption that the law can really cause 'the right of property' to pass over from B to A as a result of an act called conveyance. But is this an assumption concerning something which the lawgivers are actually capable of achieving?

Through the procedure of legislation, as we have seen, a text is ranged among other texts forming a body to which the name of 'law' is applied by common and regular usage. This has the very important effect of influencing people's ideas and consequent behaviour. When the new text refers to some mode of acquiring a right, then rights will be supposed to be acquired in the way prescribed in the text. If A and B perform a transaction according to the new law purporting the transfer of the right of property to a piece of real estate, the right of property to this piece of real estate will be supposed to be really transferred. A and B will act in conformity with the consequential ideas attached to the idea that the right of property has passed over from B to A. Other persons will do the same in so far as they come into contact with the parties and become acquainted with the transaction. The revenue authorities will require A to pay taxes for the land. At some future time legal proceedings may perhaps be instituted concerning the same piece of land; depending on the circumstances, the deed of conveyance may form part of the grounds on which the court will base its decision.

Such are the actual effects of legislation. But the transfer of the right of property is not among them. The actual effects are of a psychological nature; and the effect called 'the transfer of the right of property' cannot be described in psychological terms. That the right of property has been transferred does not mean that people have acquired some ideas and act according to them. The supposed transfer of the right of property takes place on another level. In fact, it takes place in words only. But words are powerful, and the words of the lawgivers especially so: the words of the law, solemnly enacted and publicized according to the constitution, initiate chains of causality resulting in regular behaviour of people in general and acts by courts and other organs of the state.

No conclusion concerning the existence of rights is possible. The supposed syllogism is a sequence of ideas. We get the illusion of inferring the existence of a right, when really we form an idea of a right in accordance with some rules of law. The declaration theory is based on this illusion and therefore it is exposed to endless difficulties.

Import of a judgment

If a judgment in a civil case is no declaration concerning 'existing rights', how is it then to be characterized? To get the answer we have to examine the different kinds of judgments.

An executory judgment contains a decree ordering the defendant to pay a sum of money or to do something else. This is an imperative to the defendant. There may also be an express prescription concerning execution in case the defendant does not perform what he has been ordered to do. But this is not necessary. Even if no such prescription is given, the judgment serves as a sign for the competent authorities to institute execution on the application of the winning party. The imperative to the defendant supplies a measure for the execution. If, for instance, the defendant has been ordered to pay a certain sum of money, the meaning is that this sum of money should be extracted from his property.

Thus the imperative to the defendant is significant in two directions: it exerts pressure on the defendant which often causes him to satisfy the winning party; and it puts the action of the executive authorities at the disposal of the winning party in case satisfaction is not attained. Obviously, the psychological pressure on the defendant is greatly reinforced by the threat of executive action looming in the background.

The imperative is the essential element in an executory judgment. A declaration concerning the right of the plaintiff may be included. If this is done, the declaration is supposed to contain the immediate reason for the imperative: because the plaintiff possesses a certain right against the defendant, the latter is ordered to do what the plaintiff has a right to claim. The right, then, is interposed between the facts of the case and the imperative. But the imperative may also be directly based on the facts presented to the court. It makes no difference if the court orders the defendant to pay damages simply because he has driven his car carelessly or if it inserts the phrase that the plaintiff, in consequence of the defendant's negligence, has acquired a right to obtain compensation for the loss he has suffered.

The nature of a declaratory judgment is best shown by an example. The plaintiff prays judgment declaring that a note, signed by the defendant as maker, promising to pay him £1,000 on . . . is a valid note, binding on the defendant. Admitting that he has signed the note, the defendant alleges that he was deceived into doing so, which the plaintiff denies. The defendant tries to substantiate his plea. But in the view of the court the facts presented and proven do not amount to fraud in the sense of the law. The plea is therefore rejected; and the court declares the note to be valid and binding on the defendant.

On the face of it, this judgment is a pronouncement on a property in the note. But no such property has been ascertained by the court; and it could not be ascertained since it does not exist. The dispute concerned the circumstances in which the note was made. They have been evaluated by the court according to certain legal principles with the result that they were not classed as including fraud. In giving judgment the court makes use of a traditional formula which obtains its significance through the rules attached to the fact that a judgment with such a formula has been rendered. These rules imply that the question of the circumstances at the making of the note has been definitely settled. The defendant will no more be heard with a plea that he was deceived into signing the note. If the plaintiff prays an executory judgment, this will be granted to him on the basis of the declaratory judgment if the defendant can show no other reason than the alleged deception why judgment should not be rendered against him.

We must not take all legal formulae at their face value. The language of jurists has many peculiarities; and we should, as Bentham said, try to pierce the veil it casts upon the facts. The formulae are instruments for attaining results; and the results follow because legal rules, conscientiously applied by state organs, refer to formulae having been used in a proper way by courts.

Another example is a judgment concerning the construction of a will. With regard to a particular gift there is no question as to its validity or the person to receive it; but there are different opinions regarding the amount of property passing under the gift. The words used in the will are ambiguous. To protect himself from competing demands the executor prays a declaratory judgment on the matter. Reasons are adduced by the interested parties for several different interpretations. It is impossible to find out with certainty the meaning of the testator. But the court has to make a decision. After weighing the relevant circumstances the court renders judgment to the effect that the will should be understood as giving certain defined property to X. This is clearly an imperative. Its significance is to replace, so to speak, the disputed testamentary provision. Instead of the ambiguous prescription in the will, the content of the judgment will now be the basis on which the executor has to rely in apportioning certain property out of the estate to X.

Many different formulae are used in declaratory judgments. The common feature of such judgments is that they have a directive function. First, the judgment indicates to the parties the correct behaviour on the point in dispute. Secondly, the judgment will be a legal obstacle to renewed litigation on the same question; if subsequently an executory judgment is called for, it will be based on the declaratory judgment.

Rendering declaratory judgments is therefore an exercise of state power as well as rendering executory judgments. The state takes a definite position with respect to the relations between the parties. The declaration concerning the validity of a document, the construction of a will, the breach of a contract, the discharge of a debt, the liability of an insurance company, etc., means, in the first place, laying down a law for the parties regarding the matter in dispute. In general, this will be sufficient. The parties will conform to the judgment. It will be senseless to press a claim that has been rejected by the court. To refuse to satisfy a claim that has been confirmed will also be purposeless, since the winning party can easily obtain an executory judgment on the basis of the declaratory judgment. A positive declaratory judgment is a step towards an executory one.

The actual role of the court is that of being a lawgiver for particular cases. The legal rules, whether laid down through acts of legislation or evolved in some other way, cannot supply exact patterns of behaviour for every contingency. There is always a more or less wide margin for deciding which of two or more alternatives are to be deemed lawful. The margin is so small as to be (in general) negligible when you have put your name on the back of a bill of exchange. If you have been involved in an accident when driving your car, the margin may be very wide. All of us have to apply the rules of civil law in our relations with our fellow-citizens. In a great many simple cases, for instance when we pay a tradesman's bill, we know what we have to do without asking anybody for advice. When difficulties arise, we have to consult a legal expert. But the experts may disagree. There must be some ultimate authority capable of giving a definite answer to the question of lawful behaviour in the situation. This task is entrusted to the courts. They supplement the abstract rules of law by laying down particular rules for individual cases.

Furthermore, power has to be put behind the rules of civil law. Among primitive peoples, who have not yet developed a state organization, the authority of the judge will often be sufficient to ensure obedience to his decisions. Such is the psychological situation. In modern times judgments rendered by international courts are almost invariably respected by the parties; there are very strong reasons to abide by the decision once a case has been submitted to a court. But the rules of civil law must be backed by force to be efficient; and the force is supplied by the state organization. It has to be exerted with great care, as much as possible according to definite rules, if it is to fulfil its functions. The task is therefore entrusted to select persons with high legal and ethical qualifications, acting in the light of publicity in prescribed forms under the name of courts. They lay down rules of action for the parties; at the same time they direct the eventual use of state power in the shape of executive measures.

The courts are not spectators, taking a bird's-eye view of the legal relations between contending parties and ascertaining the existence of this or that relation. They represent a dynamic force in society, moulding the relations of parties as supplementary lawgivers and directors of the executive force of the state.

When the courts make pronouncements on the rights of the parties, they act in their capacity as lawgivers. They cannot ascertain 'the existence of a right'. But they can form ideas of rights on the model of the general ideas expressed in the rules of law. This is what they do. Their pronouncements concerning rights serve to direct the behaviour of the parties in the same way as the pronouncements of the legislators.

The Element of Valuation

In wielding state power by rendering judgment a court cannot proceed solely on the basis of theoretical considerations. There is also necessarily an element of valuation.

First, the court takes position with regard to a number of theoretical questions referring both to the facts of the case and to the law. The judges find that certain allegations by the plaintiff have been proved; concerning some events the account offered by the defendant is considered true; in some respects it is found impossible to know what really happened. The court also ascertains that an expression used in a law has a technical significance differing from the meaning of the expression in common usage, that such-and-such opinions have been expressed by judges in previous cases, etc. But, however conscientiously such questions are debated and answered by the court, there is still not a sufficient basis for rendering judgment.

Let us take the case that S claims payment from B for goods delivered according to a contract of sale. The defendant denies that a contract was concluded between the parties. To substantiate his claim the plaintiff gives a description of certain talks which in his opinion implied that a bargain had been struck. The defendant offers no objection to the plaintiff's account of the facts, but he says that there was no deal. According to him the parties had only agreed on the terms of a proposed contract, but the contract was never finally concluded.

The law on sale of goods refers to the 'fact' that two parties have made a contract for sale and purchase. But the court cannot reach a decision in this case merely by comparing the facts as presented by the parties with a description in the law of how a contract is concluded. It will find no such description. In a statute on the sale of goods the concept of a contract will be presupposed. In the law reports the court will find many decisions on the question whether a contract has been concluded or not. But the present case will never be identical with any previous case; there will always be some peculiar trait in it. The textbooks will not give exhaustive information on the matter. Ultimately, the court will have to take a position itself. It has to decide whether the rules of sale and purchase should be applied in the case. Let us suppose that the court finds it to be in accordance with the letter and the spirit of the law to apply those rules when two parties have said certain things and behaved in a certain manner. This is not to take position on a theoretical question. It is a decision on a question of how to act. The court decides to apply the rules of sale and purchase and render judgment accordingly. The basis of this decision is an evaluation of the facts implying that they are of such a character that the rules referring to contracts for sale and purchase ought to be applied.

Usually, this value judgment is not made explicitly. As a rule, the court does not say directly: 'for certain reasons we find it proper to apply the rules of sale and purchase in this case'. Instead it declares that it finds a contract to have been concluded. In appearance this is a proposition concerning a theoretical question. It really implies that the name of a contract for sale and purchase is officially applied to the transaction, which in its turn serves as the reason for applying the rules of sale and purchase in the case.

The real reason for the decision to apply the rules of sale and purchase is the evaluation resulting in finding that these rules ought to be applied. Nothing substantial is added by the declaration that a contract for sale and purchase has been concluded. But this declaration is of psychological importance. Since the law refers to the apparent fact that a contract for sale and purchase has been concluded, it seems necessary that the court, before applying the law of sale and purchase to the case, declares that such a contract has really been concluded. It is not generally realized that such a declaration is made on the basis of an evaluation; the declaration is taken to be the ascertainment that a fact has taken place. The real situation is that the law, in referring to the circumstance that a contract has been concluded, presupposes a general notion of a contract which it is, however, impossible to define exhaustively in factual terms. Therefore, it is of necessity left to the courts to evaluate in each case an alleged transaction as being, or not being, of such a character that the rules of sale and purchase ought to be applied.

Another example is a claim for damages. C has suffered a bodily injury in a road accident. He imputes it to the negligence of D in driving his car and asks for judgment against D for payment of a sum of money. It should be quite obvious that 'negligence' cannot be described in factual terms. The law leaves it to the courts to class actions as implying negligence. A court cannot perform this classification without resorting to valuation. It is true that the court will take guidance from previous decisions on similar cases. When it does so, the scope of its own evaluation is narrowed down. But all previous decisions have been based on evaluations; and ultimately the court will have to make an evaluation of the facts itself.

The element of valuation is most obvious in such border-line cases as those cases where the classification of the facts as constituting a 'contract' or 'negligence' seems doubtful. In a great many cases the evaluations do not come to the fore because the court can follow standardized valuations. Thus, for instance, a sheet of paper with a certain conventional text and a signature will probably without hesitation be classified by a judge as a promissory note. There exists no doubt for him on that point—unless it be contended by a party, for instance, that he had been induced to sign his name under the impression that he was only making an application for a loan. As an operative fact, the promissory note has to be 'valid'. But the 'validity' can never be ascertained as a fact. The classification of a sheet of paper as a valid promissory note rests on valuation.

There is always an element of valuation when a court classifies some event as constituting an 'operative' fact. There are no operative facts in nature but only in legal language. Since the law refers to 'operative' facts under such names as contract, promise, payment, marriage, etc., alleged facts have to be classified by the courts under such headings. This is a step in the application of the law. It requires something more than ascertaining some facts: these facts have also to be evaluated, with the result that the court either declares them to constitute a contract, a promise, a payment, a marriage, etc., or rejects the proposed classification.

Likewise, valuations are made with regard to the law. A text is evaluated as belonging to the law in force; a previous decision is evaluated as being a precedent with bearing on the case now before the court; an utterance of a judge is evaluated as being an *obiter dictum*, etc. Laws and precedents are not 'pure facts'. Texts and pronouncements are evaluated when they are classified as laws and precedents.

Within the judiciary valuations are fairly uniform. Lawyers absorb the common stock of valuations during their formative years and subsequently apply them in the exercise of their profession. To a very large extent the valuations to be made seem quite self-evident. But in cases brought before courts debatable questions of valuation are likely to crop up with regard to the facts and/or the rules to be applied. The advocates endeavour to cause the court to accept valuations favourable to their clients.

The common valuations form, so to speak, the spirit of the law which animates the verbal expressions of rules. The same texts can acquire vastly different significance when interpreted in the light of different sets of valuations. The valuations are never rigidly fixed; they are always undergoing changes. The practical import of laws and precedents changes with them. A well-known example is the transformation of the civil law of France during the long reign of the Code Napoléon.

The Internal and the External Aspect of Law

We have now arrived at an explanation of how the idea of a right fulfils weighty functions in the organization of society despite the fact that the word 'right' lacks semantic reference. In isolation the idea would have no significance. It gains its social importance through being connected, on the one hand with the idea that 'rights' are acquired in certain ways defined by law, on the other hand with consequential ideas concerning correct behaviour, also dependent on law.

This manner of thinking is firmly embedded in our minds. The sequence of acquisition of a right, possession of a right, and consequences of having a right seems to us as natural as the regular chain of events in the physical world—the rise of the sun, light during the day, and the darkness following sunset. Rights acquired according to the law are to us as real as horses and dogs.

This is the 'internal' aspect of law, to use the convenient expression introduced by Professor Hart.[5] It is the way of thinking and talking typical of a person who feels himself to be a member of the community in which he lives, accepting its legal system, adapting, on the whole, his behaviour to current ideas of rights and duties, and judging the conduct of others, perhaps with a little more severity, according to the same standard.

[5] *The Concept of Law* (1961) 56, 86 ff., 99, 244.

A special effort is needed to place oneself, so to speak, outside the social context in order to get the 'external' aspect. From this point of view no rights or duties can be discovered. But the external observer cannot be content to look at the movements of millions of people on the face of the earth and listen to the sounds they make in talking to each other. To understand what is going on he has to interpret people's speech and penetrate their minds. He will then begin to understand their legal ideas, how they are generated, what they imply, and how they influence behaviour.

The internal aspect of law has to be integrated into the external aspect. It is a psychological phenomenon forming a part of the complex reality presented to the observer. The internal aspect of law represents a subjective view. But this subjective view is an essential part of law as fact.

In the language belonging to the internal aspect there is a peculiar form of speech which is much in use for bringing about alterations in the sphere of rights, duties, and legal qualities and which therefore deserves special study. It has recently come to be discussed in the philosophy of language under the name of 'performative utterances'.

CHAPTER 8

LEGAL PERFORMATIVES

THE late Professor J. L. Austin began his lectures on *How to do Things with Words* by pointing out that it had too long been the assumption of philosophers that the business of a 'statement' could only be to 'describe' some state of affairs, or to 'state some fact', which it must do either truly or falsely. It has long been recognized that besides sentences expressing statements there are sentences expressing questions, exclamations, commands, wishes, or concessions. But in recent years, Austin says, it has come to be seen that many perplexing words embedded in apparently descriptive statements do not serve to indicate 'some specially odd additional feature in the reality reported'. There are other possibilities of interpreting such statements. To overlook these possibilities is usually called the 'descriptive' fallacy; Austin himself prefers to employ the expression 'constative' fallacy.[1]

These reflections are not least applicable to legal language. We use a great many 'apparently descriptive statements' ostensibly indicating some 'odd additional feature in the reality reported'. Statements about rights are a case in point. It is the 'constative' fallacy that has caused the long search for a mysterious power, a *facultas moralis* or a *Willensmacht*. Only in recent time has it begun to be realised that there is a 'constative' fallacy here, which makes it necessary to explain the use of the word 'right' in a new way. But there are many other words and sentences apparently referring to 'additional features' in observable reality. Indeed, all talk about law is of this nature: government, legislation, administration, offices in the state organization, marriage, guardianship, juridical persons, etc. It pervades common discourse as well as the technical language of jurists.

Ostensibly to bring about these 'additional features' a peculiar form of speech is being employed, to which reference was made at

[1] J. L. Austin, *How to do Things with Words* (1962, cited *HTD*), 1 ff. *Cf.* Max Black, *The Labyrinth of Language* (1968). As Professor Black remarks (93) 'it is hard to understand, in retrospect, why so many able thinkers should have been able to persuade themselves that the cognative use of language was its only standard use'.

the end of Chapter 5. Making use of the term 'performatives' ('performative utterances') introduced by Austin, the expressions characteristic of this language, with a slight modification of Austin's terminology, were called 'performatory imperatives'; but the discussion of their nature was postponed to a later part of the book. The time has now come to take up this thread again. The study of the expressions in question is essential for understanding legal language.

Performatives as Imperatives

As an example of a performative utterance Austin mentions the case of a person appointed to name a ship pronouncing the phrase 'I name this ship the *Queen Elizabeth*' when smashing a bottle of champagne against the bows. Another example is taken from the marriage ceremony: 'I take this woman to be my lawful wedded wife'. A third example is the sentence occurring in a will: 'I give and bequeath my watch to my brother'.[2]

Grammatically, these utterances are in the indicative. But the form of language is misleading. The meaning of the utterances is not to state a fact. What the person naming the ship wants to say is: 'the name of this ship shall be the *Queen Elizabeth*!' In the marriage ceremony the sense of the formula used by the bridegroom is: 'this woman shall be my lawful wedded wife!' The testator means to say: 'the right of property to my watch shall be transferred to my brother!'

Thus the meaning of the sentences is that something shall be brought about: the ship shall get a name, the bridegroom a wife, and the brother the right of property to a watch. The sentences are veiled imperatives.

> This it not to say that all expressions called performatives by Austin are imperatives. As performatives Austin classifies a number of utterances like 'I bet you sixpence it will rain tomorrow', 'I apologize', 'I welcome you', and 'I congratulate you'. These expressions (excepting perhaps the first one) have no imperative sense. They are of no interest from our point of view and need not be investigated here.

As we know, imperatives can very well be expressed through sentences in the indicative, depending on the setting and on the manner of uttering them. The grammatical form of the sentences

[2] Austin, *HTD* 5; *Philosophical Papers* (1961, cited *PhP*) 222.

adduced by Austin as examples of performatives is therefore no obstacle to interpreting them as imperatives. But if they are really imperatives, these imperatives seem to be of a strange nature. They are not addressed to another person: nobody is commanded to do, or forbear from doing something when it is said that a particular word shall be the name of the ship, that the woman shall be the wife of the bridegroom, or that the watch shall be the property of the brother. The imperatives are intended to call forth the effects that the ship is to carry the name of . . . , the woman to be the wife of the man, and the watch to belong to the brother. These effects are supposed to follow from the pronunciation of the imperatives in question provided this is done in the right circumstances: and as it seems, the imperatives would make no sense if the effects could not take place.

Two questions arise with regard to these imperatives. (i) Can there be an imperative without an addressee? (ii) Can any other effect than a psychological one be called forth through an imperative?

Imperatives without an addressee

It is only a preconception that an imperative must enjoin some behaviour on an addressee. The language abounds with imperatives of other kinds. There are, for instance, imperatives imposing a feeling on an addressee, such as: 'Love thy neighbour! ' But here we are concerned only with imperatives which lack an addressee.

We find such an imperative in the first chapter of Genesis. In the beginning God said: 'Let there be light; and there was light.' The Creator did not address any human being; there was none to be addressed. Nevertheless he used the imperative form of speech. 'Let there be light' means: there shall be light. This imperative has no addressee; and it enjoins no action. The imperative is directed towards the coming into being of light.

The use of imperatives without an addressee has not been reserved for the creator of the world. They are employed in many connections; and they are especially common in legal language.

The old Roman laws contain many examples. The authority of a father over his son (the *patria potestas*) included that the father could sell the services of the son for a limited period (probably not more than five years). But when a father has sold a son thrice, the law of the XII Tables says (table IV), the son shall be free from the father. (*Si pater filium ter venum duuit, filius a patre liber esto.*) This is clearly an imperative. But it is addressed neither to the father, nor to the son or to anybody else. The imperative is directed towards a change in the status of the son: he shall be a free man! Its meaning is that a change in his status shall take place.

With regard to a *patronus* who has acted deceitfully towards a client (a dependent person) table VIII says that he shall be *sacer*. (*Patronus si clienti fraudem fecerit, sacer esto.*) There is no addressee to this imperative. Its meaning is to bring about that the deceitful *patronus* becomes *sacer*.

At the solemn act of a sale called *mancipatio*, certain conditions could be added by a pronouncement. With respect to this case table VI says that the pronouncement shall have legal force. (*Cum nexum faciet mancipiumque, uti lingua nuncupassit, ita ius esto.*) This is no command to the parties of the transactions. The provision of the law is intended to endow the pronouncement with legal validity.

According to Gaius (Inst. 2, 117) a correct expression to be used in a testament was to say: Titius shall be my heir! (*Titius heres esto!*) The meaning is not to issue a command to anybody but to institute Titius as heir.[3]

To take an example from my own country, we have an ancient record from the thirteenth century of the 'making' of a king. An essential element in the ceremony, performed on a meadow near Uppsala, was that the 'lawmen' of the different provinces, each in his turn, stepped forward and recited a formula saying: 'I pronounce thee to be king, I pronounce thee to possess the crown and the kingdom, to rule the land and the realm, to give strength to the law and to keep the peace.' Until recently this procedure was held to constitute the election of a king; but it is now generally recognized that this was a mistake: the ceremony represents no election. Beforehand it had been determined (in what way, we do not know) who was to be king. The ceremony was an act of investiture. When a lawman said: 'I pronounce thee to be king' this meant: 'I lay the name of a king upon thee' or: 'you shall have the name of a king!'

[3] *Cf.* Hägerström, 1 *Der römische Obligationsbegriff* 539 ff., 377, 391 f. Hägerström, says concerning such imperatives in Roman legislation (586): 'Typische Formen für solche Imperative sind: familiam habeto, ius potestasque esto, ei ius esto, sacer esto, heres esto, liber esto. . . . Es ist wohl klar, dass diese Imperative keine an die Menschen oder an die Götter gerichteten Vorschriften sein können. Sie *müssen* als durch imperativische Worte Menschen oder Göttern zustehende Rechte *schaffend* betrachtet werden. Sie wenden sich eigentlich an die Welt des Rechtes selbst.' *Cf.* 2 *Der römische Obligationsbegriff* 23: 'Die fraglichen Worte . . . sind nicht an gewisse *Personen* gerichtete Befehle, sondern sie sagen, dass dies oder jenes zur *Rechtsordnung selbst* gehören *soll*.' See also the same volume 35 f.

The formula was an imperative endowing the chosen man with the name and properties of a king.[4]

Imperatives bestowing on persons rights, powers, privileges, and legal qualities have always been used in legislation. It has seemed quite natural to employ this form of language in laying down rules and also to use it in concrete acts of investiture.

In the constitution of the U.S.A. there are many examples. Article I, section 1, says: 'All legislative Powers herein granted shall be vested in a Congress of the United States, which shall consist of a Senate and a House of Representatives.' Article II, section 1, provides: 'The executive Power shall be vested in a President of the United States of America.'

These imperatives do not contain any orders for the behaviour of the citizens of the U.S.A. They allocate certain powers to Congress and the President respectively.

Countless examples of similar imperatives could be gathered from all kinds of legislation. Such imperatives are also used, for instance, in nominating people to offices. Suppose a man is appointed to be a judge. This is done through a declaration of the competent authority saying, whatever words are employed: X shall be a judge. These performative imperatives are indeed so common and well known that it would be superfluous to mention further examples in support of the contention that they form part of our language.

The effect of the imperatives

In Genesis, the words of the Creator took effect according to their literal sense: 'Let there be light; and there was light.' The light came into being because He commanded so; and everything else on earth was created in the same way: by the commands of God.

In these cases the effects of the performatory imperatives were physical. The almighty Creator was supposed to be capable of bringing about light, and the herbs, the animals, etc., through His words.

The effects of the performatory imperatives with which we are concerned are not physical. They are 'legal' effects.

[4] See Karl Olivecrona, *Das Werden eines Königs nach altschwedischem Recht.* (Lunds universitets Årsskrift NF Avd. 1 Bd 44, 1948.) A brief account under the title 'Election and creation' in 1 *Studi in onore di Emilio Betti* (1962) 383 ff.

When the law of the XII Tables said that the son should be free after having been sold for the third time, the effect was supposed to be that he really became free. Similarly, the deceitful *patronus* really became *sacer*; the pronouncement made in connection with a mancipation became legally valid; and Titius really became heir when he had been instituted through the proper words of the testator. The imperatives brought about changes in the legal situation (with religious implications in the case of the *patronus* being *sacer*).

Without doubt these legal provisions had important consequences. The law of the XII Tables was the object of great veneration; its imperatives presumably directed the behaviour of the ordinary Roman citizen. Therefore, when the son had been sold thrice, he was generally regarded as a free man and treated accordingly; the deceitful *patronus* who was *sacer* could and should be killed, which probably was done; the parties to the act of mancipation adhered to the pronouncement made in conjunction with the act; and Titius was regarded as the lawful heir.

These psychological effects took place because the immediate legal effects were supposed to have occurred: that the son became free, that the *patronus* became *sacer*, that the pronouncement became legally binding, and that Titius became heir. When the son had become a free man, it followed that he should be treated as such; when the *patronus* became *sacer*, he should be killed; the legal validity of the pronouncement entailed that it should be respected; and the character of heir accorded to Titius had important consequences with regard to the property of the deceased.

Through the words of the law, certain effects were supposed to be established when some events had taken place. The legal situation became such as the law said it should be. To the idea of a certain legal situation as existing, certain consequential ideas concerning behaviour were attached; and it may be assumed that these consequential ideas were, on the whole, decisive for the conduct of a Roman citizen.

The chain of cause and effect was briefly as follows: the words of the law, visible on the Tables erected in the Forum—general reverence for this law—everybody feeling bound to obey the law—certain events, such as the three mancipations of a son, take place—the legal situation is supposed to be altered—therefore one ought to act in a certain manner. The effect of the law with regard to the general conduct of the citizens was mediated through the idea of legal situations being modelled through the law and consequential ideas attached to the ideas of different legal situations.

The imperatives of the law were also destined to guide the decisions to be rendered by judges. In this respect, too, the actual effects were mediated by the idea of legal effects, to which many rules referred. When the son had become a free citizen, other rules were applicable to his contracts than when he was subject to the parental power of his father; when Titius had been instituted heir, a great many rules became applicable with regard to him and the property of the deceased, etc. In this way decisions came to be based on the words of the law. But between the law and the decisions the ideas of legal effects were interposed. Concerning these effects, legal experts could be consulted, originally the priests, then the jurists. They were supposed to know what the effects were in a given case.

Thus we see how the performatory imperatives really were instrumental in guiding people's behaviour. Their actual effects were conditioned by the idea that the imperatives primarily gave rise to (as we say) 'legal' effects. These 'legal' effects were evidently supersensible. The performatory imperatives aimed at the creation, modification, and extinction of such effects. Their immediate psychological effect was to make people think that the supersensible legal effects really took place in accordance with the meaning of the imperatives. Consequential ideas concerning behaviour were associated with the idea that this was so; and people's conduct was largely determined by them.

The modern view is basically similar. Relatively uniform ideas of ownership, monetary claims, many other kinds of rights, corresponding duties, and legal qualities are disseminated among the general public. These rights, duties, and legal qualities are supposed to be created, modified, transferred, and extinguished through operative facts by virtue of the law. They form a supersensible world: in the sensible, natural world there are no rights, duties, or legal qualities. But there must be some connection between the natural world and the sphere of the law. The connection is established, first, by performatory imperatives. They belong to the natural world; but they are supposed to mould the supersensible sphere of rights, duties, and legal qualities. Secondly, as we have seen, a great many ideas concerning correct behaviour are attached to ideas of people actually possessing rights and legal qualities; the idea of having a duty immediately implies an idea of correct behaviour.

That effects, other than psychological ones, are brought about by mere words seems to be an absurd proposition. If the effects were supposed to be of a physical nature, the absurdity would be blatant. A rainmaker pretending to possess the power of causing the clouds to disperse their water over the earth at his command would be dismissed as being mentally disturbed. But the effects of the legal performatives are held to take place in the sphere of law. Since we are accustomed to this manner of thinking and speaking, it seems to us quite natural. In our daily life we have no reason to reflect upon the peculiarities of the performative language. But we know how to use it for practical purposes; and this is what interests us. The theoretical difficulties involved are only a plague for writers on philosophy and jurisprudence.

In the cases of the naming of a ship and of the marriage ceremony, both adduced by Austin as examples of performatives (*Philosophical Papers,* 1961, 222, 226, HTD 5,23), it is easy to see wherein the supposed and the real effects of the performatives consist.

When the wife of the president of the shipping company in the traditional way has smashed a bottle of champagne against the bow of the ship saying: 'I name this ship the Queen Elizabeth', everybody agrees that the ship carries the name of 'Queen Elizabeth'. But suppose, Austin says, that at the last moment a fellow rushes forward, snatches the bottle, and smashes it against the ship's side shouting: 'I name this ship Generalissimo Stalin'. The christening ceremony would then be held to have misfired and the ship would not really carry the name of 'Generalissimo Stalin'.

The example may be analysed as follows. In both cases, a performative sentence is pronounced with reference to the ship. In the first case, this is thought to be done in the proper way. If the president's wife, with customary ceremony, has pronounced the sentence giving the ship a name, everybody falls into line and calls the ship by this name. In the other case, this does not happen. The christening of the ship by a person not appointed to the task is regarded as an outrage and people pay no heed to it.

The difference, therefore, lies in the effect of the performative sentence on other minds. People are prepared to accept, without the slightest reflection, and to use the name given to the ship by the president's wife. This disposition follows from the prevalence of a certain custom with regard to the naming of ships. The custom has its roots in practical considerations: it is convenient that ships have names which are universally employed. Attempts at name-giving outside the rules of the custom are disregarded and even met with hostility.

The example is instructive. A person is 'appointed' to pronounce a performative formula during a ritual ceremony intended to draw attention to the pronouncement and give the impression that something important happens. The effect is psychological; it depends on people being conditioned to respond in a uniform way to the act, *viz.*, to use a certain form of speech with regard to the ship. The whole thing fulfils a social function.

Evidently it would be useless to discuss whether the ship really has the name or not. The name is not, objectively speaking, attached to the ship, even if some letters to that effect are painted on its sides. What happens is only that people use the name with reference to the ship.

For concluding marriage there are ancient and new ceremonies centring upon a few performatory words which purport to make the parties man and wife. What happens? The psychological effect is instantaneous, uniform and far-reaching. Everybody regards the newly wedded couple as man and wife, using these words. They are thereby socially classified in a new way. This entails a great many consequences of an ethical, religious, social, and legal kind. Certain ethical rules are now held to apply to the couple. They are treated socially according to customs referring to married people. In the legal sphere, a number of rules apply to them.

No mystical, supersensible bond is formed by the act of marriage. We need not, for that reason, discuss whether it is a reality or not to be married; it surely is. But the reality is not supersensible. It consists in a certain kind of place in the social context, depending on people's uniform reaction to the marriage ceremony. Take this reaction away and the performatory words are inane. We are all conditioned to respond to the act in certain ways, and we do it. Thus, when people are known to, or supposed to, have gone through the ceremony in the proper way, then the couple is, so to speak, embedded in social surroundings giving them a certain position and requiring them to conform to certain rules. At the basis of it all are the considerations as to the importance of stability in family relationships.

If the act is to call forth these effects, observance of the customary or prescribed form is essential. If the performative words of the act are pronounced at the theatre, or in jest, or in any connection except by the right person in the proper circumstances, no real marriage is held to be concluded. The act is said to be void. This expression means that the act lacks the force of producing the effect intended by the words. What actually happens is, of course, that pronouncements made outside the proper context are disregarded. This is the reverse side of our inclination to respond in a certain way to the right ceremony.

So far we have talked about the psychological effects of

performatives legal and extra-legal. But there are also 'legal' effects. Are they not something else?
Legal effects are spoken of in two different senses, which must be kept apart:
(i) Legal effects are the effects implied in the rules of law with regard to personal relations and property. Strictly speaking, the word 'effect' is inappropriate in this connection. No legal effects in this sense are caused, for instance, by the act of marriage. What takes place is an alteration in the actual situation to which the legal rules refer. A new fact has been added to the situation; and this fact entails the applicability of a number of rules referring to 'married' persons. This is the whole thing. The so-called effects are nothing but the contents of rules. The legal situation has been changed through the act of marriage in that this act is relevant according to a complex of rules; the rules applying to the couple are now different from what they were before the act.
(ii) Legal effects mean effects that take place through the action of the courts or other state agencies. A man is, for instance, sent to prison for not supporting his wife and children. The effects of this latter sort are actual effects. They are dependent on the psychological effectiveness of the legal rules; they take place because the state organs feel bound by the rules and therefore apply them carefully. All real effects of the act of marriage are therefore ultimately psychological effects.

Origin of Performatory Imperatives

The performatory imperatives have a long history. If we may trust the old tale, the first words ever spoken were performatives.

From the point of view of the narrator it was no absurdity that the omnipotent God created the world and all the living beings by his commands. We do not know how the story of the creation originated. But we can reasonably surmise that it was formed in a community where it was generally acknowledged that men with secret powers could accomplish effects through rites and words. The belief in magic is common to all 'primitive' peoples. It was only natural that the creation of the world was ascribed to the greatest magician.

Magic has been used not only to promote the fertility of the soil and the fecundity of women, to cure disease and to inflict death on enemies, etc. It has also been employed to call forth invisible effects: to confer mysterious powers on a person, to make it dangerous to transgress a boundary line, to bring down the wrath of the gods, and the like. The origin of legal rites and formulae can be traced to this usage.

When the man destined to be king was made a king on the meadow near Uppsala, this was done through a magic rite. The man was placed upon a holy stone—in all probability similar to the Stone of Scone extant in Westminster Abbey—the lawmen recited their formula, conferring kingship on him, and the result was that he became a king. This no doubt meant that he became possessed of secret powers. Therefore he should be obeyed as far as those powers went.

From all parts of the world examples can be collected of how 'rights' have been established through magical ceremonies. The following account has been given of the acquisition of land in Kenya according to tribal custom. The agricultural Kikuyu had a nomadic tribe for neighbours. Since this tribe was much weaker, the Kikuyu could easily have taken by force the land they needed when their numbers increased. But the idea of doing so did not occur to them. They were firmly convinced that the neighbours were protected by their gods; it would be impossible for the Kikuyu to cultivate the soil to their own advantage if they simply took it by force from the possessors. Therefore, negotiations were opened with a view to acquiring a tract of land. But it was not sufficient that an agreement was reached. The transfer had also to be accomplished through a series of religious ceremonies. In the first place mutual adoption had to be made so that the gods became common to both. Finally the boundary line was marked in conjunction with sacrifices to the gods and to the spirits of the forefathers.[5]

If the Romans had held the same sort of belief as the Kikuyu, they would, perhaps, never have extended their domination over Italy. But they had a more dynamic view. Gaius says that the ancients believed those things which they had taken in war to be in the highest degree their own.[6] The war had to be 'just and pious' —*iustum piumque*. In old times the Romans were very particular on this point. The war had to be agreeable to the gods.[7] What was taken in war, including all prisoners, was therefore taken, and kept, with divine assistance.

The ancient sales ceremony, the *mancipatio*, is to be seen against this background. It was rigidly formal. The most salient feature, as compared with a present-day sale and purchase, is the passivity

[5] L. S. B. Leakey, *Mau-Mau and the Kikuyu* (1953) 2 ff.

[6] Gaius, *Inst.* 4,16: *maxime sua esse credebant* [*veteres*], *quae ex hostibus cepissent*.

[7] On the Roman concept of a just war see Hägerström, 1 *Der römische Obligationsbegriff* 552 ff.

of the seller and the activity of the buyer. According to the modern view, the seller confers the right of ownership to an object on the buyer through a declaration of will. Not so in the Roman mancipation. The seller is a passive onlooker whilst the buyer performs a ceremony. In the presence of five witnesses (probably representing the Roman people) and a 'keeper of the balance' he seizes the object, which in the example is a slave, and says: 'I pronounce this man to be mine according to the law of the citizens of Rome, and let him be bought for me through this piece of copper and the copper balance.' The buyer thereafter strikes a piece of copper against the balance and gives it to the seller.[8]

Most probably the ceremony was, in the beginning, intended to represent the taking of a prisoner in war. If this hypothesis is correct, it explains the fact, otherwise strange, that only the buyer is active. However that may be, it is evident that the ceremony is a rite used for acquiring an object. The rite as a whole had to be gone through in the correct manner; as we know from Gaius (Inst. 4,11) the slightest fault in a ceremony of this kind made it void and without effect. The central element was the formula recited by the buyer. Its first part is grammatically in the indicative; but the latter part (*mihi emptus esto*!) is in the imperative. This shows that the first part, too, had the sense of an imperative. The meaning cannot have been to record the circumstance that the slave was the property of the buyer: the words were spoken before the buyer had acquired the slave. Indeed, he does not say straight out: the slave is mine. Instead he says *that he says* the slave is his: 'I pronounce the slave to be mine!' The introductory *aio*, I pronounce, serves to give the words a forceful sense similar to the imperative. The formula as a whole was a performative intended to make the slave the property of the buyer, to bring about the inclusion of the slave within his sphere of 'mine' (*meum esse*).

For the analysis of the act of mancipation see Hägerström, 1 *Der römische Obligationsbegriff* 35 ff. and in the second volume *102* f., *172* f., *308* ff., *343* ff. I have followed the interpretation of Hägerström, although with a significant modification. Different opinions have been expressed regarding the wording of the formula. Several authors have concurred in the opinion of Wlassak that the buyer said: *mihi emptus est* (not *esto*). But there is no real justification for this alteration in the text. The only manuscript extant of the *Institutes* of Gaius has *esto*

[8] Gaius, *Inst.* 1,119: *Hunc ego hominem ex iure Quiritium meum esse aio isque mihi emptus esto hoc aere aeneaeque libra; deinde aere percutit libram idque aes dat ei a quo mancipio accepit, quasi pretii loco.*

in the three places where the formula is rendered (2,104 and 3,167 besides 1,119). Wlassak adduces that Boethius in a commentary on Cicero read *est* in the formula of Gaius and that the *est* occurs in a statement by the jurist Paulus preserved in the *Fragmenta Vaticana* (28 *Zeitschrift der Savigny-Stiftung für Rechtsgeschichte, roman. Abt.*, 1907, 74). Against the threefold *esto* of the Verona manuscript of Gaius these instances carry little weight; a scribe may easily have dropped a letter, especially when he did not understand the meaning of the old formula. The chief reason put forward by Wlassak for his emendation is, indeed, that the formula becomes 'unsupportably asymmetric' if the imperative *esto* is accepted. But there is a lack of symmetry only if the first half of the formula is interpreted as narrating the fact that the slave belongs to the buyer. (Thormann, *Der doppelte Ursprung der mancipatio*, 1943, 47 f., gives good reasons for reading *esto*. See also Kaser, 1 *Römisches Privatrecht*, 1955, 38.)

Hägerström takes no position on this question; he considers the reading doubtful. In his final explanation of the formula (40) he disregards the *mihi emptus esto* and concentrates on the *aio*-sentence, which he paraphrases in the following way: 'Ich sage aus, ich stelle in Worten dar die Zugehörigkeit dieses Menschen zu mir gemäss dem Recht der Quiriten' (40).

This rendering is not convincing. The forcefulness of the sentence has been lost. The buyer is depicted as using symbolic magic. Just as the rainmaker causes thunder and rain by producing noises intended to represent thunder, the buyer is supposed to cause the slave to be his by representing (in words) the situation that the slave is his (*Ich stelle in Worten dar . . .*). As related above, Hägerström himself has shown that the Romans used imperatives to shape legal relationships. This was not a case of symbolic magic; the force of the imperative was supposed to produce the effect. As far as I can see, the *aio*-phrase (to which there are many analogies) served the same purpose. On this assumption the formula becomes coherent and symmetrical: the *aio* . . . and the *esto* correspond.

The French philologist Paul Lejay gives the following translation in his *Histoire de la littérature latine des origines à Plaute* (1924): 'Cet homme, moi je prononce qu'il est mien par le droit quiritaire et qu'il soit acheté pour moi avec ce bronze et cette balance de bronze' (61). This seems to be as adequate a rendering of the formula in a modern language as is possible.

Much fruitless speculation on the meaning of the mancipation formula might have been spared, had attention been drawn earlier to the category of performatives. Today the performatory character of the formula is obvious to us. But it is equally obvious that we have before us a typical piece of verbal magic. What else but magic is it to call forth an effect through words, solemnly recited during a ritual act in strict accordance with an ancient model? The formula was composed by the pontifical jurists at a remote time when, as we know, every aspect of life in the community of the Romans was dominated by their magico-religious beliefs. Surely, this must have been the case not least with such an important act as that of acquiring a slave as one's own. This is not to say that the same beliefs prevailed at the time of the Antonines. We cannot know what view the Romans then took of the meaning of the formula, if they reflected upon it at all. We only know that the act of mancipation was used for certain purposes up to the time of Justinian. In all probability the original meaning had long been forgotten. Only the form remained; but to the correct use of the form important legal and practical consequences were attached.

The puzzling feature of the performatory imperatives so much used in legal language is that they do not enjoin any behaviour on an addressee but are directed towards bringing about a new state of affairs. This feature is explained if we assume that the performatory imperatives were originally employed in magical formulae. If effects are to be brought about through words, forceful words evidently have to be used, not the neutral language employed in recording facts. Imperative speech must have been particularly well suited to the purpose. The desired effect could be commanded to come into being. Other moods could be used, too. An example is the mancipation formula, where the forcefulness and creative purpose of the utterance is emphasized by the *aio*: 'I pronounce' this man to be mine. But in the present context the interesting thing is to note that the apparently absurd imperatives without an addressee, directed towards calling forth effects, become completely comprehensible if we trace their origin back to the language used in verbal magic.

This is not to say, of course, that in our time the same ideas are attached to the performatory imperatives as was the case many hundreds or thousands of years ago. We have travelled a long way since the time when a ritual act representing the taking of prisoners in war was thought to be the proper form for acquiring an object or since kingship was conferred by placing the person designated on a holy stone and reciting a formula over him.

The most significant change seems to be that in ancient time effects such as making a thing 'mine' (*meum*) or endowing a man with kingship were achieved through strictly formal words and actions making up a rite which was supposed to have the power of calling forth the desired effect. This view has lapsed into oblivion. Legal effects are no longer held to be brought about through words and acts as such. The will has taken their place. Words, and to some extent acts, employed in legal transactions are thought to be means of expressing the actor's will. The will itself is supposed to be the efficient cause of legal effects. Legislative acts are represented as declarations of the will of the legitimate lawgiver. A promise is defined as a declaration of will on the part of the promisor. The will-theory in both its aspects—referring to legislative acts and legal transactions between persons—has permeated the general outlook and replaced the view properly described as magical.

Much opposition has been voiced against Hägerström's interpretation of the *mancipatio* and other formal transactions in Roman law as magical acts. Several different questions have been involved in this discussion.

Here we are only concerned with the original meaning of the acts, not with the construction put upon them by the classical jurists. There can be no doubt that the formulae devised by the priests in ancient Rome were pieces of verbal magic. No other explanation fits the facts. How the classical jurists looked upon these formulae more than five hundred years later is another question, which need not and cannot be discussed in this connection.

Kunkel's review of the first volume of *Der römische Obligationsbegriff* (49 *Zeitschrift der Savigny-Stiftung für Rechtsgeschichte, roman. Abt.*, 1929, 479 ff.) is usually cited as an authority for rejecting the magical explanation. It is therefore interesting to see what Kunkel says in another context concerning the similarity between the legalistic theology of the *pontifices* and the *ius civile*, which was also under their control: 'Die magischen Beschwörungsformeln, mit denen man den Willen der Gottheit zu beeinflussen suchte, nahmen einen ausgesprochen juristischen Charakter an; . . . in dem Bereich, in dem sich bei anderen Völkern und in anderen Religionen eine Theologie entwickelt hat, entstand in Rom eine förmliche Jurisprudenz des Verkehrs mit den göttlichen Mächten, eben das ius pontificium, dessen Struktur sich von der des gleichfalls von den Pontifices verwalteten ius civile nicht wesentlich unterschied. . . . Nur die richtige Formel konnte die übernatürlichen Kräfte bannen. . . . Genau die gleiche Vorstellung liegt aber auch dem altrömischen Formalismus auf dem Gebiete des Zivilrechts zugrunde. . . . Trotz aller Rationalisierung der Methode tritt also auch in der zivilrechtlichen Jurisprudenz der Pontifices noch die magische Natur ihres Priesteramts hervor. Sie beherrschte das ius civile ebenso wie das ius sacrum, weil sie allein die berufenen Kenner der "wirksamen" Formeln waren.' (*Schriften der Universität Heidelberg* H.3, 1948, 28 f.)

This is an admirably clear and cogent expression of the view that the ancient legal transactions were magical acts. What Kunkel says here must be applicable not least to the act of mancipation, which was one of the most important legal transactions in the *ius civile*.

The arguments Kunkel uses in the review to refute Hägerström's thesis that the act of mancipation was magical refers to other questions. Kunkel contends (485 f.):

(i) In the late republic and in the empire the ancient rites had become *vielfach unverständlich und zum leeren Ritual*. There is no difference of opinion on this point. (*Cf.* 2 *Der römische Obligationsbegriff 313:* 'Es ist allerdings wahr, dass später der fragliche Ritus [*die Mancipatio*] nur deshalb gebraucht wurde, weil es so sein musste, ohne Reflexion über seinen Sinn.')

(ii) Classical jurisprudence elevated *uralte Begriffe in eine andere, nüchterne Sphäre*. Whether this was really done is a separate question, to be distinguished from the question about the original meaning of the formula.

(iii) The words *hunc ego hominem* . . . in the mancipation rite were not a magical formula (*Zauberformel*) but a declaration of will (*Willenserklärung*); for this thesis several arguments are adduced.

If Kunkel is right in his view on the role of the priests, the mancipation formula must have been constructed by them as a magical formula (*Zauberformel*). What he says in the review refers to the character which the formula is supposed to have assumed when the classical jurists had transformed the legal concepts. Kunkel here asserts two propositions: (i) that in classical times the mancipation formula was a *Willenserklärung* and nothing else, and (ii) that the formula was regarded in this light by the jurists. Both contentions are debatable. But they do not refer to the original meaning of the formula.

Much confusion has been caused by uncertainty concerning the implications of the word 'magic'. In his work *Römisches Privatrecht* (I, 1955) Kaser says (23): 'Einen Einschlag von *Magie* enhält vielleicht der frühzeitliche *Symbolismus* der Rechtsformen. . . . Eine Stufe prälogischen Denkens mag hier geglaubt haben, die bezweckte Vollwirkung, dass der andere gebunden ist, durch einen Helfedämon herbeiführen zu können.' But the influence of magic on private law has been *masslos übertrieben* by Hägerström.

If the magical theory is interpreted in Kaser's way, it must obviously be rejected. There is no trace in the sources there of the idea that the assistance of 'auxiliary daemons' was invoked in the act of mancipation, and Hägerström does not say so. By characterizing the act as magical he means that the effect of making the slave the property of the speaker was held to be achieved through the ritual words and gestures. But this is exactly what Kaser says, too (40): 'Der mit Wort und Hand vollzogene Ergreifungsakt des Erwerbers hat rechtsbegründende Kraft: das '*meum esse aio*' wird durch den rituellen Vollzug wahr.' The words and gestures bring about the effect.

So far there is no real difference of opinion between Kaser and Hägerström. Both understand the meaning of the act in the same way: the acquisition is made by means of the words and gestures. But there are differences as regards the import of the 'acquisition' and the use of the word 'magic':

(i) For Kaser it is quite natural to say that the act really had *rechtsbegründende Kraft*. The intended effect of the act really and objectively takes place: the speaker acquires the *dominium ex iure Quiritium*. Hägerström never says so. He only speaks of the idea through which the formula can be explained, *viz.*, that the words and gestures had the power of making the slave the property of the buyer.

(ii) For both authors the word magic signifies the bringing about of certain effects by means of solemn words and ritual acts. The difference is in the nature of the effects. In Kaser's view magic consists in the invocation of daemons and in *Schadenzauber, Verhexung, Fluchtafeln, Totenbeschwörung*, etc. (23 footnote 21). For Hägerström other effects, too, are included under the word magic. The magical effects of which he speaks in his treatise on Roman law are non-psychological effects of legal acts supposed to be called forth by words and ceremonies, such as the acquisition of the *dominium ex iure Quiritium*. (The question of 'magic' will be discussed further in the next chapter.)

The Theory of Performatives

In the paper 'Other Minds' from 1946, where Austin first adumbrated the theory of performatives, he points out the fallacy of interpreting 'ritual phrases' like 'I promise', 'I do' (*sc.* take this woman to be my lawful wedded wife), 'I give' when it is mine to give, or 'I order' when I have the authority as reporting the fact that I am promising, marrying, giving something away, or issuing an order. The expressions, he says, are 'not *describing* the action we are doing.'[9]

This is obviously correct. In giving away a watch to somebody I do not describe the act of giving it away; the bridegroom does not describe the marriage ceremony.

Austin does not mention any instance where an author has committed a 'descriptive fallacy', of this kind. Examples may possibly be found. For my own part I can remember none from legal literature, where such expressions have been discussed at great length.

[9] *PhP* 71.

Returning to the example of a promise Austin later draws attention to another kind of descriptive fallacy. It is very easy to think, he says, that the phrase 'I promise to . . .', is simply 'the outward and visible (*i.e.* verbal) sign of the performance of some inward spiritual act of promising'. This view, he adds, has certainly been expressed in many classical places. As an example he mentions the utterance of Euripides Hippolytus 'My tongue swore to, but my heart did not'.[10]

In this case Austin struck upon a descriptive fallacy that is really very common in legal literature. The view on the nature of a promise which he refutes is that of the teachers of natural law. As we have seen, they regarded a promise as a *declaratio* or *signum voluntatis,* an outward sign of the inward will. This is a descriptive fallacy which has played an important role in the history of legal thinking.

> If Austin had been aware of the theory of the *declaratio voluntatis,* which he probably was not, he could have adduced a better example than the utterance of Hippolytus. It is interesting to note that two other authors, who have discussed the performatives, also find it very easy to think that the words 'I promise' are the outward sign of an inward act of promising. (Furberg, *Locutionary and Illocutionary Acts in J. L. Austin's Philosophy,* 1963, 195, and Samek, 'Performative Utterances and the Concept of Contract' in 43 *The Australasian Journal of Philosophy,* 1965, 199.) The teachers of natural law evidently had a basis for their doctrine of promises in a view which is somehow natural to us.

None of the utterances referred to is either true or false, Austin says: 'I assert this as obvious and do not argue it'.[11] The reason is evidently that the utterances do not describe anything.

At the same time Austin emphasizes that the utterances are 'not nonsensical'. This he takes as a matter of course and does not discuss the question.[12]

So far Austin says (i) that the utterances are not descriptions of facts, (ii) that they are therefore neither true nor false, and (iii) that, nevertheless, they are not nonsensical.

The next question to be raised would seem to be: what is the meaning of those utterances? If the sentences describe no facts, if they are neither true nor false, and if they are not meaningless, their

[10] *PhP* 223; *cf. HTD* 9, 13.
[11] *HTD* 6, *cf.* 12 and *PhP* 222, 224.
[12] *PhP* 222; *HTD* 4: 'The type of utterance we are to consider here is not, of course, in general a type of nonsense.'

meaning ought to be explained. That they have some meaning seems to be undeniable. We use them every day, they are pretty well understood, and they serve a lot of practical purposes. This could not be so, were they only noise without meaning. To explain their meaning should therefore be the next task.

But Austin never addressed himself to this problem. He neglected it. On the question of the meaning of the utterances he only made the negative statement that they are not nonsensical.

Instead he speaks about how we talk about these utterances: 'If a person makes an utterance of this sort we should say that he is doing something rather than merely saying something.'[13] In naming a ship, Austin says, 'I do not describe the christening ceremony, I actually perform the christening; and when I say "I do" (*sc.* take this woman to be my lawful wedded wife), I am not reporting on a marriage, I am indulging in it'.[14] 'Utterance of obvious ritual phrases, in the appropriate circumstances, is not describing the action we are doing, but doing it.'[15] This is the reason why the utterances in question are called performatives by Austin. An action is performed by uttering them.

The term 'performative utterances' serves to mark a contrast with declarative or, as Austin prefers to say, 'constative' utterances, usually called statements. The 'Performative-Constative antithesis' consists of the fact that the constative utterance has the property of being true or false while the performative is neither, its job being to perform an action.[16]

This contrast is bewildering. It seems that I perform an action in making a statement, or constative utterance, as well as when I pronounce a formula in a marriage ceremony or say that I name a ship so and so. That the uttering of the words constitutes an action is no peculiar characteristic of the so-called performatives as opposed to the constatives.

Having the property of being true or false and having the job of performing an action are not in contrast. If the two kinds of

[13] *PhP* 222; *cf. HTD* 5: 'The uttering of the sentence is, or is part of, the doing of an action, which again would not *normally* be described as saying something.'

[14] *PhP* 222; *cf. HTD* 6.

[15] *PhP* 71.

[16] 'Performative-Constative' in *Philosophy and Ordinary Language* (ed. Charles Caton, 1963, cited *PC*) 22: 'The constative utterance, under the name, so dear to philosophers, of *statement*, has the property of being true or false. The performative utterance, by contrast, can never be either: it has its own special job, it is used to perform an action.'

sentences are contrasted with regard to their meaning we should say: the meaning of constative sentences is to assert the reality of something, the meaning of performative sentences is not to assert the reality of anything. Then we should have to inquire about the meaning of the sentences mentioned as examples of 'performatives'.

It is, however, easy to comprehend why Austin chose to call the utterances in question performatives. He began by reflecting on cases where we are supposed to achieve a result through uttering certain 'ritual phrases' in appropriate circumstances.[17] One gets married through the marriage ceremony; a man and a woman become husband and wife. When I make a promise (of a legal nature) I create an obligation for myself and a right for the addressee. When a ship is christened, it gets a name: the ship thereafter carries that name. Thus we think and speak.

Now results may also be achieved by constative utterances, as when the addressee is instructed or deceived. This is a psychological effect. Such effects may also follow from performative utterances; I will feel bound when I have made a promise. But the peculiarity with the cases cited is that a non-psychological effect is supposed to follow. The effect that a marriage has been concluded is not a psychological effect; it is an effect of another kind, not to be identified with the impression made by the ceremony on those present and on others. The creation of a right and an obligation is not a psychological effect; nor is it a psychological effect that a ship has got a certain name.

Strictly speaking the non-psychological effects are not supposed to be called forth through the words alone. The words pronounced by the man in the marriage ceremony are only a part of the ceremony; and the marriage is concluded only when the ceremony has been gone through according to the law. The words 'I promise' have to be uttered in such a setting that they are deemed to satisfy the requirements of the law for a promise. The shipowner's wife has to pronounce the formula 'I name this ship . . .' in a ceremony arranged for the purpose of christening the ship. The adjective 'performative' or 'performatory' should therefore primarily apply to the act, though it might also be used to qualify the formula used in the act since the formula is its most conspicuous element.

Consequently, we might quite properly be said to 'do things with words' in the sense that marriages are concluded, ships named, and

[17] This is evident in the paper 'Other Minds', *PhP* 67 ff.

rights established through words uttered in certain circumstances. The expressions that a marriage is concluded, a ship named, or a promise made comprise the supposed non-psychological effects of the ritual acts. It was this use of language that caused Austin to create the term 'performative utterances'.[18]

But as Austin never inquired into the meaning of the 'ritual phrases', he also omitted to discuss the nature of the supposed non-psychological effects of the ritual acts. He did not raise the question what it means that two persons have got married, that a ship has got a name, or that a right has been created. Therefore, he lost sight of the fact that doing something with words consists in calling forth a supposed non-psychological effect. To do things with words became merely uttering the words ('in appropriate circumstances').

When the supposed effects of the acts had been forgotten, the category of performatives was extended. It came to include a number of utterances that are not supposed to give rise to any non-psychological effects. Phrases like 'I congratulate you', 'I advise you', etc. were also said to be performatives.[19]

Thus the category of performatives was diluted. The one remaining characteristic of the performative utterances became the fact that we often, in speaking of them, use the same verb as that which is employed in the utterance itself: we say that a man has promised something when he has said 'I promise . . .'. But this is not always the case. We may speak in other terms of the acts in which such words occur. So the category of performatives could not be definitely

[18] *PhP* 67: 'When I say "I promise" . . . I have not merely announced my intention, but, by using this formula (performing this ritual), I have bound myself to others, and staked my reputation.' A non-psychological effect of the ritual is supposed to occur, *viz.*, that of being bound (legally speaking being obligated), though it is mixed up with the psychological effect of the reputation being staked. *Cf. PhP* 224 f.: There must exist a conventional procedure to be used in uttering performatives and in a concrete case the appropriate circumstances must be present. Otherwise 'the act which we purported to perform is void, without effect'. Jurists would say that no legal effects ensue: no rights or duties are created. *Cf. PC* 23: 'Our performative, like any other ritual or ceremony, may be, as the lawyers say, "null and void". If, for example, the speaker is not in a position to perform an act of that kind, or if the object with respect to which he purports to perform it is not suitable for the purpose, then he does not manage, simply by issuing his utterance, to carry out the purported act.' Austin obviously means: carry out the act with the desired effect. Furberg points out (218) that the obligation 'is built into the notion of promising'.

[19] In his last paper on performatives (*PC* 22) Austin started by mentioning the following examples of performatives: 'I name this ship "Liberté"; I apologize; I welcome you; I advise you to do it.' Only the first phrase is an example of an utterance destined to achieve a non-pyschological effect.

circumscribed at all. Ultimately the distinction between performatives and constatives (statements) broke down.[20]

It is somewhat surprising that Austin never mentions the formulae of verbal magic though they are the most striking performatives of all. The reason for this omission is perhaps that he took it for granted that the performatives, about which he wanted to speak, were not nonsensical. He would undoubtedly have regarded magical formulae as pure nonsense. But if they had been taken into consideration, the affinity between them and many legal expressions would have attracted notice.

In the fields of law and religion and in certain other contexts we have abundant material for studying performatives in the exact sense of the word: expressions used to call forth non-psychological effects. If they are characterized as being either nonsensical, or not nonsensical, we have to ask: in what sense are they nonsensical, or not nonsensical, respectively?

It is obviously not nonsense to ascribe psychological effects to verbal utterances. But from a modern point of view it would seem absurd to assert that words could have the power of creating effects of any other kind. We are not believed to be able to 'do things with words' in that sense. This, at least, is the scientific opinion. It would not be said that a supersensible, spiritual bond between a man and woman is really established through the utterance of a few words before an official. Nevertheless, the marriage ceremony is of great social importance. The use of the appropriate words in the right circumstances is not nonsensical in the sense that this use of words is purposeless. There are countless instances of formulae having important social functions though their content is perhaps, from a modern intellectual standpoint, nonsensical. We shall return to this question in the next chapter.

In a paper called 'Austin on Performatives' in 38 *Philosophy* (1963) 222 Max Black notes that the 'conventional', 'ritual', or 'ceremonial' action performed according to Austin by uttering 'a genuine performative' are 'claim-generating'. The performer of the act '*counts* as satisfying certain demands, acquiring certain rights or privileges, becoming subject to determinable claims, etc.'. The act in question 'is taken to have a certain non-natural meaning or significance'. This refers to the legal effects of performatives.

In the paper 'Performatives' (42 *The Journal of Philosophy*,

[20] *PhP* 238. *Cf.* Walter Cerf in 75 *Mind* (1966) 262 ff.; Searle in 77 *The Philosophical Review* (1968) 405 ff.

1965, 459 ff.) A. Sesonske notes three classes of relationship between persons in which language plays a vital role and in which an utterance can alter the relation. These are psychological, generative, and formal relations. An example of a formal relation being altered is the marriage ceremony. When a minister says: 'I now pronounce you man and wife,' the formal relations between a man and woman have changed. Other examples mentioned are 'promising, introducing, appointing, hiring, firing, giving a gift, making an offer', etc., mostly, but not always, legal transactions. That formal relations are altered means that some actions that would not have been so before the words were spoken become 'permissible, appropriate, or obligatory' (465). The author points out that all the examples from which Austin starts are examples of utterances whose point is to alter 'formal relations' (466). He proposes to define performatives as precisely this kind of utterances (467).

In his recent work *Directives and Norms* (1968) Alf Ross says concerning the performatives (27): 'Because a statement creates expectations, or claims and corresponding responsibilities, it belongs to the group of linguistic acts which has been called *performative*. If this concept is to be of philosophical and not only linguistic interest, it should in my opinion be limited to the designation of locutionary acts which by virtue of a social norm create social relations of claims, obligations, and responsibilities determined in accordance with the meaning content of the act.'

CHAPTER 9

LEGAL LANGUAGE AND REALITY

No working legal system is conceivable without language. Nevertheless, the role of language in the law has attracted comparatively little attention. Only quite recently have articles and books on the subject begun to appear.[1]

The chief reason for this situation in legal theory is probably the traditional view that 'the world of law' belongs to another sphere of reality than the spatio-temporal world in which language is an ingredient. But some assumptions concerning the role of language have, of necessity, always been made. Two opposite and extreme positions can be discerned as underlying reasoning on legal matters: on the one hand the magical view and on the other hand the view belonging to classical natural law doctrine. In the former the emphasis was laid on the word, in the latter on the will, for which the word was a means of expression.

The Word and the Will

According to the magical view, words possess a mysterious force. Solemn phrases recited during a ritual act are held to be capable of producing effects. Such was the origin of the Roman verbal contracts. The *sponsio* was originally a promise made in conjunction with a libation; the wrath of the gods was called down on the one who broke his promise. In time the real libation was dispensed with; the act became symbolic. Finally, only the ancient form of words remained while their original meaning was probably forgotten.[2]

The jurists preserved the ancient formal acts and the rules pertaining to them while they developed informal contracts. When

[1] Glanville Williams's 'Language and the Law' (61 & 62 *The Law Quarterly Review*, 1945–46) was perhaps the first essay expressly devoted to the question of the role of language in the law. Dieter Horn's *Rechtssprache und Kommunikation* (Berlin, Duncker & Humblot 1966) contains an extensive bibliography. See also Julius Stone, *Legal System and Lawyers' Reasoning* (1964) and Max Black, *Models and Metaphors* (1962) ch. V ('Necessary Statements and Rules'), discussed by Jan Moline in 35 *Theoria* (1969) 168 ff.; Luigi Bagolini, 'Positivismo giuridico e analisi del linguaggio' (*Rivista trimestrale di diritto e procedura civile* 1966).

[2] Hägerström, 2 *Der römische Obligationsbegriff* 107 ff.

the jurists said that the formal contracts were concluded with words, *verbis*, and not through *consensus*, they meant what they said. They were expressing the old principle, based on magic, that the bond on the promisor was created by the words. In the case of the *mancipatio* and other 'libral' acts (acts *per aes et libram*) the legal effect was held to be brought about through the ceremony including the recitation of a formula.

Roman jurisprudence was interpretative. The jurists did not offer any theory of their own on the nature of the law or on the legal concepts. Their business was to tell what the existing law implied and develop it through interpretation. They did not speculate on the essence of law and rights. With regard to the old civil law, the *ius civile*, their principles of interpretation were extremely conservative. For many centuries the jurists continued to reason along traditional lines. No overt break with the original view occurred until the late empire, when the emperors began to discard certain remnants of the ancient law which seemed to be meaningless.[3]

In contradistinction to Roman jurisprudence, classical natural law doctrine was speculative and systematizing. Its principal purpose was not to interpret an existing positive law. The great object was to explain rationally the nature of law in general, to lay a foundation for positive law, and to show that there was an international law obtaining between nations. To this end the universal and timeless law of nature was constructed.

The law now came to be regarded as the contents of a will. The law of nature was the will of God, positive human law the will of the sovereign. For practical reasons only the will had to be signified to the subjects. (In the case of the law of nature this was not required because these commands by God were immediately apprehensible for the human mind.) The will of the lawgiver could be communicated in any suitable way; the form was unimportant.

Legal transactions between individuals were regarded in the same light. The will of the promisor to transfer a part of his liberty to the promisee and the acceptance by the latter were the creative forces in establishing a right for the promisee against the promisor. Only because the internal will as such could not be considered in social relations, was an external sign necessary. Here, too, the form was without importance; any comprehensible sign of the will was sufficient, if nothing more was required by positive law. The transfer of property rights was treated correspondingly. Over the whole field

[3] *Cf.* Jhering, II: 2 *Geist des römischen Rechts* (4. Aufl. 1883) 471.

the will was the source of rights. Words had no significance but that of communicating the content of the will to others.

There is a certain similarity between the view of natural law doctrine and the magical view. According to both theories rights and duties are said to be 'created', 'transferred', etc., through legal transactions. But there is an important difference with regard to the means of bringing about such legal effects.

No definition of 'magic' has been generally accepted. But it always seems to be understood that magic consists in producing effects through such outward means as words and gestures. In performing verbal magic the speaker is not supposed to cause an effect through his will. He makes use of a formula, generally in connection with some rite, for the realization of his purpose. The creative force is not believed to be his will but the words and acts, which are held to possess some secret power.

If this is taken to be characteristic of 'magic', as has been done in the present book, it is obviously not correct to say that the teachers of natural law entertained a magical view. They regarded the will, and not the words or gestures used, as the active force in creating and transferring rights.

There is another difference, too, between the magical view and natural law doctrine. The magician is supposed to control mystical forces outside himself, as was the case when the wrath of the gods was called down on someone who broke a promise made in connection with a libation. In natural law doctrine there is no question of directing forces outside the human mind through legal transactions. As we have seen, all rights are supposed to have their origin in promises made by free individuals. But a promise consisted in the transference of a part of the liberty, or *potestas in se*, of the promisor to the promisee. Thereby the will of the promisor became morally subject to the will of the promisee with regard to a certain action (or group of actions). This implies that legal effects consisted of alterations in the relationship between different wills. Such were the effects of every legal transaction. There is a vast difference between this theory and the magical view.

The deepest motivation for the teachers of natural law in constructing their system was perhaps a desire to overcome the magical view. For them the law was a part of a moral order of the universe, governed by the will of God. It would not be consistent with this view to ascribe legal effects to words and gestures as such. The effects must be referred to the will of free and rational beings.

Natural law doctrine, therefore, was decidedly non-magical and even anti-magical.

The will-theory was taken over by the positivists. The law of nature was discarded. But positive law was held to be the will of the supreme authority in society; and legal transactions were interpreted as declarations of will.

These dogmas have left a lasting imprint on the general outlook concerning legal and political matters. The will of the people is held to be the supreme authority, the sole source of legitimacy for lawgivers. In legal transactions the words used are not considered as having any force of their own. They are only regarded as means of expressing the will of the parties. The will is held to be the active force in establishing rights and duties. If special formalities are prescribed for a transaction, they are only regarded as the outer trappings in which the will of the parties has to manifest itself.

This view has long been so firmly established that it has been applied not only to modern law. It has also formed the basis of the interpretation of historical phenomena.

This is especially evident in the mode of treating the significance of formalities in legal transactions. The first jurist to discuss this question was Jhering. His exposition in the second volume of the *Geist des römischen Rechts* (470 ff.) has become classical. Conforming with the view inherited from natural law doctrine Jhering holds that the effects of legal transactions, ancient and modern, are brought about by the will of the parties, though the will has to be declared in some suitable way. Usually the will is free to choose the mode of expressing itself. But sometimes a definite form is prescribed. The will is always the active force. The difference between informal and formal transactions is that in the case of the latter the will has to manifest itself in a certain way.

Jhering's contemporary Sir Henry Maine held a similar view. Speaking about the development in Roman law he characterizes 'form and ceremony' as an 'external shell' to the mental engagement, signified through 'external acts', which 'gradually becomes the sole ingredient [in pacts or conventions] on which the interest of the jurisconsult is concentrated'. (*Ancient Law*, ch. IX.)

The following utterances by Kaser (1 *Römisches Privatrecht* 202) is an example of how the will-theory serves as the basis for discussing questions of legal history. Referring to the formal character of the ancient legal transactions in Roman law Kaser says:

'Die . . . dargestellten Rechtsakte beruhten auf dem ursprünglichen Formalismus eines Volkes, das sich rechtswirksames Handeln anders als formgebunden nicht vorstellen kann. Indem sich allmählich die Erkenntnis festigt, dass nicht das äussere Handeln, sondern der innere Wille dem Rechtsakt Kraft und Sinn gibt, wandelt sich jedoch die Funktion der Formen.'

It is taken to be an indubitable fact that 'the force and meaning' of legal acts stem from the inner will of the parties. In former times people did not understand this. Only at a later stage was the real character of legal transactions realized.

Recently, however, the magical theory with regard to the significance of formalities in ancient law has been gaining ground. Dulckeit adopts it for instance in the article 'Zur Lehre vom Rechtsgeschäft im klassischen römischen Recht' (1 *Festschrift Schulz,* 1951, 161 ff.). He proclaims this theory with great emphasis. The formalities were not, as they are today, a covering for the will prescribed for practical reasons; they were the creative element in the transactions. ('Die Form allein führt die Rechtsfolge herbei.') The origin of this old view is to be found in magic. 'Nicht weil die Person es will und diesen ihren Willen kundtut, tritt die Rechtswirkung ein, sondern weil die seit alters her überlieferten und "erprobten" Zauberhandlungen und magischen Formeln diese Änderung unmittelbar hervorbringen . . . Für die archaische Vorstellung ist [die Form] die magische Kraft, die sich in einer unmittelbar *geistigen* —und in diesem Sinn in der Tat zauberischen—*Veränderung der Aussenwelt* äussert.'

Just as the natural law view on legal transactions was not magical in the sense of the word used here, the view of modern jurisprudence cannot correctly be characterized as magical in this sense. It is true that rights and duties are said to be 'created' and 'transferred' through promises, conveyances, etc. But the 'legal effects' are certainly not ascribed to the words and forms as such. If any theory at all is held on the subject, the effects are supposed to depend on the law and the will of the parties. Whatever terminology is employed, there is a crucial difference between the magical and the modern view.

Hägerström, and later Lundstedt, called the legal transactions of our time 'magical'. Once Hägerström said that a housewife buying fish in the market-place performs an act of magic. ('Vergleich zwischen den Kraftvorstellungen der primitiven und der modernen Kulturvölker', *Festskrift tillägnad A. Grotenfelt,* 1933, 84.) The reason for this form of expression is that the right of property, according to Hägerström, is conceived as a mystical power over the object. He regards the ostensible handling and control of such powers as 'magic'.

The nearest approach to a definition of magic which I have found in Hägerström's writings is an utterance defending his own use of the word magic. The Romans, he says, regarded the right of property, the obligation, etc., as including a supersensible power. He has called this power 'magical' because one is concerned with such incomprehensible powers in magic. (2 *Der römische Obligationsbegriff 399:* 'Magisch habe ich [die übersinnliche Macht] genannt, weil man sich in der Magie mit solchen unbegreiflichen Kräften beschäftigt.')

Hägerström has shown that there is a fundamental difference between the concept of a right in Roman jurisprudence and in natural law doctrine, from which the modern concept of a right derives. But in both cases he found the right to be a mystical power. Therefore, he held that, just as the Roman *pater familias* was working magic in the act of mancipation, the housewife of 1930 was doing so in acquiring the right of ownership to the fish through a bargain with the fishmonger. In expressing himself thus he disregarded the difference between the Roman and the modern idea of a right. Moreover, Hägerström paid no attention here to the difference with respect to the means by which the control over mystical powers is supposed to be exercised: words and rites on the one hand, the will on the other. The same word 'magic' came to be applied indiscriminately to both views despite their different character. I think this was unfortunate.

Actually, Hägerström emphasized that Roman 'magic' was exercised by means of words and rites and that the natural law view of legal transactions as declarations of will was alien to the Romans. If this distinction had been reflected in an adequate and precise terminology, much misunderstanding would have been avoided. In fact, modern research into the history of legal ideas is moving in the same direction as Hägerström. He was a little in advance of his time; his language was unusual and sometimes difficult to understand. But his work on the views of the Romans remains an inexhaustible source of information and ideas.

Words as Tools

Both in the magical and in the natural law view words are tools. But for what?

In the magical view words are means of bringing about the creation, transference, and extinction of rights and duties and legal qualities. In the natural law view the 'legal effects' are generated by the will of the individual; and the words merely serve to make his will known to others.

Both views are based on the assumption that 'legal effects' of a supersensible kind take place. The question to be answered is supposed to be how these effects are brought about. The more ancient, magical view refers the effects to the power of words and rites. The more sophisticated natural law view implies that the effects do not consist in creating and transferring powers outside the human mind. The effects are held to consist in alterations in the moral relations between human wills; they are, therefore, supposed to be brought about through acts of will.

These two views are supposed to give an answer to an unanswerable question. The problem for legal theory must be framed in a different way. It is useless to continue discussing how supersensible effects are produced through legal acts.

How then should the question be framed? A question is an incentive to make a search in some direction. We cannot know beforehand what we will find. But the question must be related to the fund of knowledge we actually possess; the search has to begin from the point where we are standing.

We have no knowledge of any supersensible effects of legal transactions. But we know that a number of transactions called purchases, loans, conveyances, etc. take place; and we know in a general way that, in the usual course of things, they are actually followed by more or less important consequences. In these transactions certain forms of language are used.

Meaningful questions can be raised concerning the role of language in those transactions and in communications of other kinds. We can make inquiries about the origin of the language, its actual use, and the consequences thereof. Words are certainly tools in legal transactions; and we can study the function of the tools. Such problems take the place of questions about supersensible effects.

Some empirical questions concerning legal language have already been discussed. The word ' right ' as commonly used turned out to lack semantic reference. How it comes about that it nevertheless has such paramount importance in society was explained by pointing out two sets of circumstances: On the one hand, the word is used with relative consistency according to certain rules; on the other hand, consequential ideas concerning correct and obligatory behaviour are attached to the idea that somebody has a right, *i.e.*, that the right really exists and belongs to that person.

There are many other words in our legal language with similar functions. They are used according to regularized patterns, and consequential ideas attach to them when they are supposed to have been used according to those patterns. A few examples may be given.

The monetary unit

The word for the monetary unit (the pound, the dollar, etc.) is of exceptional importance. Its use has given rise to much speculation. The concept of money has often seemed to have something enigmatic about it. The reason for this is the elusive character of the monetary unit itself.

We talk of pounds, dollars, and other monetary units as if they are entities which actually exist and which can be counted in quantities. But it is difficult to identify these entities. Every attempt to do so seems to fail.

A pound sterling is not, of course, identical with a pound note; for a pound note is only held to represent a pound.

For a long time it was generally thought that a pound signified a certain quantity of gold of a certain quality. Sir Robert Peel is reported to have said in the House of Commons that he could not, 'by any effort of his own understanding, form any other idea of a pound sterling but a certain determinate weight of gold metal'. This opinion, which at the time was shared by almost all, was plausible in the heyday of the gold standard; but it cannot be upheld when notes are no longer redeemed in gold.

What, then, is a pound? On a pound note you read that the Bank of England promises to pay the bearer on demand the sum of one pound. But what happens if you ask the Bank of England to fulfil this promise? You will receive another note with the same inscription, and so on *ad infinitum*. You will never get the pound itself.

It looks as if the pound has vanished into thin air. Professor Hawtrey has compared it to the grin of the Cheshire cat which is the only thing that remains when the cat itself has disappeared.

In order to give some substance to the notion of a monetary unit it has been said that the unit signifies a certain amount of value. But what is an amount of value? How could anybody represent a quantity of value to his mind? You can represent things that you buy for a pound or a dollar; but that is something else. Moreover, what you can buy for a pound depends on how many pounds you have at your disposal.

It seems to be impossible to find anything at all that is denoted by the word 'pound' or 'dollar'. But is not this paradoxical? We count numbers of pounds and dollars; and how could this be done unless there were objects to be counted?

Yet, the difficulty of finding any objects denoted by the pound or the dollar seems to be insuperable. Another way out must be sought for.

Light is shed on the whole matter if we consider the legal and social effects of making promises to pay a sum of pounds. If I make such a promise, I place myself in a position of constraint; a trap closes on me. Unless I wish to expose myself to very unpleasant consequences, I have to perform what is called payment at the proper time. If I omit this, I will impair my reputation and suffer loss of credit. Moreover, legal consequences of a serious nature are in store for the promisor; he may be sued and his belongings may be taken from him and sold in order to satisfy the creditor.

For all this to happen, it is quite irrelevant whether or not there are any objects denoted by the word 'pound'. What matters is that one has made a promise to pay so and so many pounds; in public opinion as well as in law, a certain behaviour is required when you have made such a promise. Contrary behaviour entails the said consequences.

But wait a moment! The behaviour that is demanded from me consists in the payment of a sum of pounds. How could I perform this act if there were no objects which are characterized as being pounds? Is it not necessary that I deliver some objects, called pounds, which can be counted?

In order to meet this objection we have only to remind ourselves of how payments are performed in our society. Small payments are made by handing over certain scraps of paper or bits of metal issued by a bank for the purpose. On these scraps of paper and bits of metal there is an inscription reading 'one pound', 'one penny', and so on; in virtue of this inscription the objects are said to represent so and so many monetary units. We do not have the units themselves in our hands, only their representatives; but through delivery of the representatives the corresponding number of units is considered to be transferred.

The bulk of payments are made by means of cheques. This implies that the creditor instead of his claim against the debtor gets a claim against a bank; this claim he can use for payments of debts of his own, and so on. There is an endless chain of exchange of claims, in which low-grade claims are exchanged for high-grade claims against banks; and the mutual claims of the banks are cancelled out in the clearing-house.

The banking accounts as well as the coins and notes are very hard to acquire. That is why it is a serious step to make a promise to pay a sum of money. I must see to it that I can perform one of those acts that are considered to effect the transference of the sum promised.

Nowhere are the pounds to be found except in speech. But this form of speech is most important socially. It is quite immaterial that the pounds are not objects. The significant thing is that we talk about them in certain ways.

It is, indeed, one of the most fruitful inventions of the human mind that the objects have been eliminated while the form of speech referring to them has been retained. To handle thousands and millions of objects would be impossible; but it is easy to speak of them and to use them in book-keeping.

To fulfil its social functions, speech cannot be disorderly. There are certain rules governing its use. To be legally relevant a promise to pay a sum of money should meet the requirements of the law; a cheque must be drawn up in the form prescribed, and so on. Not without reason has the monetary system been likened to a gigantic game; it is essential that we play the game according to the rules.

The case of the monetary unit is highly illuminating. We find here a noun ostensibly used as denoting an object. But there is no object; the word has ceased to denote anything at all. It nevertheless plays an important role when employed in certain ways according to law and social custom. By means of its use the whole exchange of goods and services is mediated. In order to obtain delivery of some goods or the performance of a service, one puts oneself in a position of constraint by making a promise to pay a sum of money at a certain date; to release oneself from the position of constraint one has to carry out one of those formal acts which are deemed to bring about the transference of the sum of money promised. In this way the machinery of the economy grinds on. Nobody cares to inquire about the supposed objects designated by the word for the monetary unit; the goods, the services, the positions of constraint, and the means of release from them are the significant things.[4]

Appointments

A man is appointed judge. This is done through a performatory act by the chief of state. He signs a paper which has been prepared for him where it says in conventional language that X is 'appointed

[4] See further Appendix 2.

to be judge ' in a certain court. This act is supposed to make X a judge. We think and speak as if X had now acquired a new property: that of being a judge. He is not quite the same human being as before. There is a new aura about him.

What has happened? The performatory act has been duly accomplished and this has been made known in suitable ways. Everybody now calls X a judge, and customary respect is shown to him. A great many legal rules concerning the organization of the courts and their work become applicable to X. These rules do not directly refer to the act of appointment but to its supposed effect that somebody has become a judge. The property of being a judge is interposed between the appointment and the rules concerning judges.

Strictly and objectively speaking X has acquired no new property. But the title of a judge has been conferred on him in the way prescribed by the constitution. Both state officials and the general public then follow suit. The consequential rules attached to somebody being a judge are applied by the state authorities: and the consequential ideas connected with the idea that X is a judge are held by people in general. These attitudes result in the creation of a network of relationships for X. He becomes actually capable of conducting the business of the court according to legal rules, his decisions are applied by the authorities concerned, he gets his salary, and his social position corresponds to his functions.

Such is the case with all public officials from top to bottom of the scale. There is a word structure of different positions in the hierarchy: chief of state, ministers, civil servants, military officers. Each title is a point of reference for a group of legal rules concerning the tasks to be performed by the occupant of a position, the relevancy of his acts for other authorities and for the general public, his remuneration, and the sanctions that may be applied for neglect of duty. When the rules are, on the whole, regularly applied, each nomination places a person in a particular position where his actions become significant for other people and where he, by applying the rules himself, contributes to keep the whole system going.

Juridical persons

From the standpoint of the will-power theory rights and duties are properties in a person. The right is a power belonging to the person's will; if he is under a duty, his will is subject to the domination of another person's will. It would seem to follow that rights and duties could only belong to real living human beings, physical persons. But it was impossible, from a practical point of view, to draw this conclusion. It was necessary also to regard rights and duties as belonging to organizations of many kinds, such as churches, guilds, foundations, companies, etc. Since, however, there had to be a person possessed of the rights and subject to the duties, a person was constructed for that purpose. The rights and duties of the organization were held to belong to a fictitious person, a person existing only 'in the eye of the law'. Allegedly, this theory was based on the authority of the Roman jurists.

Critical jurisprudence was forced to seek another solution. But this proved difficult as long as the traditional concepts of rights and duties were retained in one form or other. Rights and duties in this sense can only belong to persons; but it was impossible to find any real person to whom they could be said to belong.

The actual situation is briefly the following. The 'juridical person' is primarily a word structure. A company has a name which is officially registered and legally protected. A paper organization is defined by the statutes. A corresponding actual organization is set up. Legal transactions are carried out in the name of the juridical person. Usual rules of civil law apply to them. When a property right is ascribed to a juridical person, this has the same sort of directive function in general commerce as the ascription of such a right to a physical person. The word is a red light for people in general. The rules of the organization designate persons entitled to make decisions regarding its property; for them the word has the function of a green light. In litigation the juridical person has to be 'represented' by somebody designated to the task according to the statutes. If the court orders the juridical person as defendant to pay a sum of money to the claimant, executive measures can be taken with regard to the property defined, according to the legal rules, as belonging to the juridical person.

The whole time, the regular use of the name is essential. It fits into the general use of legal language. Ascribing rights and duties to juridical persons is quite analogous to the ascription of rights and duties to physical persons. In this case, too, the use of the name is essential. Ordinarily, the person designated by the name carries out legal transactions himself under that name. But during a long life he may be represented by others (a guardian or an agent) in many transactions. The resulting 'rights' and 'duties' are ascribed to him. His name serves as a common point of reference which makes it possible to define a sphere of rights and duties as being 'his'.

> In my *Three Essays in Roman Law* (1949) I have tried to show that the Roman jurists did not have the theory of a fictitious person. For them *collegia* and other 'corporations' (*corpora*) were *corpora* in the sense of *universitates* or *corpora ex distantibus*: entities consisting of parts actually possessing their own individuality. Other examples were the people, a legion, and a herd of sheep. These entities were contrasted with such entities as a building. The planks in the building did not possess actual individuality: their individuality was merged in that of the house though they regained it when the house was pulled down. The fiction theory has been ascribed to the Romans because of a misinterpretation of D 46,1,22, which passage says that the estate of a deceased person represents the deceased (*hereditas personae vice fungitur*). On the heavily interpolated passage D 3,4,1, which has also been invoked as evidence of the fiction theory among the Roman jurists, see 5 IURA (1954) 181 ff.

Language and Social Control

The examples could be multiplied. One word after another in the legal vocabulary can be analysed in a similar way. It could be shown that many words are employed as signifying a power, a bond, or some quality in persons or things supposed to be created, modified and extinguished by performatory statements. We are in the habit of thinking that such effects really take place. Assertions concerning them are accompanied by a feeling of certainty.

But those words actually denote nothing, not even imaginary entities. They are 'hollow' words. Their function in our language is primarily to serve as guides to action. When used according to rules, or at least when supposed to be used in such a way, they become points of reference for consequential ideas concerning correct and obligatory behaviour. Such consequential ideas are inculcated from an early age, regulated through rules, and impressed by means of sanctions (social and legal). The result is that real positions of power are established, real bonds are created, and certain attitudes in relations to persons and things are formed.

These actual power positions, bonds, and attitudes are easily confounded with the ideal powers, bonds, and qualities ostensibly created by performatory pronouncements. To a great extent both kinds of powers, etc., coincide. He who is supposed to have a certain right according to the law usually possesses a corresponding actual power. But this is not always the case. In the ideal world of law, the effects take place according to the law with infallible regularity. In the empirical world of facts, the effects of legal rules, transactions between individuals, the attitudes of people in general, etc., are varied and more or less uncertain.

Legal language is not a descriptive language. It is a directive, influential language serving as an instrument of social control. The 'hollow' words are like sign-posts with which people have been taught to associate ideas concerning their own behaviour and that of others.

To serve as an instrument of social control legal language is, and must be, a regularized and repetitive language. The hollow words can function as sign-posts only if they are in some way 'authoritatively' established as such and used in accordance with some rules. Many words are used in a similar way outside the 'legal' sphere. The ship is named by a lady on whom 'authority' to do so has been conferred in conformity with custom; the rule that the ship should be spoken of under the name given by her is generally known and applied; everybody repeats the name when there is occasion to do so; and the ship is supposed to 'have' that name. A man is appointed judge by somebody 'empowered' according to the constitution to do so; he is then universally spoken of as being a judge; and the legal and social rules attached to the office of a judge are regularly applied with regard to him. The use of language for social control is not confined to the legal sphere; it plays an important role in most kinds of human relations.

Language may seem to be a frail instrument of social control. No wonder its efficiency in this respect was originally connected with the belief in mysterious forces that were manipulated by means of ritual phrases. Such beliefs have probably lingered for a long time. What remains of them today is difficult to say and cannot be discussed here.

With the emergence of the state the use of legal language became connected with the regularized use of organized power. Social history includes a process in which magical beliefs have slowly withered away while the supernatural sanctions have been replaced by hard and fast ones inflicted by the organs of the state.

But many more factors than magical beliefs and the use of sanctions must, of course, be taken into consideration in explaining how language serves as a means of social control. Upbringing, indoctrination, habits of thought and behaviour taken over by every new generation from the preceding one, propaganda of different kinds, etc., play their part.

Despite its apparent frailty, language is amazingly powerful as an instrument of social control—depending on the setting in which it is employed. In establishing a division of property, a monetary system, an interchange of goods on a vast scale, corporations for business and other purposes, an orderly government, etc., legal language plays a vital role. It is an instrument for keeping the peace, as well as for sending men to death on the battlefield in time of war.

> In a brief passage Bronislaw Malinowski has given a striking exposition on the importance of language for the organization of society. It immediately refers to the Trobriand language of magic. But the great anthropologist wants to fit this phenomenon into a general theory of language. After pointing out the importance of speech for the mastery of social relations among a people where everybody has been instructed from childhood in the intricacies of *kinship*, the taboos, etc., Malinowski goes on to discuss the problem of law 'in its verbal and pragmatic aspects'. Here the value of the word, the binding force of a formula 'is at the very foundation of order and reliability in human relations'. The marriage vows, promises and contracts are mentioned as examples. The average man need not comprehend the real function of deep belief in the sanctity of legal and sacral words and their creative power. 'But he must have this belief; it is drilled into him by the process whereby he becomes part and parcel of the orderly institutions of his community.' (From a chapter called 'The General Theory of Magical Language' in vol. II of *Coral Gardens and their Magic*, 1935, cited from *The Importance of Language*, edited by Max Black, 1962, 75.)

Conveying Information

Though legal language is in the first place a directive language it is also used for conveying information. But this practice gives rise to difficult questions.

As was pointed out in the introduction our language is full of legal terms. We think and speak of ourselves as being citizens of a country with its own government and a parliament, to which the members are elected. Laws are issued by these authorities and applied by a host of officials. We have our legal rights; one is married; disputes as to rights and duties are settled by judgments of the courts, and so on. To a large extent the news of the day is communicated in terms of legal language. The opposition party has won the elections, the government has resigned, the taxes are to be raised again, two corporations have merged, and a princess is going to celebrate her wedding.

No doubt our knowledge of the world is extended by our hearing such statements. They satisfy our curiosity, and in countless situations we act upon the knowledge we have acquired.

Yet there is some difficulty with this sort of information. It seems to be highly problematical. Let us suppose that the analysis of legal language presented here is substantially correct. Then we must conclude that precisely those key words which are the principal vehicles for conveying the information in question lack semantic reference. Citizen, government, parliament, law, right, duty, marriage, elections, taxes, corporations, and princess all belong to this category. How then is it possible that information can be communicated by means of such words?

The problem has already been discussed at length with regard to the word ' right '. As was suggested there, the crucial point is to distinguish between (i) the ostensible denotation of the word and (ii) the assumptions made when the word is taken to be employed in accordance with some presupposed rules.

The word ' right ' denotes nothing. But when X is described as being the owner of an object, and this statement is thought to be reliable, we assume that X has some ' legal title ' to the object, that he is in the position of actually being able to use the object in his own interest, that he can sell it if he likes, and so on. Every such assumption may turn out to be incorrect. The legal title may be non-existent; the supposed owner may be powerless to use the object; and if he cannot prove his title, a contract for sale by him may be without practical effect. To make certain, further inquiries have to be made on each point. Nevertheless, the statement concerning the ownership was useful because it put us on the track. We know how to gather such further information as may be of interest in the circumstances. In many connections no further inquiries are held to be required. We are content with the assumptions we make on being informed that X is owner of the object. They serve us well in numerous ways if we are aware of the importance of checking them before using them as a basis for serious decisions.

The assumptions presuppose that the word ' right ', in its directive capacity, is being used within a working legal system where the rules are, on the whole, heeded by the general public and applied by the authorities. The reliability of the assumptions depends on the efficiency of the system. The more clear the rules are, and the more consistently they are followed and applied, the higher the degree of reliability will be. When the rules are muddled, the level of general rule observance low, and the administration of justice irregular, the assumptions will evidently be less dependable. A country may find itself almost anywhere on the scale of reliability.

The informative function of other words in the legal vocabulary is to be analogously explained. Let us take the example of a President of a country.

According to the constitution the President is to be elected through certain proceedings ending in the proclamation that a certain person has been 'elected' President. Suppose X has been elected in this way. On a certain day and at a certain hour, he assumes office after taking the oath. Exactly at that hour presidential powers devolve on him. They are defined in the constitution. With infallible certainty, these paper powers are supposed to become his at that moment. But the election and the correct assumption of office also cause a change in people's attitudes. Since the constitution is generally revered and its patterns of behaviour respected, actual powers now accrue to the elected person. Everybody regards him as really being President and speaks of him in this vein. For all officers of the state it is a matter of course that the rules referring to acts of the President should be applied to his acts when performed in the correct manner prescribed by the constitution. The same opinion prevails in the country without opposition. Thanks to these attitudes, the President, and he alone, has access to certain shafts in the machinery of the state. This gives him actual power in the sense that he can efficiently direct the activities of other people in certain respects. But the import of this power cannot be described in constitutional terms. It depends on the firmness of the attitudes and on the infinitely complex political situation. Paper power and real power are different things. But the fundamental reason why real power comes to X is that people generally ascribe the paper power to him.

What information, then, is conveyed by the statement that Mr. X is President of the republic Y? This statement is not identical with an assertion that proceedings (called an election) have taken place; he is supposed to be President because he has been elected to the office. The statement is not equal to the assertion that X possesses presidential powers according to the constitution (if this would be taken to be a statement of fact); he is supposed to possess those powers because he is President. We are not told that people have particular attitudes towards X; his being President does not consist in people having these attitudes; on the contrary, the attitudes are conditioned by the general opinion that he is President. The statement does not describe his actual powers; the actual powers possessed by him depend on his ' being President ' in combination with a multitude of other factors.

So ' being President ' is reduced to—' being President '. A current expression is repeated. But when X is supposed to be correctly described as President (*i.e.* in conformity with the constitution), then a number of assumptions are made depending on what we are thinking of. We take it for granted that X has been duly elected, that he actually fulfils the functions incumbent on the President according to the constitution, and that he therefore exercises some more or less vaguely conceived power. Thus the information we receive consists in a number of assumptions we make on the premise that the title of President is correctly ascribed to X according to the constitution. Briefly speaking, the statement that X is President, when supposed to be correct, locates him in a certain position in the constitutional (paper) organization of the country. Since the working organization roughly corresponds to the constitutional one, we assume that he occupies the corresponding place in this actual organization.

The correspondence may be very close or rather remote according to historical and political conditions. In many cases the paper power of the president or monarch may be lacking a counterpart in real power; by custom and political pressures his power may be reduced to almost nothing, however great his paper powers may be. Differences in this regard do not diminish the usefulness of the title for conveying information. For it is obvious that the assumptions concerning the actual role of the holder of the title are not made solely on the basis of the use of the title and the constitution; more or less consciously everybody (provided they are not very naïve) also takes the political realities into account. But for the statement that X is President to be in any way informative concerning his present position in the country, it is always necessary that the constitution, according to which the title has been conferred on him, is functioning and that he is fulfilling his constitutional role, at least formally.

The same sort of explanation applies to other pivotal words in the legal vocabulary like ' government ', ' money ', ' marriage ', ' corporations ', etc. The regularized use of these words is an ingredient in a social machinery. When they are supposed to be correctly used, they are connected with uniform ideas about correct behaviour, fixed attitudes, and relatively common scales of value. Their use is therefore a most important, and indeed indispensable, instrument of social control. Actual government becomes possible, monetary transactions become meaningful, family life is encased in an accepted form, corporations are conducting business. But we are not, in general, conscious of the role of language in this connection; we do not reflect upon its enormous importance; a philosophical distance is needed to do so. The mediating idea that the words signify supersensible entities and qualities covers up the real function of our legal language. We vaguely assume that those entities and qualities are the important things while in reality there is only the regularized use of language in connection with the ideas of behaviour, fixed attitudes, and common scales of value. But because the ideal entities and qualities have their counterparts in real life thanks to the working of the social machinery, information ostensibly referring to them becomes a basis for making inferences concerning actual conditions in society. Though generally very vague, these inferences are useful from a practical point of view.

The various legal terms are connected with each other. Marriage entails certain rights; corporations are holders of rights and subject to duties; money enters into very many legal relations. The terms should not, therefore, be viewed as isolated words. The legal vocabulary must be treated as a whole because it functions as a whole.

The directive and the informative function cannot always be sharply distinguished. Performatory imperatives concerning rights and duties in a law are purely directive. A notice in the papers that X has become President of a country is purely informative. But in many cases a statement concerning concrete rights or duties may have both functions. The statement that X is the owner of an object may be given in a neutral way without any intention of influencing the behaviour of the addressee; but on him it may act as a signal that he must not use the object (as he perhaps thought he could do when he believed that it belonged to a near relative). Thus both functions are intermingled.

In his recent book *Speech Acts* (1969) Professor John R. Searle discusses 'institutional facts' and statements referring to them as distinguished from statements referring to 'brute facts' (essentially=physical and mental facts). 'Institutional facts' include legal acts such as acts of marriage, rendering judgment, and making a promise. Unlike brute facts, they presuppose the existence of certain human institutions. Every institutional fact is 'underlain by a system of rules' of the form '*X* counts as *Y* in context *C*'. Example: X counts as having made a promise by uttering certain words in certain circumstances (50 ff., 177 ff.). The semantic analysis of such expressions forms one of the main themes of the exposition. The book came to my notice too late to be discussed here.

Correctness and Truth

When statements concerning the existence of rights, duties, and legal qualities are made with the purpose of conveying information, they are judged as being correct or incorrect. If they are held to be correct, confidence is placed in them; and we are supposed to have acquired some information. Correctness is also required for such statements to have an influence on behaviour. Phrases like 'this is mine' or 'that belongs to A' cannot be impressive unless they are regarded as being correct.

But the correctness of these statements cannot be empirically ascertained. It is no empirical fact that I own a certain house, that A owns a car, that M and W are married, that C is a judge, or that D is President of a country. All such statements are based on the assumption of a system of rules regulating among other things the mode of acquiring the right of property, concluding marriage, appointing judges, and electing a president. The statements can only be judged as correct or incorrect according to these rules. Without reference to the rules the question about correctness would be meaningless.

The import of correctness is not that a right, duty, or legal quality really exists. Correctness according to the legal rules means that it is in conformity with these rules to ascribe a right, a duty, or a legal quality to a person. It is a question of using legal language in a certain way. The ascription of the right of property to a person is, so to speak, an echo of the rules concerning the right of property. The rules say that one acquires the right of property to an object in a certain way. When a person is believed to have 'acquired' the right of property to an object in a proper way according to the rules, we say that he possesses the right of property to it.

But there is something more to this use of language than merely uttering the proper words. The ascription of rights, duties, and legal qualities to persons is accompanied by consequential ideas concerning correct behaviour, however vague these may be in daily life.

Moreover, we know that the ascription of rights, duties, or legal qualities, when correctly made, is supported by the might of the state; for the same ascription will be made by the state authorities if a case is referred to them; and this means that the authorities will act according to consequential ideas regarding their behaviour and that state power will be used according to the law. In general we have no precise knowledge of what kind of action will be taken in certain circumstances. But we have the general idea that correct ascription of rights, duties, and legal qualities is connected with the regular use of state power, especially to the advantage of people to whom rights are ascribed. This gives such statements a peculiar character and a special weight.

Many differences of opinion naturally occur concerning the ascription of rights, duties, and legal qualities. In a great number of cases such disputes are settled one way or other between the parties themselves on the basis of their imperfect ideas about the law and (more important perhaps) their relative strength. Some cases are referred to lawyers who give their opinions and negotiate on behalf of their clients. A small minority of the disputes is submitted to the courts, which are regarded as the ultimate authorities for making decisions concerning the correct ascription of rights, duties, and legal qualities. Usually they are held to possess moral authority in this respect; in any case they wield state power. The existence and regular function of such an authority belong to the background of our legal language.

The method used by the courts in deciding disputes about rights, duties, and legal qualities was described in Chapter 7. As was pointed out there, the courts take position on a number of theoretical questions regarding the facts of the case, the contents of legal provisions, the opinion expressed in previous judgments, etc. But they also necessarily make valuations when preparing the decision of a case. A transaction is evaluated as implying a conveyance, a sale of goods, a payment, or some other 'operative fact'. This ultimately means taking the position that a group of rules ought to be applied to the facts presented to the court. Moreover, the rules themselves are evaluated as being valid, which means holding the opinion that they ought to be applied. The rules are gathered from texts of law and opinions of judges expressed in previous cases; and these rules are supplemented on the basis of valuation as demanded for the decision of new cases. The courts are entrusted with making the necessary valuations; but they are supposed to conform to certain standards of value current in the community.

In principle the same method is employed by lawyers giving their opinions on the 'existence' of rights, duties, and legal qualities. But it is also used by people in general when they take position on such questions though this is usually done in an unsophisticated, often primitive, way.

The differences of opinion concerning individual legal relationships are marginal cases. Such differences must always occur. But this should not be allowed to obscure the fact that there is a broad stream of events concerning which no doubts ever arise because the facts are known or not in dispute, the law is clear, and the valuations uniform. Very, very seldom is there any divergence of opinion on the question whether people are married, whether A owns the house he pretends to own, whether this is a bill of exchange, whether a company has been legally incorporated, whether B is a member of the Diet, or whether C is President of the country. If somebody asks for confirmation of such a statement, the answer is given with reference to the system of rules accepted as being the law of the country; and certain common valuations are silently presupposed.

The whole time the ascertainment of correctness presupposes the evaluation of a certain system of rules as valid and the adherence to some more or less common scales of value. Without such a basis every discussion on the correctness of legal statements becomes inane. People with different valuations on relevant points can never reach an agreement—unless the one side surrenders and accepts the valuations of the opposite party.

Thus correctness of legal statements always means correctness with regard to a system of rules and common valuations. We can therefore speak of correctness only in a relative sense. Outside the system of rules and the common valuations there is no ground for ascertaining the correctness of legal statements. Correctness is correctness for people living within a working legal system accepting certain fundamental valuations.

All this refers to statements asserting the 'existence' of rights, duties, and legal qualities. It follows that such statements cannot be said to be either true or false. They are always based on valuation; and in appearance only they refer to something that conceivably could exist. Though ostensibly propositions concerning objective realities, they are only ascriptions of rights, duties, and legal qualities in conformity with certain rules. Such statements are to be considered as an essential element in a working legal system. Despite appearances, they are not statements about realities within the system;

they form a part of the regularized use of language which makes the system work.

> In his *Definition and Theory in Jurisprudence* Hart says that 'the great anomaly' of legal language is our inability to define its crucial words in terms of ordinary factual counterparts (7 f.). The primary function of these words is not to stand for or describe anything; they have a distinct function (12 f.). They cannot be defined in the sense that a synonym is provided for them (14). An 'explanatory definition' is needed. It will show how words like that of a 'right' derive their meaning from the way in which they function in connection with legal rules. This is what makes these words 'different from ordinary words and hence perplexing'. (105 *Pennsylvania Law Review*, 1957, 961.)
>
> The point is that the words must not be taken alone. Following Bentham, Hart suggests that we have to elucidate whole sentences in which the words play their characteristic role (*Definition and Theory* 8). But the sentences cannot, as Bentham thought, be paraphrased in factual terms. (In Bentham's view, doing so meant that the sentences had to be paraphrased in terms calculated to raise images of 'substances' or 'emotions'.) What we can do is to specify the conditions under which the sentence that X has a right is true (15 f.).
>
> To illustrate the method, Hart takes an example from a game of cards. Under certain conditions a player is said to have 'taken a trick'. No definition of the word 'trick' can be given: a trick is not just a collective name of four cards, and it is not a fictitious entity. But we can explain under what conditions the statement 'He has taken a trick' is true (*Definition and Theory* 14 f.).
>
> The example is useful. A game of bridge is made up of a sequence of actions performed according to a set of rules. The actions are partly physical acts, as dealing and playing the cards, partly speech acts, such as bidding, passing and doubling. The utterances made in these speech acts are obviously neither true nor false. Like the physical acts they are moves in the game. According to the rules, each move has to be followed by another move of a specified kind: when a bid has been made by one player, the player to his left has to overcall or pass, etc. The play of the cards consists of a number of rounds during which each player lays down a card on the table face up. Thereafter one side is counted as winning. Conceivably the rules could include that a round should be followed by a declaration on the part of the 'winning' player to the effect that 'this is our trick'. But it would be cumbersome and annoying to have this speech act incessantly repeated. It has therefore been replaced by a physical act: one of the players on the winning side gathers the four cards and puts them face down on the table in a customary way. The action is equivalent to his saying: 'This

is our trick'. The purpose of the act is to mark off a stage in the game. The act is neither true nor false. But it can be judged as correct or not correct according to the rules of the game.

If the players are satisfied that the act was performed in conformity with the rules, they go on with the game. But suppose the player who laid down the four cards made a mistake: he did not notice that his ace of diamonds had been trumped with the two of hearts. Then there will be opposition; and according to the rules of the game it will be decided which party has to lay down the four cards on the table. It would be devoid of meaning to ask whether the laying down the cards is true or false. But it can be ascertained whether or not it conforms to the rules of the game.

Statements about the winning of tricks are not only made as acts in the game; they are also used for reporting ostensible facts. Suppose the dummy has left the table for a few minutes. When he comes back, the declarer informs him: 'We made four hearts'. The meaning of this utterance is not to state the fact that the declarer has said ten times that 'this is our trick' or laid down cards to the same effect. The utterance is made with the intention of communicating the result of a phase in the game. We speak of the result as consisting in the one party having won and now possessing a number of entities called 'tricks'. But these entities are given in our speech only. As was just said, it is an element in the game to use a certain form of speech according to the rules accepted by the players. When the declarer informs the returning dummy that they have made four hearts he makes use of this form of speech. The addressee, who is familiar with the rules, understands what stage has been reached when it is correctly said: 'We have made four hearts'. A new phase in the game has to follow; and the correct statement that the one party has made these four hearts has a certain bearing, according to the rules, on what has to be said in the following phases, and especially on the scoring.

When Hart says that we can specify the conditions under which the statement 'He has taken a trick' is true, what he has in mind is, so it seems to me, that we can specify the conditions under which it is correct, according to the rules of the game, to make that statement.

Besides propositions on the existence of rights, duties, and legal qualities there are also statements on legal matters of another character. A business man consulting his lawyer wants information concerning his own actual position in certain respects and concerning the effects of proposed lines of action. Suppose, for instance, that the question concerns a contract which the business man has concluded. He asks whether he will be considered bound by the contract despite certain misrepresentations made by the other party which caused him to sign the contract. He wants to know whether it is the wisest course for him to fulfil the contract, to repudiate it and face the possibility of litigation, or to try to settle for a compromise. The lawyer gives his advice on the basis of his knowledge of statutes and precedents and with regard to the available evidence. He will say, perhaps, that in view of a number of precedents in similar cases, a court will most probably render judgment to the effect that the contract is binding, or not binding, or that the outcome is extremely doubtful. The answer does not refer to the 'binding effect' of the contract itself, but to the likely mode of action of a court to which the case is submitted: it therefore refers to certain actual probabilities which the business man has to take into account in deciding how to act. In other situations the business man will ask how a contract for a certain purpose is to be drawn up, how a company is to be formed, etc. The answer consists in describing a course of action and preparing certain papers.

Questions of this kind must not be confounded with questions concerning the existence of rights, duties, and legal qualities. They refer to hard and fast realities; and they can be judged as true or false, or probably true or probably false.

The role of the lawyer undergoes a change if he is to represent his client in court. Then, he will not make any statement concerning the probable action of the court; this would be meaningless. Instead he will try to make the court accept valuations favourable to the client. To this purpose he will perhaps eloquently assert the existence of rights on the client's side.

Statements concerning rights, duties, and legal qualities are often made by people living outside the system. We talk about people possessing property, owing debts, occupying positions in the organization of state, etc., in foreign countries. In doing so we adopt the language used in the other country. Our language echoes the speech used within that system. If confirmation is requested, we usually refer to the opinions held by the system's own authorities. To express an independent opinion would presuppose putting oneself in the position of a member of the other community and making its valuations one's own.

If a lawyer is asked for an opinion on a question of property rights in his own country, he will perhaps assert without hesitation that X has acquired the right of property to a certain object through a transaction classified as an act of sale and purchase. But suppose the transaction has taken place in a neighbouring country the laws of which are considered applicable. Then the lawyer will probably be wary of expressing a definite opinion himself. Instead, he will refer to the opinion prevailing among the authorities in the other country; and he will perhaps find that according to their interpretation of the law the transaction is not to be classified as a valid purchase. This is what he can say without making any evaluation himself.

The valuations are essential for the 'internal aspect of law'. The 'external aspect' is the view held by a person standing outside a working legal system looking at it in a detached way, not animated by its valuations. On the whole we take the internal aspect with regard to the legal system of our own country and particular questions arising within it. The external aspect is usually applied to other countries and situations in them. Similar language is employed in both cases. But there is a fundamental difference regarding the modes of ascertaining the correctness of a statement. For those sharing the internal aspect, the assertion that a statement is correct contains a reference to fundamental valuations. Argumentation of this kind becomes meaningless from the point of view of a neutral observer. He only takes notice of what is said within the system and of the opinions held by those who are regarded as its authorities.

The distinction here made between correctness and truth may perhaps seem punctilious or even pedantic. It is alien to the common, unreflected view. As was pointed out in the introduction, our language is full of legal expressions. We speak of states, monarchs, presidents, governments, officials, courts, rights, duties, corporations, elections, appointments, crimes, etc., etc. as we talk of natural phenomena. Cannot statements about such things be true? Why say that they can only be assessed as correct with reference to a system of rules and certain common valuations? To deny the possibility that such statements can be true seems, indeed, to be eccentric.

Nevertheless the distinction between truth and correctness is of vital importance. In asserting the truth of a statement we always presuppose that the statement refers to something which is what it is, regardless of the language used about it by human beings. Ascertaining the truth of the statement does not imply ascertaining that some special terminology is being used about the object. But how is it with the statement that Mr. X is President of country A? If we try to ascertain the 'truth' of this statement, we find only that in country A there is a written text called the constitution according to which a ' President ' is to be elected in a certain way, that Mr. X is supposed to have been elected in that way, that he is universally called President, that officials and other people regulate their behaviour towards him and his actions according to a vast number of legal and social rules referring to somebody being President, and so on. Let us suppose that this language with its consequences for behaviour did not exist: the talk about Mr. X being President would then be as empty and meaningless as the claim of a man in a lunatic asylum that he is the Emperor of China. Still, the statement that Mr. X is President of country A does not refer to the said use of language as a fact. It is a repetition of that language. Ostensibly, a supersensible quality, *viz.* that of being ' President ', is ascribed to Mr. X. But this quality is nothing. There is only the regularized use of language saying that Mr. X is President and the social consequences thereof.

Within a working legal system the consistent use of the title is an ingredient in the constitutional machinery. Ordinarily there is no doubt among the population that the holder of the title really ' is ' King or President. If any question is raised in this respect, it is answered by reference to the rules of the constitution and birth or election respectively.

For the historian, the question whether a man really was King or President of a country at a certain time would be pointless. What the sources show is that the title during a certain period was generally ascribed to some personality known under a certain name. Usually no difference of opinion existed concerning the ascription. Everybody thought that Louis XIV ' was ' really King of France, called him so, and acted according to the consequential ideas attached to this use of language. But let us think of his English contemporary, James II.

When in 1688 James had fled the country, he was received as a King by Louis and was regarded as still being a King by his courtiers and by many other Englishmen, both in England and in exile. For many years he continued to exercise some royal functions from his court in St. Germain, such as creating peers and appointing bishops. Meanwhile William and Mary were made King and Queen by the Convention Parliament. James had not been deposed in a constitutional way and William and Mary had not been created monarchs strictly according to the constitution. Were they really King and Queen? Was not James the real King? The question is meaningless. It can never be answered. What we know is only that the titles of King and Queen were ascribed to William and Mary, that this ascription was accepted by most people in the United Kingdom and by most foreign governments, that the usual consequential ideas were attached to the titles, and that therefore the constitutional machinery functioned on this basis, while James lost his place at the centre of the working system.

It is also useless to ask whether Napoleon was 'really' Emperor of France. He was called so by most people in France from 1804 to 1815 and the corresponding attitudes prevailed. But to the Bourbons and the émigrés he was no real emperor: he was the usurper Napoleon Bonaparte. It cannot be decided who was right. We can only ascertain what people thought, said, and did.

The distinction between correctness and truth is generally overlooked. We talk about rights, duties, and legal qualities as of natural phenomena. The sentences are analogous, and a similar feeling of certainty is connected with them. They serve us well in general commerce. But when it comes to giving a scientific explanation of legal phenomena, *i.e.* of fitting them into a coherent, non-contradictory view of the world in which we live, the distinction is of crucial importance. Its implications are doubtless far-reaching.

JOURNEY'S END

EACH time one has taken a step forward in an inquiry, a desire arises to take yet another step; for as soon as an answer to a question is supposed to have been found, new problems present themselves. But at some point a stop has to be made. When a group of related matters have been discussed and the road seems to lead on to another group, the time has come to look back, surveying the results, and look forward at the problems that now arise.

Looking Back

Legal theory has been dominated by the will-theory at any rate since the time of the classical natural law doctrine. The law has usually been conceived of as commands by a superior power, a ' sovereign ', the people, or the state, the commands being expressions of the lawgiver's will. In this will the law resided.

According to natural law doctrine God himself was the supreme lawgiver: the law of nature as well as divine positive law was His will. Positive human law was the will of the human sovereign; the capacity of the sovereign to lay down laws for the subjects derived from the social contract, which was binding by virtue of the law of nature. So the law of nature was the ultimate foundation of positive law. The sovereign had no power but that which was conferred on him by the law of nature and the social contract.

Legal theory was split into two branches when the idea of a law of nature began to be discarded. For the positivists only positive law was real law. But the concept of positive law was taken over from the natural law doctrine.

Positivism in its turn was divided into two branches: on the one hand the theory that the law is nothing but the naked commands of an authority actually possessing supreme power, on the other hand the theory that the law is endowed with binding force in the traditional sense. Despite the rejection of the idea of a law of nature, legal positivism, especially in its latter form, was imbued by natural law concepts and ideas.

Legal positivism was beset by many difficulties. As they were exposed by the critics, differences of opinion concerning fundamental questions multiplied. A powerful revival of natural theories took place. An opposite tendency was represented by the 'Pure Theory of Law' which was a great attempt to establish a scientific view of the law on the basis of the will-theory; this was to be achieved principally by eliminating all moral and utilitarian considerations in order to grasp the essence of the law itself.

Besides the will-theory there is another current in the history of legal theory which is of equal, if not still greater, importance. It has never proved feasible to incorporate the ideas of rights, duties, and legal qualities in the will-theory. Many attempts have been made to explain how rights, duties, and legal qualities could be derived from the commands of the sovereign or the state; but they have failed. Commands are commands, and they can be followed or disobeyed; but they cannot conceivably create any rights or legal qualities. This has long been realized by acute critics. It is also obvious that a duty in the proper sense of the word cannot be identified with being commanded to do something or forbear from doing something.

Therefore, the world of rights, duties, and legal qualities has never really been fitted into the view of law based on the will-theory. The consequence is that legal theory has been characterized by a combination of two different, incompatible lines of thought. Thinking in terms of commands has alternated with thinking in terms of rights, duties, and legal qualities.

This is apparent not least in the classical natural law doctrine. Ostensibly the will-theory prevailed since the law of nature was described as the will of God and positive human law as the will of the sovereign. But no rights were held to be derived from the commands of either authority. All rights had their origin in an act of will by the individual who was absolute sovereign within his own sphere. No right for anybody else against him could be established except by the transference made by him of a part of his power over his own actions (his *potestas in se*). So the whole system of rights stood, so to speak, beside the commands of God and the sovereign. All discussions about rights were based on the idea of the original freedom of the individual or his power over his own actions, the possibility of transferring parts of this power to other persons through acts of will, and the notion of a declaration of will as the socially necessary way of making the will manifest.

Bentham was an extreme representative of the will-theory. He sought to carry it through without the slightest deviation while he—

in direct opposition to Pufendorf—contemptuously regarded rights, duties, and legal qualities as so many fictitious entities. But he could not completely free himself from dependence on the traditional concepts. Something similar is to be said of the 'Pure Theory of Law'. On the other hand, Zitelmann's theory is a good example from comparatively recent times of an attempt to construct a theory of law on the basis of thinking in terms of rights; but Zitelmann tried to derive the rights from the will of the state. The two lines of thought have always blended to some extent.

The inadequacy of the will-theory is now apparent. The rules are not 'declarations of will' or commands by a single supreme will but independent imperatives stemming from many sources. The efficacy of the rules in regulating conduct does not depend on their being imposed on people by a powerful will. It is to be explained by psychological factors causing people to respond to rules established in certain ways among which, in modern times, legislation in the form prescribed by an accepted constitution is the most conspicuous one.

We have no knowledge of how the system of rules from which the present order has grown was once created. We can only study the evolution of an infinitely vast and complicated legal system from an early stage at which life in society was regulated by venerated rules with strong magico-religious implications. Ultimately it seems necessary to assume that *homo sapiens* is endowed with a propensity to establish rules, obey rules, and enforce rules. Progress will surely be made in the study of these traits in the constitution of man.

Just like the will-theory, thinking in terms of rights, duties, and legal qualities is inadequate from a scientific point of view. The object of study cannot be these supposed 'moral entities' themselves. It can only be the ideas of rights, duties, and legal qualities, their history, their import, and their social functions. An inquiry into these questions leads to the conclusion that the use of regularized language is an integral part of a working legal system.

Looking Forward

The discussion started from the standpoint of an individual, living in a contemporary community, surrounded by people who think and speak in terms of law, state, rights, duties, and legal qualities and who comport themselves more or less consistently according to the rules summarized under the name of law. We worked our way through the theories on the nature of law and rights to the facts themselves. The investigation was concerned the whole time with the situation within a modern state. A concept of the state was therefore presupposed. Now the question arises: what is the state?

Of course, the state is not thought to be a superhuman entity. The word is being used to denote an organization of a special kind.

At present the surface of the earth is divided between some one hundred and thirty different organizations called states. Within each one of them, and across the boundaries, there are many other working organizations. But the state is distinguished from them by two characteristics: (i) It is connected with a definite territory commonly regarded as its own. (ii) Within the territory the state organization includes a monopoly of force in the shape of a military establishment and the police.

The state is a comparatively recent phenomenon in the history of mankind. Before its emergence there existed communities governed by customary rules. On this basis the states were slowly formed during centuries of struggles between unifying and disruptive elements. It is impossible to say that the state existed from this or that date. Usually the time of birth of the modern states of Western Europe is set about four or five hundred years ago. It was greatly favoured by the use of gunpowder.

The system of rules called the law of a modern state is characterized by its relation to the state. As we have seen, it is not the case that the law is given by the state. The law includes rules for introducing alterations in its system of rules. But the state does not exist independently of the law. It presupposes the law: without law and law observance there is no state.

On the other hand law observance is conditioned by the regular use of force. Our present society could not exist without a criminal law steadily applied by state organs. Without criminal law neither security to life and limb, nor the distribution of property or the multifarious activities of the state are conceivable. But the application of criminal law consists in using force according to legal rules. The sanctions of civil law are also necessary for maintaining the distribution of property as well as for the reliability of contracts, for the debt system, etc. In this sphere, too, inflicting sanctions ultimately means using state force according to rules.

The relationship between state and law is therefore characterized by interdependency. The state organization is regulated by rules and carries on its work according to rules that are, on the whole, generally respected. But at the same time the regular use of force according to criminal and civil law is necessary for keeping up the respect for the rules.

This is not to say, of course, that the threat of force is the sole reason for rule observance. Such a conclusion would be manifestly wrong. Many other factors besides the threat of force (upbringing, ethical teachings, habits, propaganda, etc.) are required to build up the state of mind conducive to rule observance. But legal sanctions cannot be dispensed with. There is an interdependency between legal sanctions and law observance.

The role of force is more or less prominent depending on the strength of the other factors by which rule observance is conditioned. In many countries the use of force is reduced to a minimum; in others it is used on a far more extended scale. This is connected with another question: the degree to which the use of force is effectively harnessed by rules of law. The discussion in this book has principally referred to countries where the legal system is constructed in such a way as to exclude arbitrary use of force by the holders of political power. This is achieved by placing the control of the use of force in the hands of a really independent judiciary.

The law in the usual sense of the word includes the rules about the organization of the state and the activities of the state. But it also comprises all other rules promulgated according to the constitution. Besides these rules of enacted law there are also the rules based on precedents. This mass of rules cannot be exactly circumscribed. The system of 'legal' rules is not a closed system which can be identified by formal criteria. It is an 'open' system without fixed boundaries. An ingredient in the legal system is also constituted by the undefinable body of principles, usages, and techniques enunciated in textbooks, transmitted in oral tradition, and employed by those who are entrusted with the application of the rules. Finally, a regularized use of language belongs to the legal system.

A definition of the supposed concept of law cannot be given. At the end of the inquiry we can only indicate some disparate but interconnected realities which are covered by the term.

We also speak of an international law or law of nations. This is a system of rules about the rights and duties of states, about the correct procedures to be used in communication between states, etc. So far international law is analogous to municipal law. But a world-wide organization of force is lacking. It is useless to discuss whether international law is ' real ' law or not. This is a question of terminology. The real difference between internal and international law is apparent.

The problems ahead are principally concerned with the monopoly of force. They require separate study. Large amounts of other material, and other methods, would be needed in order to shed some new light on such questions as the formation of the monopoly, the conditions for its maintenance, the effects and the limitations of regular use of force in human society, and the implications of the existence of several territorial monopolies which are subject to no superior power capable of ensuring peace.

Appendix 1

THE CONCEPT OF A RIGHT ACCORDING TO GROTIUS AND PUFENDORF

The moral faculty—The *suum*—The origin of rights—The declaration of will—The effect of a promise—The transfer explained—The import of a right—Some applications—Psychological basis of the theory—Supposed religious basis for the theory—*Dominium* and its transference—Vindicating the *suum* —The secondary right—Conclusion.[1]

At the beginning of his treatise on the law of war and peace, *De iure belli ac pacis,* Grotius says that his purpose is to discuss whether any war is just and what is just in war.[2] The word *ius,* he says, here signifies nothing but that which is just, *iustum*. He further says that just is that which is not unjust, *iniustum*; *iniustum* is what is repugnant to the nature of human society.[3]

The first theme of the treatise is therefore the quality of a war of being just or unjust; and the quality of being just, as Grotius points out himself, is defined in a purely negative way since *iustum* is what is not *iniustum*.

Grotius then proceeds to define *ius* in another sense: *ius* 'with reference to persons' (1, 1, 4). What he has in mind is the concept of a right (*subjektives Recht*). In this sense, he says, *ius* is a moral quality (*qualitas moralis*) to possess something or to do something justly (*iuste*). It is a quality in a person. Grotius also calls it a faculty (*facultas moralis*).

Pufendorf has the same view as Grotius. The *ius* is a moral quality or faculty.[4]

The Latin *ius* has the same double meaning as the German *Recht*: both law (*objektives Recht*) and right (*subjektives*

[1] This paper was first published in the *Festschrift für Oscar Adolf Germann zum 80 Geburtstag* (Bern 1969, Stämpfli & Cie). Here the material has been rearranged to some extent. A few additions have been made.

[2] Grotius, *De iure belli ac pacis* 1, 1, 3, 1. (Cited from the Amsterdam edition of 1712 with comments by Gronovius.)

[3] *Cf.* Hägerström, *Recht, Pflicht und bindende Kraft des Vertrages nach römischer und naturrechtlicher Anschauung*. (*Acta Societatis Litterarum Humaniorum Regiae Upsaliensis* 44:3. Uppsala 1965), 50 f.

[4] *De iure naturae et gentium* 1, 1, 19; 3, 5, 1 and 3. (Cited from the Frankfort edition of 1744 by Mascovius.)

Recht). What Grotius wants to say at the beginning of the treatise is that *ius* in the title does not signify *ius* in this latter sense. There would have been no occasion for such an explanation if Grotius had written in English, since the title of his work would then have been *The Law of War and Peace*.

The Moral Faculty

The concept of a right is defined by means of the concept of *iustum*. Since *iustum* merely signifies what is not *iniustum*, the concept of a right is also negatively defined. Having a right only means possessing something or doing something without inflicting injury on others. Absence of injury to others is the essence of a right.

According to this definition the right of property only includes that the owner does no injury to anybody else in using the object for his own purposes, or in destroying it. This 'right' would be on the same level with the 'right' to walk about and breathe the air. The import of a legal claim would only be that the creditor does no injury to the debtor in requiring him to pay the debt.

This is what follows from the definition. But is the definition really an adequate expression for the concept that Grotius harbours? Why then should he make use of the significant appellation of a *qualitas* or *facultas moralis* for a right? This expression indicates that the right is actually conceived as a positive quality in a person. The meaning must be that the right is a power, though not a physical but a moral power.

This conclusion is immediately verified by what Grotius says next. He is going to employ the term *ius* in the proper and strict sense for the *facultas* in question. Under *ius* in this sense four kinds of rights are comprised: (i) *potestas in se* (= *libertas*), (ii) *potestas in alios*, (iii) *dominium*, and (iv) *creditum*.[5] *Potestas* obviously means power. An example of *potestas in alios* is paternal power (*patria potestas*) which is also called an *imperium* (2, 5, 1). Since *dominium* and *creditum* are co-ordinated with *potestas* as species of the genus *ius*, it follows that these rights too are conceived as powers. *Dominium* is either full *dominium* (the right of property) or limited, as for instance a tenant's right. *Creditum* is a claim to which an obligation on the part of the debtor corresponds. In another context Grotius mentions civil power as the moral faculty of governing the state (*facultas moralis civitatem gubernandi*, 1, 3, 6, 1).

[5] *Cf.* Diesselhorst, *Die Lehre des Hugo Grotius vom Versprechen* 39.

It is therefore evident that the definition of a right given by Grotius is not adequate. As Hägerström points out, Grotius *says* that a right only consists in being able to possess something or to do something without injury to others, but he *means* that a right is a moral power, a positive *facultas moralis*. Absence of injury and moral power are being confused.[6]

Grotius expatiates no further on the nature of a right, but Pufendorf does. He presents an elaborate theory of moral entities (*entia moralia*) by which he means moral forces and qualities superimposed on nature by the will of God or man.[7] Rights and obligations belong to these moral entities. In the language of Pufendorf a right is a 'positive operative moral quality'. It is a power, *potestas*, in a person enabling this person to act with moral effect. The effect is that an obligation is laid on somebody else.[8]

An obligation is an inner bond on the will. It 'imbues' the will and forces us to censure our own acts. One must recognize that one deserves evil in acting contrary to an obligation.[9]

The right (*potestas, ius*) is a capacity of imposing such a bond on the will of another person; it is conceived as a power of making demands with the effect that the inner freedom of the addressee is restrained. Pufendorf calls this power an empire (*imperium*).[10] A creditor, for instance, possesses an empire over the debtor.

When a right is conceived as a moral power over the will of

[6] Hägerström 55. The reason for the confusion will be explained below 295.

[7] *Entia moralia posse definiri, quod sint modi quidam, rebus aut motibus physicis superadditi ab entibus intelligentibus* (1, 1, 3). *Cf.* Welzel, *Die Naturrechtslehre Samuel Pufendorfs* (1958), 19 ff.; Erik Wolf, *Grosse Rechtsdenker der deutschen Geistesgeschichte* (4. Aufl. 1963), 341 ff.

[8] 1, 1, 19: *Potestas est, qua quis legitime, et cum effectu morali agere potest. Qui effectus est, ut alteri adferatur obligatio aliquid exequendi aut actiones ab altero exercitas admittendi, vel non impediendi, aut ut valeat in alterum conferre facultatem aliquid agendi aut habendi, quae antea aberat.* The concept of *potestas* includes that of *ius*, 1, 1, 20. On the difference between natural and moral faculties Pufendorf says (3, 5, 3): *non quamlibet facultatem naturalem aliquid agendi proprie ius esse, sed illam demum, quae effectum aliquem moralem involvit apud alios, qui eiusdem mecum sunt naturae.*

[9] 1, 6, 5: *obligatio vero moraliter voluntatem afficiat, et peculiari quasi sensu eandem intrinsece imbuat, ut in suas actiones ipsa censuram exercere cogatur, ac malo se ipsam dignam iudicare, ni praescriptae sese normae reddiderit conformem.*

[10] *Alterum obligare=alteri pro imperio quid iniungere* (1, 6, 5). *Cf.* Hägerström 60 f. In 1, 1, 20 Pufendorf says: *Frequentissimum est, ut accipiatur (iuris vocabulum) pro qualitate illa morali, qua recte vel personis imperamus, vel res tenemus aut cuius vi aliquid nobis debetur. Videtur tamen inter vocabula potestatis et iuris id discriminis intercedere, quod illa magis insinuet actualem praesentiam dictae qualitatis in res vel personas, obscurius autem connotet modum, quo quis ea sit potitus.*

another person, all rights must be rights over persons. Strictly speaking, there can be no rights over things. The essence of the right of property will be the moral power of imposing obligations on all other persons to restore the object if they have appropriated it, to pay compensation, etc.

Nevertheless, the teachers of natural law entertained the idea that certain rights were powers over things. Concerning the right of property (*dominium*) Grotius says (2, 10, 1, 2), that others by its very existence are subject to the obligation of restitution. No demand on the part of the owner is required to give rise to this obligation. If the 'force' of the right of property (*vis dominii*) were only to create an obligation in cases where such a demand is made, the right of property would be too weak and too costly to guard. Obviously *dominium* is conceived as a power over the object which automatically engenders the obligation of restitution in every unlawful possessor.

Pufendorf distinguishes between four kinds of *potestates* (1, 1, 19). (i) *Libertas,* or the power over our own person and actions (*potestas in personam actionesque proprias*). (ii) *Dominium,* or the power over our things (*potestas in res proprias*). (iii) *Imperium,* or power over other persons (*potestas in alias personas*). (iv) *Servitus,* or power over things belonging to others (*potestas in rem alienam*). (*Cf.* also 3, 5, 4.)

Evidently it proved impossible for the teachers of natural law to fit the right of property into the conceptual framework based on the idea that a right is a moral power over another person. They were forced to assume that some rights were rights, or powers, over things.[11]

The Suum

In the state of nature there were no rights, properly speaking (no *facultates morales*) either over persons or over things (except if special agreements had been made, one must suppose). Everybody

[11] Referring to Grotius 2, 10, 1, 2 (just quoted in the text) Hägerström says (63): Für die Naturrechtslehre wäre dominium kein ius, wenn nicht der Aussenstehende, der die Sache in seinem Besitzhat, zur Rückerstattung obligiert wäre. This is no doubt correct. (It is evident for instance in Pufendorf 3, 5, 3.) But it must be added that the right of property was primarily a power over the object. From this power stemmed the obligation of restitution. More on the nature of *dominium* follows below.

was free. The right of property did not exist; it was subsequently introduced through the human will.

Nevertheless, according to Grotius everybody had his proper share which belonged to him. This was the *suum*. It comprised his life, limb, and liberty. To deprive somebody of anything appertaining to the *suum* was *iniustum*.[12]

The sphere of the *suum* could however be enlarged. It was the general practice, Grotius says, that one could appropriate things for one's own use. When this had been done, it became unjust for others to take it away.

In 2, 2, 2, 1 Grotius explains that God, at the Creation, gave men the right over all things inferior to them (which right was reaffirmed after the Deluge). Therefore everybody could appropriate for himself what he wanted. This general practice filled the role of the right of property. Nobody could, without injustice, take away what somebody else had appropriated for himself. (*Talis usus universalis iuris erat tum vice proprietatis. Nam quod quisque sic arripuerat, id ei eripere alter nisi per iniuriam non poterat.*) In the following the introduction of *proprietas* (*dominium*) is treated (2, 2, 1, 5). It took place either by an express pact, as by dividing things, or through a tacit pact, permitting occupation; for if no division was made, everybody should be held to possess as his own what he had occupied. (*Simulatque enim communio displicuit, nec instituta est divisio, censeri debet inter omnes convenisse, ut, quod quisque occupasset, id proprium haberet.*)

The reason why things could be appropriated in the state of nature was not that labour was spent on them. There is no hint of this theory in Grotius. The appropriation did not create a right of property. This would have been impossible from the point of view of Grotius. The right of property was a moral faculty over all other people. But no such faculty could conceivably be established through the unilateral appropriation of an object. Grotius simply makes use of the natural, pre-juristic idea that a thing becomes 'mine' when I lay hold on it. He quotes the saying of Cicero concerning the places in the theatre: though the theatre is common to all, nevertheless a seat in it may be said to belong to him who has occupied it.

The *suum* implies no moral faculty. It means that the ego is

[12] Grotius 1, 2, 1, 5: *Societas eo tendit ut suum cuique salvum sit communi ope ac conspiratione. Quod facile intelligi potest locum habiturum; etiamsi dominium (quod nunc ita vocamus) introductum non esset. Nam vita, membra, libertas, sic quoque propria cuique essent, ac proinde non sine iniuria ab alio impeterentur.*

somehow extended to encompass external objects. Attacks on them become attacks on the personality itself.

Nobody could, without injustice, infringe on the *suum* as long as the individual committed no injury on anybody else. But if someone committed an injury, he lost the protection for his own sphere. The offended party could, without injustice, employ force against him (1, 1, 10, 7). Except in this situation, the sphere of the *suum* was inviolable.

Pufendorf argues that the natural power to use objects and animals for one's purposes was not, properly speaking, a right. Objects and animals were under no obligation to submit to one's domination, and it would be incompatible with equality if one man were to exclude others without their express or presumptive consent. To establish the right of property a pact was required because the right of property, as a *facultas moralis,* had an effect over other people: [*Dominium*] *effectum habet in ordine ad alios homines*; . . . *omnino praesupponit factum humanum, et pactum aliquod tacitum vel expressum* (4, 4, 4).

Concerning appropriation in the state of nature Pufendorf concurs with the opinion of Grotius (4, 4, 9) though he changes the meaning by introducing a tacit pact to the effect that a thing should belong to the one who has appropriated it for his own use. Pufendorf therefore assumes the existence of a mixture of community of goods and right of property 'which should be comprehensible even to mediocre minds'. The substance of things is common; but the fruits belong to those who have picked them. The oak is nobody's property; but the acorns become the property of the one who has taken them (4, 4, 13). This mixed state of things is supposed to have existed before the social contract.

The result is that Pufendorf's position comes very close to that of Grotius. Even in the state of nature, one has the right to use force in preserving things belonging to oneself (one's *bona* or *res,* 2, 5, 1 and 3).

Hägerström defines the *suum* as 'die Sphäre des nicht verbotenen Handelns' (53), 'die Bewegungsfreiheit, die dem einzelnen in der Weise zukommt, dass ein Verfahren innerhalb dieser Sphäre durch das Gesetz nicht verboten ist' (55 f.). No reference is made to the important statement of Grotius in 2, 2, 2, 1. The *suum* is described by Grotius as primarily consisting of one's life, limb, and liberty (= *potestas in se*). This is not the same thing as the sphere of not forbidden activities. The *suum* has positive significance.

The Origin of Rights

When everybody possessed original freedom, how then could a right be established over the individual? How could he become subject to the moral power, the *facultas moralis,* of another person?

There was only one way to achieve this: an act of will on the part of the individual himself. He could voluntarily submit himself to the moral power of someone else.

According to Grotius there was only one exception to the principle that all rights over persons or things derived from an act of will including consent (2, 5, 1). Parents, he thought, held an *imperium* over their children because they had generated them. (The parents held the *imperium* jointly though in case of disagreement the decision lay with the husband because of the superiority of his sex.)

Pufendorf strongly objects to the theory of generation as a source of power. The reason for the act of generation, he points out, is only the pleasure it affords; and this is no ground for the parents to claim obedience from their children. No doubt the children are subject to the empire of their parents. But this is because the parents love them so dearly and have to educate them; besides, the children presumably consent in the domination of their parents 6, 2, 4).[13]

The Declaration of Will

Thus rights over things or persons—which always implied a moral obligation on another person, or on other persons—had their origin in acts of will. But the internal act of will was not sufficient. The will had to be declared. It would not be consistent with human nature to attribute legal effects to the internal acts of will as such, Grotius says, because the internal acts cannot be known to others. The will has to be indicated through some external sign. This is the *declaratio* or *signum voluntatis.*

But another complement was needed too. Grotius points out that outward signs only create some *probability* regarding the real content of the will. People may say something they do not mean or simulate something through their actions. But it would be inconsistent with human society if acts of will made known through outward signs

[13] The issue became important when Filmer made parental authority the basis of political power. *Cf.* Laslett's remarks in his edition of Locke's *Two Treatises of Government* (1960) 36, 196.

should have no effect. Therefore, what has been sufficiently indicated is held to be true against the one who has indicated it.[14]

These are the conditions under which the acts of will are effective in human society. The efficient cause is supposed to be the internal act of will. But an act of will cannot be recognized in society unless it has been made known to others by some outward *sign*; and when such a sign has been offered, it is supposed to be a *true* sign of the content of the will. In this way the theory was made to meet the requirements of society. Pufendorf takes the same position (4, 9, 2–3).

The Effect of a Promise

A promise was a declaration of will. The ground of its binding force could easily, as it seems, be explained from the point of view of the teachers of natural law. In his introduction Grotius states that the obligation to implement a promise is an element in the law of nature (prol. 8). The reason why promises are binding according to the law of nature is that there must be among men some mode of creating obligations; and no other natural mode could be imagined (prol. 15).

This should be sufficient. When Grotius came to the chapter on promises in the second book of the treatise (ch. 11), he could simply have referred to those fundamental statements in the introduction. But he did not do so. Instead, he offered an elaborate disquisition on the nature of a promise in order to explain how the promisor becomes bound. Why is this done? The trouble seems to be superfluous.

Grotius never tells the reader why a general reference to the principles of natural law is insufficient. But his reason can be gathered from his argument. What he wants to explain is how a *right* for the promisee can arise out of a promise. The law of nature only says that the promisor is *obligated* to fulfil his promise; it says nothing about any right for the promisee. The great problem for

[14] Grotius 2, 4, 3. *Iuris effectus, qui ab animo pendent, non possunt tamen ad solum animi actum consequi, nisi is actus signis quibusdam indicatus sit. Quia nudis animi actibus efficientiam iuris tribuere non fuerat congruum naturae humanae, quae nisi ex signis actus cognoscere non potest: qua de causa etiam interni actus meri legibus humanis non subiacent. Signa autem nulla de animi actibus certitudinem habent mathematicam, sed probabilem tantum: nam et verbis eloqui aliud possunt homines, quam quod volunt et sentiunt, et factis simulare. Neque tamen patitur natura humanae societatis, ut actibus animi sufficienter indicatis nulla sit efficacia. ideo quod sufficienter indicatum est, pro vero habetur adversus eum qui indicavit.* The wording indicates that a declaration was not necessary in the case of a vow to God since God immediately had cognizance of the inner act of will. Such was the opinion of St. Thomas. (See Diesselhorst, *Die Lehre des Hugo Grotius vom Versprechen*, 1959, 22 f.)

Grotius is to explain how a right in the sense of a *facultas moralis* is established through a promise. How can such a declaration of will create a moral power in the other party?

Strange as it may seem, Grotius explains the creation of a right in the promisee as a case of a *transference* of a right (2, 11). No new right is created. An existing right is made over. This is the gist of the theory of Grotius on the nature of a promise. Pufendorf agrees. It is generally recognized, says he, that rights are transferred to others through promises and pacts.[15]

For a modern jurist it no doubt sounds absurd to interpret a promise as an act purporting the transference of a right. If I borrow a sum of money from another person and promise to pay it back, the creditor is said to acquire the right of claiming payment from me. In no sense is this right held to exist beforehand. It is an entirely new right, created through the transaction. No transference of a right could take place. Rights are created, not transferred, through promises.

Such is the modern view. But to understand the teachers of natural law, we must avoid reading their expositions in the light of our own conceptions or preconceptions. We have to take their views as they are set forth, regardless of their being rational or irrational from the standpoint of modern jurisprudence.

The Transfer Explained

In his chapter on promises Grotius is intent on refuting the doctrine of the French jurist Franciscus Connanus (1508–51). According to him, as Grotius relates his view (2, 11, 1), agreements (*pacta*) without reciprocal benefit (*synallagma*) are not binding either in the law of nature or in the law of nations (*ius gentium*); it is only honest, not obligatory, to fulfil them. If this were correct, Grotius says, no pacts between kings or different peoples would be binding as long as no implementation had been made on either side.[16] Moreover, it could not be explained how the laws, being, so to speak, pacts of the whole people, could add obligatory force to pacts between individuals.

[15] 3, 5, 2: *Caeterum cum apud omnes in confesso sit, per promissa et pacta ius in alios transferri* . . . Vgl. Hägerström 70 f. Hobbes, among others, shared this opinion (*Leviathan* ch. 14.) *Cf.* Diesselhorst, *Ursprünge des modernen Systemgedankens bei Hobbes* (1968) 19, 28 f.

[16] Grotius expresses himself too briefly. Connanus had taught that the Roman innominate contracts were binding according to the *ius gentium* when either party had done something to implement the contract. This is what Grotius refers to. *Cf.* Diesselhorst, *Die Lehre des Hugo Grotius vom Versprechen* 33.

With these remarks Grotius wants to show that the theory of Connanus leads to absurd consequences. It would rob many covenants between sovereigns of their binding force; and it would destroy the very basis of positive law, the binding force of the social contract.

But these purely negative arguments are not sufficient. It remains for Grotius to show positively why promises, even without *synallagma,* are binding irrespective of positive law, and how rights can be established through them.

To solve the problem Grotius refers to the ' recognized principle ' that *the right of property* can be transferred through an act of will which has been sufficiently indicated. He goes on to say that we have a right over our actions equal to our right over things belonging to us. Why then, he asks, should it not be possible to transfer such a right, *i.e.,* a right over one's own actions, to another person (2, 11, 1, 3)? His further reasoning is rather complicated.

Grotius makes a distinction between a promise to transfer the right of property at a future time (*promissio dandi*) and a promise to do something (*promissio agendi* or *faciendi*).

The distinction is somewhat confusing; for to transfer the right of property is of course to do something. But there is a reason why this distinction is made.

Grotius argues that the right of property includes the right of transferring it to somebody else. Therefore it is evident that this latter right can be transferred: when the right of property can be transferred, it must be possible to transfer the minor, inherent right, too (2, 11, 1, 3).

In this way the effect of a *promissio dandi* is explained. Such a promise marks the beginning of an alienation of the right of property itself (*est via ad alienationem rei*, 2, 11, 4, 1). The implication is that the rest must follow.

The nature of a promise to do something (*promissio faciendi*) is explained as analogous to a transfer of property. Our right over our own actions is equivalent to our rights over things. Therefore, we can transfer a right over our own actions to another person as well as we can transfer the right of property. The effect is similar (*perfecta promissio, . . . similem habens effectum qualem alienatio dominii*).

Thus it appears that in promising to do something, as for instance to pay a sum of money, one desists from the power of decision over this action; it is conferred on the other party. In so doing, one alienates a part of one's liberty: an *alienatio particulae nostrae libertatis* takes place. It is a *moral* power that is transferred. The promisee now has a moral power over the promisor as regards the action promised. This action is no longer subject to the free will of the promisor. He is morally bound to execute it when required by the promisee.

The underlying idea is that the will cannot create anything out of nothing; it can only transfer something within its own sphere of domination. The promise draws its strength, Grotius says, from the right of the promisor (2, 11, 8, 1).

Thus it is explained how a promise can be viewed as effecting the transference of a right. The theory is different with regard to a *promissio dandi* and a *promissio faciendi*. In the first case a right inherent in the right of property is transferred. In the second case the object of transfer is a part of the *libertas* of the promisor in the sense of his right, or power, over his own actions. In neither case is any new right created. An existing right is alienated by the promisor and conferred on the other party. This is done through an act of will sufficiently declared.

Pufendorf (3, 5, 3 ff.) closely follows the exposition of Grotius though he does not repeat the argument from analogy with the transference of *dominium*. The possibility of alienating a part of one's liberty is taken to be self-evident. The promisor confers on the promisee the power of prescribing what he shall do, suffer, or omit.[17]

> Pufendorf's reasoning concerning the source of God's *imperium* over men is revealing (1, 6, 12). He first invokes the bounties which God has showered upon us. As Barbeyrac observes, this is a weak argument: past favours are no ground for future obedience. Perhaps Pufendorf has a feeling of something more being needed to establish the moral power of God. After mentioning God's benevolence towards us and his superior wisdom, Pufendorf finally suggests that God, in creating us, could circumscribe a part of our freedom with regard to his own right. (*Qui homini dedit, ut libere posset agere, quare non is iure suo aliquam eius libertatis particulam circumscribere queat?*) The analogy with the establishment of a right for another person through a promise is evident. The promisor transfers a part of

[17] 3, 5, 4: *In quo igitur proprie consistat translatio, et adquisitio iuris, planius fiet, si praemittatur, quod quaedam iura respiciant homines, quaedam res; . . . In homines adquiritur ius, si alter expresse aut tacite consentiat, ut ipsi, quid agere, pati aut omittere debeat, possim prescribere: per quod simul se obligat, quod ultro ad implendam meam voluntatem velit conniti; simulque potestas mihi conceditur tergiversantem metu mali adigendi.*

> his freedom to the promisee. God reserves, at Creation, a part of Man's liberty as a right for himself. These are the two sources of the force of obligations, which are understood to impose an inner bond on the freedom of our will. (*Ex hisce duobus fontibus manare arbitramur vim obligationum, quae intrinsecum velut vinculum voluntatis nostrae libertati iniicere intelliguntur.*)

To complete the transfer of a right, the promise has to be accepted by the promisee just as acceptance is necessary for the transference of *dominium*.[18] Therefore, the promise may, without injustice, be recalled as long as it has not been accepted. Until then the right has not been transferred.[19]

In both cases the reason for the requirement of acceptance is the same. When *dominium* is transferred, the will of the recipient has to be active in order to assume domination over the object. Similarly, the promisee cannot acquire a *facultas moralis* over an action of the promisor without his will being active.

The Import of a Right

The import of a right in the sense of a *facultas moralis*, as conceived by the teachers of natural law, is now clear. The right is a moral power for one person over another. By virtue of the right its possessor can command the other party to perform or omit a certain action, with the consequence that it becomes morally necessary for this party to behave as required. The right has its origin in a promise (either a direct promise from A to B or the promise implied in the social contract). A promise consists in the alienation by the promisor of a part of his *potestas in se*, his power over his own actions. Consequently, the right is a part of the obligated party's *potestas in se* as now possessed by the promisee and exercised by him. The power of decision concerning a certain action has passed to the promisee.[20]

[18] Grotius 2, 11, 14. *Ut autem promissio ius transferat, acceptatio hic non minus quam in dominii translatione requiritur.*

[19] Grotius 2, 11, 16. *Sequitur hinc* (from the necessity of acceptance), *ante acceptationem, quippe iure nondum translato, revocari promissum posse sine iniustitia.*

[20] Diesselhorst remarks on the theory of Grotius: 'Gegenwärtiges und zukünftiges menschliches Handeln sind für Grotius der souveränen Herrschaft der Person ebenso unterworfen wie Sachen, die sich in ihrem Besitz befinden.' (*Die Lehre des Hugo Grotius vom Versprechen* 51.) This is exactly what Grotius thinks. The idea of having power over one's own future actions and the possibility of transferring this power to someone else form the basis of his doctrine of promises. But this is not clearly brought out in Diesselhorst's exposition. Instead, the author tries to show that the ground of the binding force of a promise was of a religious nature. See below.

Some Applications

An interesting passage (2, 11, 8) may serve to illustrate the view of Grotius.

For a promise to be effective, Grotius says, its object (that which is being promised) has to be within the power of the promisor (*in iure promittentis* = *in potestate* as Gronovius comments). For this reason promises to do something illicit are void; nobody has a right to do something illicit. (*Non valent promissa facti per se illiciti*: *quia ad illa nemo ius habet nec potest habere.*) A promise derives its strength from the right (power) of the promisor and it has no effect beyond that. (*At promissio, ut supra diximus, vim accipit ex iure promittentis, nec ultra extenditur.*)

In the case of a promise to transfer the right of property to a thing that does not yet belong to the promisor, the effect is suspended because the promise is to be understood as given under the condition that the promisor becomes owner of the object. As was mentioned above, a promise to transfer the right of property at some future time is a transference of a right inherent in the right of property. It cannot, therefore, be transferred until the promisor is actual owner of the object.

Grotius adds that the civil law, for reasons of utility, has made many conditional promises invalid though they are valid in the law of nature. A case in point is the promise of a married man to marry some woman at a future time. As long as the state of matrimony subsists, neither party has the right to marry another person; for a new marriage would be an illicit act. Therefore no present right to marry somebody else can be transferred. But according to the law of nature the right of deciding to marry anew after the dissolution of the existing marriage can be conferred on another person. This would be the import of a promise by a man to marry another woman after the death of his present wife. The decision to marry her or not to marry her would no longer be in his power. The woman would possess the power of making this decision; she would be able to claim that the marriage act be performed, and it would be a moral necessity for the man to play his part. But for certain reasons the civil law has deprived his conditional promise of its natural effect.

The whole time the basis of the argument is the tenet that a promise implies the transference of a right. But a right can be transferred only if it exists. If it does not at present belong to the promisor, it can only be conditionally transferred.

Even when the promise has been extracted by coercion, the alienation of a part of the liberty has taken place (2, 11, 7). The promisee therefore acquires a right through such a promise, and the promisor is bound. But if the promisee has exercised coercion himself, and done so unjustly, he is bound to liberate the promisor if the latter asks for it. The promise is not void. It has its usual effect. But the promisee has done an injury which he is bound to repair. If the coercion was exercised by a third party, there is no remedy in the law of nature but only in civil law.

Pufendorf differs from Grotius in the treatment of coercion. His reason is not that the will of the promisor is inefficient in this case. In the person of the promisor everything required for the transference of a right is present. But the promisee is prohibited from accepting it. Therefore the obligation of the promisor becomes void.[21] In this ingenious way Pufendorf avoids the conclusion drawn by Grotius from the nature of a promise.

Psychological Basis of the Theory

In the explanation of the nature of a promise and its ability to confer a right on the promisee, neither the maxims of natural law, nor the social nature of man or the commands of God are relevant. The promise becomes so to speak self-sufficient. It is conceived as an act of will through which the promisor, in an almost mechanical way, transfers part of his liberty, in the sense of his power to decide over his own actions, to the promisee. The effect is caused by the will itself, though the will has to be signified in some adequate way, through words or gestures.

This sounds no doubt absurd. But the theory was not snatched out of the air by the teachers of natural law. There was a psychological basis for it.

When one has made a promise, it is natural to feel bound. I therefore regard my liberty of action as being circumscribed through the promise. I *must* do as I have promised, at least if the other party insists upon it. This is a feeling of being under a moral necessity, or having a duty. Correspondingly, the promisee is regarded as possessing some sort of power over me. By making a demand, he actualizes my obligation; he can let it drop, if he so wishes. In natural law theory these subjective feelings and views are objectivized and trans-

[21] 3, 6, 12: *Non sufficit, ut in me sint requisita ad obligationem producendam necessaria, sed ab altero quoque abesse vitia debent, quae iuris in ipso adquisitionem intercipiant.*

formed into entities in a supersensible sphere (by Pufendorf called the sphere of the *entia moralia*).

Supposed Religious Basis for the Theory

After stating that a *promissio dandi* is the beginning of the alienation of the right of property and a *promissio faciendi* an alienation of a *particula libertatis,* Grotius adds that the 'divine oracles' give us significant proof (*insigne argumentum*) for what he has said because they show that God himself, who can be bound by no posited law (*lex constituta*), would act contrary to his own nature if he did not implement his promises (2, 11, 4, 1). This shows that the principle that promises should be kept stems from immutable justice, which is common to God and rational beings.

Referring to this passage Diesselhorst suggests (rather vaguely) that the ground of the binding force of a promise, according to Grotius, was of a religious nature.[22] This is no doubt mistaken.

In his discussion of the nature of a promise Grotius makes a distinction between acts of will that only establish a duty for oneself and acts that confer a right upon another person (2, 11, 2–4). There are three modes of speaking about future things which are in our power or may come into it. The first one is simply to declare one's present intentions with regard to the future. This is in no way binding since one has the right of altering one's mind. The second mode consists in the self-determination of the will regarding the future with the addition of a sufficient sign of the necessity to persevere in one's intention. This is called *pollicitatio.* It is obliging independently of the civil law. But it confers no right on anybody; it occurs in many cases that there is an obligation in us though no corresponding right in another person. (*Multis enim casibus evenit, ut obligatio sit in nobis, et nullum ius in alio.*) Grotius here refers to purely moral duties as opposed to legal obligations; examples are the duty to have pity and the duty to be thankful.

The third mode is marked by the addition (to an act of the second degree) of a sign of the will to *confer a right* on somebody else. Then

[22] The most important thing for Grotius was his *religiöse Überzeugung von der bindenden Kraft eines Versprechens.* The passage just cited (2, 11, 4, 1) *zeigt mit grosser Klarheit den tragenden religiösen Grund seiner Naturrechtskonzeption.* (*Die Lehre des Hugo Grotius vom Versprechen* 39 f. Wieacker shares Diesselhorst's view, *Privatrechtsgeschichte der Neuzeit,* 2. Aufl. 1967, 293 f.) *Cf.* also Stig Jørgensen, 'Grotius's doctrine of contract' in 13 *Scandinavian Studies in Law* (1969) 112.

there is a perfect promise; its effect is similar to the alienation of *dominium*, i.e. that of transferring a right. (*Tertius gradus est, ubi ad determinationem talem*—of the second grade—*accedit signum volendi ius proprium in alteri conferre: quae perfecta promissio est, similem habens effectum qualem alienatio dominii.*)

The significant difference between utterances of the second and third degree is that *rights* are established through utterances of the third degree only. What Grotius says about God's fidelity to his own promises could possibly be an argument why promises should be kept even if the promisee has acquired no right to claim fulfilment; it could in no way corroborate the statement that an utterance of the third degree confers a right on the promisee. Grotius cannot have been of the opinion that God, through his promises, alienated a part of his liberty to men and gave them a moral power, a *facultas moralis*, over himself. The phrase about the promises of God is a lofty, though irrelevant, argument thrown in as an afterthought to embellish the rather crude theory that rights are conferred through promises by way of alienating a part of one's liberty.

Pufendorf rightly scorns the reasoning of Grotius on this point. The alienation of a part of one's liberty takes place in promises among men only, he says. It is impossible that the divine promises should not be fulfilled; but it would be too arrogant for a mortal to presume that he had acquired a right over God (3, 5, 7; *cf*. 2, 1, 3: *Sic quod Dei promissa non fallunt, id non inde est, quod eius libertas fuerit circumscripta per obligationem ex promisso ortam* . . .). The sole reason why a promise confers a right on the opposite party is that the promisor by an act of will effectuates the transfer of a part of his liberty.

Dominium and its Transference

The whole doctrine of promises and contracts is based on the theory of the transference of part of one's liberty. This theory in its turn rests on the assumption that the right of property can be transferred through an act of will. But how is this thesis substantiated?

As was mentioned above, the right of property does not belong to the law of nature. But when it has been introduced, Grotius says, the law of nature includes the possibility of its transference, for this is inherent in it (in full *dominium* 2, 6, 1, 1; *cf*. 1, 1, 10, 4). In a later passage he says that *nothing is more natural* than that the will of the owner to transfer his right to someone else should be held valid (2, 11, 1, 4).[23]

No attempt is made to derive the rule from the social disposition of Man. The argument is simply that it is 'quite natural' that an owner should have the power of transferring his right to another person.

Thus the concept of *dominium* is still more fundamental in the theory of Grotius than the concept of a promise. For a promise to transfer the right of property is the transference of a right inherent in the right of property; by analogy, other promises become valid as implying the transference of a part of one's liberty. Nevertheless, the right of property is grounded on a pact between the members of society—either an express pact of division or the tacit agreement that whatever anyone had occupied should be his own (2, 2, 2, 5). Grotius actually explains the effect of a promise through the nature of *dominium* though the basis of *dominium* is a pact, which consists of reciprocal promises.

It is easy to understand how this circularity came about. There is an affinity between the concept of *dominium* and the concept of the *suum,* that which naturally belongs to oneself. As we have seen, originally the *suum* consisted of one's life, limb, and liberty; but it could be enlarged by the appropriation of outside objects. The notion of *dominium* includes the notion of *suum. Dominium* is the *suum* as far as it consists of objects outside one's own person, corroborated through a pact between the members of society. It is a power over those objects of the same kind as the power over one's own actions.

The idea that one can separate a physical object from the *suum* and transfer it to another person is quite natural. In assuming that this is possible one is on firm ground, Grotius believes. The power over our own actions and the power over physical objects included in the *suum* are of the same kind. Therefore, by analogy it must be possible to transfer to somebody else the power over a certain action as well as the power over a physical object. Such is the reasoning of Grotius.

The essence of *dominium* is the domination by the will over an object. This is clear from Grotius' exposition concerning the origin

[23] In both passages Grotius refers to Iust. Inst. 2, 1, 40. As Diesselhorst remarks (44) what is set forth in this place is the requirements of *tradition* for the transference of *dominium* in Roman law. For Grotius this becomes an authority for his thesis that *dominium,* according to the law of nature, can be transferred *through an act of will.*

of *dominium*. A pact was necessary. The will to possess an object could not be sufficient by itself because others could not know what somebody wanted to have as his own, and several persons could want the same thing (2, 2, 2, 5). We find here the usual idea that the internal act of will, though it was the *force creatrice*, could not, for practical reasons, alone be relevant in society. Something more had to be added. (*Cf.* Pufendorf 4, 4, 9.) *Dominium* was established through the will to have dominion over a thing plus the act of occupation or a pact to divide a number of things among the members of society.

If the will to dominate a thing was the essential element in the right of property, it would seem to follow that the right of property could not be vested in a small child or a lunatic. Grotius accepts this conclusion. In the law of nature *dominium* can only appertain to those who possess full mental faculties. But for reasons of utility the law of nations has made it possible even for children and lunatics to acquire and retain the right of property.[24] Pufendorf is of the same opinion (4, 4, 15).

As will be seen, *dominium* differs from personal rights in that it has a double character. It is a *facultas moralis* because it implies an obligation on everybody but the owner himself. But this obligation refers to the 'fact' that the object 'belongs' to the owner. The 'belonging', the *suum esse*, is the primary element in *dominium*. It is a power of the will with regard to the object of the same nature as one's power over one's own actions (the *potestas in se*). The *facultas moralis* has been added through the social contract.

Vindicating the Suum

The *suum* represents a sacred sphere for the individual. Everybody who trespasses on the *suum* commits an injury. In consequence the trespasser forfeits the ideal protection for himself. He becomes exposed to a reaction from the injured party, who has a right to defend his sphere.

In the state of nature the right of vindicating the *suum* through force is exercised by the injured party himself.[25] This is called

[24] 2, 3, 6: *Si solum ius naturale spectamus, dominium non dari nisi in eo, qui ratione utitur.* (Gronovius comments: *Quia ad dominium actus animi requiritur agnoscentis aliquid pro suo et habendi voluntas.*) *Sed ius gentium ob utilitatem communem introduxit, ut et infantes et furiosi dominia accipere et retinere possent, personam illorum interim quasi sustinenti humano genere.*

[25] *Grotius* 1, 1, 10, 7: *Ius suum per vim consequendi ante positas leges. Cf.* Pufendorf 2, 5.

private war by Grotius, *bellum privatum* (1, 3, 1). With the formation of society the right in question has been transferred to the civil power to be exercised through the courts. But the original right of using force is retained by the individual in so far as the delay caused by recourse to court would entail danger or loss; it also remains with him in places like uninhabited islands, where no community exists.

According to Grotius, the right of reacting against an injury is limitless (2, 1, 10, 1). The evil inflicted on the aggressor need not be proportionate to the injury he has done. In order to avert a box on the ear I am entitled, in the law of nature, to kill the aggressor if there is no other way of warding off the attack.

Pufendorf enlarges on this subject (2, 5, 3). He vividly depicts how insupportable life would be if one were exposed to daily beatings, however slight, or daily pilferings from another man and there were no possibility of getting rid of him. Surely, it must be permitted to kill such a fellow. Life would become ' insociable (*insociabilis*) in the state of nature if limits were set to the right of reacting against injuries.

The right of using force to vindicate the *suum* is no *facultas moralis*. There is no question here of putting forward a demand with the effect of imposing an obligation. The meaning of the ' right ' is only that inflicting evil is not *iniustum* when it is done in response to an injury. Then there is no moral obstacle to the use of force.

> In speaking about the box on the ear, Grotius employs the expression *facultas moralis* for the right of defence: *Qui iniuriam me parat afficere, is mihi eo ipso dat ius, hoc est, facultatem quandam moralem adversus se in infinitum, quatenus aliter malum illud a me arcere nequeo* (2, 1, 10, 1). Here Grotius seems to have got his terminology mixed up. In a corresponding context Pufendorf employs the expression that the aggressor gives the injured party an illimited *licence* against himself: *dat mihi, quantum in se, adversus se licentiam in infinitum* (2, 5, 3).
>
> Regarding the right of sovereigns to vindicate their rights through force Grotius discusses the question whether a war could be just on both sides (2, 23, 13). Here he makes a distinction. A war could not be just on both sides in the sense that each belligerent held a *facultas moralis* over the other party; this would involve a contradiction. But both parties could act without injustice; for nobody acts unjustly without being aware of doing something wrong. Therefore it is possible for the belligerents on both sides to act justly (=without injustice; *iustum* =*non iniustum*).
>
> In this connection Grotius clearly realizes that the right of

waging war in defence of one's rights is no *facultas moralis*. It is only a right in the sense that the use of force is not *iniustum*. At the beginning of his work, Grotius expressly makes a distinction between a right in the sense of what is not *iniustum* (*negantis magis sensu quam aiente*, 1, 1, 3, 1) and a right in the sense of *facultas moralis* (1, 1, 3, 4). The right of war in the former sense makes up the theme of the second book.

The right of the civil power to inflict punishment ultimately derives from the right of the individual to vindicate the *suum*. Pufendorf therefore draws a correct conclusion when he says that the culprit is under no obligation to submit to the punishment (3, 5, 1; 8, 3). The right of punishing is not a right in the usual sense of an *imperium* over the will of another person. In the social contract, the members of society have not consented to being punished; they have only engaged not to impede the execution of sentences, everybody thinking that he will never be subjected to punishment himself (8, 3, 1). After a long discussion Pufendorf finally ends up by saying that it is one's own fault if one exposes oneself to punishment in deliberately committing a crime (8, 3, 6).

Grotius mentions a criminal act (*delictum*) as a cause of subjection without consent. But in the chapter on punishment he actually derives the right of punishing from the implied consent of the culprit: whoever deliberately commits a crime implicitly concedes that he deserves a penalty (2, 20, 2, 3).

The Secondary Right

The *facultas* is no actual, irresistible power. As we have seen, it is a moral power enabling its possessor to make demands on another party with the effect that an obligation, an inner necessity, is created for the latter. But recalcitrance is always possible. Therefore, the *facultas moralis* has to be supported by force. A secondary right is attached to it. The possessor of the *facultas moralis* has the right to pursue it with force. This is an essential element in a perfect right.[26]

As the *facultas moralis* always derives from a voluntary submission through a *declaratio voluntatis*, so this is the case with the secondary right too. In alienating part of one's liberty, one also

[26] Pufendorf 1, 1, 19. *Dividitur potestas ratione efficaciae in perfectam et imperfectam. Illa est, cuius exercitium etiam per vim adseri potest aversus illos, qui eandem illegitime impedire aggrediuntur (vis autem in civitatibus exseritur potissimum per actionem, extra civitates per bellum).*

concedes to the other party the right to inflict evil on oneself if the claim is not complied with.[27]

This secondary right is of the same kind as the right of vindicating the *suum* through force in the state of nature. It is not a power of commanding somebody else to do something. A new command would be without purpose when the first one has been disobeyed. Now it is a question of getting, by means of force, what one has a right to receive or at least of punishing the aggressor. No injury is done to him when force is used to this purpose. In society this secondary right is exercised by the civil power through the courts.

Hägerström has not brought out the distinction between the primary and the secondary right. He characterizes the right to use force as a *ius* in the same sense as the right to prescribe an action to another person. In both cases the right is said to be an ideal power (*ideelle Potenz, ideelle Macht*). Hägerström sums up his results in the following way (64): 'Damit ist nun der Begriff des privaten subjektiven Rechts im Sinne der Naturrechtslehre vollständig bestimmt. Es ist ein der Person zugehöriges ideelles Potenz, wodurch eine andere Person *moralisch* zu einem bestimmten Handeln *verpflichtet wird*, verbunden mit einer ideellen Macht, im Falle der Pflichtverletzung den zu Entschädigung und Sicherheit erforderlichen Zwang auszuüben.' I can find no convincing evidence that the right to use force in vindicating the primary right was conceived as an 'ideal potency'. It seems to have implied nothing more than the absence of injury to the other party. Quite certainly it was no *facultas moralis*.

Conclusion

We can now understand the confusion pointed out by Hägerström between a right in the sense of *facultas moralis* and a right in the sense of being able to possess something or do something without inflicting injury on anybody else. The scholars talked about two different rights: the primary and the secondary one; but the same word *ius* was applied to both of them. In his definition Grotius tried to embrace both concepts at the same time. Therefore the definition lacked coherence.

The *facultas moralis* is the moral power of imposing an obligation on another person through a command. With the possible exception of the rights of parents over their children it always derives, directly

[27] A *translatio iuris* through a *promissio* includes according to Pufendorf 3, 5, 4 that *potestas mihi conceditur tergiversantem metu mali adigendi*. *Cf.* Grotius 2, 11, 3. *Pollicitatio* differs from *perfecta promissio* in that he who has made a *pollicitatio* cannot be compelled to implement his promise.

or indirectly, from an act of will by means of which the obligated party has alienated a part of his original liberty. The *facultas moralis* is a part of his original power over his own actions now belonging to the other party.

The secondary right is no *facultas moralis.* Its significance is purely negative. It makes no sense to say that the creditor does not commit an injury in requiring his debtor to pay up. But it makes good sense to say that he who pursues with force his *suum* or his primary right against an aggressor does him no injury.

The import of the secondary right is that the use of force meets with no moral obstacle. The aggressor has lost the protection accorded to him by the law of nature. His sacred sphere has dissolved in relation to the injured party and he is exposed to the infliction of evil.

APPENDIX 2

THE MONETARY UNIT

THE concept of money is as intriguing as the concept of a right. It has been a subject of controversy in a vast amount of literature. Now, interest in the problem has almost petered out though it cannot be said that a satisfactory solution has been reached.

It is obvious that the monetary system is based on law. The issuing of money is strictly regulated by legal rules and there are legal rules governing money obligations. Our monetary system can exist only within a working legal system. To make the nature of money perfectly clear and comprehensible, its legal basis has therefore to be investigated.

When speaking of money most people probably have physical money in mind, at least in the first place. Physical money consists of tiny discs of metal and small rectangular bits of paper with an inscription indicating that the disc or bit of paper is valid for a certain number of pounds, dollars, etc., or for some fractions of such a unit. These discs and scraps of paper, called coins and notes, are used for paying off debts. Therefore physical money is called money of payment.

Debts are obligations fixed in a unit like the pound, the dollar, or their equivalents in different countries. Both debts and physical money therefore presuppose the use of such a unit. These units are called monetary units. Every monetary system includes a unit of this kind.

Obviously, the monetary unit cannot be identified with a coin or note representing one unit. A pound note is not the same thing as 'one pound'. The inscription on the note refers to a unit that is supposed to exist as a separate entity.

This entity is usually called an ideal unit. It serves as a unit for the calculation of prices and debts. Accounts are kept in terms of this unit. It is therefore customary to speak of money of account in contradistinction to money of payment.

But how is this ideal unit to be defined? What is a pound or a dollar? This is a difficult problem.

For a long time the unit was identified with a certain quantity of gold or silver. This was the idea underlying the system called the classical gold standard (the gold coin standard) which was introduced in Britain in 1819.

The gold coin system was designed to maintain the identity of the monetary unit with a definite quantity of pure gold. To this end it was prescribed that the legal medium of payment should be a gold coin, called, in Great Britain, the sovereign. The difference between a sovereign and an unminted quantity of gold of the same weight was only to be that the gold in the sovereign had been moulded in a certain form and endowed with an inscription. The purpose of the inscription was to guarantee that the piece contained so much gold. Everybody could have gold minted free of costs at the Royal Mint. There was no prohibition against melting down sovereigns. The import and export of gold ingots and gold coins was completely free.

Thanks to these arrangements gold was allowed to flow in and out of the monetary system with the least impediment possible. The medium of exchange was to be gold. Those small discs with their inscriptions were made in order to spare people the trouble of weighing the gold and assessing its fineness at every transaction.

Besides gold coins banknotes were also issued to serve as media of payment. But they were regarded as mere substitutes for gold. At any time they could be exchanged for gold; and to make certain that this would always be possible, their amount was strictly limited.

The system was intended to ensure the stability of the value of money by debarring the political powers from debasing the coin or issuing paper money that was not securely backed by gold. But had the media of payment really and effectively been restricted to coins and notes, they would have been insufficient to meet the needs of business; the growth of the economy would have been stifled. And so other media of payment were created, silently as it were. Most important were cheques. They had already been in use for a couple of hundred years. But the practice of paying by cheque increased rapidly during the nineteenth century. Thereby commerce was supplied with media of payment to an amount far exceeding the supply of coins and notes.

In spite of this actual situation the monetary unit was still identified with a quantity of gold. Payment by cheque was regarded as a substitute for payment with legal tender money.

The gold coin standard was adopted in most economically developed countries during the latter half of the nineteenth century and functioned without serious disturbance until the outbreak of the First

World War. But in some countries, among them Austria, there was a paper standard which seemed to work well. This raised some doubts about the necessity of identifying the monetary unit with a quantity of precious metal. In opposition to the 'metallistic' theory, 'nominalistic' theories on the significance of the monetary unit began to appear. Later events gave them further impetus. The gold coin standard broke down during the war, and its modified successor, the 'Gold Bullion standard', suffered the same fate in 1931.

Nominalistic theories then became prevalent. When gold coins were no longer in use and banknotes could not be exchanged for gold, it was obvious that the monetary unit could not be defined in terms of a quantity of gold. The term 'nominalism' is applied to theories including a non-metallistic definition of the monetary unit.

Nominalism is therefore negatively defined. With regard to the positive content, the nominalistic theories differ.

Many nominalists have tried to define the monetary unit in terms of value in the sense of purchasing power. Thus Irving Fisher said that 'the dollar is what the dollar buys'. But this is no fixed quantity. What I can buy if I have 100,000 dollars is not 100,000 times what I can buy if I have only 1 dollar. In the latter case, I can only buy a few small things. If I have 100,000 dollars at my disposal, my range of choice is immeasurably widened, and I can command more favourable prices for the same objects.

The definition is in fact circular. When speaking of the possibility of buying for dollars, a monetary system with the dollar as its unit is supposed to exist. The ability to buy things for a certain number of dollars follows from the regular functioning of this system. The dollar cannot be defined in terms of the consequences of its being used as a monetary unit.

In the course of the discussion several variations on the unit-of-value theme have been proposed. They all suffer from the fault of being circular.

Some nominalists have abandoned this line of thought without offering any other definition. They have given up the attempt to explain what the name for the monetary unit signifies. Thus a distinguished economist (Hawtrey) has suggested that the pound sterling can only be defined as the English unit for the calculation of debts: 'A pound is a pound.' Nothing more can be said.

This amounts to stating that the monetary unit is inexplicable. But why should it be so? Such a negative position cannot be readily accepted. It should be possible to give a positive, comprehensible explanation of the seemingly mysterious unit.

To do this, we should first take a look at the system of debts and payments now prevailing. In most advanced countries payments are effected on a large scale by means of cheques (with the addition of postal orders and credit cards). Strictly speaking, the medium of payment is not the cheque itself; it is a current account in the bank on which the payer is drawing. The cheque is an instrument for letting the payee make use of a claim against the bank: he can get notes for the cheque, or he can have his own account credited with the amount (if he does not use the cheque for payment of a debt of his own).

Current accounts now constitute by far the largest medium of payment. They are aptly called book money. Physical money is used chiefly for small payments in daily life where payment by cheque would be impractical. As people began to realize about fifty years ago, it would be theoretically possible to dispense altogether with physical money, though this would not be practically feasible, even with the use of computer technique.

Current accounts represent debts owed by the banks to their customers. When I pay a debt of my own by drawing a cheque on my bank, the creditor receives a claim on the bank in place of his claim against myself. My debt is exchanged for the debt owed by the bank.

In a modern system, therefore, payments for the most part consist in transferring claims. Receiving payment is taking one claim in exchange for another. The debt of the bank takes the place of the debt of the payer. Cash payments play a subsidiary role.

The exchange of claims goes on without a stop. No 'final' payment is ever made. There is only the endlessly revolving exchange of claims and debts.

But how is this possible? How can payment largely consist in the exchange of one claim for another without any final payment? The reason for this is that the claims differ with regard to their liquidity. It is advantageous to exchange a claim with a low grade of liquidity for one with a higher grade. Claims on banks possess the highest degree of liquidity. Therefore they are readily accepted in payment of less liquid debts.

The mutual claims of the banks are for the most part cancelled by being set off against each other. Residual debts are left standing for the time being if they are not discharged by cheques drawn on other banks or, in the last resort, on a central bank.,

This is the background against which the meaning of the word for the monetary unit is to be understood. What is its significance in such a system?

Promises to pay money, cheques used for payment, and book-keeping transactions in the banks refer to sums of monetary units. These units seem to be some entities which can be counted. How else could we speak of sums of monetary units? Is not a promise to pay a sum of pounds or dollars a promise to transfer a number of entities called pounds or dollars to the promisee?

But where are these entities to be found? Every conceivable sort of answer to this question has been proposed—without success. The search for the entities called monetary units has been in vain and must be so. No such units are in existence. The word for the monetary unit has no semantic reference at all.

This no doubt sounds paradoxical. We reckon in monetary units, we promise to pay quantities of such units, etc. Surely there must be entities denoted by the word pound or dollar. But if we try again to find these entities, the result will be the same. Nothing will be found.

In order to seek a way out of the dilemma, let us ascertain the implications of a promise to pay a sum of money.

Even if there are no pounds in existence, a promise to pay a sum of 1,000 pounds is no idle playing with words. The promisor puts himself in a situation of constraint. When the debt falls due, he has to pay it off. Unless he does so, he will expose himself to unpleasant consequences. He will be pressed for payment, and his credit will suffer. Ultimately, the creditor may resort to legal proceedings, procure an order for payment, and have executive measures taken. The debtor will discover that he is in the iron grip of the law.

Such are the consequences of promising to pay a sum of money. The promisor makes use of a conventional formula in saying or writing 'I promise to pay 1,000 pounds' or something similar. The expressions are not rigidly fixed as they used to be in ancient times (for instance in the Roman *stipulatio*). But they are formulae. To create the situation of constraint a formula of the proper kind is sufficient. This is not to say that every use of such an expression will have that effect. It may be said on the stage or in jest that 'I promise'. This will entail no serious consequences. Certain conditions must be fulfilled. Broadly speaking the words have to be uttered under such circumstances that the legal requirements for a 'binding' promise are met. If this is the case, the situation of constraint will normally be established.

The ideal units ostensibly designated by the word 'pound' are purely fictitious. The word is 'hollow', it is a word that denotes nothing. But when it is used in certain contexts, according to certain rules, practical consequences of great importance follow.

Though the word for the monetary unit is hollow, we think and speak as if it denoted some entities that can be counted. This is important for making talk about the unit function. The ideas connected with the monetary unit are, indeed, an element in our monetary system.

Notes and coins are supposed to be symbols of the monetary unit to the amount indicated by the inscription. When notes representing the sum of 1,000 pounds are handed over in payment of a debt, 1,000 ideal units are held to be transferred from payer to payee. In our imagination the transfer of the symbols brings about the transfer of the symbolized units.

Payment with book-money is looked upon in a different light. We think and speak of 'having' a sum of money 'in the bank'. When the account of the payee is credited with an amount of money at the order of the payer, a sum of ideal units is thought to be directly transferred from the sphere of the latter to that of the former. The payee now 'has' the amount in question in the bank. What really takes place is an alteration in the network of situations of constraint. Instead of owing a debt to the payer, the bank now owes a debt to the payee.

The assumption of debts through promises and the payment of debts are corresponding actions, both according to our ideas and with regard to their practical effects. As we think and speak, one promises to transfer a sum of ideal units at a future date and fulfils the promise either by handing over symbols of the units or by causing a bank to effectuate a direct transfer of a sum of units to the creditor. The practical effect of the promise is to establish a situation of constraint for the promisor; the effect of payment is to release him from the constraint.

The exchange of goods and services is mediated by people undertaking and discharging these nominal or artificial obligations. In order to obtain delivery of some goods or the performance of some service, one puts oneself in a position of constraint by making a promise to pay a sum of money; and release from the situation of constraint is obtained by carrying out an act which, according to the rules, is deemed to bring about the transference of ideal units to the amount promised. Nobody cares to inquire about the objects ostensibly denoted by the word for the monetary unit. The system works, and that is the important thing.

The system is based on the observance of rules. This is what has made it possible to dispense with the precious metals as media of exchange. Instead of them we have the different ways of assuming artificial obligations expressed in terms of monetary units, the ways of discharging these obligations, and the consequences of not discharging them. Everything is regulated by rules. Without reference to the rules, promises and payments would be meaningless sounds and gestures. The rules are not only such rules as those we called legal. These rules are supplemented by social rules, and in some connections only social rules may be relevant. But rules there must be.

The fictitious monetary unit is a marvellous invention, comparable to the symbol for zero in the Hindu-Arabic numerical system. Without it the economy of the industrial age would be inconceivable. On the other hand, its use presupposes the highly developed legal system of the industrial state and its vast network of banking organization.

The rules on which the system is based include certain legal and prudential rules concerning the 'creation' of money by the central bank, which is done through extending credit to the state and/or the banks. This is the weak point in the system. The possibility of creating enough money for the expansion of the economy is an inestimable advantage. But it has its reverse in the ease with which too much money is created. Inflation is the consequence and ultimately the whole system may collapse.

In international relations gold is still used as the ultimate medium of payment. Efforts are now being made to supplement it, and eventually to replace it by an international medium of payment with a world bank fulfilling the role of the central bank in each country. The great difficulty is that rule observance cannot be as firmly established among nations as within the framework of a state.

The foregoing is a summary of the argument set forth in the book *The Problem of the Monetary Unit* (New York, Macmillan 1957, & Stockholm, Almqvist & Wiksell).

BIBLIOGRAPHICAL INDEX

Abe, Hamao, 'Feeling of Being Bound and Role of State Organs.' *Festskrift til Alf Ross 10 Juni 1969.* Copenhagen 1969.

Affolter, A., 'Zur Normentheorie.' 32 *Archiv für öffentliches Recht* 1908.

Ago, R., 'Droit positif et droit international.' 3 *Annuaire de droit international* 1957. (Also in 51 *American Journal of International Law* 1957.)

Allen, C. K., *Law in the Making.* 7th ed. Oxford 1964.

Aubert, J.-M., *Le droit romain dans l'œuvre de Saint-Thomas.* Paris 1955.

Austin, J., *Lectures on Jurisprudence.* Ed. R. Campbell. 5th ed. London 1929.

The Province of Jurisprudence Determined and The Uses of the Study of Jurisprudence. With an introduction by H. L. A. Hart. London 1954.

Austin, J. L., *Philosophical Papers.* Oxford 1961.

How to Do Things with Words. Oxford 1962.

'Performative-Constative.' *Philosophy and Ordinary Language.* Ed. Charles Caton. Urbana 1963.

Bagolini, L., 'Positivismo giuridico e analisi del linguaggio.' *Rivista trimestrale di diritto e procedure civile* 1966.

Battifol, H., 'Sur la positivité du droit.' 1 *Mélanges en l'honneur de Jean Dabin.* Bruxelles & Paris 1963.

Beling, E., 'Vom Positivismus zum Naturrecht und zurück.' 133 *Archiv für die civilistische Praxis* 1931. *Beilageheft. Festschrift für Heck, Rümelin und Schmidt.*

Bentham, J., *A Comment on the Commentaries.* Ed. Ch. W. Everett. Oxford 1928.

The Limits of Jurisprudence Defined. Ed. Ch. W. Everett. New York 1945.

The Theory of Legislation. Translation by R. Hildreth. Ed. C. K. Ogden. London 1931.

A Fragment on Government. Ed. W. Harrison. Oxford 1948.

Bergbohm, K., *Jurisprudenz und Rechtsphilosophie. Kritische Abhandlungen.* I:1. Leipzig 1892.

Bierling, E., *Juristische Prinzipienlehre.* I. 1894. Neudruck Tübingen 1961.

Binder, J., 'Wille und Willenserklärung im Tatbestand des Rechtsgeschäftes.' 6 *Archiv für Rechts- und Wirtschaftsphilosophie* 1912–13.

Rechtsnorm und Rechtspflicht. Leipzig 1911.

Philosophie des Rechts. Berlin 1925.

Black, M., *Models and Metaphors.* Ithaca, N.Y. 1962.
'Austin on Performatives.' 38 *Philosophy* 1963.
The Labyrinth of Language. London 1968.
Bobbio, N. *Giusnaturalismo e positivismo giuridico.* Milano 1965.
'Sur le positivisme juridique.' 1 *Mélanges en l'honneur de P. Roubier.* Paris 1961.
Bohnert, H. G., 'The Semiotic Status of Commands.' 12 *Philosophy of Science* 1945.
Bonnecase, J., *La pensée juridique française de 1804 à l'heure présente.* I–II. Bordeaux 1933.
Borchard, E., *Declaratory Judgments.* 2 ed. Cleveland 1941.
Brie, S., 'Der Volksgeist bei Hegel und in der historischen Rechtsschule.' 2 *Archiv für Rechts- und Wirtschaftsphilosophie* 1908–09.
Bruns, R., *Zivilprozessrecht.* Berlin & Frankfurt a/M. 1968.
Bucher, E., *Das subjektive Recht als Normsetzungsbefugnis.* Tübingen 1965.
Bülow, O., 'Die neue Prozessrechtswissenschaft und das System des Civilprozessrechts.' 27 *Zeitschrift für deutschen Zivilprozess* 1900.
'Klage and Urteil.' 31 *Zeitschrift für deutschen Zivilprozess* 1903.

Campbell, A. H., Review of Lundstedt, *Legal Thinking Revised.* 21 *Modern Law Review* 1958.
Carré de Malberg, R., *Contribution à la théorie générale de l'état.* Paris 1920–22.
Catalano, P., *Contributi allo studio del diritto augurale.* I. Torino 1960.
Cattaneo, M. A., *Il positivismo giuridico inglesi. Hobbes, Bentham, Austin.* Milano 1962.
Centenaire, Le, du doyen François Gény. Paris 1963.
Cerf, W., Review of J. L. Austin, *How to Do Things with Words.* 75 *Mind* 1966.
Charmont, J., *La renaissance du droit naturel.* Paris 1910. 2nd ed. Paris 1927.
Cohen, Felix S., 'Transcendental Nonsense and the Functional Approach.' 35 *Columbia Law Review* 1935. (Also in M. & F. S. Cohen, *Readings in Jurisprudence and Legal Philosophy.*)
Cohen, M. & F. S., *Readings in Jurisprudence and Legal Philosophy.* New York 1953.
Cohen, Morris R., *Law and the Social Order.* New York 1933.
Comte, A., *Cours de philosophie positive.* I. Paris 1830.
Corbin, A. L., 'Legal Analysis and Terminology.' 29 *Yale Law Journal* 1919.
On Contracts. I. St. Paul 1950.
Cuche, P., 'A propos du "positivisme juridique" de Carré de Malberg.' *Mélanges R. Carré de Malberg.* Paris 1933.

Davit, Th. M., *The Nature of Law.* St. Louis & London 1951.

Dias, R. W. M., *Jurisprudence*. London 1964.
Diesselhorst, M., *Die Lehre des Hugo Grotius vom Versprechen*. Köln 1959.
Ursprünge des modernen Systemgedankens bei Hobbes. Stuttgart 1968.
Dubischar, R., *Grundbegriffe des Rechts*. Stuttgart 1968.
Duguit, L., *Traité de droit constitutionnel*. I. Paris 1921.
Dulckeit, G., 'Zur Lehre vom Rechtsgeschäft im klassischen römischen Recht.' 1 *Festschrift Fritz Schulz*. Weimar 1951.
Dunning, W. A., *A History of Political Theories*. New York & London 1928.
Dvornik, Fr., *Early Christian and Byzantine Political Philosophy. Origins and Background*. Washington 1966.

Ehrlich, E., *Fundamental Principles of the Sociology of Law*. Cambridge, Mass. 1936.
Engisch, K., *Einführung in das juristische Denken*. Stuttgart 1959.
Esser, J., *Grundsatz und Norm in der richterlichen Fortbildung des Privatrechts*. Tübingen 1956.
Evers, H.-U., 'Zum unkritischen Naturrechtsbewustsein in der Rechtsprechung der Gegenwart.' 16 *Juristenzeitung* 1961.

Francisci, P. de, *Primordia civitatis*. Romae 1959.
Friedmann, W., *Legal Theory*. 4th ed. London 1960.
Fuller, L. L., 'Positivism and Fidelity to Law. A reply to Professor Hart.' 71 *Harvard Law Review* 1957–58.
The Morality of Law. New Haven & London 1964.
Furberg, M., *Locutionary and Illocutionary Acts*. Stockholm 1963.

Gagnebin, M., 'Le rôle du législateur dans les conceptions politiques de Rousseau.' *Etudes sur le contrat social de Jean-Jacques Rousseau*. Paris 1964.
Gagnér, S., *Studien zur Ideengeschichte der Gesetzgebung*. Uppsala 1960.
Gavit, B. C., 'The Code Cause of Action: Joinder and Counterclaims.' 30 *Columbia Law Review* 1930.
Gény, Fr., *Méthode d'interprétation et sources en droit privé positif*. 2nd éd. Paris 1919.
Science et technique en droit privé positif. Paris 1914–24.
'La notion de droit en France.' 1 *Archives de philosophie du droit et de sociologie juridique* 1931.
Germann, O. A., *Methodische Grundfragen*. Basel 1946.
Probleme und Methoden der Rechtsfindung. Bern 1965.
Gierke, O. von, *Naturrecht und deutsches Recht. Rektoratsrede*. Breslau 1883.
'Labands Staatsrecht und die deutsche Rechtswissenschaft.' 7 *Jahrbuch für Gesetzgebung, Verwaltung und Rechtspflege des deutschen Reiches. N.F.* 1883.
Deutsches Privatrecht. I. Leipzig 1895.
Giorgianni, V., *Neopositivismo e scienza del diritto*. Roma 1956.
Goldschmidt, J., *Der Prozess als Rechtslage*. Berlin 1925.

Grotius, H., *De jure belli ac pacis.* Ed. J. F. Gronovius. Amsterdam 1712.

Gurvitch, G., *L'idée du droit social.* Paris 1931.

Hägerström, A., *Der römische Obligationsbegriff im Lichte der allgemeinen römischen Rechtsanschauung.* I. Uppsala 1927. II. Uppsala 1941. (*Skrifter utgivna av humanistiska vetenskapssamfundet i Uppsala* 23 & 35.)

Das magistratische Ius in seinem Zusammenhang mit dem römischen Sakralrechte. Uppsala 1929. (*Juridiska fakultetens i Uppsala minnesskrift 1929.*) Uppsala 1929.

'Vergleich zwischen den Kraftvorstellungen der primitiven und der modernen Kulturvölker.' *Festschrift Professor A. Grotenfelt zugeeignet.* Helsinki 1933.

Inquiries into the Nature of Law and Morals. Translated by C. D. Broad. Uppsala 1953. (*Skrifter utgivna av humanistiska vetenskapssamfundet i Uppsala* 40.)

Rätten och staten. Stockholm 1963.

Recht, Pflicht und bindende Kraft des Vertrages nach römischer und naturrechtlicher Anschauung. Herausgegeben von Karl Olivecrona. Uppsala 1965. (*Skrifter utgivna av humanistiska vetenskapssamfundet i Uppsala* 44:3.)

Haines, Ch. G., *The Revival of Natural Law Concepts.* Cambridge, Mass. 1930.

Hall, J., 'The Present Position of Jurisprudence in the United States.' 44 *Virginia Law Review* 1958.

'From Legal Theory to Integrative Jurisprudence.' 33 *University of Cincinnati Law Review* 1964. (Also in 1 *Mélanges en l'honneur de Jean Dabin.* Bruxelles & Paris 1963.)

Hare, R. M., *The Language of Morals.* Oxford 1952.

Review of Warnock, *Contemporary Moral Philosophy.* 77 *Mind* 1968.

Hart, H. L. A., *Definition and Theory in Jurisprudence.* Oxford 1953.

'The Separation of Law and Morals.' 71 *Harvard Law Review* 1957–58.

'Analytical Jurisprudence in Mid-Twentieth Century: A Reply to Professor Bodenheimer.' 105 *University of Pennsylvania Law Review* 1957.

The Concept of Law. Oxford 1961.

'Legal Positivism.' *Encyclopedia of Philosophy.* New York & London 1968.

Hawtrey, R. G., *The Gold Standard in Theory and Practice.* 5th ed. London 1947.

Hegel, G. W. F., *Philosophie des Rechts.* Ed. J. Hoffmeister. Hamburg 1955.

Hellwig, K., *System des deutschen Zivilprozessrechts.* I. Leipzig 1912.

Henke, W., Review of Gagnér, *Zur Ideengeschichte der Gesetzgebung.* 28 *Rabel's Zeitschrift für ausländisches und internationales Privatrecht* 1964.

Henkel, H., *Einführung in die Rechtsphilosophie.* München 1964.
Henle, R., *Lehrbuch des bürgerlichen Rechts.* I. Berlin & Rostock 1926.
Héraud, G., 'Regards sur la philosophie du droit française contemporaine.' 2 *Le droit français,* éd. R. David. Paris 1960.
Herrfardt, H., 'Der Positivismus in der Rechtswissenschaft.' 7 *Studium generale* 1954.
Hobbes, Th., *Leviathan.* Ed. M. Oakeshott. Oxford 1951.
Hoebel, E. A., *The Law of Primitive Man.* Cambridge, Mass. 1954.
Holland, Th. E., *The Elements of Jurisprudence.* Oxford 1888.
Holmes, O. W., *Collected Legal Papers.* London 1920.
Horn, D., *Rechtssprache und Kommunikation.* Berlin 1966.
Hughes, G., Review of Shuman, *Legal Positivism.* 9 *Natural Law Forum* 1964.
Hugo, G., *Lehrbuch des Naturrechts als einer Philosophie des positiven Rechts.* Berlin 1798.

Interpretations of Modern Legal Philosophies. Essays in Honor of Roscoe Pound. New York 1947.

Jaehner, Th., *Der Mythos vom Recht und seine empirischen Grundlagen.* München 1933.
Jellinek, G., *Gesetz und Verordnung.* 1887. Neudruck Tübingen 1919.
Allgemeine Staatslehre. Berlin 1914.
Jennings, W. I., *The Law of the Constitution.* 5th ed. London 1959.
Jhering, R. von, *Geist des römischen Rechts auf den verschiedenen Stufen seiner Entwicklung.* II:1. 4. Aufl. Leipzig 1880. II:2. 4. Aufl. Leipzig 1883. III:1. 4. Aufl. Leipzig 1888.
Der Zweck im Recht. 5. Aufl. Leipzig 1916.
'Die Reflexwirkungen oder die Rückwirkung rechtlicher Thatsachen auf dritte Personen.' 10 *Jahrbücher für die Dogmatik des heutigen römischen und deutschen Privatrechts* 1871.
Jolowicz, H. F., *Lectures on Jurisprudence.* Ed. by J. A. Jolowicz. London 1963.
Jordan, Z. A., *The Evolution of Dialectical Materialism.* London 1967.

Kaser, M., *Römisches Privatrecht.* I. München 1955.
Kaufmann, A., *Naturrecht und Geschichtlichkeit.* Tübingen 1957.
Kelsen, H., *Hauptprobleme der Staatsrechtslehre.* Tübingen 1911.
Allgemeine Staatslehre. Berlin 1925.
Die philosophischen Grundlagen der Naturrechtslehre und des Rechtspositivismus. Berlin 1928.
Reine Rechtslehre. 2. Aufl. Wien 1960.
General Theory of Law and State. Cambridge, Mass. 1946.
'On the Basic Norm.' 47 *California Law Review* 1959.
'Was ist juristischer Positivismus? ' 20 *Juristenzeitung* 1965.
Pure Theory of Law. Berkeley & Los Angeles 1967.
Kipp, Th., Über Doppelwirkungen im Recht. *Festschrift der Berliner juristischen Fakultät für F. von Martitz.* Berlin 1911.

Koschaker, P., *Europa und das römische Recht.* 3. Aufl. München & Berlin 1958.

Kunkel, W., Review of Hägerström, *Der römische Obligationsbegriff* I. 49 *Zeitschrift der Savigny-Stiftung für Rechtsgeschichte. Romanistische Abteilung* 1929.

'Von den römischen Juristen.' 3 *Schriften der Universität Heidelberg.* Berlin & Heidelberg 1948.

Kuttner, S., 'Sur les origines du terme "droit positif".' 15 *Revue historique de droit français et étranger* 1936.

Larenz, K., *Methodenlehre der Rechtswissenschaft.* Berlin 1960. 2. Aufl. Berlin 1969.

'Der Rechtssatz als Bestimmungssatz.' *Festschrift für Karl Engisch zum 70 Geburtstag.* Frankfurt a/M 1969.

Laslett, P., Introduction to the edition of John Locke, *Two Treatises of Government.* Cambridge 1960.

Leakey, L. S. B., *Mau-Mau and the Kikuyu.* London 1953.

Leclercq, J., 'Suggestions for Clarifying Natural Law.' 2 *Natural Law Forum* 1957.

Lejay, P., *Histoire de la littérature latine des origines à Plaute.* Paris 1923.

Llewellyn, K. N., *Jurisprudence.* Chicago 1962.

Lloyd, D., *Introduction to Jurisprudence with Selected Texts.* London 1959.

Lundstedt, V., *Die Unwissenschaftlichkeit der Rechtswissenschaft* I–II:1. Berlin 1932–36.

Grundlinjer i skadeståndsrätten. II:1. Uppsala 1944.

Legal Thinking Revised. Stockholm 1956.

Maihofer, W. (Ed.), *Naturrecht oder Rechtspositivismus.* Bad Homburg 1962.

Maine, H. S., *Ancient Law* (1861). London 1919.

The Early History of Institutions (1874). London 1890.

Malinowski, B., 'The Language of Magic.' *The importance of Language,* Ed. Max Black. Englewood Cliffs, N.J. 1962. (From 2 *Coral Gardens and Their Magic.* New York, Cincinnati & Chicago 1935. Pp. 231 ff.)

Manning, C. A. W., 'Austin To-Day.' *Modern Theories of Law.* Ed. W. I. Jennings. London & Oxford 1933.

Marini, G., *L'opera di Gustav Hugo nella crisi del giusnaturalismo tedesco.* Milano 1968.

Mazeaud, L., 'De la distinction des jugements déclaratifs et des jugements constitutifs des droits.' *Revue trimestrielle de droit civil* 1929.

Merkel, A., 'Über das Verhältnis der Rechtsphilosophie zur "positiven" Rechtswissenschaft und zum allgemeinen Teil derselben.' 1 *Zeitschrift für das Privat- und öffentliche Recht der Gegenwart* 1874.

Millar, R. W., *Civil Procedure of the Trial Court in Historical Perspective.* New York 1952.

Moline, J., 'An Approach to the Analysis of Rules.' 35 *Theoria* 1969.
Mommsen, Th., *Römisches Staatsrecht*. III: 1. 3. Aufl. Leipzig 1887.
Montesquieu, Ch. L., *De l'esprit des lois*. Genève 1749.
Morison, W. L., 'Some Myth about Positivism.' 68 *Yale Law Journal* 1958–59.

Naturrecht oder Rechtspositivismus? See Maihofer.
Naturrecht, Das, in der Politischen Theorie. See Schmölz.

Olivecrona, K., *Law as Fact*. Copenhagen 1939. Reprinted by Wildy & Sons. London 1962.
Domen i tvistemål. Lund 1943.
Das Werden eines Königs nach altschwedischem Recht. Lund 1947.
'Is a Sociological Explanation of Law possible?' 14 *Theoria* 1948.
Three Essays in Roman Law. Lund 1949.
'"Corpus" and "collegium" in D.3,4,1.' 5 *IURA* 1954.
'Zur Frage des magischen Charakters der älteren Rechtsvorstellungen.' *Bulletin de la société royale des lettres de Lund 1956–57*. Lund 1957.
The Problem of the Monetary Unit. New York & Uppsala 1957.
Rätt och dom. 1960. 2nd ed. Stockholm 1966.
'Election and Creation.' 1 *Studi in onore di Emilio Betti*. Milano 1961.
'Legal Language and Reality.' *Essays in Honor of Roscoe Pound*. Indianapolis & New York 1962.
Rättsordningen—Idéer och fakta. Lund 1966.
Orestano, R., *I fatti di normazione nell'esperienza romana arcaica*. Torino 1967.

Pagenstecher, M., *Zur Lehre von der materiellen Rechtskraft*. Berlin 1905.
Pattaro, E., 'Riflessioni su Olivecrona.' *Rivista trimestrale di diritto e procedura civile* 1968.
'Diritto, morale e concezione realistica del diritto.' *Rivista trimestrale di diritto e procedura civile* 1969.
Petrazycki, L., *Law and Morality: Leon Petrazycki*. Translated by Hugh W. Babb. With an introduction by Nicholas S. Timasheff. Cambridge, Mass. 1955.
Pound, R., Review of E. Jenks, *The New Jurisprudence*. 47 *Harvard Law Review* 1933–34.
Jurisprudence. St. Paul, Mo. 1959.
Promulgation, La. See Waline.
Puchta, G. F. *Das Gewohnheitsrecht*. Erlangen 1828.
Cursus der Institutionen. Leipzig 1841.
Pufendorf, S. L. B. A., *De jure naturae et gentium*. Ed. G. Mascovius. Frankfurt & Leipzig 1744.

Radbruch, G., *Rechtsphilosophie.* 4. Aufl. Stuttgart 1950.
Reinach, A., *Die apriorischen Grundlagen des bürgerlichen Rechts.* Halle a.d.S. 1913. (Reprinted 1953) *Zur Phänomenologie des Rechts.* München 1953.
Rieg, A., *Le rôle de la volonté dans l'acte juridique en droit civil français et allemand.* Diss. Strasbourg 1958. Paris 1961. (Also an article with the same title in 3 *Archives de philosophie du droit* 1958.)
Rosenberg, L., *Die Beweislast auf der Grundlage des bürgerlichen Gesetzbuchs und der Zivilprozessordnung.* 3. Aufl. München & Berlin 1953.
Lehrbuch des deutschen Zivilprozessrechts. 7. Aufl. München & Berlin 1956.
Ross, A., *On Law and Justice.* London 1958.
'Tû-Tû.' 70 *Harvard Law Review* 1956–57. (Also in *Festskrift til Professor Henry Ussing,* Copenhagen 1951, and in 1 *Scandinavian Studies in Law,* Stockholm 1957.)
'Status i rettighedsdiskussionen.' 38 *Svensk Juristtidning* 1953.
'Naturret contra retspositivisme.' 76 *Tidsskrift for Rettsvitenskap* 1963.
Review of Karl Olivecrona, *Rättsordningen—Idéer och fakta.* 80 *Tidsskrift for Rettsvitenskap* 1967.
Directives and Norms. London 1968.
Roubier, P., *Théorie générale du droit.* Paris 1946.
Rousseau, J. J., *Du contrat social.* (*Oeuvres complètes,* tome premier. Paris 1835.)

Sagnac, Ph., *La législation civile de la révolution française* (1789–1804). Paris 1898.
Salmond, J., *Jurisprudence.* London 1893. 9th ed. London 1937.
Samek, R., 'Performative Utterances and the Concept of Contract.' 43 *Australasian Journal of Philosophy* 1965.
Sartorius, R., 'The Concept of Law.' *Archiv für Rechts- und Sozialphilosophie* 1966.
Savatier, R., 'Observations sur les modes contemporains de formation de droit positif.' 1 *Mélanges en l'honneur de Jean Dabin.* Bruxelles & Paris 1963.
Savigny, Fr. C. von, *Vom Beruf unserer Zeit für Gesetzgebung und Rechtswissenschaft.* Heidelberg 1814.
System des heutigen römischen Rechts. I. Berlin 1840.
Das Obligationenrecht. I. Berlin 1851.
Schlossmann, S., *Der Vertrag.* Leipzig 1876.
Schluep, W. R., *Das Markenrecht als subjektives Recht.* Basel 1964.
Schmölz, F.-M., *Das Naturrecht in der politischen Theorie.* Wien 1963. (Also in 13 *Österreichische Zeitschrift für öffentliches Recht* 1964.)
Schreiber, R., *Die Geltung von Rechtsnormen.* Berlin 1966.
Schwarz, A. B., 'John Austin and the German Jurisprudence of his time.' 1 *Politica* 1934.

Searle, J., *Speech Acts.* Cambridge 1969.
Sesonske, A., 'Performatives.' 62 *The Journal of Philosophy* 1965.
Sforza, C., 'Sul significato degli imperativi giuridici.' *Rivista italiana per le scienze giuridici* 1957–58.
Shuman, S. I., (with Richard A. Falk) 'The Bellagio Conference on Legal Positivism.' 14 *Journal of Legal Education* 1961–62.
Legal Positivism. Its Scope and Limitations. Detroit 1963.
Simpson, A. W. B., 'Analysis of Legal Concepts.' 80 *Law Quarterly Review* 1964.
Sjögren, W., 'Die Formen des Unrechts.' 35 *Jahrbücher für die Dogmatik des heutigen römischen und deutschen Privatrechts* 1896.
Sorokin, P., *Contemporary Sociological Theories.* New York & London 1928.
Stoljar, S. J., 'More Thinking on Law and Morals.' *Current Legal Problems.* London 1961.
Stone, J., *The Province and Function of Law.* Cambridge, Mass. 1950.
Legal System and Lawyers' Reasoning. Stanford 1964.
Human Law and Human Justice. Stanford 1965.
Sundby, N. Kr., 'Legal Right in Scandinavian Analyses.' 13 *Natural Law Forum* 1969.

Tammelo, I., 'Contemporary Developments of the Imperative Theory of Law: A Survey and Appraisal.' 49 *Archiv für Rechts- und Sozialphilosophie* 1963.
Taylor, P. W., *Normative Discourse.* Englewood Cliffs, N.J. 1961.
Thieme, H., *Das Naturrecht und die europäische Privatrechtsgeschichte.* Basel 1947.
Thon, A., *Rechtsnorm und subjectives Recht.* Weimar 1878.
Thormann, K. F., *Der doppelte Ursprung der Mancipatio.* München 1943.
Timasheff, N. S., *An Introduction to the Sociology of Law.* Cambridge, Mass. 1939.
Tuhr, A. von, *Der allgemeine Teil des bürgerlichen Rechts.* II:1. Leipzig 1914.

Ullmann, W., Review of Gagnér, *Studien zur Ideengeschichte der Gesetzgebung.* 29 *Tijdschrift voor Rechtsgeschiedenis* 1961.
Undén, O., 'Några synpunkter på begreppsbildning inom juridiken.' *Festskrift tillägnad Axel Hägerström den 6 september 1928.* Uppsala 1928.
Uren, W. J., 'Criteria of Legal Positivism.' *Archiv für Rechts- und Sozialphilosophie* 1969.

Verdross, A., *Abendländische Rechtsphilosophie.* Wien 1958.
Villey, M., 'Essor et décadence du volontarisme juridique.' *Archives de philosophie du droit* 1957.
Leçons d'histoire de la philosophie du droit. Paris 1962.
La formation de la pensée juridique moderne. Paris 1968.

Virally, M., *La pensée juridique*. Paris 1960.

Wagenwoort, H., *Roman Dynamism*. Oxford 1947.

Waline, M., 'Positivisme philosophique, juridique et sociologique.' *Mélanges Carré de Malberg*. Paris 1933.

La promulgation, la signature et la publication des textes législatifs en droit comparé. Ed. J.-B. Herzog & G. Vlachos. Avec une introduction par Marcel Waline. Paris 1961.

Warnock, G. J., *Contemporary Moral Philosophy*. London 1967.

Welzel, H., *Naturrecht und materiale Gerechtigkeit*. 4. Aufl. Göttingen 1962.

Die Naturrechtslehre Samuel Pufendorfs. Berlin 1958.

'Naturrecht und Rechtspositivismus.' *Naturrecht oder Rechtspositivismus*. Ed. W. Maihofer 1962.

An den Grenzen des Rechts. Die Frage nach der Rechtsgeltung. Köln & Opladen 1966.

Wieacker, Fr., *Privatrechtsgeschichte der Neuzeit*. 2. Aufl. Göttingen 1967.

Williams, G., 'Language and the Law.' 61–62 *Law Quarterly Review* 1945–46.

Windscheid, B., *Lehrbuch des Pandektenrechts*. I. 9. Aufl. von Th. Kipp. Frankfurt a/M 1906.

Gesammelte Reden und Abhandlungen. Leipzig 1904.

Wlassak, M., 'Der Gerichtsmagistrat im gesetzlichen Spruchverfahren.' 28 *Zeitschrift der Savigny-Stiftung für Rechtsgeschichte. Romanistische Abteilung* 1907.

Wolf, E., *Grosse Rechtsdenker der deutschen Geistesgeschichte*. 4. Aufl. Tübingen 1963.

Das Problem der Naturrechtslehre. Karlsruhe 1964.

Wolff, Chr., *Jus naturae methodo scientifica pertractatum*. I—IX. Frankfurt & Leipzig 1740–48.

Wright, G. H. von, *Norm and Action*. London & New York 1963.

Zitelmann, E., *Irrthum und Rechtsgeschäft*. Leipzig 1879.

INDEX OF NAMES

INDEX OF SUBJECTS